Subtypes of Learning Disabilities

Theoretical Perspectives and Research

Subtypes of Learning Disabilities

Theoretical Perspectives and Research

Edited by

Lynne V. Feagans
The Pennsylvania State University

Elizabeth J. Short
Case Western Reserve University

Lynn J. Meltzer
Institute for Learning and Development

LEA LAWRENCE ERLBAUM ASSOCIATES, PUBLISHERS
1991   Hillsdale, New Jersey   Hove and London

Lawrence Erlbaum Associates, Inc., Publishers
365 Broadway
Hillsdale, New Jersey 07642

Library of Congress Cataloging-in-Publication Data

Subtypes of learning disabilities : theoretical perspectives and research / edited by
Lynne V. Feagans, Elizabeth J. Short, Lynn Meltzer.
    p.   cm.
Includes bibliographical references and indexes.
ISBN 0-8058-0602-4
1. Learning disabilities—United States—Congresses. I. Feagans, Lynne. II.
Short, Elizabeth J. III. Meltzer, Lynn.
LC4705.S83 1991
371.9—dc20   90-22510
                                                                         CIP

Printed in the United States of America
10   9   8   7   6   5   4   3   2   1

Contents

Preface   vii

List of Contributors   xi

I. Theoretical and Conceptual Issues in Subtyping

1. Subtypes of Learning Disabilities: A Review   3
   Lynne V. Feagans & James D. McKinney

2. Retreat, Regroup, or Advance? An Agenda for Empirical
   Classification Research in Learning Disabilities   33
   Deborah L. Speece & David H. Cooper

3. A Dimensional Approach to Cognition and Academic Performance
   in Children with Medical Problems or Learning Difficulties   53
   John W. Hagen, George Kamberelis, & Stuart Segal

4. A Behavioral Genetic Approach to Learning Disabilities and Their
   Subtypes   83
   Robert Plomin

II. Current Research on Subtyping

5. Genetic Etiology of Individual Differences in Reading Disability   113
   R. K. Olson, J. P. Rack, F. A. Conners, J. C. DeFries, & D. W. Fulker

6. Can Learning-disabled Children Become Good Information
   Processors? How Can We Find Out?   137
   Michael Pressley

7. Problem-solving Strategies and Academic Performance in Learning-
   disabled Students: Do Subtypes Exist?   163
   Lynn Meltzer

8. Arithmetic Disability: Theoretical Considerations and Empirical
   Evidence for This Subtype   189
   Sylvia R. Morrison & Linda S. Siegel

9. A Subgroup Analysis of Learning-disabled and Skilled Readers'
   Working Memory: In Search of a Model for Reading
   Comprehension   209
   H. Lee Swanson

10. Subtypes as Prototypes: Extended Studies of Rationally Defined
    Extreme Groups   229
    Joseph K. Torgesen

Author Index   **247**
Subject Index   **259**

Preface

The field of Learning Disabilities has changed dramatically over the last 20 years and this volume hopefully reflects these changes and will help lead the way to new advances as we near the 21st century.

The term *specific learning disabilities* was first used in the United States in 1963 to describe a variety of disorders related to language, reading, and social communication that could not be attributed to sensory handicaps, mental retardation, emotional disturbance, or environmental disadvantage (Kirk, 1963). The advent of the term "learning disabilities" (LD) reflected the realization by scientists, educators, and parents that some children presented an exceptional pattern of development that did not fit existing categories, but the term "learning disability" also reflected a general lack of consensus about its principal manifestations and etiology. Consequently with these considerations in mind, the current Federal definition as articulated in Public Law (PL) 94-142, the Education for All Handicapped Children Act, includes a wide range of conditions that are generally associated with neurological factors and establishes eligibility for special education services by the exclusion of other handicaps.

> "Specific learning disability" means a disorder in one or more of the basic psychological processes involved in understanding or in using language, spoken or written, which may manifest itself in an imperfect ability to listen, think, speak, read, write, spell, or to do mathematical calculations. The term includes such conditions as perceptual handicaps, brain injury, minimal brain dysfunction, dyslexia, and developmental aphasia. The term does not include children who have learning problems which are primarily the result of visual, hearing, or motor handicaps, of mental retardation, of emotional disturbance, or of environmental, cultural, or economic disadvantage. (U.S. Office of Education, August 23, 1977)

The past decade has witnessed phenomenal growth in the field of learning disabilities, to the point where it now represents approximately 40% of the handicapped students receiving special education nationally. According to a 1984 report to Congress by the Office of Special Education programs, the percentage of the school population classified as LD was 3.82 for the 1983 school year, compared to less than 2% in 1978.

Because all known forms of exceptionality were excluded from the present definition of learning disabilities, researchers in the field have had the arduous task of trying to specify exactly how LD children are handicapped apart from their failure to profit from regular classroom instruction. As a result, an extensive LD literature has evolved, cataloging the various deficits displayed by such children.

Gallagher (1966) first described learning-disabled children as displaying an uneven pattern of development, with both abilities and disabilities. Many have tried to quantify the nature of this pattern both across different areas of development and over time. This quantification process has both theoretical and methodological problems associated with it, most of which have been grappled with in the last few years. Thus, both the etiology of the disorder as well as its manifestations are thought to be basically multivariate. Although it is widely believed that different types of learning disabilities exist, relatively few attempts have been made to classify subtypes of LD students within this heterogeneous population. In our view, this factor has frustrated previous research efforts to obtain a generalizable body of knowledge in the field.

At present, the most compelling evidence for the hypothesis of distinct subtypes of learning disabilities comes from studies that have successfully subdivided children by using various classification procedures (see Feagans & McKinney, this volume). Although this research is still in an embryonic stage of development, it does demonstrate the feasibility of creating more homogeneous subtypes of LD students that may have important theoretical and practical implications. Preliminary evidence suggests that students with specific disabilities can be differentiated from those with other handicaps and from underachievers without obvious learning handicaps. In addition, if LD subtypes could be defined reliably, future research on intervention could test the efficacy of "trait × treatment" paradigms individually designed for children. These research paradigms might lead to the development of better program-planning models for individualizing instruction for different types of learning disabilities.

An additional, serious problem with most of the subtyping approaches is that they are atheoretical and exploratory. Hopefully, this book will help build some multivariate models and theories of learning disabilities that can help future researchers carefully specify the kinds of subtypes they expect to find.

The book is divided into two parts. The first part presents basic reviews and theoretical approaches used to subtype learning disabled children. The chapters range from a behavior genetics approach to a dimensional approach in understanding learning disabilities. The chapters can be seen as an integration of approaches across educational, psychological, and medical areas. It is hoped that these chapters will set the stage for the second part of the book.

Part II of this book presents actual research approaches using some of the theoretical approaches espoused in Part I. These more data-based chapters reflect both the growing diversity of approaches to subtyping, as well as the different content areas that have used a subtyping approach. These chapters focus on problem-solving strategies, memory, reading, and arithmetic, to name a few. Although some of the chapters focus on intervention, most of the chapters only hint at how effective interventions might be developed from the subtyping literature. One outcome of this book might be the development of intervention approaches that capitalize on the information gleaned from the subtype approach. The ultimate goal of both the conference and book will be achieved when the basic research presented here is translated into programs that help learning-disabled children.

We thank the National Institutes of Child Health and Human Development, the National Institute for Neurological and Communicative Disease and Stroke, and the Center for the Study of Child and Adolescent Development for their financial support for this project. Dr. Sally Broman and Dr. David Gray, representing their respective agencies, helped and participated in the conference. Thanks also to the other participants who made the conference[1] so successful and to the authors for their willingness to contribute thoughtful chapters. Finally, thanks go to the staff at the Department of Human Development and Family Studies at Penn State for helping with all parts of the preparation of this book.

Lynne V. Feagans

REFERENCES

Gallagher, J. J. (1966). Children with developmental imbalance: A psycoeducational definition. In W. M. Cruickshank (Ed.), *The teacher of brain injured children.* Syracuse, NY: Syracuse University Press.

Kirk, S. (1963). Behavioral diagnosis and remediation of learning disabilities. *The Conference on the exploration into the problems of the perceptually handicapped child.* Evanston, IL: Fund for the Perceptually Handicapped child.

[1]The chapters in this book stem from the First Annual Conference on Research and Theory in Learning Disabilities held May 31-June 7, 1988 at The Pennsylvania State University.

List of Contributors

Frances A. Conners
Department of Psychology
Hamilton College
Clinton, NY 13323

David H. Cooper
Department of Special Education
University of Maryland
College Park, MD 20742

John C. De Fries
Institute for Behavioral Genetics
University of Colorado
Boulder, CO 80309

Lynne V. Feagans
The Pennsylvania State University
Department of Human Development and Family Studies
South-110 Henderson Building
University Park, PA 16802

David W. Fulker
Institute for Behavioral Genetics
University of Colorado
Boulder, CO 80309

John W. Hagen
Center for Human Growth and Development
300 North Ingalls, 10th Floor
Ann Arbor, MI 48109-0406

George Kamberelis
Center for Human Growth and Development
300 North Ingalls, 10th Floor
Ann Arbor, MI 48109-0406

James D. McKinney
School of Education
University of Miami
Merrick Bldg.
P.O. Box 248065
Coral Gables, FL 33124

Lynn Meltzer
Institute for Learning and Development
One Courthouse Lane
Chelmsford, MA 01824

Sylvia R. Morrison
The Ontario Institute for Studies in Education
252 Bloor Street West
Toronto, M5S 1V6
Canada

Richard K. Olson
Department of Psychology, Box 345
Institute for Behavioral Genetics
University of Colorado
Boulder, CO 80309

Michael Pressley
College of Education
Department of Human Development
University of Maryland
3304 Benjamin Building
College Park, MD 20742-1131

Robert Plomin
The Pennsylvania State University
Department of Human Development and Family Studies
South-110 Henderson Building
University Park, PA 16802

John P. Rack
Institute for Behavioral Genetics
University of Colorado
Boulder, Co 80309

Stuart S. Segal
Center for Human Growth and Development
300 North Ingalls, 10th Floor
Ann Arbor, MI 48109-0406

Elizabeth J. Short
Department of Psychology
Case Western Reserve University
Cleveland, OH 44106

Linda S. Siegel
The Ontario Institute for Studies in Education
252 Bloor Street West
Toronto, M5S 1V6
Canada

Deborah L. Speece
Department of Special Education
University of Maryland
College Park, MD 20742

H. Lee Swanson
The University of British Columbia
Faculty of Education
2125 Main Mall
University Campus
Vancouver, B.C., Canada V6T 1Z5

Joseph K. Torgesen
The Florida State University
Department of Psychology R-54
Tallahassee, FL 32306-1051

THEORETICAL AND CONCEPTUAL ISSUES IN SUBTYPING

1 Subtypes of Learning Disabilities: A Review

Lynne V. Feagans
The Pennsylvania State University

James D. McKinney
University of Miami

INTRODUCTION

The field of learning disabilities is one which is diverse and varied in its focus. There are few theories that would be agreed upon, and children with learning disabilities have been described in a number of different ways depending upon the theoretical or conceptual framework of the researchers. One overarching assumption in most of the work is that children with learning disabilities display a diverse pattern of disabilities.

The history of the field reflects this diversity with figures such as Kurt Goldstein (1939) who described the brain-injured adult in World War I. His description of the behavior of these adults has been used even today to describe the distractibility and hyperactivity of the learning disabled child. Strauss and Werner (1942) later used Goldstein's work to structure the environment of children who displayed the Goldstein characteristics. By the 1950s and 1960s, emphasis had shifted away from behavior to investigating the cognitive and perceptual processing capabilities of the children as the work of Marianne Frostig and Samuel Kirk appeared in the literature. This focus emphasized the deficits in basic processing skills which were presumably linked to poor academic skills like math and reading (Frostig & Horne, 1964; Kirk, McCarthy, & Kirk, 1968). Recently there has been another shift in research which has emphasized the importance of executive processes and metacognition (Ryan, Short, & Weed, 1986; Wong, 1985) while another has emphasized the specific decoding abilities needed in reading (Bradley & Bryant, 1983; 1985; Stanovich, 1988; Wagner & Torgensen, 1987).

All of these streams of work within the field reflect the diversity of work

3

but with an awareness that learning disabilities may affect a number of different basic and academic processes. This emphasis on the multidimensionality of learning disabilities was first articulated by James Gallagher (1966). He postulated that learning disabled children have an uneven pattern of development across a number of different domains. In this way they differed from the mentally retarded children who showed a depressed but even pattern of development. This led to a number of different theoretical approaches that emphasized one set of variables over another but always with the recognition that learning disability was implicitly a multidimensional concept. Thus, today it seems appropriate that different forms of subtyping within the area of learning disabilities have become a popular way to describe the diversity within this disability.

The kinds of subtyping that have occurred are many and many might challenge the usefulness of some of the approaches. Yet the acknowledgment of the different kinds of learning disabilities has elevated the argument among theoreticians and researchers to a higher level. For instance, researchers can now argue for an attention deficit subtype while others can argue for a phonological decoding subtype without disputing the validity of either as a valid dimension of learning disabilities. At the same time, the argument still remains about what proportion of children display each of these diverse characteristics and the extent to which they relate to academic achievement.

The purpose of this chapter is to review some of the research which has addressed the subtyping issue and to critically examine its importance in our growing knowledge about learning disabilities. We will distinguish three main types.

First, there are clinical inferential subtypes derived from clinical practice. These subtypes are empirically derived from test performance. The most common approach to subtyping in this fashion has been the analysis of subtest scatter on tests such as the Wechsler Intelligence Scales for Children (WISC) and the Illinois Test of Psycholinguistic Abilities (ITPA). The subtypes characterized by this approach represent uneven patterns of abilities which diverge from normal. Thus, a child might do well on the vocabulary portion of the WISC-R but perform below average on picture completion and digit span, which may indicate either cognitive deficits or developmental lags associated with learning disabilities.

The second approach to subtyping is to study children with a particular kind of disability. For instance, some learning disabled children have been described as either having a particular reading problem or math problem, or as having either attention or memory deficits. Each single variable is used to identify a specific subtype of learning disabilities that is of interest to the investigator. This kind of subtyping is especially beneficial in an experimental treatment design in which children are selected who perform similarly on the blocking variable. This approach has been represented in the literature by Torgesen (1982) who has been interested in memory subtypes and Stanovich (1988; Bradley & Bryant, 1983; Wagner & Torgensen, 1987) who have been interested in a specific phonological subtype.

The last approach to subtyping research is the most recent and will be discussed most thoroughly; it is the use of multivariate empirical classification procedures to group individuals who perform similarly over several different measures. This approach is different from the first and second because the way subtypes are formed does not depend upon *a priori* theories or clinical inferential thinking about the existence of specific subtypes. Rather, it uses empirical techniques like Q-factor analysis and Cluster analysis to define subtypes that are then validated with external measures of theoretical and practical relevance such as sociodemographic, neurological/ historical, and academic variables.

At some level all these three approaches have proven useful in advancing knowledge in the field because they incorporate the underlying assumption that learning disabilities is a multiple variable syndrome that is marked by heterogeneity as one of its major features. Obviously, there is still much controversy over which of the many variables are most important and account for which aspects of child behavior and academic performance. This theme will be elaborated in the following sections of the review.

CLINICAL/INFERENTIAL SUBTYPES

Subtest Scatter

In the 1950s and 1960s there was interest in providing a portrait of the learning-disabled child based on the concept of developmental imbalances (Gallagher, 1966). A number of investigators examined scatter on the WISC-R in order to document some imbalance in the developmental process (Bannatyne, 1979). The verbal/performance discrepancy on the IQ test was the most popular way to document an imbalance and is still used in many clinical settings as a way to identify a child with possible learning problems. In addition, subtest scatter has been examined in order to find strengths and weaknesses within the verbal or performance areas. Much of this work grew out of existing clinical practice and was driven less by theory than by a need to find an abnormal pattern of strengths and weaknesses consistent with the concept of developmental imbalance.

The early research on the retarded reader, who might now be classified as learning disabled, revealed some of these developmental imbalances. Altus (1956), Vance, Gayor, and Coleman (1976), and Kallos, Grabow, and Guarino (1961) presented similar patterns of WISC subscale scores in retarded readers. They all found that within the retarded-reader group, Coding was especially low in comparison to the other mean subscale scores and Arithmetic and Information were slightly lower. In an early study, Burks and Bruce (1955) compared 11 good readers with 31 poor readers and reported poorer performance by the poor readers on the Information, Arithmetic, and Coding subscales of the WISC. An intellectual profile of retarded readers on a larger scale was done by Belmont and Birch (1966). They examined 150 retarded readers and 50 normal readers who were boys of 9-10 years of age and found that all the subscales of the WISC differentiated the groups but one (Coding). Moreover, they reported that retarded readers were less variable in subtest scatter.

Earlier studies generally relied on clinic populations for their samples of children and most did not include a normal comparison group. Thus, there were questions about the interpretation of the scatter and discrepancy scores, both because the clinic sample might not be representative of all learning disabled children and because there was no normative comparison. More recent work has placed in doubt some of the early work on profiles. Hammill and Larsen (1974) found that the ITPA scatter did not predict learning disabilities and that patterns were not different in a normal population of children. Other studies have also questioned the use of the IQ subtest scatter. Ysseldyke and his colleagues in a series of studies have questioned the entire definition of the disorder with particular attention to the use of standardized tests like the WISC-R to define the disorder. In one study they found that in a normal sample of 248 children almost 20% could be identified as learning disabled by the usual definitions of subtest scatter and other profile analyses (Ysseldyke, Algozzine, & Epps, 1983).

Feagans and McKinney (1981) examined a population of school identified learning disabled children who were matched with normal children in their regular classroom (58 pairs). The WISC-R profiles revealed that the LD children had generally lower scores on the subtests of the WISC-R but an analysis of the pattern differences revealed no differences except on Comprehension.

In order to try to replicate some of the previous findings with respect to the question of subtest scatter, Feagans and McKinney (1981) examined two common indexes that have been used in diagnostic practice with the Wechsler scales. One measure that was often taken as indicative of learning disabilities was a 15-point discrepancy between Verbal and Performance IQ (Black, 1974; Holroyd & Wright, 1965) Eight LD and 13 non-LD students had discrepancies of this magnitude. Another common index of subtest scatter was the difference between the highest and lowest scale scores earned by a given child (Kaufman, 1976). The mean discrepancy in scale scores of LD children was 7.79 points and that for non-LD children was 7.53 points. Again, significant differences were not found between groups on this index of subtest scatter, and it was noted that these average differences in scale scores were comparable to those reported by Kaufman (1976) for 2,200 children on the WISC-R.

Finally, in this same study, another and more defensible way to assess the dispersion of individual scores was reported which examined the differences between within-cell variability. An analysis of spread or variability within each group showed that LD students were less variable with respect to both Verbal and Performance scores than normally achieving students.

Although these recent studies question the validity of interpretative Wechsler subtest scatter as an index of LD, this procedure still enjoys wide acceptance in the field. Thus, a few recent review articles have been published supporting the caution needed in using IQ for diagnostic purposes. Kaufman (1981) reviewed the literature on the WISC-R with respect to factor analytic studies, subtest recategorization, and scatter analysis and concluded that there was little evidence for a stereotypical pattern that could define LD. More recently, Kavale and Forness (1984) conducted a meta-analysis of 94 studies of the validity of Wechsler scatter analysis and recategorization and reached the same conclusion.

IQ-Achievement Discrepancy

Most definitions of LD attribute the disorder to deficiencies in the "basic psychological processes" that underlie school learning. Research has yet to produce consensus on exactly what psychological processes define the condition or how these processes should be measured. Lack of consensus on the major indicators of LD and the failure of psychometric and etiological classification procedures to provide useful indexes has led to an increased reliance, especially by state agencies, upon IQ/achievement discrepancy formulas as the principal index of LD. Most states have either revised their rules and regulations to require discrepancy criteria or are in the process of doing so. Although the use of discrepancy criteria has the advantage of providing a more objective index of underachievement, this approach to classification also presents a host of methodological, conceptual, and practical problems.

Most of the research on the use of IQ/achievement discrepancies to identify LD children has involved the comparison of various formulas and assessment of the effects of different cut-off criteria (Cone & Wilson, 1981; Forness, Sinclair, & Gutherie, 1983; Shepard, 1980). In general, none of the available methods for calculating discrepancy scores is without serious methodological limitations. Most authors favor the regression method because it is the most robust statistically; however, it is the most difficult to implement practically. Nevertheless, the choice of methods has been shown to be critical since different methods identify different children as well as different numbers of children (Alberg, 1985).

For example, Alberg (1985) recently compared the use of a standard score difference method and regression analysis. She found that the standard score method identified fewer children, but over-identified bright children compared to regression analysis. The extent to which the same children were identified by the two methods was related to IQ level such that there was more agreement in the average range and less agreement at the extremes of the IQ distribution. Ysseldyke et al. (1983) found that most of the IQ achievement discrepancy formulas resulted in increasing percentages of children being identified at higher grade levels. Moreover, in a three year longitudinal study McKinney (1987) found that discrepancy at the time of identification for special education was not prognostic of later academic outcomes. In sum, while IQ/achievement discrepancies may provide an index of under-achievement generally, it does not appear to be a valid index of LD specifically.

Academic Subtypes

Other researchers have focussed attention on the identification and description of LD by examining only academic performance, especially reading. Ingram (1969) proposed that three different types of reading disabilities could be distinguished according to the pattern of deficits in visuospatial and auditory-linguistic skills. Subsequently, Ingram, Mann, and Blackburn (1970) examined patterns of children's reading errors retrospectively and sorted the sample into three groups: auditory dyslexia, visuospatial dyslexia, and mixed. Johnson and Myklebust (1967) proposed two reading subtypes, visual and auditory dyslexia. Later, Myklebust (1978) included several additional subtypes that combined the two into crossmodal subtypes of dyslexia.

One of the first large scale studies to subdivide children using a clinical inferential method was by Boder (1970, 1973). She examined the reading and spelling errors of over 100 reading disabled children who ranged in age from 8 to 16. Based on her clinical impressions of error patterns, she classified 93% of the sample into three subtypes.

The largest subtype (*Subtype 1*) was classified as dysphonetic. This subgroup had particular difficulty analyzing words phonetically and tended to use a visual approach in which they read words globally rather than analytically. A much smaller subtype (*Subtype 2*) was described as dyseidetic. They read very laboriously as if they were "word blind." Boder (1973) classified the last subtype (*Subtype 3*) as alexic (mixed dysphonetic-dyseidetic). The latter group was the most severely impaired group in terms of overall reading achievement.

Camp and Dolcourt (1977) administered Boder's reading and spelling tests to a sample of 34 average to above average fifth graders and a group of 18 fourth-to-sixth grade retarded readers who were placed in special programs. Using *a priori* decision rules, the sample was first divided into high, average, and low reading groups and then classified as either normal, dyseidetic, dysphonetic, or alexic. Although Camp and Dolcourt's (1977) diagnostic classification was fairly reliable (76% - 91% agreement), the proportional membership in each subtype did not replicate Boder (1973). Also, the low reading group contained approximately as many normal children as those in atypical subtypes, although the latter findings could be attributed to differences in samples.

In a second study based on Boder's subtypes, Obrzut (1979) used the classification procedures developed by Camp and Dolcourt (1977) to subdivide a sample of 144 second and fourth grade boys into subgroups of 45 normal readers, 18 nonspecific poor readers, and 80 dyslexic readers. The dyslexic group was further classified into Boder's three subtypes. Obrzut administered dichotic listening tasks and bisensory memory tasks (visual and auditory). Results showed that normal and dyseidetic readers performed better than dysphonetic and alexic: readers, thereby suggesting that Boder's subtypes were related to performance on tasks other than those that were used to classify the children diagnostically.

Recently, Bayliss and Liversey (1985) used the Camp and Dolcourt classification procedure to study visual memory strategies in 8 dysphonetic, 11 dyseidetic, and 11 normal readers. In the first experiment in this study, no differences were obtained between combined dyslexics and normals on both easy to label and hard to label items. However, when broken out of subtype, dyseidetic children performed better than dysphonetics on hard to label items but not easy to label items; presumably because they used different memory strategies. This hypothesis was confirmed in a second experiment which showed that dysphonetics tended to remember items spatially, whereas dyseidetics preferred a serial recall strategy. However, this study suggested that normals were as heterogeneous in their learning styles as dyslexics. When the two subtypes were combined they did not differ from normals.

Neuropsychological Classification

The framework for this subtyping research was based on the literature which has examined children and adults with brain injuries, soft neurological signs (minimal brain dysfunction), and related research on the behavioral correlates of brain function as assessed by neurological evaluation and methods such as electroencephalograms. Although the neuropsychological tradition has a long and controversial history in the study of learning disabilities, it has generated a number of interesting research studies which have been used as the basis for classification and intervention with learning disabled children

Mattis, French, and Rapin (1975) studied 113 children between the ages of 8 and 18 who were diagnosed as brain-damaged dyslexics ($n = 53$), brain-damaged readers ($n = 31$), and non-brain-damaged dyslexics ($n = 29$) by pediatric neurologists, electroencephalograms, and educational assessment.

Children were given a battery of neuropsychological tests that indexed general ability (WISC), visual-spatial abilities, perceptual-motor performance, and language. *A priori* decision rules were developed to classify children. They identified a language disorder subtype (39%, *Subtype 1*), an articulation-graphomotor dyscoordination subtype (37%, *Subtype 2*), and a visual-perceptual disorder subtype (16%, *Subtype 3*). Within the various diagnostic groups selected by Mattis et al. (1975), language disorders were more common among brain-damaged dyslexics, while articulation and graphomotor disorders were more frequent among brain-damaged readers. Disorders of visual perception were less common and spread evenly across diagnostic groups.

Mattis (1978) attempted to replicate the earlier study with a sample of 163 minority children who were diagnosed as dyslexic and identified the same subtypes in 78% of the sample. Unlike the first study, 63% of the minority children were classified as language disordered, only 10% presented articulation-graphomotor problems, and 5% had visual-perceptual impairments. Unfortunately, neither study reported data on the reliability of classification procedure nor on the external validity of the subtypes.

Denckla (1972) described three clinical syndromes that were similar to those reported by Mattis et al. (1975): a language disordered group (*Subtype 1*), a visual-spatial disorder group (*Subtype 2*), and a dyscontrol (*Subtype 3*). However, unlike Mattis, she noted that 70% of her clinic sample of disabled readers either did not fit subtypes described elsewhere in the literature or presented mixed patterns of deficits. Later, Denckla (1977, 1978) proposed six subtypes with the following characteristics: (*Subtype 1*) Global-mixed language disorder (generally low language abilities); (*Subtype 2*) Articulation-graphomotor disorder (poor articulation and fine motor skills); (*Subtype 3*) Anomic-repetition disorder (poor naming, digit span, and sentence repetition); (*Subtype 4*) Dysphonemic sequencing disorder (similar to subtype 3 but characterized by phonetic errors and problems with syntax); (*Subtype 5*) Verbal learning disorder (general low verbal ability); and (*Subtype 6*) Correlational disorder (absence of atypical reading patterns but reading below that expected from IQ scores).

Although a number of Denckla's subtypes resemble those reported in the clinical literature of the time, they appear to be based primarily on clinical impressions and evidence was not offered concerning external validity (Doehring, Triter, Patel, & Fiedorowicz, 1981; Satz & Morris, 1981).

Summary of Clinical Inferential Classification

There is difficulty in summarizing literature in this area because of the diverse use of measures and approaches. Overall, it appears that there is a clear language subtype, but there are a number of other different subtypes based on the variables of interest but few common subtypes across many approaches. In evaluating the utility of these studies, the first problem encountered was the nature of the research samples themselves. As Satz and Morris (1981) pointed out, most of the clinical-inferential studies did not include appropriate comparison groups of normal readers to determine whether clinical subtypes were indeed deviant or idiosyncratic of learning disabled children. As noted in the next section, it was common to find "normally appearing" subtypes in empirical studies of LD samples. In addition, most of the samples were preselected and subject to referral and diagnostic bias. These clinic-based samples may not have represented the range of child and socio-demographic characteristics in more typical school-identified samples.

Attention to the issues of reliability and validity was notably absent from reports reviewed in this section. The specific criteria used to classify individuals was obscure in many of these studies and appeared to rely on the visual inspection of complex multivariate profiles.

A final issue in evaluating the utility of this work was the lack of evidence concerning external validity. For example, we often do not know whether the subtypes described in this section differed according to age, sex, race, IQ, and school performance. At the same time, research on the clinical-inferential classification of LD subtypes appears to have had heuristic merit in stimulating more objective research.

RATIONALLY DEFINED SUBGROUPS

An alternative approach to subtyping an entire sample is to select a subgroup of children who have the same characteristic in common. This technique is well suited for experimental studies in which the investigator wishes to determine the effects of a specific type of learning problem on performance and/or how performance varies under different task demands or treatments. Thus, child characteristics are varied along a single variable, as opposed to the multiple variable strategy used in most subtype studies.

One of the best examples of research in this vein can be found in a series of studies by Torgesen and his colleagues on memory (Torgesen, 1982). Another recent example can be found in the work of Bradley and Bryant (1983) who studied backward readers and normals as a function of whether they could both read and spell words that varied in difficulty. Also, Rourke (1982) used this approach to subtype children who showed different patterns of deficits on reading, spelling, and arithmetic subsets.

The experiments by Torgesen (1982) and his colleagues compared the performance of three subgroups. The target group (*Subtype 1*) was composed of LD children who showed severe deficits in short-term memory (STM) capacity as measured by a digit span task. This group was compared to two comparison groups composed of (*Subtype 2*) LD children who did not show memory deficits and (*Subtype 3*) average achievers. In an initial series of 13 experiments, it was demonstrated that the performance deficits of the target group were stable across tasks and materials, and were unaffected by incentives or the use of mnemonic strategies (see Torgesen, 1982). Having demonstrated that children with STM deficits formed a relatively homogeneous subgroup who exhibited stable performance on experimental tasks, Torgesen then showed a relationship between STM group membership and academic problems (Torgesen & Houck, 1980; Torgesen, Rashotte, Greenstein, Houck, & Portes, 1987).

Recently, research on phonological processing deficits also illustrates the utility of the rationally defined approach to subtyping. Phonological processing deficits have been causally linked to the reading process in a number of studies and reviews of studies (Bradley & Bryant, 1978; Stanovich, 1988; Wagner & Torgesen, 1987). This particular kind of learning disability may constitute a rather large proportion of learning disabled children who have reading problems. There are a number of research studies which have examined this issue.

For instance, Fox and Routh (1980, 1983) examined 45 first grade children who were at risk for reading disabilities on a phoneme segmentation task. Children who were good readers had no problem with this task while the poor readers could almost never perform this task correctly. In a follow-up study of these same children, the children who could not do the phoneme segmentation task in first grade were considered severely disabled readers, performing almost two years behind IQ matched controls.

Also, Foster and Torgesen (1980) related phonological processing and short term memory (STM) deficits demonstrating differences between the LD-STM and LD-normal STM group as a function of study methods. LD-STM children had great difficulty learning to spell new words in both free and structured study conditions, whereas difficulty for the LD-STM normal group was apparent only in the free study condition. Finally, the sound blending performance of the LD-STM group was shown to diminish as the number of phonemes in words increased in relation to that shown by LD-STM normal and average achieving children (Torgesen, 1982).

Feagans and Merriwether (1990) examined 63 LD and 66 normally achieving children who had visual perceptual problems at 6 or 7 years of age, as assessed by a letter-like forms task. The children who were categorized as having these perceptual problems did not differ from the other children on demographic characteristics or on measures of verbal IQ. The perceptual deficit children (both LD and non-LD) performed more poorly on the non-verbal IQ measure. They also performed more poorly on reading tests over the early elementary school years and at the end of elementary school. This demonstration of the long-term effects of a particular deficit was a significant contribution to this kind of literature by using external measures over time for validating the importance of this rationally defined subtype.

Finally, Rourke (1975, 1982) and his colleagues studied three rationally defined subgroups of children who showed different combinations of deficits on the Wide Range Achievement Test (WRAT). *Subtype 1* had reading, spelling, and arithmetic scores below the 19th percentile on all three subtests. *Subtype 2* (reading- and spelling-disabled) displayed good arithmetic scores and poor reading and spelling scores. *Subtype 3* (arithmetic-disabled) showed good reading and spelling combined with lower arithmetic scores.

Rourke and Finlayson (1978) and Rourke and Strang (1978) compared the three subtypes on neuropsychological tests and found that *Subtype 3* children had adequate verbal skills, but poorer visual-perceptual and tactile skills. *Subtype 2* children displayed better visual-spatial skills but poorer linguistic skills. *Subtype 1* who were deficient in all three achievement areas showed severe verbal deficits. Recently, Fletcher and Satz (1985) and Siegel and Linder (1984) reported differences between Rourke's achievement subgroups on memory tasks.

Summary of rationally defined subgroups. The studies reviewed here illustrate several approaches to subtyping that involve the classification of more homogeneous subgroups of LD children along a single dimension. Also, they demonstrate the importance of controlling sample heterogeneity as opposed to simply comparing heterogeneous groups of LD and NLD children. However, as noted by Torgesen (1982), this approach is not without its limitations. The major one being that although children within a subgroup may have a given characteristic in common, they are likely to vary greatly with respect to other characteristics which are not controlled in selecting the target group and which are often not measured as part of the research design. In addition, since children are usually selected according to preselected performance on one or a few variables, it is difficult to estimate the number of children who exhibit these given characteristics in relation to those who exhibit other types of problems. Nevertheless, the rationally defined subgroups approach represents an important advance over heterogeneous group comparisons because it (a) facilitates experimental replication, (b) provides more confined paradigm for testing specific hypotheses, and (c) allows the investigator to explore more subtle and complex relationships between processing deficits and performance because of reduced within group heterogeneity.

MULTIVARIATE EMPIRICAL CLASSIFICATION

The studies reviewed in this section used multivariate statistical classification techniques to subdivide heterogeneous LD samples into more homogeneous subtypes based on their performance across an array of variables. These classification procedures were at times theoretically driven but were often empirically driven by the subtypes that emerged from the statistical procedures.

Generally, there are two basic empirical techniques for accomplishing the task of grouping individuals together across multiple variables: Q-factor analysis and cluster analysis. The Q-factor technique is conceptually similar to traditional factor analysis (sometimes called the R-technique). However, the Q-technique involves the factor analysis of correlations among subjects. Thus, the Q-technique results in factors that describe groups of similar children rather than groups of similar tests. Cluster analysis, on the other hand, is an iterative technique which successively matches children who display either a similar level of response or a similar pattern of response across an array of variables. Although the definition of similarity and the rules for joining subjects may vary, the basic technique operates in such a fashion as to increase the homogeneity within subsets of children while decreasing the overlap among subsets. Thus, over successive iterations, the variance within subsets becomes small in relation to variance among subsets. It is important to note that although these techniques are empirical, the investigator has no *a priori* knowledge concerning the number of factors or clusters that may be obtained. Accordingly, some theoretical perspective should guide the selection of variables and samples to ensure interpretable results.

A more complete discussion of empirical classification methods can be found in Aldenderfer and Blashfield (1984), Anderberg (1973). Everitt (1980), and Lorr (1983), and its application to subtyping LD students has been discussed by Fisk and Rourke (1983), Morris, Blashfield, and Satz (1981), Rourke (1985), and Lessig, Williams, and Gil (1982).

Q-Factor Research

Q-factor analysis has been used as the primary classification strategy in two major research studies. The general approach taken in the McGill studies was to first classify subjects according to their reading deficits and then to assess linguistic and neuropsychological correlates. The Windsor studies classified on neuropsychological measures and then sought neurological and educational correlates.

The first study by the McGill group (Doehring & Hoshko, 1977) involved a sample of 34 reading disabled children who were given a battery of reading-related measures (letters, words, syllables, and sentences) that assessed visual and auditory-visual matching, oral reading, and visual scanning. Q-factor analysis of this sample yielded three subtypes: *Subtype 1* were children with an oral reading problem (35%) who were described as poor in word, phrase, and sentence reading with near normal silent reading; *Subtype 2* were children with an intermodal association problem (32%) who were described as poor in matching spoken and printed letters, words, and syllables; and *Subtype 3* were children with sequential relation problems (23%;) who were described as poor in visual and visual-auditory matching of words and syllables compared to letters. Doehring and Hoshko verified these three subtypes in a sample of 31 children with mixed handicaps including mental retardation. Also, they found a fourth subtype that reflected visual-perceptual problems that was not represented in the original reading disabled sample.

The second study compared the Doehring and Hoshko (1977) sample to a sample of normal readers in grades 1 - 11 who had been given the same classification measures (Doehring, Hoshko, & Bryans, 1979). Unlike children in the reading disabled sample who were classified into three distinct subtypes, normal readers were not classified into discrete subtypes, and represented as many as six different performance patterns that were distributed evenly across the range of individual differences in the sample. In addition, Doehring et al. (1979) matched 31 normal readers to 31 disabled readers on age and sex. *Q*-factor classification of the combined sample revealed little overlap. Doehring et al. (1979) concluded that subtypes of reading disabled children did not simply represent exaggerated patterns of normal individual differences Moreover, it appeared that the patterns of skill deficits among disabled readers were not characteristic of young beginning readers in the normal sample.

In the last study, Doehring et al. (1981) explored the characteristics of their subtypes more fully and related reading-skill subtypes to those formed by linguistic and neuropsychological measures. Doehring replicated the same three subtypes found previously with a clinic-referred sample of 88 children and young adults. They administered 22 language measures and showed a general language deficiency in the reading disordered sample compared to the 70 normal achievers. However, their measures of language failed to discriminate the three subtypes of reading disability. *Q*-factor analysis did not produce any characteristic neuropsychological profiles for the reading disabled sample across 22 measures. However, neuropsychological measures did discriminate the three reading disability subtypes such that the oral reading subtype was least impaired and the intermodal association subtype was most impaired.

The second set of *Q*-factor studies was the Windsor studies. Petrauskas and Rourke (1979) classified a sample of 133 clinic-referred reading disabled eight- and nine-year-olds who were compared to 27 normal readers. Their neuropsychological test battery included 44 measures of tactile, sequencing, motoric, visual-spatial, auditory-verbal, and abstract-conceptual ability. Although six subtypes were found, reliable classification was obtained for only three. *Subtype 1* had poor auditory language skills relative to good visual-perceptual skills. *Subtype 2* had mixed linguistic sequencing deficits with impaired memory for sentences, visual-spatial memory, and verbal fluency. *Subtype 3* had poor verbal fluency, sentence memory, and eye hand coordination. The fourth subtype was composed mainly of normal readers, but it was not replicated across separate analyses. The follow-up study in this series involved 264 clinic-referred children who ranged in age from 9 to 13 years (Fisk & Rourke, 1979). *Q*-factor analysis with the same 44 measures yielded three reliable subtypes that accounted for 54% of the sample; 20% was unclassified and 26% was classified unreliably.

Cluster Analytic Research

The cluster analytic approach to subtyping is represented by four major research efforts: the Florida Longitudinal Project on Underachievement, the Northwestern studies, the studies at Boys Town Institute for Communication Disorders, and the Carolina Longitudinal Project

The Florida Study. The Florida Longitudinal Study reported by Satz and Morris (1981) and Morris, Blashfield, and Satz (1981) followed an initial classification study by Darby (1978). This study was unique because cluster analysis was first used to identify LD children within a larger ($n = 236$) sample of typical fifth graders who were assessed at the endpoint of a six-year longitudinal study. Two subgroups ($n = 89$) that had average or better IQ scores and were two or more years behind in achievement were classified as LD and retained for further analysis. Also these two subgroups contained children with a larger number of "soft" neurological signs compared to the other five clusters.

Children in the two LD subgroups were then clustered on a battery of neuropsychological measures (see Fletcher & Satz, 1979, 1980). The following five subtypes were identified: *Subtype 1* (30%) Global language impairment; *Subtype 2* (16%) Specific language impairment in fluency; *Subtype 3* (11%) Mixed global language and perceptual impairment; *Subtype 4* (26%) Visual and perceptual-motor impairment; and *Subtype 5* (13%) No neuropsychological impairment. *Subtypes 1* (global language), *3* (language and perceptual), and *4* (perceptual-motor) showed a higher proportion of children with soft neurological signs compared to *Subtypes 2* (specific language) and *5* (no neuropsychological problems). Also, the parents of children in *Subtypes 2* and *5* scored higher on the WRAT reading subtest than those of children in the other three subtypes. Satz and Morris (1981) speculated that *Subtype 5* (no impairment) might be explained by motivational or emotional factors, but were unable to find evidence for this hypothesis with personality tests.

Most recently, Satz, Morris, and Fletcher (1985) reported a retrospective analysis in which children in the Florida Project in grades five, two, and K were clustered separately on the same cognitive measures. The authors reported that *Subtypes 3* and *4* were also found essentially unchanged among younger children. However, *Subtype 2* and *Subtype 5* showed an improvement from grades K to five in cognitive performance. It was noted previously (Satz & Morris, 1981) that the latter two subtypes had fewer soft neurological signs and tended to come from higher SES homes. Satz et al. suggested that subtype membership may be related to later outcomes, but cautioned that longitudinal research would be required to address the issue of the relationship to later outcomes.

The Northwestern Study. The second set of studies was led by Lyon and his colleagues at Northwestern. These studies were based on school-identified samples of LD children who met PL 94-142 criteria and who were receiving special education services. This is in contrast to most of the other studies reviewed thus far who used clinic referred samples. Lyon and Watson (1981) administered a battery of diagnostic measures to a sample of 100 LD and 50 normal 11- to 12-year-olds in the public schools. The battery included measures of receptive and expressive language, visual-spatial ability, perceptual-motor ability, and visual memory. Cluster analysis yielded six subtypes: *Subtype 1* (combined auditory and visual deficits, 11%); *Subtype 2* (combined linguistic and perceptual-motor deficits, –13%); *Subtype 3* (expressive language deficits, –13%); *Subtype 4* (visual perceptual deficits, –34%); *Subtype 5* (auditory sequencing deficits, –13%); and *Subtype 6* (normal diagnostic profile, –17%).

Lyon and Watson (1981) found that *Subtypes 1* and *5* scored lower on both the reading recognition and comprehension subtests of the PIAT compared to *Subtypes 2, 3,* and *4*. As expected *Subtype 6* scored higher than all other subtypes on achievement measures. Like Satz and Morris (1981), they speculated that *Subtype 6* may represent children who perform poorly in school because of social or emotional factors but could not offer evidence to that effect. Subsequently, Lyon, Watson, Reitter, Porch, and Rhodes (1981) found that *Subtypes 1, 3,* and *5* made more errors on the function, names, and dictation subtests of Porch Index of Communicative Ability than the other subtypes and *Subtypes 1* and *3* performed more poorly than other subtypes on the graphic spelling subtest.

In addition, Lyon, Stewart, and Freedman (1982) expanded their eight test battery to 10 measures of linguistic and visual perceptual skills which they administered to 75 LD readers and 42 normal readers between six and nine years of age. The results of cluster analysis with this younger sample and additional measures were substantially different from those reported by Lyon and Watson (1981) and Lyon et al. (1981). This study yielded five rather than six subtypes: *Subtype 1* (24%) - visual perceptual deficit; *Subtype 2* (13%) - auditory linguistic deficit; *Subtype 3* (16%) - normal diagnostic profile; *Subtype 4* (20%) auditory sequencing; and *Subtype 5* (12%) - mixed phonetic and perceptual deficits.

Analysis of Woodcock reading tests showed that *Subtypes 4* and *5* scored lower on the word attack subtest than all other subtypes while *Subtypes 2* and *4* obtained lower word comprehension scores. Also, children in *Subtypes 2* and *4* showed the lowest scores on the passage comprehension subtest. Children in *Subtype 1* were younger than those in *Subtypes 2* and *4*, and those in *Subtype 5* were younger than those in *Subtype 4*. Thus, it appeared visual perceptual and auditory-verbal deficits were associated with younger LD children, while language comprehension and conceptual deficits were characteristic of older LD children.

The Boys Town Study. The third set of studies was conducted at the Boys Town Institute for Communication Disorders. Watson, Goldgar, and Ryschon (1983) cluster analyzed 65 LD children who ranged in age from 7 to 14 years. Included were measures of reading and spelling, language, visual perception, and memory. Watson et al. (1983) factor analyzed their data initially revealing an achievement test factor, a language factor, a visual factor, and a memory factor. Accordingly, their clusters appeared to represent different combinations of deficit performance across the various factors or combinations of variables that were assessed.

Subtype 1 (30%) showed a general visual perceptual deficit compared to average performance on all language measures with uniformly poor reading achievement. *Subtype 2* (26%), in contrast, displayed a general language disorder but average performance on visual perceptual tasks. This cluster also showed a deficit on memory tasks and uniformly poor achievement. *Subtype 3* (43%) was interpreted as a "minimal deficit" subgroup with subaverage performance on four of the 23 measures. Since many of the children in this subgroup had only very mild reading problems, Watson et al. argued that they may represent the lower end of the reading distribution without any outstanding deficits in underlying abilities.

The North Carolina Study. The last set of studies was conducted as part of the Carolina Longitudinal Project (McKinney & Feagans, 1982, 1984) containing 63 newly identified first and second graders who were placed in special education resource settings in public schools. When each LD child was identified, s/he was matched by sex and race to a randomly selected normally achieving child (from the same mainstream classroom). In order to determine the developmental processes that distinguish LD and NLD children, and to isolate distinct subtypes of learning disabilities, both groups were followed longitudinally over a three-year period with multiple measures of linguistic, cognitive, and behavioral competence. In addition to school achievement, data were also obtained on health and educational histories of the children and a variety of descriptive family variables.

Apart from the prospective longitudinal design, a unique feature of this project with respect to research on subtypes was the multivariate, multiple domain approach to assessment. This feature is important because it provided the capability for the external validation of LD subtypes on sets of independent measures that assessed the same processes measured by the classification variables. For example, behavioral data on the same instrument were collected from both classroom teachers and special educators as well as from independent classroom observations. Similarly each task selected for the cognitive and language batteries had another conceptually similar task that could be used for validation purposes. Also, given the longitudinal focus, the opportunity existed to assess the stability of subtypes over time as well as their prognostic value with respect to academic outcomes.

It has been well documented that some LD children have short attention spans and other behavior that can be maladaptive in the classroom (Hallahan, Kauffman, & Lloyd, 1985). Earlier studies in the Carolina Learning Disabilities Project showed that LD children, as a heterogeneous group, displayed maladaptive behavior patterns in the classroom that predicted academic failure over the elementary grades (McKinney & Feagans, 1983, 1984; McKinney & Speece, 1983).

The first cluster analytic study in this project by Speece, McKinney, and Appelbaum (1985) involved the classification and validation of behavioral subtypes in the Carolina Longitudinal sample based on classroom teacher ratings of independence/dependence, task-orientation/distractibility, extroversion/introversion, and considerateness/hostility. The resulting subtypes were interpreted as follows: *Subtype 1* (28.6%) - Attention Deficit; *Subtype 2* (25.4%) Normal Behavior; *Subtype 3* (14.3%) - Conduct Problems; *Subtype 4* (11%) Withdrawn Behavior; *Subtype 5* (9.5%) - Normal Behavior; *Subtype 6* (6.3%) - Low Positive Behavior; and *Subtype 7* (4.8%) - Global Behavior Problems.

The interpretation of *Subtypes 2* and *5* as normal patterns of behavior was supported by the fact that 85% of the normal comparison sample were classified into these two subtypes by the forecasting technique. Contrasts among the subtypes on the SCAN observational system (McKinney, Mason, Perkerson, & Clifford, 1975) generally confirmed hypotheses about classroom behavior generated from the cluster descriptions of classroom teachers. For example, subtypes 3, 6, and 7 (problem behavior types) differed from all others with respect to gross motor inappropriate behavior and aggression. Similarly, the frequency of observed off-task behavior differentiated the normal clusters from the other five as well as *Subtypes 4, 6,* and *7* from the others. Comparable ratings from LD resource teachers also differentiated the subtypes; however, more importantly, the cluster profiles generated from LD teachers showed the same shape as those obtained from classroom teachers with some minor differences in elevation.

It was interesting that the seven subtypes did not differ in academic achievement the first year the LD children were placed in special education (Speece, McKinney, & Appelbaum, 1985). However, in a previous study, McKinney and Feagans (1984) reported that children in the same longitudinal sample, as a heterogeneous group, declined over a three year period compared to average achievers. In order to assess the longitudinal stability and academic consequences of subtype membership, McKinney and Speece (1986) reclassified the LD sample over the next three years of elementary school and assessed academic progress longitudinally. This analysis showed that although children in the various subtypes did not differ in achievement in the first and second grades, they were differentiated over the next two years such that those in normal behavior subtypes and those in the withdrawn subtype showed linear progress on the PIAT, while those in the attention deficit subtype and those exhibiting problem behaviors showed a declining pattern of progress.

Also, McKinney and Speece (1986) report evidence for the longitudinal stability of behavioral subtypes as assessed two distinctly different ways. The first approach was the use of a forecasting technique to reclassify children in subsequent years based on their original subtype membership. When viewed in terms of clinically significant variations (i.e., normal, attention deficit, withdrawn, and conduct problems), it was more likely for a child to be classified as maladaptive at both year 1 and year 3 (55%) than to move from a maladaptive subtype to an adaptive one (11%). In addition, McKinney and Speece (1986) showed that classroom teachers in subsequent years produced the same profile patterns that defined each subtype the first year of the study. In the same vein, external validation was also obtained longitudinally with respect to the ratings of LD teachers who produced essentially the same profiles as classroom teachers each year of the study.

Feagans and Appelbaum (1986) used the same cluster procedures described above to subtype the Carolina Longitudinal sample. This study was unique because the authors had *a priori* clusters they believed would exist from theories of language as well as how these clusters would perform on reading over the elementary school years. In addition, this study divided language skills into 6 separate areas to evaluate the importance of each within the clusters. Six measures which assessed syntax, semantics, and discourse (narrative) skills were used. This study used several experimental tasks to assess language. One of the major tasks was one to assess narrative skill. The comprehension and production of oral narratives was assessed by using a task that has shown to differentiate LD and non LD children as well as disadvantaged and normal children. Furthermore, performance on the narrative and discourse tasks have been related to school achievement, especially reading (Feagans & Farran, 1981; Feagans & Short, 1984, 1986). In this task, children were shown a toy grocery store with dolls and various props. They were read a series of stories about the store and people and then were asked to act out each story with the props provided. The comprehension measure was the number of trials required to act out the story correctly while the major production measure was the number of critical information units in their paraphrase. Other measures of their productive language abilities included the number of words (verbal output) used to paraphrase the story and the complexity of the child's syntax (the proportion of subordinate clauses). Additional measures included a syntax test (Feagans, 1980) and the vocabulary subtest of the WISC-R. On the basis of previous studies, it was predicted that children who were relatively competent on the discourse/narrative comprehension and production part of the task compared to syntax and vocabulary would perform better on the reading tests.

Feagans and Appelbaum (1986) identified the following six language subtypes: *Subtype 1* (superior syntax relative to poor narrative ability - 16%); *Subtype 2* (superior vocabulary relative to poor narrative/language skill - 16%); *Subtype 3* (superior linguistic output and complexity relative to average narrative skill - 14%); *Subtype 4* (good narrative skill relative to poorer syntactic/semantic skill - 27%); *Subtype 5* (superior narrative skill relative to average syntactic skill - 16%); and *Subtype 6* (superior syntactic/semantic skill relative to average narrative skill - 9%).

As in the Speece et al. (1985) study, the interpretation of normal subtypes in this study was supported by forecasting procedures which classified 71% of the NLD sample into normal appearing LD clusters. The six clusters did not differ in nonverbal IQ; however, consistent with results from studies of high-risk children (Feagans & Farran, 1981), the structural deficit subtype contained a higher number of lower SES children. Based on previous studies (Feagans, 1983; Feagans & Short, 1984), Feagans and Appelbaum (1986) hypothesized that children with poorer narrative language skills would score lower on reading tests initially and make less progress longitudinally compared to those with better narrative skills relative to poorer structural skills. This was substantiated by the results. *Subtypes 1, 2,* and *6* had lower achievement scores than *Subtypes 4* and *5* when the children were classified in the first and second grades. Similarly, longitudinal analyses showed that LD children with poorer narrative language (*Subtypes 1, 2,* and *6*) progressed at a slower rate over the three years of the study compared to those with poorer structural language and hyperverbal children (*Subtypes 3, 4,* and *6*).

Two other studies from the Carolina project have been completed that examine various skills within cognition and perception. The first used the longitudinal school-identified sample and a battery of perceptual, problem solving, and linguistic measures (McKinney, Short, & Feagans, 1985). The second study used a sample of reading disabled third and fourth graders and a theoretically based battery of information processing measures (Speece, 1987).

The McKinney et al. study used six measures to index the following processes: visual recognition (match-to-sample), sequential problem-solving (bits of information), perceptual-motor skills (WISC-R coding), linguistic comprehension (trials to criterion in an instructional problem), linguistic production (information units), and semantics (WISC-R vocabulary). Children in the Carolina Longitudinal sample were clustered by using the same procedures as other studies in this section; the following subtypes were identified: *Subtype 1* (11%) Normal; *Subtype 2* (7%) - Severe Perceptual Deficit; *Subtype 3* (,'7%) Severe Language Comprehension Deficit; *Subtype 4* (22%) - *Normal*; *Subtype 5* (14%) - Mixed Perceptual-Linguistic Deficits; and *Subtype 6* (18%) - Marginal Perceptual/Semantic Problems.

The results of this study were similar to others in this section which reported distinct perceptual, linguistic, and mixed perceptual-linguistic subtypes (e.g., Lyon & Watson, 1981; Satz & Morris, 1981). However, the low prevalence of severe perceptual deficits (7%) (*Subtype 2*) compared to language deficits (27%) (*Subtype 3*) was unexpected. In this regard, it was interesting that 29% of the average achieving sample was forecasted into *Subtype 2* (Perceptual deficit), while 63% were classified into normal-appearing LD clusters. The six subtypes did not differ in reading achievement initially in the first and second grades; however, *Subtypes 2, 3*, and *5* scored lower on math than *Subtypes 1, 4,* and *6*. As with the other longitudinal studies described above, the various perceptual/linguistic subtypes showed different patterns of academic progress. *Subtypes 2, 3,* and *5* showed a declining pattern of progress in reading compared to *Subtypes 1* and *4*. Interestingly, *Subtype 6* maintained its relative superiority in math but fell behind in reading.

In the second study in the cognitive domain, Speece (1987) sought to identify theoretically based subtypes by using experimental measures of information processing that were related to various single deficit hypotheses of reading disability. The seven measures were selected to index sustained attention, phonetic and semantic encoding, speed of recoding (naming), short-term memory capacity, and strategic organization in memory. The study sample contained 59 third and fourth grade school identified LD children who were 1.5 years or more behind on the Gray Oral Reading Test and were average or better in Verbal IQ. Also, data were collected on 21 average achievers for comparison purposes. Six clusters were identified: *Subtype 1* (Short-term Memory Deficit - 15%); *Subtype 2* (Speed of Recoding Deficit - 20%); *Subtype 3* (Mild Recoding/Attention Deficit -17%); *Subtype 4* (Mild Encoding/Severe Recoding Deficit -17%); *Subtype 5* (Marginal Performance - 15%); and *Subtype 6* (Mild Memory/Recoding Deficit -15%).

Although, Speece (1987) found no differences among her information-processing subtypes on the WISC-R or reading subtests of the Woodcock-Johnson Achievement Battery, her study does provide important information on the relative frequency of various information-processing deficits that have been reported in the experimental literature, but studied from a univariate as opposed to a multivariate perspective.

Related Studies

A specific study of memory processes in learning disabled children was conducted by Swanson (1988). He gave 50 LD students and 25 nondisabled students a battery of 7 memory tasks to assess various aspects of overall memory. These dependent measures from the tasks were further analyzed, producing 8 factor scores representing elaboration, short term memory for specific word features, depletion of elaborative processing resources, central processing capacity, selective attention, resource allocation during effortful encoding, organization, and low effort/secondary recall. The Cluster solution chosen produced 8 clusters, although over half of the LD sample $(n = 26)$ was contained in a single cluster. Thus, the remaining 7 had between 2 and 7 members.

These included: *Subtype 1* (4%), selective attention deficits; *Subtype 2* (6%), elaboration and central processing deficits; *Subtype 3* (52%), elaboration deficits; *Subtype 4* (12%), no memory deficits; *Subtype 5* (6%), depletion of elaborative processing deficit; *Subtype 6* (4%), effortless encoding and central processing deficits; *Subtype 7* (10%), central and deficits; and, *Subtype 8* (6%), selective attention and central processing deficits. The large subtype (3) contained children who were primarily deficient in accessing structural resources during elaborative encoding. This group's performance differed significantly from the non-disabled group on these measures. It was difficult to interpret the rest of the subgroups because of the small number of students in each group. External validation for intelligence and achievement was discriptively presented but not analyzed, presumably because of the small numbers in the subgroups. This study was valuable in demonstrating that not all LD children have the same memory problems but that a majority appear to have difficulty forming multiple connections between task material and information in memory.

A final study of some importance is the only long term replication study of cluster analysis performed on a group of LD children at 10 years and again at 24 years of age (Spreen & Haaf, 1986). The instruments used at 10 years included a sentence repetition task, left-right orientation, the Wide Range Achievement Test (WRAT), and a number of scaled scores from the WISC-R. The cluster analysis at 10 years produced six clusters. There were two small clusters: *Subtype 1* represented overall excellent performance (13%) and *Subtype 2* represented overall very poor performance (8%). The other clusters included *Subtype 3*—an arithmetic disability cluster (19%), *Subtype 4*—a reading disability cluster (14%), *Subtype 5*—a linguistic disability cluster (17%), and *Subtype 6*—a visuo-perceptual cluster (14%). The remaining 15% could not be clustered. At the adult follow-up there was support for a replication of the clusters found at 10 years of age except for the linguistic subtype. Although a replication of this subtype was not obtained, the original members of the linguistic subtype fell into the very low performing groups as adults. All the LD groups performed more poorly than a non-LD group of adults, indicating the persistence of problems into adulthood.

Evaluation of Empirical Classification

The research on empirical classification demonstrates the importance of creating more homogeneous subtypes of specific learning disability since it clearly shows the intra-individual differences among children with learning disabilities. However, since different investigators have taken different approaches with respect to classification procedures and have used different types of measures, it is not possible to draw firm conclusions at this time about the existence of particular subtypes, the number of subtypes that characterize the LD population, or the number of children they represent.

In a recent critique of this empirical approach, Kavale and Forness (1984) raised some further limitations of this approach. They argued that clustering techniques did not reflect developmental change and that the clusters that emerged reflected the measures chosen for the study. These are valid criticisms, although they could also be levelled at almost all the studies of learning disabilities.

Particular aspects of clustering approach are also problematic, including the logic of the procedures. The number of clusters chosen to interpret is clearly made by the researcher, since cluster analysis results in n clusters. In addition, the similarity metric (distance, pattern, or scatter) have implications for the kind of clusters that will emerge (Kavale & Forness, 1984). These problems can only be solved by *a priori* hypotheses about the kind of clusters one is trying to find and some thought about which similarity metric one believes is important to describe the phenomena. A few studies have addressed this issue but not most (Feagans & Appelbaum, 1986; McKinney & Speece, 1986; McKinney, Speece, & Appelbaum, 1985).

Finally and most importantly, many of the cluster analytic studies are really atheoretical with no real hypotheses about the clusters to be found. Without this guiding framework the resulting clusters may be merely an empirical fishing expedition. With all these limitations in mind, several common patterns have emerged from this diverse set of studies that are worthy of comment.

Most of the empirical classification studies that have used both perceptual and linguistic measures have reported specific visual perceptual and/or perceptual-motor subtypes that display average to above average language abilities. The prevalence of this pattern ranged from 24% to 34% of the samples in the majority of studies, although McKinney et al. (1985) and Mattis et al. (1975) reported low prevalence figures of 7% and 8%. The rather consistent evidence for specific perceptual subtypes provides some support for early single deficit theories that emphasized perceptual processes in reading (Benton, 1975; Hallahan & Cruickshank, 1973).

As with the general domain of perceptual processing, the majority of studies that classified children with measures from both domains reported subtypes with specific auditory and linguistic deficits combined with intact perceptual and/or perceptual-motor skills. The prevalence of linguistic and/ or auditory processing subtypes varied from 13% to 41% of the samples studied.

Although less prevalent than specific deficit patterns across either perceptual or linguistic measures, all but one of the empirical studies with appropriate measures reported mixed deficit subtypes that comprised from 8% to 23% of the sample. The presence of mixed deficit subtypes as well as specific deficit subtypes in one domain but not another suggests that the performance of all LD children (or even most of the population) cannot be explained by a single syndrome theory, and that all LD children do not subdivide neatly within the larger domains of perceptual and linguistic processes.

At the same time, evidence has been found for the existence of subtypes that reflect attentional disorders (Speece et al., 1985) and memory deficits (Speece, 1987; Torgesen, 1982), as well as those defined by perceptual and linguistic measures on more traditional psychoeducational and neuropsychological test batteries. Also, the data from at least two studies indicate that specific subtypes can be found within domains of psychological processes such as language (Feagans & Appelbaum, 1986) and information processing (Speece, 1987).

Finally, most of the studies report at least one cluster, containing children who functioned within the normal range on a variety of measures. Conclusions about these clusters cannot really be made because of the limited kind of variables used in most of the studies (Kavale & Forness, 1984).

CONCLUSION

The research on subtypes of learning disabilities reflects the diversity of theoretical viewpoints represented in the field. Thus, the heterogeneity of both the children and researchers is evident. Since most of studies were designed with a certain perspective on what a learning disability is, the sample selected and the measures chosen reflected this thinking. Thus, it is difficult to compare even studies using the same base methods of analyses. For instance, the Florida study (Morris, Blashfield, & Satz, 1981; Satz & Morris, 1981; Satz, Morris, & Fletcher, 1985) and the Carolina study (Feagans & Appelbaum, 1986; McKinney, Short, & Feagans, 1985; McKinney & Speece, 1986; McKinney, Speece, & Appelbaum, 1985) both used cluster analysis. Yet because the Florida group had a neuropsychological approach to learning disabilities, they used a battery of measures that reflected the search for "soft" neurological signs. On the other hand, the Carolina study had a more psychological/environmental approach, using measures which reflected basic processes in development.

Although several common trends in the findings from these studies were noted, the generality and potential for application of this body of research is severely limited by its diversity. Some investigators have sought more homogeneous subgroups of children within a particular domain of functioning such as language or academic performance, while others have used clinically based psychoeducational and neuropsychological test batteries. Rarely, however, have various investigators given a clear theoretical rationale for the use of a particular method or the selection of a particular set of measures.

The issue of diversity among methods and measures is difficult to deal with scientifically because traditionally the individual investigator has the prerogative to choose those methods and measures which in his/her professional judgement best address the research question of interest. On the other hand, there may be a real danger that the method or measure will drive the science. We have seen this with the use of the popular use of the IQ measure.

With all these limitations, it is clear that the subtyping research has advanced the field of learning disabilities by providing some replications of certain subtypes and suggesting that some of these subtypes have implications for later academic and life functioning. Hopefully, future work in this area will yield more important information through larger scale studies which include more comprehensive measures given over time. In addition, it is hoped that many of the studies will examine the precursors to learning disabilities in very young children. With the subtypes derived from these future studies, we may truly be able to design prevention and intervention programs which are targeted at those processes that appear to be implicated in later academic achievement and life functioning.

REFERENCES

Alberg, J. (1985). *Evaluation of alternative procedures for identifying learning disabled students.* Unpublished doctoral dissertation, University of North Carolina, Chapel Hill.

Aldenderfer, M. S., & Blashfield, R. K. (1984). *Cluster analysis.* Beverly Hills, CA: Sage Publications.

Altus, G. T. (1956). A WISC profile for retarded readers. *Journal of Counseling Psychology, 20,* 155–156.

Anderberg, M. R. (1973). *Cluster analysis for applications.* New York: Academic Press.

Bannatyne, A. (1979). Spatial competence, learning disabilities, auditory-vocal deficits, and a WISC-R subtest recategorization. *Journal of Clinical Child Psychology, 8,* 194–200.

Bayliss, J., & Liversey, P. J. (1985). Cognitive strategies of children with reading disabilities and normal readers in visual sequential memory. *Journal of Learning Disabilities, 18*(6), 326–332.

Belmont, L., & Birch, H. G. (1966). The intellectual profile of retarded readers. *Perceptual and Motor Skills, 22,* 787–816.

Benton, A. L. (1975). Developmental dyslexia: Neurological aspects. *Advances in Neurology, 7,* 1–41.

Black, F. W. (1974). WISC verbal-performance discrepancies as indicators of neurological dysfunction in pediatric patients. *Journal of Clinical Psychology, 30,* 165–167.

Boder, E. (1970). Developmental dyslexia: A new diagnostic approach based on the identification of three subtypes. *The Journal of School Health, 40,* 289–290.

Boder, E. (1973). Developmental dyslexia: A diagnostic approach based on three atypical reading-spelling patterns. *Developmental Medicine and Child Neurology, 15,* 663–687.

Bradley, L., & Bryant, P. (1978). Difficulties in auditory organization as a possible cause of reading backwardness. *Nature, 271,* 746–747.

Bradley, L., & Bryant, P. (1983). Categorizing sounds and learning to read—A causal connection. *Nature, 301,* 419–421.

Bradley, L., & Bryant, P. (1985). *Rhyme and reason in reading and spelling.* Ann Arbor: University of Michigan Press.

Burks, H. F., & Bruce, P. (1955). The characteristics of poor and good readers as disclosed by the Wechsler Intelligence Scale for Children. *Journal of Educational Psychology, 46,* 486–493.

Camp, B. W., & Dolcourt, J. L. (1977). Reading and spelling in good and poor readers. *Journal of Learning Disabilities, 10*(5), 46–53.

Cone, T. E., & Wilson, L. R. (1981). Quantifying a severe discrepancy: A critical analysis. *Learning Disability Quarterly, 4,* 359–371.

Darby, R. O. (1978). *Learning disabilities: A multivariate search for subtypes.* Unpublished doctoral dissertation, University of Florida, Gainesville.

Denckla, M. B. (1972). Clinical syndromes in learning disabilities: The case for "splitting" vs. "lumping." *Journal of Learning Disabilities, 5,* 401–406.

Denckla, M. B. (1977). Minimal brain dysfunction and dyslexia: Beyond diagnosis by exclusion. In M. E. Blaw, J. Rapin, & M. Kinsbourne (Eds.), *Child neurology.* New York: Spectrum.

Denckla, M. B. (1978). Critical review of "electroencephalographic and neurophysiological studies in dyslexia." In A. L. Benton & D. Pearl (Eds.), *Dyslexia: An appraisal of current knowledge.* New York: Oxford University Press.

Doehring, D. G., & Hoshko, I. M. (1977). Classification of reading problems by the technique of factor analysis. *Cortex, 13,* 281–294.

Doehring, D. G., Hoshko, I. M., & Bryans, B. N. (1979). Statistical classification of children with reading problems. *Journal of Clinical Neuropsychology, 1,* 5–16.

Doehring, D. G., Triter, R. L., Patel, P. G., & Fiedorowicz, C. A. M. (1981). *Reading disabilities: The interaction of reading, language, and neuropsychological deficits.* New York: Academic Press.

Everitt, B. (1980). *Cluster analysis* (2nd ed.). New York: Halsted Press.

Feagans, L. (1980). Children's understanding of some temporal terms denoting order, duration, and simultaneity. *Journal of Psycholinguistic Research, 9*(1), 41–57.

Feagans, L. (1983). Discourse processes in learning disabled children. In J. D. McKinney & L. Feagans (Eds.), *Current topics in learning disabilities* (Vol. 1, pp. 87–115). Norwood, NJ: Ablex.

Feagans, L., & Appelbaum, M. I. (1986). Language subtypes and their validation in learning disabled children. *Journal of Educational Psychology, 78*(5), 358–364.

Feagans, L., & Farran, D. (1981). How demonstrated comprehension can get muddled in production. *Developmental Psychology, 17,* 718–727.

Feagans, L., & McKinney, J. D. (1981). Pattern of exceptionality across domains in learning disabled children. *Journal of Applied Developmental Psychology, 1*(4), 313–328.

Feagans, L., & Merriwether, A. (1990). Discrimination of letter-like forms in learning disabled and normal children: A subgroup analysis and validation. *Journal of Learning Disabilities. 23,* 417–425.

Feagans, L., & Short, E. J. (1984). Developmental differences in the comprehension and production of narratives by reading disabled and normally achieving children. *Child Development, 55,* 1727–1736.

Feagans, L., & Short, E. J. (1986). Referential communication and reading performance in learning disabled children over a 3-year period. *Developmental Psychology, 22,* 177–183.

Fisk, J. L., & Rourke, B. P. (1979). Identification of subtypes of learning disabled children at three age levels: A neuropsychological, multivariate approach. *Journal of Clinical Neuropsychology, 1,* 289–310.

Fisk, J. L., & Rourke, B. P. (1983). Neuropsychological subtyping of learning-disabled children: History, methods, implications. *Journal of Learning Disabilities, 16*(9), 529–531.

Fletcher, J. M., & Satz, P. (1979). Unitary deficit hypotheses of reading disabilities: Has Vellutiono led us astray? *Journal of Learning Disabilities, 12,* 155–159.

Fletcher, J. M., & Satz, P. (1980). Developmental changes in the neuropsychological correlates of reading achievement: A six-year longitudinal follow-up. *Journal of Clinical Neurology, 2*(1), 23–37

Fletcher, J. M., & Satz, P. (1985). External validation of learning disability typologies. In B. P. Rourke (Ed.), *Neuropsychology of learning disabilities* (pp. 40–64). New York: The Guilford Press.

Forness, S. R., Sinclair, E., & Gutherie, D. (1983). Learning disability discrepancy formulas: Their use in actual practice. *Learning Disability Quarterly, 6,* 107–114.

Foster, K., & Torgesen, J. K. (1980). *Learning to spell under two study conditions by learning disabled children.* Unpublished manuscript.

Fox, B., & Routh, D. K. (1980). Phonemic analysis and severe reading disability in children. *Journal of Psycholinguistic Research, 9,* 115–119.

Fox, B., & Routh, D. K. (1983). Reading disability, phonemic analysis, and dysphonic spelling: A follow-up study. *Journal of Clinical Child Psychology, 12,* 28–32.

Frostig, M., & Horne, D. (1964). *The Frostig program for the development of visual perception: Teacher's guide.* Chicago: Follett.

Gallagher, J. J. (1966). Children with developmental imbalances: A psycho-educational definition. In W. M. Cruickshank (Ed.), *The teacher of brain-injured children.* Syracuse, NY: Syracuse University Press.

Hallahan, D. P., & Cruickshank, W. M. (1973). *Psychoeducational foundations of learning disabilities.* Englewood Cliffs, NJ: Prentice-Hall.

Hallahan, D. P., Kauffman, J. M., & Lloyd, J. W. (1985). *Introduction to learning disabilities* (2nd ed.). Englewood Cliffs, NJ: Prentice Hall.

Hammill, D. D., & Larsen, S. C. (1974). The effectiveness of psycholinguistic training. *Exceptional Children, 41,* 5–14.

Holroyd, J., & Wright, F. (1965). Neurological implications of WISC and Bender Gestalt test in predicting arithmetic and reading achievement for white and non-white children. *Journal of Consulting Psychology, 29,* 206–212.

Ingram, T. T. S. (1969). Developmental disorders of speech. In P. J. Vinken & G. W. Bruyn (Eds.), *Handbook of clinical neurology* (Vol. 4). Amsterdam: North Holland.

Ingram, T. T. S., Mann, A. W., & Blackburn, I. (1970). A retrospective study of 82 children with reading disability. *Developmental Medicine and Child Neurology, 12,* 271–282.

Johnson, D. J., & Myklebust., H. R. (1967). *Learning disabilities.* New York: Grune & Stratton.

Kallos, G. L., Grabow, J. M., & Guarino, E. A. (1961). The WISC profile of disabled readers. *Personnel and Guidance Journal, 39*, 476–478.

Kaufman, A. S. (1976). A new approach to the interpretation of test scatter on the WISC-R. *Journal of Learning Disabilities, 9*, 160–168.

Kaufman, A. S. (1981). The Wechsler Scales and learning disabilities. *Journal of Learning Disabilities, 14*(7), 397–398.

Kavale, K. A., & Forness, S. R. (1984). A meta-analysis of the validity of Wechsler Scale profiles and recategorizations: Patterns of parodies? *Learning Disability Quarterly, 7*, 136–156.

Kirk, S. T., McCarthy, J., & Kirk, W. (1968). *Illinois Test of Psycholinguistic Abilities.* (rev. ed.) Urbana: University of Illinois Press.

Lessig, E. E., Williams, V., & Gil, E. (1982). A cluster-analytically derived typology: Feasible alternative to clinical diagnostic classification of children? *Journal of Abnormal Child Psychology, 10*, 451–482.

Lorr, M. (1983). *Cluster analysis for social scientists.* San Francisco: Jossey-Bass, Inc.

Lyon, R., Stewart, N., & Freedman, D. (1982). Neuropsychological characteristics of empirically derived subgroups of learning disabled readers. *Journal of Clinical Neuropsychology, 4*, 343–365.

Lyon, R., & Watson, B. (1981). Empirically derived subgroups of learning disabled readers: Diagnostic characteristics. *Journal of Learning Disabilities, 14*(5), 256–261.

Lyon, R., Watson, B., Reitter, S., Porch, B., & Rhodes, J. (1981). Selected linguistic and perceptual abilities of empirically derived subgroups of learning disabled readers. *Journal of School Psychology, 19*(2), 152–156.

Mattis, S. (1978). Dyslexia syndromes. A working hypothesis that works. In A. Benton & D. Pearl (Eds.), *Dyslexia: An appraisal of current knowledge* (pp. 43–58). New York: Oxford.

Mattis, S., French, J. H., & Rapin, I. (1975). Dyslexia in children and young adults: Three independent neuropsychological syndromes. *Developmental Medicine and Child Neurology, 17*, 150–163.

McKinney, J. D. (1987). Research on the identification of learning-disabled children: Perspectives on changes in educational policy. In S. Vaughn & C. S. Box (Eds.), *Research in learning disabilities. Issues and future directions* (pp. 215–237) Boston: Little, Brown, & Co.

McKinney, J. D. (1988). Research on conceptually and empirically derived subtypes of specific learning disabilities. In M. C. Wang, H. J. Wolberg, & M. C. Reynolds (Eds.), *The handbook of special education: Research and practice* (pp. 253–281). Oxford, England: Pergamon Press.

McKinney, J. D., & Feagans, L. (1980, July). *Learning disabilities in the classroom.* Final report: Bureau of Education for the Handicapped, U. S. Department of Health, Education, and Welfare, Grant No. G00-76-0-5224, Washington, DC.

McKinney, J. D., & Feagans, L. (1982, March). *Longitudinal research on learning disabilities.* Paper presented at the Association for Children and Adults with Learning Disabilities, Chicago, IL.

McKinney, J. D., & Feagans, L. (Eds). (1983). *Current topics in learning disabilities* (Vol. 1). Norwood, NJ: Ablex Corp.

McKinney, J. D., & Feagans, L. (1984). Academic and behavioral characteristics: Longitudinal studies of learning disabled children and average achievers. *Learning Disability Quarterly, 7*(3), 251–265.

McKinney, J. D., Mason, J., Perkerson, K., & Clifford, M. (1975). Relationship between classroom behavior and academic achievement. *Journal of Educational Psychology, 67*, 198–203.

McKinney, J. D., Short, E. J., & Feagans, L. (1985). Academic consequences of perceptual-linguistic subtypes of learning disabled children. *Learning Disabilities Research, 1*, 6–17.

McKinney, J. D., & Speece, D. L. (1983). Classroom behavior and the academic progress of learning disabled students. *Journal of Applied Developmental Psychology, 4*, 149–161.

McKinney, J. D., & Speece, D. L. (1986). Longitudinal stability and academic consequences of behavioral subtypes of learning disabled children. *Journal of Educational Psychology*, *78*(5), 365–372.

Morris, R., Blashfield, R., & Satz, P. (1981). Neuropsychology and cluster analysis: Potentials and problems. *Journal of Clinical Neuropsychology*, *3*, 79–99.

Myklebust, H. R. (1978). Toward a science of dyslexiology. In H. R. Myklebust (Ed.), *Progress in learning disabilities* (Vol. 4, pp. 1–39). New York: Grune & Stratton.

Obrzut, J. E. (1979). Dichotic listening and bisensory memory skills in qualitatively diverse dyslexic readers. *Journal of Learning Disabilities*, *12*, 304–314.

Petrauskas, R., & Rourke, B. (1979). Identification of subgroups of retarded readers: A neuropsychological multivariate approach. *Journal of Clinical Neuropsychology*, *1*, 17–37.

Rourke, B. P. (1975). Brain-behavior relationships in children with learning disabilities. *American Psychologist*, *30*, 911–920.

Rourke, B. P. (1982). Central processing deficiencies in children: Toward a developmental neuropsychological model. *Journal of Clinical Neuropsychology*, *4*(1), 1–18.

Rourke, B. P. (Ed.). (1985). *Neuropsychology of learning disabilities: Essentials of subtype analysis*. New York: Guilford.

Rourke, B. P., & Finlayson, M. A. J. (1978). Neuropsychological significance of variations in patterns of academic performance: Verbal and visual-spatial abilities. *Journal of Abnormal Child Psychology*, *6*(1), 121–133.

Rourke, B. P., & Strang, J. D. (1978). Neuropsychological significance of variations in patterns of academic performance: Motor, psychomotor, and tactile-perceptual abilities. *Journal of Pediatric Psychology*, *3*(2), 62–66.

Ryan, E. B., Short, E. J., & Weed, K. A. (1986). The role of cognitive strategy training in improving the academic performance of learning disabled children. *Journal of Learning Disabilities*, *19*, 521–521.

Satz, P., & Morris, R. (1981). Learning disability subtypes: A review. In F. J. Pirozzolo & M. C. Wittrock (Ed.), *Neuropsychological and cognitive processes in reading*. New York: Academic Press.

Satz, P., Morris, R., & Fletcher, J. M. (1985). Hypothesis, subtypes, and individual differences in dyslexia: Some reflections. In D. Gray & J. Kavanagh (Eds.), *Biobehavioral measures of dyslexia*. Parkton, MD: York Press.

Shepard, L. (1980). An evaluation of the regression discrepancy method for identifying children with learning disabilities. *Journal of Education*, *14*, 79–80.

Siegel, L. S., & Linder, A. (1984). Short-term memory processes in children with reading and arithmetic disabilities. *Developmental Psychology*, *20*, 200–207.

Speece, D. L. (1987). Information processing and reading in subtypes of learning disabled children. *Learning Disability Research*, *2*, 91–102.

Speece, D. L., McKinney, J. D., & Appelbaum, M. I. (1985). Classification and validation of behavioral subtypes of learning disabled children. *Journal of Educational Psychology*, *77*, 67–77.

Stanovich, K. E. (1988). Explaining the difference between the dyslexic and the garden-variety poor reader: The phonological-core variable-difference model. *Journal of Learning Disabilities*, *21*, 590–612.

Spreen, O., & Haaf, R. G. (1986). Empirically derived learning disability subtypes: A replication attempt and longitudinal patterns over 15 years. *Journal of Learning Disabilities*, *19*, 170–180.

Strauss, A. A., & Werner, H. (1942). Disorders of conceptual thinking in the brain injured child. *Journal of Nervous and Mental Disease*, *96*, 153–172.

Swanson, H. L. (1988). Memory subtypes in learning disabled readers. *Learning Disability Quarterly*, *11*, 342–257.

Torgesen, J. K. (1982). The use of rationally defined subgroups in research on learning disabilities. In J. P. Das, R. F. Mulcahy, & A. E. Wall (Eds.), *Theory and research in learning disabilities*. New York: Plenum Press.

Torgesen, J. K., & Houck, D. G. (1980). Processing deficiencies of learning-disabled children who perform poorly on the Digit Span Test. *Journal of Educational Psychology, 72*, 141–160.

Torgensen, J. K., Rashotte, C. A., Greenstein, F., Houck, G., & Portes, P. (1987). Academic difficulties of learning disabled children who perform poorly on memory span tasks. In H. L. Swanson (Ed.), *Memory and learning disabilities: Advances in learning and behavioral disabilities* (pp. 305–333). Greenwich, CT: JAI Press.

Vance, H., Gayor, P., & Coleman, M. (1976). Analysis of cognitive abilities for learning disabled children. *Psychology in the Schools, 13*, 477–483.

Wagner, R. K., & Torgesen, J. K. (1987). The nature of phonological processing and its causal role in the acquisition of reading skills. *Psychological Bulletin, 101*, 192–212.

Watson, B. V., Goldgar, D. E., & Ryschon, K. L. (1983). Subtypes of reading disability. *Journal of Clinical Neuropsychology, 5*(4), 377–399.

Wong, B. Y. (1985). Meta cognition and learning disabilities. In D. L. Forrest-Pressley, G. E. MacKinnon, & T. G. Waller (Eds.), *Metacognition, cognition, and human performance* (Vol. 2, pp. 137–180). New York: Academic Press.

Ysseldyke, J., Algozzine, B., & Epps, S. (1983). A logical and empirical analysis of current practice in classifying students as handicapped. *Exceptional Children, 50*, 160–165.

2

Retreat, Regroup, or Advance? An Agenda for Empirical Classification Research in Learning Disabilities

Deborah L. Speece
David H. Cooper
University of Maryland at College Park

The purpose of this chapter is to identify the themes that have evolved from the recent methodological and substantive papers on empirical classification research. As we reviewed the literature on the application of cluster analysis methods to the field of learning disabilities, we were impressed by the amount of territory already covered. There are a number of content reviews summarizing findings of both clinical and empirical classification research (Fletcher & Morris, 1986; McKinney, 1988; Satz & Morris, 1981); papers addressing general research issues in learning disabilities that invariably include a solid rationale for identifying valid taxonomies (e.g., Keogh, 1987a; Lyon, 1987; Torgesen, 1982); discussions of classification methodology specific to learning disabilities (e.g., Adams, 1985; Lyon & Risucci, 1988; Speece, 1990); and, indeed, entire volumes such as the present one devoted to classification and learning disabilities (e.g., Hooper & Willis, 1989; Rourke, 1985). When we did not impose the restriction of learning disabilities in our selection of readings, we found an even wider array of material encompassing methodological and developmental concerns (e.g., Milligan & Cooper, 1985, 1987; Cross & Paris, 1988; French, 1988; Taylor, Asher, & Williams, 1987). Given the breadth of this literature, our coverage is necessarily selective but representative of the published work. The goal is to present the methodological issues and to offer a research agenda for consideration by investigators concerned with applied problems in classification research with children.

The themes for this chapter are organized with respect to the directions research on classification might take: retreat, regroup, or advance. The first position is not merely the proverbial "straw man," despite the generally positive regard afforded classification research. Public critics of empirical subtyping are few at this point, but their reservations need to be considered and addressed to maintain a balance of perspective. Also, we believe there are some approaches to subtyping that may be profitably abandoned with little loss of explanatory power. The "regroup" position is an active one and not suggestive of stagnation. Here we review methodological considerations that may inform research in classification. Advancing classification research is the position with the greatest currency. This position may be best examined in light of observations under the retreat and regroup analyses. From our perspective, "advance" connotes a number of interpretations, including both horizontal movement (e.g., replication of previous results with different samples or parallel variables, and extended validation efforts) and vertical movement (e.g., multiple domains, broader sampling, developmental analysis, differential interventions).

The context of this discussion is whether empirical classification approaches are part of the problem or part of the solution to our understanding of learning disabilities. In both instances, the operational term is *part*. Just as single-deficit hypotheses are inadequate to capture the data generated on children identified as learning disabled (Applebee, 1971; Speece, 1987), the confusion that surrounds both research and practice in learning disabilities will not be clarified by a single methodological approach.

The application of cluster analysis techniques to a data set becomes part of the problem (i.e., adds to the conceptual confusion) when the design of the study perpetuates methodological inadequacies that are well known to our field. Thus failure to explicate the theoretical rationale guiding the study, use of samples of convenience including school-defined children, selection of technically inadequate tests and procedures, misapplication of statistical tests, and statements of conclusions that bear no resemblance either to the stated purpose of the research or to the results, singly and in combination, add up to poor science regardless of type of data analysis used. Users of cluster analysis techniques are no more immune to these problems than are any other investigators. The point we wish to emphasize is that cluster analysis techniques, in and of themselves, have no more valence than correlation coefficients or F ratios.

Empirical classification techniques are useful in research on learning disabilities to the extent that one regards as interesting and important the variance among children generally and specifically those identified as learning disabled. Of course there are several ways of addressing sample heterogeneity other than empirically (Keogh, Major–Kingsley, Omori–Gordon, & Reid, 1982; Shepard, Smith & Vojir, 1983; Torgesen, 1982, 1987). Some of these approaches are evident in this text. The primary difference between empirical classification and other types, such as the rational methods proposed by Torgesen (1982), is focus. Empirical efforts, even within single domains, are broadly conceived with the intent of capturing variability across the entire sample. Rational methods focus specifically on an aspect of child functioning and select only those children exhibiting the desired behavior for further study (control and comparison groups notwithstanding). Both approaches serve as entry points to the study of children and do not end either with replicable classification schemes or with selection of subjects. As several authors have noted, these methods are not mutually exclusive but rather complementary (Kavale & Forness, 1987; Torgesen, 1982). The results of valid empirical classification research may be used to define a subset of children for further experimentation whereas results based on detailed analyses of a rationally defined subgroup may lead to new insights for variable selection in a cluster analysis study.

It is within this context that we detail the potential advantages and disadvantages of empirical classification methodology. That is, we view classification as an important activity within the broader spectrum of research on learning disabilities but we are not so naïve or narrow as to champion only one approach to classification or only one methodology as *the* correct solution. Empirical methods, although not necessarily more rigorous than clinical or rational approaches, are not as well understood and, in fact, have been misinterpreted and inappropriately criticized by some. With this in mind we first consider the retreat position with regard to empirical classification.

RETREAT

While the calls for retreat from subtyping and classification efforts have been sounded in the literature, the message was clearest to us in a recent anonymous critique of a manuscript that reported a subtyping study. The reviewer stated, "This study is for all practical purposes a heuristic statistical exercise. . . . Such classification or fractionation activities make sense only to the extent that there are interventions differentially effective with the different subtypes." A second but similar position, expressed by Forness (1990), placed the call for retreat in the context of research on aptitude-by-treatment interaction. In a critique of subtyping research, Kavale and Forness (1987) provided a transdisciplinary perspective on classification. Their conclusion, representing a third perspective, was that subtyping research, rather than contributing to the description of LD, rather must await "more formalized description" of learning disabilities before proceeding (p. 380). A final set of criticisms accuses subtyping research of reflecting "the reductive fallacy," regarded as a dangerous position (Rettinger, Waters & Poplin, 1989, p. 309). According to this view, subtyping efforts pursue causes of LD "in hopes of discovering cause-specific interventions."

We will address each of four retreatist positions: (1) subtyping is a senseless heuristic; (2) subtypes equal aptitudes; (3) subtyping is not descriptive; and (4) subtyping is reductionist, and therefore dangerous.

A Senseless Heuristic?

At issue is whether classification per se is of sufficient scientific merit to warrant continued effort. Classifications have been criticized as "arbitrary" (Kavale & Forness, 1987, p. 376) and irrelevant to intervention (Forness, 1988). The proposed pre-eminence of intervention over classification is nowhere more clearly stated than Forness's (1988) assertion that "we probably have more to learn even from a less well controlled ... intervention study than from yet another study on diagnosis or classification" (p. 423). We assume that Forness is not advocating poorly controlled studies as opposed to ones that are adequately designed and executed. Yet, scientific control in the design of intervention studies may be enhanced by refinement in the identification of the target populations. By now it is a truism that the so-called LD population is heterogeneous, its common feature being limited to unexplained levels of achievement below expectation. Further complicating the identification process are data that strongly suggest the absence of a clearly differentiating boundary between LD and non-LD students (e.g., Holcomb, Hardesty, Adams, & Ponder, 1987; Taylor, Satz & Friel, 1979). Thus, even an otherwise *well*-controlled intervention study of school-identified "LD" subjects will inevitably fail the test of external validity since its sample characteristics cannot be generalized (Cook & Campbell, 1979). In this regard, classification studies have the potential to make a direct contribution to intervention studies by removing one threat to external validity that may be difficult for interventionists alone to remove.

Is that enough? Or must the empirical classification study also be required to test its mettle in the intervention arena? Kaplan's (1964) judgment in the matter is clear: "The statistical approach in general has the merit of providing warrant for a conceptualization which may have heuristic value even though it does not wholly solve the scientific problem to which it is addressed" (p. 51).

Kaplan's quotation, embedded in a discussion of correlational approaches to the discovery of underlying constructs, also provides a satisfying response to our anonymous reviewer whose denigrating evaluation of "heuristic" work places him or her squarely in the "good science is applied science" camp. This position cannot be expected to find support among theoreticians such as Meehl, who has devoted considerable time to the development of a theory-based method of classification (taxometrics) that makes no mention of applications derived from the classification thereby obtained (Meehl, 1978).

Are Subtypes Aptitudes?

Pointing to the "unfulfilled promise" (Rettinger et al., 1989, p. 309; Forness, 1990) of aptitude-by-treatment interactions (ATI), critics warn that subtyping researchers are leading the field down that same failed path. This is a red herring. In its state of the art, subtyping is a multivariate classification technique, the results of which are profiles of individuals' strengths and weaknesses across an array of conceptually driven measures. Classification of subjects is carefully evaluated by tests for internal and external validity. On the other hand, the aptitudes investigated in ATI research studies were univariate and of suspect reliability and validity (Cronbach & Snow, 1977; MacMillan, Keogh, & Jones, 1986). The "unfulfilled promise" of ATI may well be attributable to a lack of rigor in classification not shared by well-designed and -analyzed subtyping studies.

A further misrepresentation of subtyping research mistakenly equates it with modality assessment (Forness, 1990). In a paragraph criticizing subtyping research for failure to produce classroom applications, Forness cites the negligible effects found in a meta-analysis of 39 studies of "learning style or demonstrated preference." While sharing Forness's disaffection for modality assessments, we are reserving judgment on *subtype*-by-treatment interactions until they have been adequately evaluated. At a minimum, this will require valid, replicable subtypes exposed to extensively documented, theory-driven interventions conducted over sufficient periods of time and with enough fidelity of treatment to demonstrate an effect.

Is Subtyping Descriptive?

Kavale and Forness (1987) called for (a) a halt in subtyping research until LD is adequately described (i.e., defined), and (b) a common set of variables to be adopted by the field. We interpret this position as suggesting that a definition and differential diagnosis of LD is first to be validated; only then can the LD population be subtyped along the defining dimensions. Kavale and Forness are not explicit in recommending a methodology for differential diagnosis of LD. Regardless of the approach, however, it is apparent that the acknowledged heterogeneity of the LD population has to be confronted directly rather than postponed, if definition is the goal. The characteristics that define LD will certainly prove to be (a) multivariate, (b) from more than one domain (e.g., neuropsychological, information-processing, linguistic, behavioral, normative achievement, etc.), (c) evident in non-LD children to some degree, and (d) subject to developmental change. In each instance, and certainly with respect to the heterogeneity issue, subtyping methodologies have the potential to contribute to the descriptive knowledge base.

Is Subtyping Dangerous?

Two recent issues of the *Journal of Learning Disabilities* (Vol. 21, No. 7; Vol. 22, No. 5) featured opinion pieces on constructivism versus reductionism. In that context, Rettinger et al. (1989) refer to the "wasted energy, and the dangers of the current rage to subtype learning disabilities" (p. 309). Further, Rettinger et al. characterize subtypes as detecting "minuscule

differences" (p. 309) of questionable reliability, validity and meaning. However, evidence to support this position was not provided even though 45 pages
were made available for the opinions expressed. Contributors to the substantive and methodological subtyping literature have done a rather thorough job
of addressing the issues of significant differences (Lyon, Stewart, & Freedman, 1982), reliability (Morey, Blashfield, & Skinner, 1983), and validity
(Speece & Cooper, 1990), as well as typologies that are interpretable from the
interventionists' standpoint (Feagans & Appelbaum, 1986).

REGROUP

While retreatists may favor abandoning or postponing classification efforts,
a more balanced approach may be to acknowledge both strengths and
weaknesses of research in classification. To advocate this type of regrouping
strategy is not analogous to "circling the wagons" to ward off all opponents.
Instead, the emphasis is on placing the work in perspective with the purpose
of analyzing what has and has not been accomplished and what is feasible.

   To this end, it is instructive to review the general progression of scientific
topics set forth by Blashfield and Aldenderfer (1988) in a review of cluster
analysis methodology. They identified four chronological phases of scientific
endeavor: early exploration, discovery, consolidation, and accommodation.
Early exploration and discovery are associated with the birth of a new line of
inquiry and later increases in the number of papers on the topic in the
literature. The consolidation phase reflects the appearance of critical reviews
on the topic, including identification of poorly executed studies and excesses
associated with the discovery phase; accommodation reflects acceptance of
the topic as denoted by inclusion in leading textbooks as a chapter or point of
discussion. It is important to note that Blashfield and Aldenderfer place
cluster analysis methodology in the initial stages of the consolidation phase.
The beginning of the early exploration phase in psychology was set around
1935, more than 50 years ago.

   While it may be disheartening to be reminded that advances in scientific
knowledge are better characterized as proceeding at a snail's pace rather than
in explosive bursts, the four-phase framework is helpful in gaining perspective on the results of subtyping efforts in learning disabilities. It appears that
the interpretation of this literature has moved more rapidly than one would
expect, given the history of scientific advances. However, premature attempts
to force consolidation at this juncture strain the credibility of our current
knowledge. This is true for two reasons. First, advances in content knowledge
cannot logically precede the chronology of the methodology. Second,
documented advances in cluster analysis methodology (e.g., Milligan &
Cooper, 1985; Skinner, 1978) are only beginning to be integrated into the

designs of classification studies (Speece, 1990; Speece & Cooper, 1990). The latter point does not necessarily imply that previous work in the area should be disregarded. Rather, the studies should be evaluated with respect to our current knowledge of the methodology and placed in proper perspective. Given the twin facts that our more time-honored statistical techniques are frequently abused and that these types of studies are either deleted from or exposed in literature reviews as a topic matures, we can be reasonably confident that same will hold true for empirical classification studies.

What we must deal with presently is the unbridled enthusiasm associated with the discovery phase of scientific endeavor. While enthusiasm may be generally regarded as a positive personal characteristic, when it is coupled with scientific concerns there is a tendency to overstate one's case. This leads to needless proselytizing, placing the offender in an untenable position, usually at the end of a limb. Appropriately, critics eliminate the deadwood with a sharp saw, regardless of the health of the nascent blooms closer to the trunk. The field of learning disabilities has ample evidence of this phenomenon, most recently associated with the usefulness of interventions derived from neuropsychology (see Lyon & Moats, 1988; Obrzut & Boliek, 1986; Sandoval & Happmanen, 1981; Torgesen, 1986, for critiques).

With regard to subtyping, this enthusiasm is captured in Weller and Strawser's (1987) attempt to derive common "adaptive" subtypes from a disparate group of empirical and clinical studies. The commonalities identified across the studies reviewed are neither apparent nor real and many important differences, both methodological and conceptual, are lost in an effort to forge consensus at too early a stage in the scientific development of the topic.

To elaborate, the authors collapsed findings from studies with subjects who collectively spanned the developmental spectrum from 6 to 15 years old. In addition, results of studies that used empirically and clinically derived subtypes as well as individual case studies were combined. On a general level these differences may be unimportant if common findings emerge. However, Weller and Strawser's interpretation of work, with which we are familiar, leads us to believe otherwise. For example, a subtype of 6- and 7-year-old LD children described as exhibiting a withdrawn behavioral pattern (Speece, McKinney, & Appelbaum, 1985) was included in Weller and Strawser's (1987) "Nonverbal Organization Disorders Subtype." Their description of the latter subtype included the following:

> These individuals are characterized by adequate to above-average verbal skills which are used to compensate for their difficulties in visually, spatially, and motorically organizing their environment. Although highly verbal, often they can make little use of this skill in academic areas. (Weller & Strawser, 1987, pp. 108–109)

With regard to the Speece et al. (1985) subtype, it should be noted that there were no academic or aptitude differences across the seven clusters during year one of a 3-year study, nor were any measures of the type described by Weller and Strawser used. Further, the longitudinal analyses of these data (McKinney & Speece, 1986) indicated that, in fact, the children associated with the withdrawn pattern tended to earn higher achievement scores than other subtypes across 3 years. Weller and Strawser's misinterpretation and overgeneralization of these findings is compounded by their recommendations for intervention and career planning. To the authors' credit, they repeatedly refer to the preliminary nature of the available evidence; but, this caution is negated when they further assert, "However, there is sufficient evidence for teachers, counselors, vocational rehabilitation specialists and psychologists to consider adaptive behavior subtypes in their programming for learning disabled individuals" (Weller & Strawser, 1987, p. 113).

Although we would certainly wish that this state of affairs was true, our interpretation of the existing literature suggests otherwise. The major stumbling block is that the necessary intervention research has not yet been conducted. The data on behavioral dimensions of learning disabilities are consistent enough to include these types of variables in further classification studies as well as to begin intervention studies as an additional form of cluster validation. As the evidence accumulates in these areas, we will be in a better position to make claims regarding the consistency and educational utility of results from empirical classification research.

In addition to a healthy dose of caution, if not skepticism, when surveying classification results to date, it is also imperative to take stock of the differences among studies with respect to purpose, design and, within design, application of statistical methods. The variability across studies in these dimensions is difficult to capture in a straightforward manner, lending further credence to the position that a meaningful substantive summary awaits further empirical work.

Purpose

Investigators pursuing classification research may adopt the goals of specifying interventions or understanding etiology (Lyon & Risucci, 1988) as well as explicating the developmental course of a particular problem (e.g., learning disabilities). Classification research in learning disabilities reflects treatment, etiological, and developmental orientations, although this information is generally implicit rather than explicit, or comes to light only in the discussion section of the paper. While any orientation may be scientifically defensible, the problem is lack of well-articulated theoretical frameworks to guide the research.

A contributing factor to the fugitive theoretical orientations in classification studies is the dependence on secondary analyses. That is, cluster analysis techniques have been applied to existing data bases that were not specifically developed for classification research. These studies tend to be exemplary with respect to the application of cluster analysis methods (e.g., Morris, Blashfield, & Satz, 1986) and yield important insights to meaningful differences among children classified as learning disabled (e.g., Speece et al., 1985; McKinney & Speece, 1986). In some cases, secondary analyses have been conducted with positive results under strong theoretical rationales (Feagans & Appelbaum, 1986).

For the most part, however, classification research has evolved from retrospective rather than prospective designs. This, of course, limits the investigators' selection of subjects, classification variables, and validation approaches. To date, secondary analyses have demonstrated the utility of an empirical approach to classification that should not be regarded as trivial knowledge. The recommendation is to pursue analyses of extant data bases only if (a) a theoretical orientation exists to provide guidance with respect to variable selection from a larger set, (b) the number of subjects is sufficient to test replication of subtypes, and (c) variables or procedures external to the classification measures are available to validate the subtypes. A particularly thorny issue is the role of testing hypotheses. This is certainly a legitimate goal of classification research although the current body of knowledge is more exploratory than definitive, making predictions tenuous at best. We would add the caution not to become too wedded to hypothesized subtypes in order to allow for identification of unanticipated profiles and, hence, further insights into the heterogeneity of children. Although it could be argued that this perspective is too generous (i.e., all subtyping studies are interesting and worthy of consideration), we would counter that it is this degree of uncertainty that will fuel advances in our understanding of learning disabilities.

The purpose of a particular classification study, derived from a theoretical orientation if not from a theory, should lead to clear guidelines for the usual methodological issues of subject and variable selection and, with respect to classification, validation procedures. Regarding the relationship between purpose and subjects, Keogh's position is insightful:

> I have ceased to be troubled by the definitional problem, as I am convinced that definition has meaning only when it is tied to purpose. Because there are multiple purposes in the LD field there will continue to be multiple definitions. The problem comes when we mix definitions and purposes, as is the case of research conducted with preselected ("system identified") subjects rather than subjects selected according to study-relevant criteria. (1987b, p. 97)

While it may be true that this position, taken to its extreme, would produce subtypes as varied as individual investigators and, hence, not yield converging evidence on any particular topic, the point is that there should be greater concern with purpose of research rather than with subjects per se. It does not appear that a consensus on who the learning disabled are will be reached in an a priori manner but rather from careful descriptions of participants chosen on the basis of compelling conceptual orientations to the problem. The energy devoted to hand-wringing on this issue would be better spent in the collection of comprehensive subject data. As cogently noted by Fletcher and Morris (1986), researchers concerned with learning disabilities tend to ignore the fact that current definitions are no more than assumptions that need to be put to empirical tests.

Developmental Perspectives

Although several purposes for classification exist, it is instructive to analyze from a developmental perspective the results of clinical classification studies designed to predict school achievement. A developmental perspective is often missing in these studies and in definitions of LD because investigators are interested in identifying linear models that cannot accommodate the changing organism. The goals of such studies are important as they relate to early identification of school failure with the implicit inference of secondary, if not primary, prevention. However, the extant data from these studies are not as straightforward as has been suggested. The point of examining problems in early classification is to emphasize the apparent fragility of classification procedures that do not account for developmental change or the heterogeneity of the sample.

For example, the hit-rate model is often used to assess the validity of a classification scheme (Lichtenstein & Ireton, 1984). A sample of children is classified at two points in time, and the agreement between the earlier (predictive) and the later (criterion) classification is quantified in terms of percentage correct and incorrect. Correct predictions are hits and are typically reported as the sum of the percentage of correct cases (those with the disorder) and correct noncases (those without the disorder). Somewhat less frequently reported are the sensitivity index, reported as the percentage of cases correctly predicted, and the specificity index, the percentage of noncases correctly predicted. Occasionally, false positive and false negative predictions are also reported, or may be calculated given the other indexes. Several problems exist with this technique including: (a) failure to account for the role played by chance, (b) lack of consensus on definitions of disability, and (c) the assumption of error-free *criterion* classification.

As an illustration, Stevenson, Parker, Wilkinson, Hegion, and Fish (1976) examined predictive accuracy relative to children's standardized achievement test scores in grade 3, based on kindergarten performance. By our calculations from the data in Table 7 (p. 394) and using the lowest 10% (the authors' criterion) of the frequency distributions for reading achievement, sensitivity was a mere 33%. Specificity was 96%; however, the false positive rate was 55% with an overall hit rate of 90%. Comparable results were evident for mathematics achievement. Despite the impressive hit rate and specificity, the classification of children during kindergarten incorrectly identified as underachievers 55% of the children who turned out to be average achievers. Furthermore, the impressive overall hit rate (90%) is little better than one could have achieved by *randomly* classifying 10% of the kindergartners into the underachieving group. By this method, an overall hit rate of 84% is possible. This situation always obtains when the prevalence of classified cases (those actually having the disorder according to the outcome criterion) is relatively low. Correct hits, then, are largely due to the large *chance* probability of correctly identifying the noncases.[1] Despite the high rate of false positives and the low sensitivity, the authors concluded that "the stability of achievement was remarkably high" (p. 398). While in a strictly correlational sense this may have been true, the classification results do not support this conclusion.

The perils of early classification were also evident but, in contrast to Stevenson et al., not ignored by Butler, Marsh, Sheppard, and Sheppard (1982) in their longitudinal study of kindergartners through their third-grade year. Butler et al. demonstrated clearly the effect of manipulating early classification definitions. Using a strict definition (i.e., the bottom 10% of students), their reported hit-rate, sensitivity, and false positive classifications were 87.5%, 42%, and 37.5%, respectively. Loosening the definition to the bottom 30% of kindergartners improved the reported sensitivity (88%) but at the high cost of increasing false positives (51%). Butler et al. stated conclusions with appropriate caution, noting the unacceptably high levels of misclassification that would result from overreliance on their predictive method.

A paper by Satz, Taylor, Friel, and Fletcher (1978) illustrates a number of concerns of general interest to classification researchers. First, the sensitivity, specificity, and hit-rate results are relatively high and taken alone, would appear to support the predictive validity of the kindergarten classifications. However, the prevalence data are noteworthy in that the range across seven analyses (18% to 42%) is significantly above most accepted estimates of the prevalence of disabled children. Second, the rates of false positive classifications (range: 32% to 55%) suggests that the kindergarten classification

---

[1]Chance hit rates are calculated as follows: First, the actual prevalence of cases (p) is fixed as the proportion of cases identified by the criterion or outcome classification method. This same proportion is then used to *randomly* classify, or predict, cases and noncases. Of those *randomly* classified as cases, a fixed proportion equal to the actual prevalence will be correct by chance alone. Similarly, of those randomly classified as noncases, a fixed proportion (q) equal to one minus the prevalence will be correct by chance. The sum of "correct" classifications, divided by the sample size gives the chance hit rate. This is also equal to $p^2 + q^2$.

definition was far too liberally applied. Third, comparison of the reported hit rates with the chance hit rates provides a benchmark against which to judge the effectiveness of the earlier classifications. Taking as an example the best hit rate relative to chance (reported in Satz et al., Table 3), improvement over chance was 23 percentage points, but at the cost of 32% false positives and an incredibly high prevalence of 42%.

These classification models may fail to predict accurately at the level of the individual due to reliance on a two-group scheme—children with or without a problem. That clinical classification is not a black or white phenomenon was recently demonstrated by Osborne and Schulte (1989) and Walker et al. (1988). These authors reported sizable proportions of children, originally identified as learning disabled, as either failing to qualify for services or being reclassified into another category of exceptionality over time. The position we advocate is that longitudinal analysis of subtype stability and change, from an empirical classification perspective, may address some of the problems of clinical prediction by assessing shades of gray via analysis of multiple groups.

For example, McKinney and Speece (1986) viewed instability of subtype membership across 3 years as illuminating developmental processes rather than as error. They found that LD children tended to become members of more impaired subtypes as they progressed through school. For example, children initially classified into an attention deficit subtype were more likely to switch to another abnormal subtype than to the normal one. In another interesting pattern, LD children in the normal behavior cluster at year one were reclassified into the attention deficit cluster at year three. Along the same lines, Cross and Paris (1988) have applied cluster-analytical methods in the evaluation of treatment effects that represents a novel application of empirical classification. In that study, cluster discontinuity was taken as evidence of a treatment effect. While critics may be tempted to use these findings against empirical subtyping, a pre-emptive response can be offered. Clinical classification studies have simply ignored discontinuity when it is clearly evident in the data. Thus empirical classification studies, in the recognition and interpretation of discontinuity, do not claim to have found more enduring traits to classify. Rather, the descriptive evidence is used in the service of theory building and elucidation of the widely acknowledged heterogeneity of learning disorders.

Design

Subjects. For the purpose of subject selection, it is necessary to state explicitly whether the goal of a particular classification study is developmental, etiological, or geared toward intervention. With regard to any of these, the role of children not experiencing academic problems must also be considered in the design. It would be imperative to include such children when the focus is developmental or etiological to determine the degree to which members of the target group (i.e., "LD") diverge from their peers. As noted by Speece (1990), normally achieving children rarely have been included as part of classification samples, thereby begging the question of overlap and uniqueness among subtypes. The role of normally achieving children has been relegated to a backup position for interpretation of subtypes, with the implicit assumption that the skills of these children are somehow more homogeneous than those of the target group. Evidence from a classification study of first-grade children at risk for school failure and average-achieving peers suggests this is not the case (Speece & Cooper, 1990).

Inclusion of normally achieving children in classification studies aimed at intervention is less necessary if one assumes that normally achieving children are not in need of differential intervention or that selection of an average comparison group for future experimentation will fulfill the requirements of a particular design. The latter rationale still presupposes homogeneity, an assumption that would need to be adequately defended.

The position that multiple perspectives are desirable for research generally and classification research specifically will be troubling for those who view the problem in terms of identifying the ultimate classification scheme for LD (Kavale & Forness, 1987) or who believe that intervention is the only legitimate focus of classification (Forness, 1988). Research purposes and, hence, subjects cannot be defined by fiat, but rather by theory, logic, and data. As elaborated by Golden and Meehl,

> There is no possibility, and fortunately there is no need, of showing that what appears to be a powerful cluster method . . . guarantees that it will always work in all situations (e.g., subjects). . . . But it must be remembered that, even in this case (research derived from theorems and postulates) the abstract possibility of cooking up some alternative conjecture is always present. All that the scientist can say to someone who adduces that possibility is to invite him (her) to present his (her) substantive alternative conjecture and subject it to tests as the first investigator has done [parenthetical information added]. (1980, p. 494)

Variables. Given the variability of purpose, the fact that there has been little consensus to date with respect to the operationalization of classification variables is to be expected. This is, however, an issue of growing concern in the field of learning disabilities (Alexander, 1989) that will not be easily resolved. The barriers to consensus are again tied to purpose, but even within a single purpose differences are the rule.

Based on an analysis of variables used in past classification studies, two suggestions are warranted. First, the measurement of variables must meet usual standards of reliability and validity. While hardly a novel perspective, it is often the case that this information is either not reported or nonexistent.

Certainly this situation undermines the utility of any resulting classification (Forness, 1990). As a case in point, we refer to the use of subtests of the Wide Range Achievement Test (WRAT) as classification variables. The psychometric weaknesses of this measure are well known (e.g., Salvia & Ysseldyke, 1985) but apparently ignored (see review by Fletcher & Morris, 1986).

A second recommendation is to view academic failure more broadly than the assumption of within-child deficits allows. As noted earlier, definitional disclaimers that include failure to learn "despite adequate instruction" must be treated as testable hypotheses. Ehri (1989) makes a convincing argument for this position with respect to reading disabilities. At issue is the role the environment, especially instruction, plays in a child's academic difficulties. If the theoretical framework guiding a study is based on within-child deficits, the investigator must demonstrate (i.e., by selection of variables) that instruction was not a contributing factor. Thus, the onus is to provide evidence that instruction was somehow adequate for the child's needs, not merely "usual" in the sense that everyone received similar methods. The same difficult task also awaits investigators who assume the environment may be a contributing factor. Regardless of the orientation adopted, variables that tap instructional differences are needed. Lyon (1985) provided preliminary evidence in support of instructional manipulation as a validation procedure. Speece and Cooper (1990) included instructional variables as part of a multiple domain classification study. While both studies define instruction in a narrow way that may not be representative of all classroom instruction, continued efforts in this direction may lead to more comprehensive views of learning problems generally and learning disabilities specifically.

Cluster Analysis Methodology. It is beyond the scope of this chapter to provide a detailed review of the methodology, but many good sources are available (e.g., Anderberg, 1973; Blashfield & Aldenderfer, 1988; Lorr, 1983; Skinner, 1978, 1981). A critical aspect of cluster analysis is the establishment of the internal consistency (reliability) of the classification scheme before proceeding to the validation stage of analysis. Methods of addressing this issue were described by Speece (1990). There are a number of ways to establish converging evidence for replicability, the best of which is to use an independent sample. The methods of cluster analysis are not as primitive and/or esoteric as some may believe, but because the methods are not based on inferential statistics, one cannot take solace in the results of an *F* test. Rather, it is necessary to plan this stage of the analysis carefully regardless of the theoretical framework and purpose guiding the study. Unfortunately, this aspect of cluster analysis is often ignored or only scant evidence is provided. Users (and consumers) of empirical methods must thoroughly understand the dangers of this situation which are analogous to use of unreliable measurements.

Perhaps the biggest problem in the application of cluster analysis methods is that critical information on correct usage is scattered across a wide literature—a single comprehensive text does not exist. Thus, the investigator must be diligent in identifying and monitoring the appropriate literature. To make matters worse, there exists published misinformation which, at best, serves to confuse and mislead (see Milligan, 1985, for a description). The interested researcher would be well advised to seek agreement on a particular approach from several independent sources.

ADVANCE

The conclusion to be drawn from our analysis of the retreat and regroup positions is that it is time to advance classification research. Suggestions for an agenda that may guide this advance follow.

The foregoing section detailed a number of issues that must be addressed if empirical classification research is to add to our understanding of learning disabilities. Interestingly, the problems identified are largely not unique to classification efforts. However, the broad aims of such work magnify the inadequacies present in research within the traditions of description and experimentation. For example, Kerlinger and Pedhazur (1973) urge that results of multiple regression analyses be replicated, preferably on large samples, within a single study. This advice is rarely heeded but is absolutely essential for a cluster analysis investigation. The time is past when a study without internal replication can be seriously considered as contributing to the knowledge base. This is also true of studies that reanalyze a data base without the benefit of a conceptual orientation or that simply describe subtypes without any indication of the concurrent, predictive, or construct validity of the taxonomy (see Skinner, 1981, for elaboration of the latter point).

Instead, we must take advantage of the methodology without losing sight of the purpose for the research. It is important to remember that it is the quality of ideas and not the intricacies of analysis that lead to meaningful advances in any field. As with any line of research, classification efforts must be programmatic, not simply single demonstrations of feasibility (Kavale, 1987).

The need exists as well for investigators to build breadth and depth in their programs. Lyon and Risucci (1988) noted in a review of substantive studies that use of experimental measures makes adoption of the variables by other investigators difficult. They suggested that investigators develop parallel measurement systems as a method of collecting evidence for reliability. This approach also implies a need to be more concerned with constructs that may underlie school failure than with an adherence to a favorite set of specific measures.

It is imperative to shake loose the shackles related to school-identified children. Though such samples may be warranted for some purposes, it is incumbent upon the investigator to provide a strong rationale for this procedure. The limits on generalizability of results are well known (e.g., McKinney, 1987). When children are selected on a logical basis, the investigator must report the number of children screened to arrive at the final sample size. This detail is often overlooked but provides a sense of the prevalence of different combinations of subject characteristics.

We would also advocate a broader view of learning problems that includes recognition of environmental influences. Many writers have emphasized this seemingly obvious need but the necessary data have yet to appear. It is curious that the field of learning disabilities has remained relatively resistant to this despite more than two decades of research on environmental influences and despite the heavy reliance on IQ scores as a major criterion for identification. It is difficult to ignore the evidence that intelligence scores are influenced by environmental factors and are not simply a within-child phenomenon. However, there are little or no data to support this ubiquitous assumption in definitions of learning disabilities. Although the measurement issues are staggering, it remains an empirical question.

If subtyping is to make further contributions to the understanding and remediation of children with LD, then the record of longitudinal research will need to be cautiously accelerated, building on the solid foundation set by McKinney and others (McKinney & Speece, 1986; McKinney & Feagans, 1984; Satz, Morris, & Fletcher, 1985). A recent review (Tramontana, Hooper, & Selzer, 1988) of longitudinal studies of achievement concluded: "prediction studies . . . show virtually no linkage with the growing research literature on the analysis of learning disability subtypes" (p. 136). Exceptions are indeed few (e.g., McKinney & Speece, 1986; Spreen & Haaf, 1986) and reveal a high degree of developmental discontinuity in cluster membership (Speece & Cooper, April, 1990). This only serves to emphasize the importance of a developmental perspective in *all* research that depends on classification, whether of subgroups or of LD itself.

Despite Forness's (1988) claims to the contrary, classification research is not "quick" (p. 423). In fact, it is such a labor-intensive endeavor that the interesting questions of validation often appear quite distant when one is dealing with issues of replication. A possible solution to the time factor is the sharing of classification functions among investigators. That is, these functions are transportable and could be used to test the similarity of constructs measured differently by separate research groups. In a like manner, researchers interested in clinical application could use the functions to identify specific subtypes of children and to design appropriate experiments to test the utility of differential interventions.

The use of classification functions across investigators demands, of course, that the functions on which the subtypes were identified have more than a modest degree of reliability. However, this suggestion may provide the means of widening classification efforts to include those investigators who are not interested in classification per se but rather the ramifications. It will also facilitate advancing our knowledge of the utility of the approach. For example, if the purpose of a classification study is developmental, necessitating a longitudinal design, by the time the original investigators identify the critical patterns related to success or failure in early years, the children will be considerably older and perhaps exhibit a different set of characteristics. What would appear to be a feasible set of interventions to test when the children were in the first grade may no longer be relevant at the third grade. Given reliable subtypes, the original classification functions could be used to identify a new sample of first graders by any investigator for further study.

Undergirding this discussion is the need for communication among various research "camps." Despite differences in purpose and related issues, there is much to be learned, whether it be insights on variable selection or advances in analysis strategies. This suggestion extends beyond classification research although there is much work to be done here. No single orientation can be identified as "the best" at this point so it is necessary to identify the strengths of various perspectives and build upon them. It is only in this way that the multivariate nature of learning disabilities will be ultimately understood.

ACKNOWLEDGMENT

The authors acknowledge the invaluable contribution of Carolynn Rice to the preparation of this chapter.

REFERENCES

Adams, K. M. (1985). Theoretical, methodological, and statistical issues. In B. P. Rourke (Ed.) *Neuropsychology of learning disabilities* (pp. 17–39). New York: Guilford Press.

Alexander, D. (1989, June). *NICHHD research initiatives in learning disabilities.* Paper presented at the 1989 Joint Conference on Learning Disabilities, Ann Arbor, MI.

Anderberg, M. R. (1973). *Cluster analysis for applications.* New York: Academic Press.

Applebee, A. N. (1971). Research in reading retardation: Two critical problems. *Journal of Child Psychology and Psychiatry, 12,* 91–113.

Blashfield, R. K., & Aldenderfer, M. S. (1988). The methods and problems of cluster analysis. In J. R. Nesselroade (Ed.), *Handbook of multivariate experimental psychology* (2nd ed., pp. 447–473). New York: Plenum Press.

Butler, S. R., Marsh, H. W., Sheppard, M. J., & Sheppard, J. L. (1982). Early prediction of reading achievement with the Sheppard School Entry Screening Test: A four-year longitudinal study. *Journal of Educational Psychology, 74,* 280–290.

Cook, T. D., & Campbell, D. T. (1979). *Quasi-experimentation: Design and analysis issues for field settings.* Boston: Houghton Mifflin.

Cronbach, L. J., & Snow, R. E. (1977). *Aptitudes and instructional methods.* New York: Irvington.

Cross, D. R., & Paris, S. G. (1988). Developmental and instructional analyses of children's metacognition and reading comprehension. *Journal of Educational Psychology, 80,* 131–142.

Ehri, L. C. (1989). The development of spelling knowledge and its role in reading acquisition and reading disability. *Journal of Learning Disabilities, 22,* 356–364.

Feagans, L., & Appelbaum, M. I. (1986). Validation of language subtypes in learning disabled children. *Journal of Educational Psychology, 78,* 358–364.

Fletcher, J. M., & Morris, R. (1986). Classification of disabled learners: Beyond exclusionary definitions. In S. J. Ceci (Ed.), *Handbook of cognitive, social, and neuropsychological aspects of learning disabilities* (pp. 55–80). Hillsdale, NJ: Lawrence Erlbaum Associates.

Forness, S. R. (1988). Reductionism, paradigm, shifts, and learning disabilities. *Journal of Learning Disabilities, 21,* 421–424.

Forness, S. R. (1990). Subtyping in learning disabilities: Introduction to the issues. In H. L. Swanson & B. K. Keogh (Eds.), *Learning disabilities: Theoretical and research issues* (pp. 195–200). Hillsdale, NJ: Lawrence Erlbaum Associates.

French, D. C. (1988). Heterogeneity of peer-rejected boys: Aggressive and nonaggressive subtypes. *Child Development, 59,* 976–985.

Golden, R. R., & Meehl, P. E. (1980). Detection of biological sex: An empirical test of cluster methods. *Multivariate Behavioral Research, 15,* 475–496.

Holcomb, W. R., Hardesty, R. A., Adams, N. A., & Ponder, H. M. (1987). WISC–R types of learning disabilities: A profile analysis with cross-validation. *Journal of Learning Disabilities, 20,* 369–373.

Hooper, S. R., & Willis, W. G. (1989). *Learning disability subtyping.* New York: Springer–Verlag.

Kaplan, A. (1964). *The conduct of inquiry: Methodology for behavioral science.* New York: Harper & Row.

Kavale, K. A. (1987). Theoretical quandaries in learning disabilities. In S. Vaughn & C. S. Bos (Eds.), *Research in learning disabilities* (pp. 19–33). Boston: College–Hill Press.

Kavale, K. A., & Forness, S. R. (1987). The far side of heterogeneity: A critical analysis of empirical subtyping research in learning disabilities. *Journal of Learning Disabilities, 20,* 374–382.

Keogh, B. K. (1987a). A shared attribute model of learning disabilities. In S. Vaughn & C. S. Bos (Eds.), *Research in learning disabilities* (pp. 3–18). Boston: College–Hill Press.

Keogh, B. K. (1987b). Response to Senf. In S. Vaughn & C. S. Bos (Eds.), *Research in learning disabilities* (pp. 97–101). Boston: College–Hill Press.

Keogh, B. K., Major-Kingsley, S., Omori-Gordon, H., & Reid, H. P. (1982). *A system of marker variables for the field of learning disabilities.* Syracuse, NY: Syracuse University Press.

Kerlinger, F. N., & Pedhazur, E. J. (1973). *Multiple regression in behavioral research.* New York: Holt, Rinehart, & Winston.

Lichtenstein, R., & Ireton, H. (1984). *Preschool screening: Identifying young children with developmental and educational problems.* Orlando, FL: Grune & Stratton.

Lorr, M. (1983). *Cluster analysis for social scientists.* San Francisco: Jossey–Bass.

Lyon, G. R. (1985). Educational validation studies of learning disability subtypes. In B. P. Rourke (Ed.), *Neuropsychology of learning disabilities* (pp. 228–253). New York: Guilford Press.

Lyon, G. R. (1987). Learning disabilities research: False starts and broken promises. In S. Vaughn & C. S. Bos (Eds.), *Research in learning disabilities* (pp. 69–85). Boston: College–Hill Press.

Lyon, G. R., & Moats, L. C. (1988). Critical issues in the instruction of the learning disabled. *Journal of Consulting and Clinical Psychology, 56,* 830–835.

Lyon, G. R., & Risucci, D. (1988). Classification of learning disabilities. In K. Kavale (Ed.), *Learning disabilities: State of the art and practice* (pp. 44–70). San Diego: College–Hill Press.

Lyon, G. R., Stewart, N., & Freedman, D. (1982). Neuropsychological characteristics of empirically derived subgroups of learning disabled readers. *Journal of Clinical Neuropsychology, 4,* 343–365.

MacMillan, D. L., Keogh, B. K., & Jones, R. L. (1986). Special education research on mildly handicapped learners. In M. C. Wittrock (Ed.), *Handbook of research on teaching* (3rd ed., pp. 686–724). New York: Macmillan.

McKinney, J. D. (1987). Research on the identification of learning disabled children: Perspectives on changes in educational policy. In S. Vaughn & C. S. Bos (Eds.), *Research in learning disabilities* (pp. 215–237). Boston: College–Hill Press.

McKinney, J. D. (1988). Research on conceptually and empirically derived subtypes of specific learning disabilities. In M. C. Wang, H. J. Walberg, & M. C. Reynolds (Eds.), *The handbook of special education: Research and practice* (Vol. 2, pp. 253–281). Oxford, England: Pergamon Press.

McKinney, J. D., & Feagans, L. (1984). Academic and behavioral characteristics: Longitudinal studies of learning disabled children and average achievers. *Learning Disability Quarterly 7,* 251–265.

McKinney, J. D., & Speece, D. L. (1986). Academic consequences and longitudinal stability of behavioral subtypes of learning disabled children. *Journal of Educational Psychology, 78,* 365–372.

Meehl, P. (1978). Theoretical risks and tabular asterisks: Sir Karl, Sir Ronald, and the slow progress of soft psychology. *Journal of Consulting and Clinical Psychology, 46,* 806–834.

Milligan, G. W. (1985). [Review of *Cluster analysis for researchers*]. *Journal of Classification, 2,* 133–137.

Milligan, G. W., & Cooper, M. C. (1985). An examination of procedures for determining the number of clusters in a data set. *Psychometrika, 50,* 159–179.

Milligan, G. W., & Cooper, M. C. (1987). Methodology review: Clustering methods. *Applied Psychological Measurement, 11,* 329–354.

Morey, L. C., Blashfield, R. K., & Skinner, H. A. (1983). A comparison of cluster analysis techniques within a sequential validation framework. *Multivariate Behaviorial Research, 18,* 309–329.

Morris, R., Blashfield, R. K., & Satz, P. (1986). Developmental classification of learning disabled children. *Journal of Clinical and Experimental Neuropsychology, 8,* 371–292.

Obrzut, J. E., & Boliek, C. A. (1986). Lateralization characteristics in learning disabled children. *Journal of Learning Disabilities, 19,* 308–314.

Osborne, S. S., & Schulte, A. C. (1989, April). *Longitudinal study of learning disabled students in mainstream and resource programs.* Paper presented at the annual meeting of the American Educational Research Association, San Francisco.

Rettinger, V., Waters, W., & Poplin, M. S. (1989). Constructing a response to responses. *Journal of Learning Disabilities, 22,* 309–313.

Rourke, B. P. (Ed.) (1985). *Neuropsychology of learning disabilities: Essentials of subtype analysis.* New York: Guilford Press.

Salvia, J., & Ysseldyke, J. E. (1985). *Assessment in special and remedial education* (3rd ed.). Boston: Houghton Mifflin.

Sandoval, J., & Happmanen, R. M. (1981). A critical commentary on neuropsychology in the schools: Are we ready? *School Psychology Review, 10,* 389–393.

Satz, P., & Morris, R. (1981). Learning disability subtypes: A review. In F. J. Pirozzolo & M. C. Wittrock (Eds.), *Neuropsychological and cognitive processes in reading* (pp. 109–141). New York: Academic Press.

Satz, P., Morris, R., & Fletcher, J. M. (1985). Hypotheses, subtypes and individual differences in dyslexia: Some reflections. In D. Gray & J. Kavanagh (Eds.), *Biobehavioral measures of dyslexia* (pp. 25–40). Parkton, MD: York Press.

Satz, P., Taylor, H. G., Friel, J., & Fletcher, J. M. (1978). Some developmental and predictive precursors of reading disabilities: A six-year follow-up. In A. L. Benton & D. Pearl (Eds.), *Dyslexia: An appraisal of current knowledge* (pp. 315–347). New York: Oxford Press.

Shepard, L. A., Smith, M. L., & Vojir, C. P. (1983). Characteristics of pupils identified as learning disabled. *American Educational Research Journal, 20,* 309–331.

Skinner, H. A. (1978). Differentiating the contribution of elevation, scatter, and shape in profile similarity. *Educational and Psychological Measurement, 38,* 297–308.

Skinner, H. A. (1981). Toward the integration of classification theory and methods. *Journal of Abnormal Psychology, 20,* 68–87.

Speece, D. L. (1987). Information processing subtypes of learning-disabled readers. *Learning Disabilities Research, 2,* 91–102.

Speece, D. L. (1990). Methodological issues in cluster analysis: How clusters become real. In H. L. Swanson & B. K. Keogh (Eds.), *Learning disabilities: Theoretical and research issues* (pp. 201–213). Hillsdale, NJ: Lawrence Erlbaum Associates.

Speece, D. L., & Cooper, D. H. (1990). Ontogeny of school failure: Classification of first grade children at risk. *American Educational Research Journal, 27,* 119-140.

Speece, D. L., & Cooper, D. H. (1990, April). *Stability and change in subtype membership and the relation to special education placement in the primary grades.* Paper presented at the annual meeting of the American Educational Research Association, Boston.

Speece, D. L., McKinney, J. D., & Appelbaum, M. I. (1985). Classification and validation of behavioral subtypes of learning-disabled children. *Journal of Educational Psychology, 77,* 67–77.

Spreen, O., & Haaf, R. G. (1986). Empirically derived learning disability subtypes: A replication attempt and longitudinal patterns over 15 years. *Journal of Learning Disabilities, 19,* 170–180.

Stevenson, H. W., Parker, T., Wilkinson, A., Hegion, A., & Fish, E. (1976). Longitudinal study of individual differences in cognitive development and scholastic achievement. *Journal of Educational Psychology, 68,* 377–400.

Taylor, A. R., Asher, S. R., & Williams, G. A. (1987). The social adaptation of mainstreamed mildly retarded children. *Child Development, 58,* 1321–1334.

Taylor, H. G., Satz, P., & Friel, J. (1979). Developmental dyslexia in relation to other childhood reading disorders: Significance and clinical utility. *Reading Research Quarterly, 15,* 84–101.

Torgesen, J. K. (1982). The use of rationally defined subgroups in research on learning disabilities. In J. P. Das, R. F. Mulcahy, & A. E. Wall (Eds.), *Theory and research in learning disabilities* (pp. 111–131). New York: Plenum Press.

Torgesen, J. K. (1986). Learning disabilities theory: Its current state and future prospects. *Journal of Learning Disabilities, 19,* 399–407.

Torgesen, J. K. (1987). Thinking about the future by distinguishing between issues that have resolutions and those that do not. In S. Vaughn & C. S. Bos (Eds.), *Research in learning disabilities* (pp. 55–67). Boston: College–Hill Press.

Tramontana, M. G., Hooper, S. R., & Selzer, S. C. (1988). Research on the preschool prediction of later academic achievement: A review. *Developmental Review, 8,* 89–146.

Walker, D. K., Singer, J. D., Palfrey, J. S., Orza, M., Wenger, M., & Butler, J. A. (1988). Who leaves and who stays in special education: A 2-year follow-up study. *Exceptional Children, 54,* 393–402.

Weller, C., & Strawser, S. (1987). Adaptive behavior of subtypes of learning disabled individuals. *The Journal of Special Education, 21,* 101–115.

A Dimensional Approach to Cognition and Academic Performance in Children With Medical Problems or Learning Difficulties

3

John W. Hagen
George Kamberelis
Stuart Segal
University of Michigan

> Such expressions as the famous one of Linneaus . . . that characters do not make the genus but that the genus gives the characters, seem to imply that something more is included in our classifications than mere resemblance. I believe that something more is included, and that the propinquity of descent—the only known cause of the similarity of organic beings—is the bond, hidden as it is by various degrees of modification, which is partially revealed to us in our classifications.
>
> *On the Origin of Species* (Darwin, 1859)

> Coyote said, "I am going to choke the Giant with this tamarack tree." The woman said, "You might as well throw that stick away. Don't you know you are already in the Giant's belly?"
>
> Flathead Myth (Coffin, 1961)

INTRODUCTION

The tension reflected in the juxtaposition of these two quotations is not unlike the tension felt by many researchers and clinicians with respect to traditional practices of diagnostic categorization. Diagnostic categories give clinical specialists ways of construing physical, psychological, and other difficulties by reducing an individual's problematical behaviors into relatively familiar patterns. Typically, these categorical descriptions are constructed based on results from assessment instruments at a single level of analysis, often by means of convergent validation. For example, a cognitive battery is generally used to diagnose learning disabilities while a neurological one is used to

53

diagnose seizure disorders. Seldom do researchers and clinicians develop comprehensive diagnostic systems that operate at several levels of analysis (e.g., neural, cognitive, developmental, environmental). Yet recent work in critical theory, cybernetics, and the philosophy of science suggests that an adequate account of behavior must include analyses of all levels of systemic organization present in the interaction between any individual system and the environment in which the system operates (Bateson, 1972, 1979; Cole & Scribner, 1974; Foucault, 1965, 1972; Salmon, 1971; Whitehead, 1960). In particular, it has been argued that analyses should include the consideration of systemic levels at least one step below and one step above the level or levels at which any phenomenon is typically explained (Rubinstein, Laughlin, & McManus, 1984; Wimsatt, 1980).

Diagnostic categories guide practitioners in applying established interventions as well as in developing new ones. These interventions are related quite specifically to the diagnostic categories themselves—categories which are typically derived from convergent validation at a single level of analysis. The outcome of clinical work depends on the efficacy of these interventions, so their effectiveness is related to proper diagnosis. Yet virtually all clinical interventions are culturally and socially situated. Thus, outcomes also depend to some extent on the fit between the meanings ascribed to them by both clients and practitioners (Fabrega, 1974; Foster & Anderson, 1978; Harwood, 1981; Smith, Osborne, Crim, & Rhu, 1986). However, because interventions are so closely related to diagnostic practices, they are usually designed to deal with deficits detected at a single level of analysis with little, if any, attention paid to other systemic levels. For example, interventions for learning disabilities focus on remediating or compensating for cognitive processing deficits, and interventions for seizure disorders focus on changing biochemical or physiological processes. While these interventions are necessary, they are not sufficient from the more comprehensive point of view we are espousing in this chapter. Seldom do such interventions include the consideration of various contextual variables such as developmental differences, task situations, social conditions, or political realities.

The development of a more satisfactory understanding of medical problems and learning difficulties in children depends on the inclusion of these contextual variables. If research questions and clinical practices are developed without considering all relevant levels of analysis, it is unlikely that understanding will be improved no matter how sophisticated the methods used. In this chapter, suggestions are offered about how this can be done. The approach is, first, to focus on the logic of inquiry of diagnostic categorization, and second to focus on particular methods.

Our view is that the conceptual integration of approaches and methods from different disciplines (e.g., medicine, psychology, sociology, social work, education) is necessary because the focus of any single discipline often leads researchers to overly simplified accounts of the problems they seek to understand. These accounts almost always operate at a single level of analysis. The main reason for the inadequacy of such accounts is that they derive from data that are artificially limited to a very narrow range of experience. This limiting occurs because observations are directed toward normatively appropriate data and away from data that are potentially anomalous to the focus of the discipline (Argyris, 1980; Campbell, 1978; Foucault, 1965, 1972; Rubinstein, et al., 1984). In connection with this latter point, the specialized knowledge and methods for knowledge acquisition of particular disciplines or areas of study come to be held as almost sacred entities. This further constrains the kinds of data and data collection techniques viewed as legitimate from a particular disciplinary perspective.

Perhaps the best way around this problem is to keep theoretical models as open as possible to new information. One way of doing this has already been suggested, namely making sure that our theoretical models include several levels of analysis. Focusing on a single level almost always leads to the confounding and normalizing of scientific models rather than to their improvement (Kuhn, 1962; Newell, 1973; Pacey, 1983; Quine, 1964; Schön, 1983). Each level affects the others, especially adjacent ones. Thus, for example, cognitive performance is affected in significant ways by neurological integrity on the next lower level (e.g., Rourke, 1981) and environmental variables such as experimental tasks and situations at a higher level (e.g., Cole & Scribner, 1974), but perhaps very little by political or societal structures. Exactly which systemic levels are important to include varies as a function of the researcher's interest and concerns.

Another important consideration in research is the recognition that scientific understanding, including the development of diagnostic categories, is a process alternating between inductive and deductive thinking (Giere, 1988; Habermas, 1971; Kuhn, 1962; Phillips, 1978; Simon, 1983). Any research finding is a product of this process and thus is abstracted from ongoing activity. Indeed, such findings can help to construct categories, such as the ones that make up typological systems, but it is important to remember that these categories are reifications of processes that do not exist independently of the purposes for which they are developed. Thus, diagnostic categories should be considered tentative, provisional, and should remain open to new knowledge and newly construed problems.

The evaluation of diagnostic categories is one way to illustrate the importance of interdisciplinary perspectives and multileveled analyses in research on medical and learning problems. In this chapter we ask questions about the nature and meaning of several diagnostic categories and pursue answers to those questions by using a variety of quantitative and qualitative methods from several disciplines. The chapter is divided into several parts. First we discuss different ways to think about diagnostic categorization. Second, we discuss the history of diagnostic categorization using learning disabilities as an example. Third, an alternative model is described, including three levels of analysis: diagnostic categorization, the developmental level of the child, and various aspects of the child's social and cultural life. Fourth, to illustrate the model, data from research on learning difficulties and medical problems are briefly considered. The results provide initial support for the model. Finally, we draw some conclusions about the logic of inquiry that guides research and clinical practice in the areas of learning difficulties and chronic illness; future directions for research and practice are considered.

The Logic of Diagnostic Categorization

Diagnosis and diagnostic categorization are terms that derive from the medical literature. Within that literature, Feinstein (1973, p. 212) proposed a definition of diagnosis that seems to embody the tension inherent in practices of diagnostic categorization that constitutes the main focus of this chapter. He referred to diagnosis as the "process of converting observed evidence into the names of disease. The evidence consists of data obtained from examining a patient; the diseases are conceptual medical entities that identify or explain abnormalities." Operationally, typologies of diagnostic categories define diseases or problems according to particular sets of evidence. The ontological and epistemological statuses of typologies and diagnostic categories, however, remain open questions. They can be interpreted from different disciplinary, theoretical or philosophical perspectives. Two particular contrasting perspectives are relevant to the present discussion.

The first perspective is rooted in normative practices and takes a realist stance, positing that diagnostic categories define ontologically real, epistemologically neutral entities. The second perspective is derived from more pragmatic concerns and takes a constructivist position, claiming that diagnostic categories are socially constructed and epistemologically relative classifications.

From the first perspective, typologies provide the basis for the objective classification of physiological and behavioral functioning, thus allowing us to tell what functioning falls outside of the range of normal activity. In addition, this perspective maintains that typologies are composed of natural categories whose boundaries exist and simply need to be discovered. Clinical typologies then provide names for these objectively identified, real entities the functioning of which deviates from biological or behavioral norms (e.g., Boorse, 1975).

From the second perspective, typologies are made of culturally and socially grounded categorizations of biological activity and behavior considered to be healthy or unhealthy, normal or abnormal. In addition, this position maintains that category boundaries are always socially constructed to some extent. Clinical typologies provide arbitrary names for biological and behavioral patterns that do not fit with the expectations arrived at by social and cultural consensus (e.g., Ysseldyke, et al., 1983).

Following the first perspective, psychological researchers and clinicians devote their energy, time, and material resources devising typologies that systematize their specialized knowledge. The results of these efforts are volumes such as the Diagnostic Statistical Manual. Based on the assumption that typologies are indexes of natural disease entities, the classifications in these volumes are derived from the convergent validation of biological and behavioral pathology. Among the aims of these typologies are improved statistical record keeping, more consistent diagnoses, and more efficacious procedures for intervention.

In contrast, following the second perspective, more anthropological and sociological minded researchers and clinicians focus on understanding the contexts in which the meanings of categories get constructed. Much of this work illuminates the fact that, in practice, diagnostic categories are used as explanatory systems for dealing with the individual's difficulties. This work also shows that these practices introduce biases that limit the kinds of data that clinicians and researchers collect and consider when attempting to make sense of an individual's experience and behavior. Finally, this work also points out that diagnostic categories get formed and reformed through the processes of social construction and that these processes are related to the contexts in which they take place (Berger & Luckmann, 1967; Conrad & Schneider, 1980; Fabrega, 1974; Feinstein, 1974; Henriques, Hollway, Urwin, Venn, & Walkerdine, 1984; Hufford, 1982; Penfold & Walker, 1983; Smith, et al., 1986). Thus, normative, disciplinary, social, economic, and political forces can influence the construction and use of diagnostic categories.

Both approaches to typologies acknowledge that for practitioners to deal effectively with their clients' difficulties they must be able to classify them according to some system and thereby to identify constellations of problematical processes as particular kinds of problems. The primary difference between the two perspectives involves the status granted to those problems. This is particularly important because of the implications for clinical practice. On the one hand, the realist interpretation of typologies leads to a world view of clinical practice that advocates a reliance on technology for "objective" problem assessment, an emphasis on the role of specialized knowledge, a limited acceptance of the individuals' reports of their own experience, and little concern for the contexts in which the problems occur. On the other hand, the constructivist approach supports the world view of clinical practice that sees technology as socially and culturally situated, expert knowledge as incomplete and emergent, individuals' reports of their experience as authentic and important to the processes of diagnosis and intervention, and contextual variables as critical in understanding individuals' problems. It is these and other similar features that form the cultural contexts of typologies, contexts which are all but ignored by the first perspective.

Next, we illustrate the conflict between these two perspectives by examining the development and attempts to validate (biologically and psychometrically) the diagnostic category, learning disabilities. In addition to illustrating the functioning of these two different views of typologies, our analysis should provide an understanding of the operation of single-leveled and multileveled analyses in the development of typological systems.

Diagnostic Categorization of Learning Disabilities

The term *learning disabilities* (LD) was introduced and formally defined by Kirk as

> A retardation, disorder, or delayed development in one or more of the processes of speech, language, reading, writing, or arithmetic resulting from possible cerebral dysfunction and/or emotional or behavioral disturbance and not from mental retardation, sensory deprivation, or cultural or instructional factions. (1962, p. 263)

Children labeled LD have traditionally been thought of as being afflicted with some kind of neurological dysfunction. For the past 25 years, attempts have been made to validate LD as a biological entity (see Broman, 1985, and Coles, 1987, for critical reviews). Indeed, the diagnostic category itself grew out of research on mental retardation. It was because of the heterogeneity within this group that the LD label was developed in the first place. In attempting to validate biologically and psychologically the category LD, the general strategy has been to seek consistent differences between "normal" and LD children (Kavale & Nye, 1986).

Several approaches have been used to demonstrate that LD is a distinct pathological entity. Some researchers have focused on discrepancies between the verbal and performance scales on intelligence tests, while others have investigated intelligence-achievement discrepancies. More recently some have focused on differential patterns of information processing (Speece, 1987; Torgesen, 1988), and still others have tried to document abnormal neurological functioning in presumed LD individuals and to demonstrate that these students experience maturational delay in central nervous system (CNS) structure and functioning (Rourke, 1985). Due to a variety of methodological problems, convergent validity has seldom been achieved in most research programs. Even when it has, none of these approaches has provided explanations that have stood the test of time. Indeed, even a cursory review of the literature shows that instead of becoming more precise, definitions of LD have become more nebulous and criteria for assessment more varied (e.g., Coles, 1987).

Since the original definition of LD, many others have been put forth. While they differ in important ways with respect to details, most still assert that CNS dysfunction plays a major role (Interagency Committee on Learning Disabilities, 1987). Furthermore, the search for both the true or generic LD condition and its source continues in the research and practice of many.

More recently, attempts have focused on developing subtypes of LD. DSM-III, for example, does not attempt to present a single comprehensive definition of LD. Rather, it organizes a general category called "Specific Developmental Disorders" into four distinct subcategories, each with its own definition: academic, speech, language, and motor skills. Along the same lines, much of the research in LD is currently devoted to subtyping (Del Dotto & Rourke, 1985; Feagans & Appelbaum; 1986; McKinney, Short, & Feagans, 1984; Satz & Morris, 1981; Torgesen, 1982; Wolfus, Moscovitch, & Kinsbourne, 1980, and many others).

The conceptual move represented by subtyping creates the possibility that the learning problems can be validated with greater specificity. Using statistical procedures such as the Q-Factor Analysis and Cluster Analysis to analyze results from biological and psychological measures these researchers are able to group subjects that demonstrate similar cognitive profiles, thus forming more valid and definitive groups. From these new and more specific definitions or group labels, more specific intervention plans have been formulated.

It is our view that subtyping represents an important conceptual advance over thinking about LD as a homogeneous disorder. Indeed, the chapters by Torgesen and McKinney and Feagans, in this volume illustrate, albeit in different but complementary ways, the utility and promise of subtyping research. Yet we believe that subtyping also has some drawbacks. First, as with the attempts to validate the more general LD categories, much subtyping research still holds on to central nervous system dysfunction as a major underlying cause of learning problems. While, as Torgesen (1986) has noted, researchers tend to operationalize LD problems according to three basic paradigms (neuropsychological, information-processing, and applied behavior analysis), many maintain neurological dysfunction as an underlying cause.

Second, with few exceptions, researchers who do not underscore neurological causation often tend to organize their research at a single level of analysis, usually cognitive. These researchers may include measures of language, perception, and motor skills, but seldom do they include measures a level below the cognitive level (i.e., neurological) and a level above the cognitive level (i.e., environmental).

Third, as Cormack (1971), Everitt (1979), and Kavale and Forness (1987) have noted, there are serious potential problems with some techniques used to arrive at subtypes. Cluster analysis is the most widely used technique for determining subtypes. Yet it is a technique that suffers from several methodological difficulties. Cluster analysis is a category for a variety of methods. Not all of these methods have been built upon firm statistical theory, and many of them have not been critically evaluated and tested. Many data sets do not warrant the use of cluster analyses. Yet there are hundreds of nondiscriminating software packages available that provide few guidelines concerning their informed use. Moreover, because of the weak theoretical foundations and evaluations of many cluster analysis techniques, even statistically savvy researchers may have a difficult time determining whether their data are appropriate for cluster analysis. Finally, clusters are derived from particular sets of dependent measures. Thus, data sets in which the kinds of measures used are limited to a single dimension (e.g., neuropsychological, linguistic, psychoeducational) or even a single level of analysis (e.g., neurological, cognitive, behavioral, environmental) yield clusters which are limited to a single dimension or level of analysis. As Kavale and Forness (1987) have pointed out, there is a troublesome relationship in subtyping research between the measures used and the subtypes identified. Their secondary analyses revealed an almost perfect correlation ($r = .983$) between the instruments (i.e., names of the instruments used to determine subtypes) and outcomes (i.e., names of subtypes). For example, in their subtyping efforts, Del Dotto and Rourke (1985) used 21 neurological measures to derive three neurological subtypes. Similarly, Feagans and Appelbaum (1986) used 6 linguistic measures to yield five language-based subtypes. And Satz and Morris (1981) used two measures of perceptual-motor functioning and two measures of linguistic functioning to identify five perspectual-motor, linguistic, or mixed subtypes.

Fourth, most research on subtyping develops assessment batteries specific to their own research goals. From these batteries they derive several specific subtypes. Yet the batteries from these different programs are often quite different. Thus it would not be surprising to find that children assessed using more than one of these batteries might be classified as more than one subtype. In other words, the way that subtyping research has proceeded could easily result in threats to the validity of subtyping constructs. Research using various batteries on the same children would help to guard against this potential problem.

Fifth, notably absent in most subtyping research are any measures of developmental or environmental variables. Like the search for the true LD example, the search for true subtypical examples has been burdened by traditional assumptions of inherited typologies and the notable absence of various environmental considerations, including development, socioeconomic status, family structure and function, and the politics of schooling. This is true despite ruminations by the field's old guard as well as many newcomers that more attention needs to be paid to these variables. Hallahan and Cruickshank (1973, p. 13), for example, stated that "children who have learning problems due to environmental conditions should not be excluded from learning disability programs." Similarly, Adelman and Taylor (1986, p. 603) noted "the increased recognition that significant numbers of learning problems do not arise from problems within the individual; rather, many problems are seen to stem from a pathological or inadequate environment."

Yet, little attention has been paid to environmental variables. For example, Torgesen (1986) has noted that it will require many variables to construct or define various subtypes. Among the variables to consider include focus symptoms, anxiety, motivation, development, IQ, cognitive style, memory and attention, and interactions among these variables. Indeed, Torgesen's suggestions extend the considerations of most subtyping research. Yet even these considerations do not stretch current paradigms far enough. There is a need to include an even wider range of variables, especially social-environmental ones.

In contrast to biological and psychometric attempts to validate LD as a specific pathological entity, research carried out using a multileveled perspective suggests that developmental factors, the role of the social environment, and the role of other environmental factors are critical for the identification of students with legitimate LD (Adelman & Taylor, 1986; Coles, 1987; Deci & Chandler, 1986; Hagen & Kamberelis, 1989; Reason & Rowan, 1981; Sleeter, 1986; and many others). Moreover, many of these researchers have demonstrated that children labeled LD may display diagnostically significant behaviors in some social and learning situations but not in others (Palincsar & Brown, 1984, 1987; Poplin, 1988; Ryan, Short, & Weed, 1986). Still others have suggested that children get labeled LD for behavioral rather than academic reasons (Smith, et al., 1986). Naturalistic studies have pointed out that the academic performance of children labeled LD varies widely across task settings and instructional situations. Indeed, some studies have found students labeled LD compare quite favorably in learning situations with children considered to be gifted (Gunderson, Maesch, & Rees, 1987). Other studies (Deci & Chandler, 1986; Pflaum & Pascarella, 1982; see also Licht, 1983, for a review) have noted the importance of perceived self-competence, motivation, independence and self-attributions in the performance of both non-LD and LD children. Finally, several researchers (Coles, 1987; McKnight, 1982; Sleeter, 1986) have argued that there is no convincing evidence from neurological, psychometric, or behavioral research to support the use of the LD label, and that LD has become a mythical scapegoat used to cover up the failure of American education to serve a significant segment of its population.

In light of these concerns and findings, several groups of researchers have expanded their programs of research at several levels of analysis and in context-sensitive ways. Smith et al., (1986) investigated the processes by which children get categorized as LD and found that whether or not a given child is labeled LD depends on whether or not the diagnosis consists of one or a combination of determinations by psychologists, teachers, school administrators, doctors, or parents. Moreover, they found that different experts and lay people defined LD quite differently and in ways consistent with their own academic training, work experience, cultural world views, job requirements, and social positions vis-à-vis the child. Similar findings were reported by Ysseldyke and his colleagues (e.g., Ysseldyke et al., 1983). These investigators questioned whether or not LD could be considered a legitimate diagnostic entity. They offered a number of alternative explanations—labeling as a form of social control of deviance, for example—to account for the difficulties faced by these children. Each alternative explanation suggested that many children labeled did not have specific disorders and that a major source of their problems lay in the social context in which the LD diagnosis was made.

The work of Ysseldyke and his colleagues offers perhaps the most convincing argument for the use of a multileveled perspective in research and clinical work with LD children. Using multiple measures and very large samples, these researchers were not able to differentiate students labeled LD from low-achieving students not labeled LD. They concluded that the LD category does not meet the criteria for a classification system. The only characteristic common to the LD students in their sample was low achievement. Rather, LD was best defined as "whatever society want[ed] it to be, need[ed] it to be, or [would] let it be" (p. 89). These researchers also noted that variables such as gender, race, socioeconomic status, and physical appearance influenced the labeling decisions of clinical experts. It was also found that clinical experts could distinguish between LD-labeled students and non-LD underachievers only at chance level. Interestingly, naïve adults were successful in making this judgment three-quarters of the time.

Finally, these researchers concluded that student learning problems must be viewed from an ecological perspective that considers child variables, home variables, classroom variables, and instructional variables in student problems, and that research and clinical efforts would be better spent on teaching than on testing and labeling.

In our own research, we have also had a difficult time distinguishing between students labeled LD and non-LD underachievers. Additionally, we have found many more similarities than differences on cognitive, academic, developmental, and environmental measures across groups of children with either medical or learning problems. Moreover, we have found that teachers, psychologists, administrators, and parents differ in making judgments about LD and non-LD students. These general findings have led us to our current research, which is aimed at developing psychosocial learning profiles of children with learning problems and children with medical problems. This research is guided by a theoretical model called the dimensional model, which takes into account diagnostic categories, developmental level, and various environmental factors, including home, school, and peer group.

Several features of our approach distinguish it from most subtyping research. First, our approach tends to be more theory-driven than much subtyping research. While some programs of research on subtyping are guided by theoretical notions about the kinds of subtypes that will be found (see McKinney & Feagans, this volume, for a review), most subtyping research depends heavily on statistical techniques to derive subtypes. In other words, subtypes tend to be empirically, rather than theoretically, defined. Second, the measures typically used to construct the subtypes are often limited to a single psychological dimension and almost always to a single level of analysis. The dimensional approach employs multiple measures at three levels of analysis (categorical, developmental, and environmental). Finally, our empirical research has consistently yielded large overlaps on most measures of cognition and academic performance among children in different diagnostic categories. Thus we have been less inclined toward seeking subtypes and more inclined toward trying to explain within-group differences and between-group similarities. In doing so we have perceived a need to include a wide range of variables, especially social-environmental ones.

The dimensional approach represents one attempt to design a research program on learning problems that maintains many traditional measures while adding a number of contextual measures. This approach is relatively new, and it is still evolving. Noticeably absent in the present model is a neurological dimension. Since we had to delimit our focus and since so much attention had already been paid to neurological aspects of LD, we decided to emphasize context and de-emphasize neurology. As we develop the model we may include a neurological dimension. A description and developmental history of the dimensional approach is provided in the next section.

The Dimensional Model

During the past 15 years, children with chronic physical illnesses have increasingly attracted the attention of pediatricians and psychologists interested in the impact of these illnesses on adaptation in school and in the family. The pioneering work of many researchers (Hobbs & Perrin, 1986; Pless & Pinkerton, 1975; Stein & Jessop, 1982, 1984) has argued for a noncategorical, or generic, approach to understanding the impact of chronic illnesses. One assumption of this general approach has been that regardless of the particular illness category, certain common considerations underlie the understanding

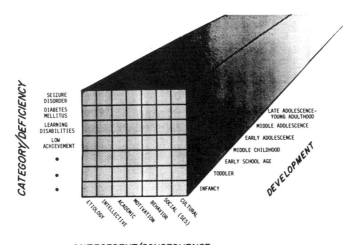

FIG. 3.1.   A dimensional model of cognitive deficiencies (adapted from
Hagen, Saarnio & Laywell, 1987).

of causes, treatment, and possible cures of many disorders. These include
etiology, age of onset, duration, medical management, relative visibility, and
family response.

The dimensional approach has grown out of an intellectual alliance with
proponents of the noncategorical approach.   Much of our research and
writing has focused on attempting to understand the complex relationships
that exist among biological, psychological, and social dimensions of human
performance, especially with respect to children identified as exhibiting
atypical patterns of cognitive development and learning (Barclay & Hagen,
1982; Hagen, Barclay, & Schwethelm, 1982). More recently, we have formalized some of our thinking into the dimensional model of cognitive and
academic performance (Hagen, Saarnio, & Laywell, 1987; Hagen &
Kamberelis, 1989). The current version of this model is represented dia-
grammatically in Fig. 3.1.

Categorical descriptions of children make up the first dimension of the
model. In the work reported in this chapter we have included children
diagnosed to have either one of two chronic illnesses (diabetes mellitus or
seizure disorders) or one of two learning problems (academic underachievement or learning disabilities). However, any diagnostic category
could be included in this dimension. The second dimension of the model
includes relevant antecedent and consequence variables. These include
factors typically considered internal to the child as well as ones normally
considered environmental. The third dimension of the model is the developmental level of the child under consideration. The segmentation of this
dimension is based on the consideration of the various factors that operate to
form qualitatively distinct periods in life-span development (e.g., Havinghurst,

1972). From the point of view of the model, any individual's developmental level interacts with factors in each of the other two dimensions.

At the heart of the dimensional model is the characterization of cognitive skills as they relate to academic, behavioral, and social variables. The cognitive-developmental approach inherent in the model permits a concentration on observed, potentially correctable problems in cognitive performance in various task settings. For example, we know that the development of short term memory progresses through stages from inactive to mediational deficient to active, efficient memorizing (Hagen & Stanovitch, 1977). Yet, some children with learning disabilities exhibit a delayed version of this pattern; other LD children exhibit a qualitatively different pattern, symptomatic perhaps of an actual deficit or defect (Hagen et al., 1982). And some of these children can make remarkable gains when task situations and other environmental factors are modified to accommodate differences in learning styles (Palincsar & Brown, 1984; Schumaker, Deshler, & Ellis, 1986). Thus, it seems clear that developmental differences and environmental influences are critical to understanding cognitive and academic performance, especially in children at risk for academic problems. The dimensional approach provides a framework within which to consider these different factors.

Empirical Support for a Dimensional Approach

We have studied four different groups of children using the dimensional approach: children with learning disabilities (LD), academic underachievers (UA), children with diabetes mellitus (DB), and children with seizure disorders (SD). Descriptive information on the subjects in each of these groups, along with a comparison group (C), is shown in Table 3.1.

TABLE 3.1
Subject Information

| | | Subjects | | |
	C	UA	DB	LD	SD
Number	30	14	30	23	29
Sex					
Male	14	10	13	14	11
Female	16	4	17	9	13
Age in years					
Mean	12.6	13.5	12.7	12.8	11.3
S.D.	2.6	2.3	2.7	2.0	2.5
Range	8.1	8.4-	8.0-	6.3-	6.8
	16.6	16.9	16.3	18.5	16.8

C = comparison
UA = underachievement
DB = diabetes mellitus
LD = learning disabilities
SD = seizure disorders

The age range for each group was wide and included children who were as young as 6 years and as old as late adolescence. The mean age at diagnosis was roughly the same for the different groups as was mean duration of the major presenting problem that led to diagnosis. Interestingly, at least 35% of the children in each of the groups, including the C group, reported learning or medical problems additional to the one that defined their membership in a particular diagnostic category (or in the C group). The UA group is small because that study is still in progress.

The battery of instruments used in our research included two measures of memory: the Central/Incidental Serial Recall Task (e.g., Hagen, 1967) and the Pause-Time Free Recall Task (e.g., Belmont & Butterfield, 1969). These measures were chosen because, together, they include both pictorial and verbal stimuli and both forced-choice and free recall conditions. Both instruments allow researchers to study the development of active strategy use which has been shown to play a key role in memory performance. Also included in our battery were selected tests of the Wechsler Intelligence Scale for Children–Revised (WISC–R), (Wechsler, 1974) and the Reading Comprehension and Mathematics subtests of the Peabody Individual Achievement Test (PIAT), (Dunn & Markwardt, 1970). Additionally, the Perceived Competence Scale (Harter, 1978) and the Moos Family Environment scale (Moos, 1974) were administered. Finally, information concerning the developmental, medical, and school histories of children participating in the research program was obtained from extensive interviews conducted with children and parents.

Families of the DB and SD children were recruited by investigators at a research facility which is physically and administratively separate from the hospital. The children were patients seen on a regular basis for routine medical follow-up at the pediatrics clinic at the University of Michigan. Children with LD and UA children were recruited through the university's Reading and Learning Skills Center as well as through community agencies and other referral sources.

All children and siblings participated in a single 3-hour session of testing and interviewing. One investigator worked with each child. While the children were being tested and interviewed, a structured interview was conducted with one or both parents. Parent(s) also completed a series of questionnaires. Sessions were scheduled at times that were convenient for the families who participated in the project.

The quantitative data from our battery were analyzed, using ANOVAs, regression analyses, and principal components analysis. ANOVAs revealed no significant differences among groups for age, gender, or head of household occupation, which we used as proxy for SES. General findings from the studies relevant to the basic argument in this chapter are provided below.

Wechsler Intelligence Scale for Children–Revised

A profile of performance on selected tests of the WISC–R for each group is provided in Figure 3.2. Note the gradually decreasing performance as a function of group.

The children in the comparison group scored the highest, and they were followed in order by the UA, DB, LD, and the SD children. It is important to note this ordering, as it shows up repeatedly in the data

The majority of the analyses across groups for performances on the subtests of the WISC–R were highly significant. Pairwise comparisons revealed many interesting similarities and differences between and among groups, as shown in Table 3.2.

Most of the differences were between the C group and the LD group and between the C group and the SD group, with the C children doing better. In addition, the UA children scored significantly higher on the Information and Vocabulary subtests than both the DB children and the SD children. DB children scored much higher than SD children on the Comprehension and Block Design subtests. The LD children scored significantly higher than SD children on the Block Design subtest. Otherwise, the aptitude profiles of children in these two groups looked very similar. Similarly, the aptitude

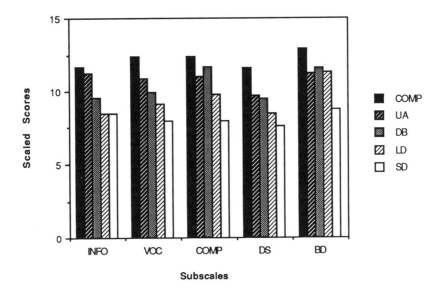

FIG. 3.2. Results from selected subscales of the WISC-R.

TABLE 3.2
WISC-R: Scheffé Comparisons

	Info	Vocab	Comp	Digit Span	Block Design
COMP × LD	•	•	•	•	
COMP × VA					
COMP × DB	•	•			
COMP × SD	•	••	••	•	••
LD × VA					
LD × DB					
LD × SD					•
VA × DB					
VA × SD	•	•			
DB × SD			•		•

•p < .05
••p < .01

profiles of children with DB and the UA children were quite similar. The performance of the C group was the highest overall, with little deviation across subtests.

If we gather together these results, the following continuum of performance is observed: C–UA–DB–LD–SD. This continuum demonstrates that many variables from the antecedent/consequence dimension of our theoretical model *cut across* chronic illness and learning problem categories. Additionally, there was a lot of within-group variance in the data, suggesting that the boundaries between diagnostic categories were by no means clear-cut.

Peabody Individual Achievement Test

The results obtained from all groups on the Peabody Individual Achievement Test are presented in Fig. 3.3.

The two scores reported for each group are percentile ranks by age for the Mathematics and the Reading Comprehension subtests. Overall, the analysis of variance for groups was significant. Results from pairwise comparisons are shown in Table 3.3. These comparisons revealed patterns of differences similar to those found on the WISC–R.

Children in the LD and SD groups performed significantly lower than the C group on both subtests. In addition, children in the LD group did not perform as well as the UA children and the DB children on the Reading Comprehension subtest. The SD children did not score as well as the UA children or the DB children on the Mathematics subtest. LD children and SD children looked quite similar, receiving the lowest scores on both subtests. Note, however, that the lower and higher scores for each group were reversed. For the SD group, mathematics was higher. This is not surprising

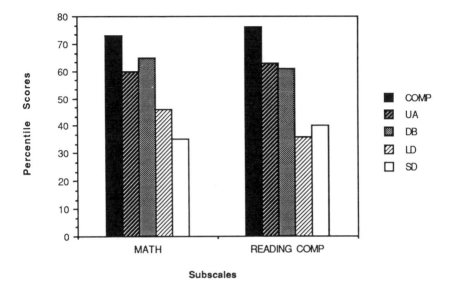

FIG. 3.3. Results from selected subscales of the PIAT.

since the major problem presented by children with LD involves processing and producing written language.

Overall, the continuum of performance observed among the groups, C–UA–DB–LD–SD, was the same on the PIAT as on the WISC–R. Also, there was considerable scatter in the data, suggesting ill-defined boundaries among diagnostic categories.

TABLE 3.3
PIAT: Scheffé Comparisons

	Math	Reading
COMP × LD	*	**
COMP × VA		
COMP × DB		
COMP × SD	**	**
LD × VA		*
LD × DB		*
LD × SD		
VA × DB		
VA × SD	*	
DB × SD	*	*

*p < .05
**p < .01

Central Incidental Serial Recall Task

Significant differences among groups were found for overall central recall on the Central-Incidental Serial Recall Task. However, pairwise comparisons revealed significant differences between two groups only: C and SD. It should be added that children in the C group scored well above children in all other groups on total recall and children in the SD group received particularly low scores on this task.

While there were no overall significant differences in incidental recall among the groups, children in the four focus groups, but not the C group, had higher recall on the incidental task than on the central task. These children appear to have utilized less effective selective attention strategies in this task. This finding corroborates work by Torgesen (1988), Pressley, Borkowski, and Schneider (1987), and others that has indicated poor strategy use as playing a key role in low performance on cognitive and academic tasks.

Serial recall performance varied significantly across some groups only, especially in the primacy positions. Pairwise comparisons revealed differences between the C group and the LD group and between the C group and the SD group in these positions, with the comparison children doing significantly better. This finding was expected, since children in the SD and the LD groups have differed consistently from children in the comparison group and have appeared repeatedly at opposite ends of the performance continuum. Children in the LD and SD groups, who have already been identified as looking similar on other tasks, performed alike on this task, demonstrating virtually no primacy effects. This finding is consistent with the interpretation that they did not approach this serial recall task strategically. As on other tasks, considerable within-group variance was found resulting in large overlaps between some diagnostic categories.

The continuum of performance among the groups on this task was quite similar to that found for the WISC–R and the PIAT: C–DB–UA–LD–SD. Note that the UA and DB groups have reversed position here. This finding is consistent with the idea that the boundaries between adjacent diagnostic categories tend to be fuzzy rather than clear-cut.

Pause-time Free-recall Task

On the Pause-time Free-recall Task, significant differences among groups were found for the primacy and medial positions. Pairwise comparisons revealed that the C children performed better than the UA children in the primacy positions and better than the children with seizure disorders in both primacy and medial positions. The continuum of performance among the groups on this task showed the familiar pattern: C–UA–DB–LD–SD. Additionally, as on other tasks, within-group variance was large, suggesting unclear boundaries among diagnostic categories on free-recall memory performance. Thus, the use of information-processing strategies was only moderately predictable as a function of group membership.

In addition to measuring correct recall on the Pause-time task, latency times were also recorded. Latency, or pause times, represent the amount of time children pause from the off-set of one stimulus item on a given trial to the self-selection or onset of the next item. Thus, pause-times can serve as proxies for strategy use. ANOVAs and pairwise comparisons revealed no significant differences as a function of group membership for latency times on the Pause-Time task. However, the groups were by no means identical. The patterns of performance suggested that the C and DB children were using optimal active–passive rehearsal strategies while the LD and UA children were not being flexible in their strategy use, but appeared to be using lower-level strategies. The children in the SD group exhibited almost no evidence of any active strategy use.

Perceived Competence Scale

While most children scored in the normal range on all four subscales (cognitive, social, physical, and general self-esteem) of the Perceived Competence Scale, significant differences were found among groups on the cognitive and social subscales. Pairwise comparisons revealed differences between the C and LD groups and between the DB and the LD groups on the cognitive subscale, with the LD children performing more poorly. In addition, DB children received significantly higher scores than the SD children on the social subscale.

Especially interesting to note are the relatively low self-ratings of cognitive competence among the SD, LD, and the UA children. These results were consistent with other findings in our research derived from interviews with both children and parents. Children in these groups not only performed poorly on many cognitive and academic tasks, they also were aware of their difficulties in these areas. Over time one would expect that low perceived competence and poor performance might mutually reinforce one another, resulting in the continued depression of both.

It is also interesting to note that in regression analyses the cognitive subscale of the Perceived Competence Scale often accounted for as much or more of the variance than did group membership. For example, on the Reading Comprehension subtest of the PIAT, group membership accounted for 12% of the variance while the cognitive subscale of the Perceived Competence Scale accounted for 14%. It may turn out that perceived cognitive competence is an important factor in understanding some children and perhaps in defining some groups. The role played by perceived cognitive competence in the regression analyses suggests some important performance–environment interactions that need to be explored.

Family Environment Scale

Most scores on the Family Environment Scale were within the normal range for both parents and children. However, some interesting results were obtained when we compared children's and parents' scores on certain subscales. Compared with their parents and to the instrument's norms, learning-disabled children and academic underachievers scored quite low on the Expressiveness and Independence subscales. Similarly, on the Control subscale, LD children and UA children scored much higher than their parents. In other words, children in these families perceived the social environment to be controlling and to offer few opportunities for independence and expressiveness, while their parents had nearly opposite perceptions. It would be useful to know whether these results reflect general trends concerning the power structure of typical American families or whether they are peculiar to families having children with certain kinds of problems or families from different cultural and socioeconomic groups. Since we did not have scores from this instrument for both parents and children in the other three groups, and since our research does not focus on ethnicity or SES, it was not possible to answer these questions.

Interview Data

Interviews and questionnaires that were completed by children in our studies, as well as their parents and siblings, included both quantitative and qualitative information. Particularly important were questions concerning the effects of the problems of one family member on family structure and functioning and family responses to the special needs of one family member. While the analyses of the interview and questionnaire data are still in progress, several findings provide insight into families' perceptions and beliefs. For example, parents of SD children were much more likely to indicate that their child's condition was in "good control" than parents of children in any of the other groups. Parents of children in all groups except the C group reported that their children's learning and achievement problems were serious. Except for families with underachieving children, reports from both parents and siblings concerning having a child with a learning or a medical problem in the family were remarkably similar across groups. Families of underachieving children expressed a good deal of hostility toward the affected child because they expected that this child could change if he or she wanted to. For families of children in the other groups, however, responses indicated that families joined together in an effort to change family routines to accommodate the needs of the affected child. Moreover, most siblings and parents viewed this accommodation process as time consuming but not as a sacrifice. Families of SD children expressed the most concern about their children's abilities to relate to their peers. Parents of underachieving children also expressed some concern about peer relations but usually it involved thinking that their children did not choose their friends wisely. From the preliminary analyses that we have done, it is evident that while some parental concerns, beliefs, and responses are especially prevalent in certain groups, many concerns, beliefs, and responses cut across group boundaries. Indeed, more analyses of environmental variables, including family, peer, and school experience variables, should provide useful information in understanding cognitive and academic performance in children with medical and learning problems.

Principal Components Analysis

We now turn to discussion of the similarities that cut across category boundaries in the entire data set. A principal components analysis was performed to arrive at another view of our data set. Principal components analysis is a variable-directed, mathematical technique that allows researchers to reduce the dimensionality of a problem space. While this analysis has no predictive value, it is useful in suggesting directions for future research and theorizing. We have not used principal components analysis to develop the dimensional approach, but to try to simplify the variable structure in our data in order to inform the direction of future research.

Four principal components emerged as particularly descriptive and together accounted for 53% of the variance in the data. The first principal component, which accounted for 22% of the variance, was composed primarily of all the WISC–R and PIAT subscales along with the cognitive subscale of the Perceived Competence Scale. Group membership also loaded on this principal component, but not as heavily as the other elements. Principal component 1 appears to represent ability and achievement variables and relationships. This finding, taken together with the ANOVA results on the WISC–R and the PIAT, suggests that while IQ and achievement are important predictors of cognitive and academic performance, they are only mildly distributed as a function of group.

Principal component 2, which accounted for 15% of the variance, was composed of Pause-Time latency scores only. Since these are proxies for strategy use, it appears that this component represents the deployment of information-processing strategies. This finding, along with the ANOVA results reported here, leaves us with the sense that, as Torgesen and others have suggested, strategy use is a critical variable in cognitive and academic performance.

Principal component 3, which accounted for 9% of the variance, was composed of age and results from information processing tasks (which are not normed for age). Therefore it appears that this component reflects developmental level, one of the major factors in the dimensional approach.

Principal component 4, accounting for 7% of the variance, was composed of gender and the Cognitive and Social subscales of the Perceived Competence Scale. This component appears to represent differential socialization and motivation, an area that a number of researchers (e.g., Deci & Chandler, 1986) have found to be critical in understanding learning problems and one that requires further attention.

Three findings from the principal components analysis are especially interesting: (1) the relative absence of Group Membership in any of the principal components, (2) the extent to which Perceived Cognitive Competence contributed to the principal components structure, and (3) the importance of understanding information-processing strategies insofar as they relate to cognitive and academic performance.

Preliminary descriptions of the groups we have studied are now considered. Table 3.4 presents a summary of the characteristics of the various groups.

TABLE 3.4
Group Characteristics

Comparison
High-normal IQ distribution
No specific deficits
Relatively high achievement
Few behavioral problems
High perceived competence

Underachievement	*Diabetes Mellitus*
High-normal IQ distribution	Normal IQ distribution but with
No specific deficits	developmental delay in early onset
Average achievement but not meeting	Memory and attention deficits
parental and school expectations	especially in early onset
IQ and achievement drop off with age	Average achievement but with
Perceived cognitive competence	developmental delay in early onset
diminishes with age	High perceived competence
Conflict with family members	Insulin reactions and hypoglycemia
and school personnel	
Low motivation	
Learning Disabilities	*Seizure Disorders*
Low-average verbal IQ; High-average	Low-average IQ with large variance
performance IQ with large variance	Delayed information-processing
on both	strategies
Developmental delay and large variance	Below-average math and reading
in IQ	achievement
Deficits in verbal processing and long-	Seizures
term memory	
Delayed information-processing strategies	Distractibility
Average math achievement; Below-average	Drug toxicity reactions
reading achievement	Low perceived cognitive competence
Developmental delay in achievement	
Distractibility	
Some acting out	
Low perceived cognitive competence	

The table is organized according to continuum of cognitive and academic performance described. As this summary of results demonstrates, while there are some characteristics specific to single groups, most characteristics accrue across two or more of the groups.

An additional set of analyses was done to pursue possible similarities across groups of children with chronic illnesses and learning problems. Children with medical problems were collapsed into one group as were children with learning problems. These two larger groups were then compared with one another as well as to the comparison group. Table 3.5 presents a summary of these comparisons.

While children with either learning problems or with chronic illnesses were different from the comparison children, they were not different from one another. Next, we collapsed the data according to the similarities across groups that we found in main effects analyses. Results from comparisons of these new groups are shown in Table 3.6. Children with seizure disorders and

TABLE 3.5
Scheffé Comparisons: Comparison vs. Learning Problems vs.
Chronic Illness

	PIAT Math	PIAT Reading	WISC-R Vocab	WISC-R Comp	WISC-R DS	WISC-R BD	WISC-R Info	Harter Cog	Hagen Primacy	Pause-time Primacy	Pause-time Medial
Comp vs. Learning	*	**	*	*	*			*		*	*
Comp vs. Illness	*	**	**	**	*	*		*		*	*
Learning vs. Illness								*			

* $p < .05$
** $p < .01$

TABLE 3.6
Scheffé Comparisons: Comparison vs. UA/DB vs. LD/SD

	PIAT Math	PIAT Reading	WISC-R Vocab	WISC-R Comp	WISC-R DS	WISC-R BD	WISC-R Info	Harter Cog	Hagen Primacy	Pause-time Primacy	Pause-time Medial
COMP vs. UA/DB			*	*			*			*	
COMP vs. LS/SD	*	**	**	*	**	**	**	*	*	*	*
UA/DB vs. LD/SD	*	*	*	*	*	*	*	*			

* $p < .05$
** $p < .01$

children with learning disabilities formed one group while children with diabetes mellitus and children who were underachievers formed another.

From this table it is clear that children with diabetes mellitus and underachievers cohered quite well as a group. Similarly, children with learning disabilities and children with seizure disorders formed a fairly homogeneous group.

Summary Comments

Findings support the use of the dimensional model in trying to understand patterns of cognitive and academic performance among chronically ill children and children with learning problems. The model stresses the developmental level of the child. This dimension was particularly important in interpreting our data. Not only was development per se an important factor in cognitive and academic performance, but developmental delay and developmental regression were important as well. Evidence indicating patterns of developmental delay was found on IQ, achievement, and information-processing measures for the learning disabilities group and a subset of the diabetes group, those for whom the chronic illness was diagnosed prior to 4 years of age. Patterns of developmental regression were found on these same measures for the underachievers.

The dimensional model questions the usefulness of diagnostic categorization. In relation to this, group membership or diagnostic category accounted for very little variance in the data when compared with other factors. In general, there was more variability within groups than across them. This was especially true for groups adjacent to one another on the continuum of cognitive and academic performance we observed. Additionally, there were many similarities across groups. In particular, each of the chronic illness groups appeared more similar to one or the other of the learning problem groups than to the other illness group. The seizure disorders children looked very similar to the learning-disabled children and the diabetic children looked similar to the underachievers on many measures. Finally, family responses and coping patterns of children with medical and learning problems were remarkably alike.

Future research should include increased attention to several aspects of learning and development among children at risk for academic success. More and better measures of self-concept, attribution, and motivation are needed. More attention needs to be paid to environmental factors, including school, family, and peer relations. Longitudinal research is needed to determine more fully the long-term consequences of various kinds of problem conditions under investigation. The inclusion of more chronic illness groups as well as more learning-problem groups would be useful. Additionally, after more studies of various groups have been completed, meta-analyses could be attempted. Finally, more sensitive measures of information processing need to be developed and used to determine more accurately the relative presence or absence of strategy use among groups, as well as the particular kinds of strategies used. In addition, these measures should be designed to tap practical intelligence or everyday cognition.

While our research has only begun to address these needs, the dimensional model contributes to a greater understanding of chronic illnesses and learning problems by providing a way to take into account cognitive potential, academic performance, and behavioral and environmental information within and across diagnostic labels. In relation to this point, research generated by the model builds upon and extends subtyping research which sometimes glosses over similarities across groups and gives short shrift to developmental and environmental factors.

In light of the findings of this chapter we would suggest conceptualizing diagnostic categories in terms of a continuum rater than as distinct entities. While many differences might exist among groups on either end of the continuum, few exist among groups that lie closer together. Basing prescriptions on labels without adequate descriptions is risky and not fair to the children who are labeled. Yet the continuum of cognition and academic performance found in our research suggests that current diagnostic categories, including subtypical ones, are not without at least some utility. However, they have limited predictive value with respect to many aspects of learning and development. More definitive criteria for these categories are needed, and we have to keep in mind that the categories that we derive are partial and tentative constructs of our always incomplete empirical work. In light of this, we suggest augmenting underspecified clinical categories with comprehensive learning profiles of all students. Included in such profiles should be information about the use of information-processing strategies in various cognitive modalities: verbal, perceptual, numerical. Also included should be careful descriptions of the task structures and the social contexts in which learning and instruction take place, and analyses of data relevant to peer group relations and family structure and functioning.

In this chapter, we have presented a model and empirical work that, we feel, provides one approach to dealing efficiently with these problems. It is compelling that the performance of children in different diagnostic categories overlaps as much as it does. This is especially true with respect to the many similarities observed between children with seizure disorders and LD children and between children with diabetes mellitus and underachieving children. Taking into account several levels of analysis is important in trying to understand problems as complex as cognition and academic performance in children at risk for educational outcomes.

In conclusion we shall return to some of the points made at the beginning of the chapter. Research findings and clinical judgments are always based on incomplete information, and thus will always be fallible. When we rely on measures from a single level of analysis we can develop the mistaken impression that we have a better understanding of how to think about problematical situations than we really do. Thus we develop a false sense of the adequacy of resulting diagnostic categories. Ignoring the relationships among the various systemic levels within and outside the child means that our information is always going to be incomplete. Because we rely upon the continued development of diagnostic categories, one consequence of failing to include measures at several levels of analysis is that our categories will always be underspecified.

Diagnostic categories are usually considered to be scientific and objective, and thus not culture-dependent or culture-specific. This blurs the fact that all behavior is appropriate or inappropriate only in relation to specific contexts and in relation to the meanings that people give to those contexts. More attention needs to be directed toward the idea that what counts as normal or abnormal, or as desirable or undesirable behavior is socially constructed, reflecting the beliefs, values, and norms basic to an individual's social and cultural context.

Finally, it is important to understand that diagnostic categories result from research that is always in process and that involves both inductive and deductive thinking. While the categories that we abstract from our research can be quite useful in making clinical judgments, they remain reifications of socially situated research processes and do not exist independently of the purposes for which they were developed. Thus, diagnostic categories must always be treated as tentative and provisional. As researchers in a field so closely related to clinical practice, we must be careful not to become too enamored of our methods and constructs, and we must continuously guard against narrowing our field of vision to the extent that we ignore critical questions and variables.

REFERENCES

Adelman, H. S., & Taylor, L. (1986). Moving the LD field ahead: New paths, new paradigms. *Journal of Learning Disabilities, 19*, 602–608.

American Psychiatric Association (1987). *Diagnostic and statistical manual of mental disorders* (3rd ed., revis.). Washington DC: Author.

Argyris, C. (1980). *Inner contradictions of rigorous research.* New York: Academic Press.

Barclay, C. R., & Hagen, J. W. (1982). The development of mediated behavior in children: An alternative view of learning disabilities. In J. P. Das, R. F. Mulcahy, & A. E. Wall (Eds.), *Theory and research in learning disabilities* (pp. 61–84). New York: Plenum Press.

Bateson, G. (1972). *Steps to an ecology of mind.* New York: Ballantine.

Bateson, G. (1979). *Mind in nature: A necessary unity.* Toronto: Bantam Books.

Belmont, J. M., & Butterfield, E. C. (1969). The relations of short-term memory to development and intelligence. In L. P. Lipsitt & H. W. Reese (Eds.), *Advances in child development and behavior* (Vol. 4). New York: Academic Press.

Bergen, P. L., & Luckmann, T. (1967). *The social construction of reality: A treatise in the sociology of knowledge.* Garden City, NY: Doubleday.

Boorse, C. (1975). Health as a theoretical concept. *Philosophy of Science, 44,* 542–573.

Broman, S. (1985). *Low achieving children: The first seven years.* London: Lawrence Erlbaum Associates.

Campbell, D. (1978). Qualitative knowing in action research. In M. Brenner, P. Marsh, & M. Brenner (Eds.), *The social context of method.* New York: St. Martin's Press.

Cole, M., & Scribner, S. (1974). *Culture and thought: A psychological perspective.* New York: Wiley.

Coles, G. (1987). *The learning mystique.* New York: Pantheon Books.

Conrad, P., & Schneider, J. (1980). *Deviance and medicalization: From badness to sickness.* St. Louis: C. V. Mosby.

Deci, E. L., & Chandler, C. L. (1986). The importance of motivation for the future of the LD field. *Journal of Learning Disabilities, 19,* 587–594.

Del Dotto, J. E., & Rourke, B. P. (1985). Subtypes of left-handed learning disabled children. In B. P. Rourke (Ed.), *Neuropsychology of learning disabilities: Essentials of subtype analysis* (pp. 89–130). New York: Guilford Press.

Dunn, L. M., & Markwardt, F. C., Jr. (1970). *Peabody Individual Achievement Test.* Circle Pines, MN: American Guidance Service.

Everitt, B. S. (1979). Unresolved problems in cluster analysis. *Biometrics, 35,* 169–182.

Fabrega, H. (1974). *Disease and social behavior.* Cambridge, MA: MIT Press.

Feagans, L., & Appelbaum, M. (1986). Language subtypes and their validation in learning disabled children. *Journal of Educational Psychology, 78*(5), 358–364.

Feinstien, A. (1973). An analysis of diagnostic reasoning. *Yale Journal of Biology and Medicine, 46,* 212–232, 264–283.

Feinstien, A. (1974). An analysis of diagnostic reasoning. *Yale Journal of Biology and Medicine, 47,* 5–32.

Foster, G., & Anderson, B. (1978). *Medical anthropology.* New York: Wiley.

Foucault, M. (1965). *Madness and civilization: A history of insanity in the age of reason* [trans. R. Howard]. New York: Pantheon Books.

Foucault, M. (1972). *The archeology of knowledge* [trans. by A. M. Sheridan]. London: Pantheon Books.

Giere, R. N. (1988). *Explaining science: A cognitive approach.* Chicago: University of Chicago Press.

Gunderson, C. W., Maesch, C., & Rees, J. W. (1987). The gifted/learning disabled student. *Gifted Child Quarterly, 31*(4), 158–160.

Habermas, J. (1971). *Knowledge and human interests.* Boston: Beacon Press.

Hagen, J. W., & Stanovitch, K. E. (1977). Memory: Strategies of acquisition. In R. V. Kail, Jr. & J. W. Hagen (Eds.), *Perspectives in the development of memory and cognition.* Hillsdale, NJ: Lawrence Erlbaum Associates.

Hagen, J. W. (1967). The effect of distraction on selective attention. *Child Development, 38,* 685–694.

Hagen, J. W., & Kamberelis, G. (1990). Cognition and academic performance in children with learning disabilities, low academic achievement, diabetes mellitus, and seizure disorders. In H. L. Swanson & B. Keogh (Eds.), *Learning disabilities: Theoretical and research issues,* (pp. 299–314). Hillsdale, NJ: Lawrence Erlbaum Associates.

Hagen, J. W., Barclay, C. R., & Schwethelm, B. (1982). Cognitive development of the learning-disabled child. In N. R. Ellis (Ed.), *International review of research in mental retardation* (Vol. 2). New York: Academic Press.

Hagen, J. W., Saarnio, D., & Laywell, E. D. (1987). A dimensional approach to cognitive deficiencies. In H. L. Swanson (Ed.), *Memory and learning disabilities: Advances in learning and behavioral disabilities* (pp. 123–145). Greenwich, CN: JAI Press.

Hallahan, D. P., & Cruickshank, W. M. (1973). *Psychological foundations of learning disabilities*. Englewood Cliffs, NJ: Prentice–Hall.

Harter, S. (1978). *Perceived competence scale*. Denver: University of Denver (Colorado Seminary).

Harwood, A. (Ed.). (1981). *Ethnicity and medical care*. Cambridge, MA: Harvard University Press.

Havinghurst, R. L. (1972). *Developmental tasks and education* (3rd ed.). New York: McKay.

Henriques, J., Hollway, W., Urwin, C., Venn, C., & Walkerdine, R. (1984). *Changing the subject: Psychology, social regulation, and subjectivity*. London: Methuen.

Hobbs, N., & Perrin, J. (Eds.). (1986). *The constant shadow: Serving chronically ill children and their families*. San Francisco: Jossey–Bass.

Hufford, D. J. (1982). *The terror that comes in the night: An experience centered study of supernatural assault traditions*. Philadelphia: University of Pennsylvania Press.

Interagency Committee on Learning Disabilities. (1987). *Learning disabilities: A report to the U. S. Congress.*

Kavale, K. A., & Forness, S. R. (1987). The far side of heterogeneity: A critical analysis of empirical subtyping research in learning disabilities. *Journal of Learning Disabilities, 20*, 374–382.

Kavale, K. A., & Nye, C. (1986). Parameters of learning disabilities in achievement, linguistic, neuropsychological, and social/behavioral domains. *Journal of Special Education, 19*, 443–458.

Kirk, S. (1962). *Educating exceptional children*. Boston: Houghton Mifflin.

Kuhn, T. S. (1970). *The structure of scientific revolutions* (2nd ed.). Chicago: University of Chicago Press.

Licht, B. G. (1983). Cognitive-motivational factors that contribute the achievement of learning disabled children. *Journal of Learning Disabilities, 16*, 483–490.

McKinney, J. D., Short, E. J., & Feagans, L. (1985). Academic consequences of perceptual-linguistic subtypes of learning disabled children. *Learning Disabilities Research, 1*(1), 6–17.

McKnight, R. T. (1982). The learning disability myth in American education. *Journal of Education. 164*(4), 351–359.

Moos, R. H. (1974). *Family environment scale: Form R.* Palo Alto, CA: Consulting Psychologists Press.

Newell, A. (1973). You can't play 20 questions with nature and win. In R. Chase (Ed.), *Visual information processing*. New York: Academic Press.

Pacey, A. (1983). *The culture of technology*. Cambridge, MA: MIT Press.

Palincsar, A. S., & Brown, A. L. (1984). Reciprocal teaching of comprehension fostering and comprehension monitoring activities. *Cognition and Instruction, 1*(2), 117–175.

Palincsar, A. S., & Brown, D. A. (1987). Enhancing instructional time through attention to metacognition. *Journal of Learning Disabilities, 20*, 66–75.

Penfold, P. S., & Walker, G. (1983). *Women and the psychiatric paradox*. Montreal: Eden Press.

Phillips, D. C. (1978). *Philosophy, science, and social inquiry*. Oxford, England: Pergamon Press.

Pless, I. B., & Pinkerton, P. (1975). *Chronic childhood disorder: Promoting patterns of adjustment*. Chicago: Yearbook Medical Publishers.

Poplin, M. S. (1988). Holistic/constructivist principles of the teaching/learning process: Implications for the field of learning disabilities. *Journal of Learning Disabilities, 21*, 401–416.

Pflaum, S. W., & Pascarella, E. T. (1982). Attribution retraining for learning disabled students:

Some thoughts on the practical implications of the evidence. *Learning Disabilities Quarterly,* 5, 422–421.

Pressley, M., Borkowski, J. G., & Schneider, W. (1987). Cognitive- strategies users coordinate metacognition and knowledge. In R. Vasta & G Whitehurst (Eds.), *Annals of Child Development* (Vol. 4, pp. 89–129). Greenwich, CT: JAI Press.

Reason, P., & Rowan, J. (Eds.). (1981). *Human inquiry: A sourcebook of new paradigm research.* New York: Wiley.

Rourke, B. P. (1981), Neuropsychological assessment of children with learning disabilities. In S. B. Filskov & T. J. Boll, (Eds.), *Handbook of clinical neuropsychology.* New York: Wiley Interscience.

Rourke, B. P. (Ed.) (1985). *Neuropsychology of learning disabilities: Essentials of subtype analysis.* New York: Guilford.

Rubinstein, R. A., Laughlin, C. D., & McManus, J. (1984). *Science as cognitive process: Toward an empirical philosophy of science.* Philadelphia: University of Pennsylvania Press.

Ryan, E. B., Short, E. J., & Weed, K. A. (1986). The role of cognitive training in improving the academic performance of learning disabled children. *Journal of Learning Disabilities, 19*(9), 521–529.

Salmon, W. C. (1971). *Statistical explanation and statistical relevance.* Pittsburgh: University of Pittsburgh Press.

Satz, P., & Morris, R. (1981). Learning disability subtypes: A review. In F. J. Pirozzolo, & M. C. Wittrock (Eds.), *Neuropsychological and cognitive processes in reading* (pp. 109–141). New York: Academic Press.

Schön, D. (1983). *The reflective practitioner.* New York: Basic Books.

Schumaker, J. B., Deshler, D. D., & Ellis, E. S. (1986). Intervention issues related to the education of LD adolescents. In J. K. Torgesen & B. Y. Wong (Eds.), *Psychological and educational perspectives on learning disabilities.* New York: Academic Press.

Simon, H. A. (1983). *Reason in human affairs.* Stanford, CA: Stanford University Press.

Sleeter, C. E. (1986). Learning disabilities: The social construction of a special education category. *Exceptional Children, 53*(1), 46–54.

Smith, M. L. (1982). *How educators decide who is learning disabled.* Springfield, IL: C. C. Thomas

Smith, R. W., Osborne, L. T., Crim, D., & Rhu, A. H. (1986). Labelling theory as applied to learning disabilities: Survey findings and policy suggestions. *Journal of Learning Disabilities, 19,* 195–202.

Speece, D. L. (1987). Information processing subtypes of learning disabled readers. *Learning Disabilities Research, 2,* 91–102.

Stein, R. E. K., & Jessop, D. J. (1982). A non-categorical approach to chronic childhood illness. *Public Health Reports, 94,* 354–362.

Stein, R. E. K., & Jessop, D. J. (1984). General issues in the care of children with chronic physical conditions. *Pediatric Clinics of North America, 31,* 189–198.

Torgesen, J. K. (1982). The use of rationally defined subgroups in research on learning disabilities. In J. P. Das, R. F. Mulcahy, & A. F. Wall (Eds.), *Theory and research in learning disabilities* (pp. 111–131). New York: Plenum Press.

Torgesen, J. K. (1988). Studies of children who perform poorly on memory span tasks. *Journal of Learning Disabilities Quarterly, 21,* 605–612.

Wechsler, D. (1974). *Wechsler Intelligence Scale for Children–Revised.* New York: Psychological Corp.

Whitehead, A. N. (1960). *Process and reality.* New York: W. W. Norton.

Wimsatt, W. (1980). Reductionistic research strategies and their biases in the units of selection controversy. In T. Nichols (Ed.), *Scientific discovery, Vol. 2: Historical and scientific case studies.* Dordrecht, Holland: D. Reidel.

Wolfus, B., Moscovitch, M., & Kinsbourne, M. (1980). Subgroups of developmental language impairment. *Brain and Language, 10*, 152–171.

Ysseldyke, J. E., Thurlow, M., Graden, J., Wesson, C., Algozzine, B., & Demo, S. (1982). *Generalizations from five years of research on assessment and decision making.* Research Report No. 100, Minneapolis: University of Minnesota Institute for Research on Learning Disabilities.

A Behavioral Genetic Approach to Learning Disabilities and Their Subtypes

y

Robert Plomin
Department of Human Development and Family Studies
College of Health and Human Development
The Pennsylvania State University

Not much is known about the genetics of learning disabilities and their subtypes. The few relevant twin and family studies—primarily of reading disability—have been reviewed previously (e.g., Smith, 1986). Rather than reviewing these studies again, the purpose of this chapter is to consider behavioral genetic theory, methods, and results in a related field about which much more is known: cognitive abilities. The goal is to abstract hypotheses about subtypes of learning disabilities that can be tested using current behavioral genetic techniques.

This might sound like the story of the person in the dark of night looking for a lost wallet under a lamppost where the light was good even though the wallet was lost in a dark alley. Although examination of the genetics of cognitive abilities will not yield conclusions concerning the genetics of learning disabilities, it may be useful in this early stage of research on the genetics of learning disabilities to have hypotheses to guide the exploration. Furthermore, the genetics of cognitive abilities is relevant to the study of learning disabilities because learning disabilities are cognitive in nature.

The chapter considers behavioral genetic research on cognitive abilities in relation to the following issues: univariate analysis, multivariate analysis, longitudinal analysis, shared and nonshared environmental variance, single genes and polygenes, and the relationship between the normal and abnormal. For each of these issues, an attempt is made to draw explicit hypotheses from research on cognitive abilities that are relevant to the exploration of learning disabilities and their subtypes.

Much must be excluded in this brief chapter. For example, it is not possible to review basic methods of human behavioral genetics, such as family, twin, and adoption designs and combinations of them, more recent advances such as model-fitting analyses, or the exciting techniques of the "new genetics" of recombinant DNA. Discussion of these topics and other background issues can be found in a recent textbook on behavioral genetics (Plomin, DeFries, & McClearn, 1990).

UNIVARIATE ANALYSIS

The following description of what is known about the genetics of cognitive abilities is abstracted from a recent review that can be consulted for details and documentation (Plomin, 1988). For more recent studies, see Plomin and Rende (in press).

IQ

Behavioral genetic IQ data for nearly 100,000 individuals converge on the conclusion that heredity significantly affects individual differences in IQ scores. For example, identical twins are substantially more similar than fraternal twins (0.86 versus 0.60). Indeed, identical twins are nearly as similar as the same persons' IQs tested twice; test–retest correlations for IQ tests are generally between 0.80 and 0.90. Reared-apart identical twins are very similar (0.72). Although few data of this sort have been reported, this result is being confirmed in ongoing studies of reared-apart identical twins in Minnesota and in Sweden. Adoption data show that resemblance among nonadoptive family members for IQ is due in nearly equal parts to hereditary and environmental factors. For example, the correlation between children and their "genetic-plus-environmental" parents (0.42) is nearly equal to the sum of the correlations for "genetic" parents (0.22) and "environmental" parents (0.19).

Estimates of heritability from these pieces of the puzzle vary from about 0.30 to about 0.70. One source of this variability in heritability estimates has recently been pointed out. Direct estimates of heritability derived from the correlations for adopted-apart relatives are generally greater than indirect heritability estimates based on the difference between two correlations, such as the difference between identical and fraternal twins or the difference between nonadoptive and adoptive relatives (Plomin & Loehlin, 1989). The reason for this difference is not yet known. Another unsolved source of variability in estimates of heritability for IQ scores is that older studies yield higher estimates of heritability than do more recent studies (Plomin & DeFries, 1980). On balance, however, these data suggest that the heritability of IQ scores is about 0.50, which means that genetic differences among individuals account for about half of the variance in individuals' performance on IQ tests. The most recent model-fitting analysis that takes into account all of the data as well as complicating factors such as assortative mating and nonadditive genetic variance yields a heritability estimate of .51 (Chipuer, Rovine, & Plomin, 1990). Assortative mating is substantial for IQ and some evidence for nonadditive genetic variance is found which is supported by research on inbreeding depression among offspring of consanguineous matings.

Points to notice in relation to learning disabilities include the following. General cognitive ability, which is bound to have pervasive effects on learning disabilities, shows substantial genetic influence. Although about half of the variance in IQ scores is genetic, it is just as important to emphasize that an equal part of the variance in IQ scores is not genetic in origin. Thus, these same data suggest an important role for environmental factors as well as genetic factors. Adoption studies of first-degree relatives (of which there are none in the field of learning disabilities) provide the most convincing evidence for genetic influence. However, to the extent that nonadditive genetic variance is important, identical twins are required to detect genetic influence because, unlike first-degree relatives, identical twins are genetically identical for all genetic factors, no matter how complex the interaction among genes. Assortative mating is substantial for cognitive abilities and must be taken into account because it leads to underestimates of heritability in twin studies and overestimates of heritability in adoption studies.

Specific Cognitive Abilities

For cognitive abilities as well as for learning disabilities, the IQ score, by no means conveys all that needs to be known. Phenotypic research on specific cognitive abilities has revealed a personality style of lumpers and splitters. Some, such as Jensen, emphasize Spearman's *g*, general cognitive functioning, some focus on Thurstone's group factors, and others, as Guilford, look for highly differentiated abilities. In the area of cognitive abilities, a hierarchical model is generally accepted that is tolerant of different levels of analysis (Vernon, 1979). The lesson to be learned from this is that fruitless arguments about which components or subtypes are *really* learning disability can be avoided by thinking in terms of a hierarchical model that incorporates different levels of analysis.

Although some behavioral genetic research has begun to consider information-processing variables, most research has focused on group factors of specific cognitive abilities, especially verbal, spatial, memory, and perceptual speed factors. There are few adoption data relevant to specific cognitive

TABLE 4.1
Twin Correlations for Tests of Specific Cognitive Abilities

Ability	Number of Studies	Twin Correlations Identical	Fraternal
Verbal comprehension	27	.78	.59
Verbal fluency	12	.67	.52
Reasoning	16	.74	.50
Spatial visualization	31	.64	.41
Perceptual speed	15	.70	.47
Memory	16	.52	.36

From Nichols, 1978, p. 163.

abilities, but dozens of twin studies have been conducted. Table 4.1 summarizes results for three types of verbal tests (verbal comprehension, verbal fluency, and verbal reasoning), spatial visualization, perceptual speed, and memory (Nichols, 1978). All of these tests suggest heritabilities on the order of 40%.

Are some cognitive abilities more heritable than others? The data on twins in Table 4.1 suggest that the answer to this question is no. However, data from the largest twin and family studies suggest that verbal and spatial abilities show greater genetic influence than do perceptual speed tests and especially memory tests. For example, the largest study of specific cognitive abilities is the Hawaii Family Study of Cognition (DeFries et al., 1979). In this study, 15 tests were administered to assess verbal, spatial, perceptual speed, and memory abilities. The sample consisted of more than 6,000 individuals in nearly 2,000 nuclear families. For both parent–offspring and sibling comparisons, familial resemblance was greater for verbal and spatial tests than for perceptual speed and memory tests. The Hawaii data also point to an issue that needs more attention: Tests within each specific cognitive ability show dramatic differences in familial resemblance. For example, independent of reliability, one spatial ability test yields high familial correlations, another spatial ability test shows low familial correlations, and three other spatial tests show moderate familiality. This suggests that there is a need to consider more finely differentiated abilities.

These results for specific cognitive abilities convey two points especially relevant to research on subtypes of learning disabilities. First, nearly all cognitive domains show appreciable genetic influence. Second, some domains may show somewhat greater heritability than others, although such differential heritability is difficult to detect because all domains show some genetic influence.

This latter point should be expanded because demonstrating differential heritability is likely to be a goal of subtype research. Hundreds of twin pairs are required to show that heritabilities of .00 and .40 differ significantly;

thousands of pairs are needed to detect significant heritability differences on the order of .20 vs. .40. Studies with small sample sizes are mischievous in that they are likely to show significant heritability for some subtypes but not for others because their power to detect significant heritability is low. By no means should such findings be construed to mean that the heritability differs significantly for the subtypes.

MULTIVARIATE ANALYSIS

A development of considerable relevance to the study of subtypes of learning disabilities is multivariate behavioral genetic analysis (DeFries & Fulker, 1986). Behavioral genetic analyses have traditionally been univariate, decomposing the phenotypic variance of traits considered individually into their genetic and environmental components of variance. Multivariate behavioral genetic analysis focuses on the covariance between traits rather than the variance of each trait considered by itself.

Multivariate analysis is important for research on subtypes of learning disabilities because it addresses the critical issue of heterogeneity in terms of etiology rather than symptomatology. It estimates the extent to which genetic factors that affect a particular symptom or disorder also affect another symptom or disorder. If genetic effects on one disorder are not correlated with genetic effects on another disorder, the two disorders are genetically distinct. If genetic effects on two disorders are perfectly correlated, the disorders are genetically the same disorder. In this way, multivariate analysis can test the etiological distinctness of proposed subtypes.

The purpose of multivariate behavioral genetic analysis is to decompose the phenotypic covariance among traits into genetic and environmental components of covariance. Two types of questions can be asked: To what extent is the phenotypic correlation between traits mediated genetically? To what extent do genetic factors that affect one trait correlate with genetic factors that affect another trait? The second question defines the genetic correlation—the extent to which genetic deviations on one trait correlate with genetic deviations on another regardless of the heritability of the traits. The main source of such genetic correlations is pleiotropy, the manifold effects of genes.

The first question weights the genetic correlation by a function of the heritabilities of the two traits; this has been called the phenotypically standardized genetic covariance (Plomin & DeFries, 1979). The difference between these two types of questions lies with the possibility that the genetic correlation between two traits can be high even though the heritabilities of the two traits are low and thus the genetic contribution to phenotypic covariance between the two traits is low. In other words, even though genetic effects on two traits are slight, the genetic effects on one trait can be essentially the same as those on the other trait. Conversely, the heritabilities of two traits can be high but the genetic correlation between them can be low. That is, genetic factors substantially affect both traits but genetic effects on one trait differ from those that affect the other.

Multivariate behavioral genetic analysis is a straightforward extension of the traditional univariate approach (Plomin & DeFries, 1979). Instead of analyzing the correlation for the same trait for two relatives, the unit of analysis is the "cross-correlation" between one trait for one relative and a different trait for the other relative. These cross-correlations can be used in the usual manner to decompose the phenotypic covariance between two traits into genetic and environmental components of covariance. For example, genetic covariance between two traits is implicated if the identical twin cross-correlation exceeds the cross-correlation for fraternal twins.

In relation to specific cognitive abilities, for example, it is possible that one set of genes influences all of these abilities or that independent sets of genes are specific to each ability. Multivariate analysis of specific cognitive abilities generally indicates that the answer appears to be in the middle—the genetic covariance structure among abilities is neither very broad nor very narrow. In fact, the genetic covariance structure is similar to the phenotypic structure (LaBuda, DeFries, & Fulker, 1987; Tambs, Sundet, & Magnus, 1986). Because heritabilities are similar for most cognitive abilities, this finding emerges for both types of questions described earlier—for genetic correlations themselves and for phenotypically standardized genetic covariances.

In other words, if two tests are highly correlated phenotypically, the genetic correlation between them tends to be high, as does the genetic contribution to the phenotypic correlation. The implication is that the phenotypic covariance structure among cognitive ability tests gives a rough approximation of the genetic structure because the phenotypic correlations are primarily due to genetics. This leads to the hypothesis that phenotypically derived subtypes of learning disabilities reflect genetic subtypes.

The multivariate approach is also applicable to dichotomous variables, such as diagnoses of learning disabilities and their subtypes. For example, the oldest multivariate behavioral genetic analysis found that there is no more schizophrenia in relatives of manic–depressive cases than in the general population, indicating that the two disorders are genetically distinct (Rüdin, 1916). Similar multivariate analyses suggest subtypes of affective disorders. For example, relatives of manic–depressive individuals have higher rates of manic–depressive disorder than do relatives of unipolar depressive individuals (Vandenberg, Singer, & Pauls, 1986). In contrast, classical phenotypic subtypes of schizophrenia do not breed true (Farmer, McGuffin, & Gottesman, 1984), as seen most dramatically in a follow-up of the Genain quadruplets who were concordant for schizophrenia but showed different symptoms and subtypes of schizophrenia (DeLisi, Mirsky, Buchsbaum, van Kammen, &

Berman, 1984). This implies that the classical subtypes of schizophrenia are not found at a genetic level of analysis.

Unlike the example of subtypes of schizophrenia, data for specific cognitive abilities suggest that their phenotypic structure reflects their genetic structure. This leads to the hypothesis that phenotypically derived subtypes of learning disabilities reflect genetic subtypes. It should be noted, however, that the opposite argument has recently been made for genetic subtypes of reading disability on the basis of two types of data (Decker & Bender, 1988). First, similar reading disability profiles were found for boys with the XXY chromosomal anomaly and for cotwins of reading-disabled identical twins. From this, it was concluded that different genotypes can produce similar phenotypes. Although it is true that polygenic effects do not necessarily imply that the same set of genes has equal effects for all individuals in the population, this does not negate the possibility of finding genetically uncorrelated subtypes that are reflected in phenotypically distinct subtypes. The second finding involved pairs of identical twins in which at least one cotwin was diagnosed as reading disabled. Because the cotwins showed a wide range of performance on reading-related tests, it was concluded that the same genotype can produce different phenotypes. However, this is merely a restatement of the fact that heritability is less than 1.0 and presents no problem for the hypothesis that phenotypically derived subtypes of learning disabilities reflect genetic subtypes.

There are few relevant developmental data concerning specific cognitive data, but there is a hint that genetic as well as phenotypic differentiation of cognitive abilities occurs during childhood (Plomin, DeFries, & Fulker, 1988). Parent–offspring comparisons suggest that genetic effects of parents' specific cognitive abilities on offspring in early childhood are diffuse. For example, parental verbal ability correlates nearly as much with offspring spatial ability as it does with offspring verbal ability. Multivariate analyses in the field of developmental psychopathology also indicate that genetic effects of parental disorders on their children tend to be diffuse rather than specific to a syndrome (Plomin, Rende, & Rutter, in press). For example, children of depressed parents show greater attentional and conduct disorders as well as affective disorders (Orvaschel, Walsh–Allis, & Ye, 1988). Adopted-away offspring of alcoholics show increased risk for attention deficit disorder and conduct disorder (Earls, 1987). This emerging finding suggests the possibility that in the field of learning disabilities genetic effects of parental disorders on their children may be diffuse rather than syndrome-specific.

DEVELOPMENTAL ANALYSIS

Another set of techniques of special utility for the study of learning disabilities and their subtypes has emerged from the new subdiscipline of developmental behavioral genetics (Plomin, 1986, 1989). Two types of developmental questions can be addressed. First, do genetic and environmental components of variance change during development? Behavioral genetic analyses describe genetic and environmental components of variance and, like any descriptive statistic, these can change for different populations and cohorts as well as for different ages.

Most developmentalists would probably guess that, as children develop and experience more diverse environments, environmental variance will increasingly account for phenotypic variance. In other words, heritability is expected to decrease during development. To the contrary, when age-related changes in the magnitude of genetic influence are observed, heritability increases rather than decreases (Plomin, 1986). For example, the heritability of general cognitive ability increases linearly during infancy and early childhood in twin and adoption studies (Fulker, DeFries, & Plomin, 1988). Not as much is known about the development of specific cognitive abilities, although it appears that heritability is generally low in infancy and early childhood and increases during middle childhood and especially during adolescence (Plomin, 1986). These results lead to the hypothesis that learning disabilities and their subtypes will show increasing heritability with age. For example, it could be predicted that reading disability in adolescence will show greater heritability than in childhood.

The second type of developmental question requires longitudinal data and assesses the etiology of age-to-age change and continuity. Multivariate concepts and methods discussed in the previous section are just as relevant for the study of covariance between the "same" behavior at two occasions of measurement as they are to the analysis of the covariance between two behaviors at a single measurement occasion. For longitudinal data, age-to-age genetic change is seen as the extent to which genetic factors that affect the trait at one age are not correlated with genetic factors that affect the trait at another age. As in multivariate analysis, we can also estimate the extent to which phenotypic stability from age to age is mediated genetically.

In this context, parent–offspring data can be viewed as an "instant" longitudinal study from childhood to adulthood. If heritabilities of a disorder in childhood and in adulthood are known, genetic correlations between childhood and adulthood can be estimated from parent–offspring correlations. In the case of IQ, genetic correlations from childhood to adulthood are surprisingly high, suggesting that genetic effects on IQ scores in childhood are much the same as genetic effects on IQ scores in adulthood (DeFries, Plomin, & LaBuda, 1987). That is, although heritability of IQ scores is low in early childhood, the genes that affect IQ scores in early childhood continue to affect IQ scores in adulthood. Because heritabilities are less than .50 especially in childhood, the genetic contribution to phenotypic stability from childhood to adulthood is only modest. Although specific cognitive abilities yield lower heritabilities than IQ in childhood, genetic correlations from childhood to adulthood appear to be high for most specific cognitive abilities (Plomin, DeFries, & Fulker, 1988). These findings lead to the hypothesis that genetic effects on learning disabilities in childhood are highly correlated with genetic effects later in life even though heritability increases.

SHARED AND NONSHARED ENVIRONMENT

One of the most important discoveries in behavioral genetics involves nurture rather than nature: Environmental factors important to development are experienced differently by children in the same family. Resemblance within families has been reasonably assumed to be caused by environmental factors shared by children growing up together in the same family. However, behavioral genetic research indicates that, for the most part, siblings resemble each other for genetic reasons. What mainly runs in families is DNA, not shared environmental influences. However, environmental variance is important even though experiences shared by siblings are not important. The implication is that environmental variation important to behavioral development lies in experiences not shared by siblings. This category of environmental influence has been called nonshared, E_1, within-family, individual, unique, or specific. Evidence for the importance of nonshared environment has been discussed elsewhere (Plomin & Daniels, 1987).

Until recently, cognitive abilities were thought to be an exception to the rule that environmental factors that affect behavioral development are of the nonshared variety. For example, a direct test of the extent to which shared experiences make children in the same family similar is provided by adoptive siblings, genetically unrelated children adopted into the same families early in life. Because these siblings are not genetically related, their similarity can be caused only by shared family environment. The correlation between adoptive siblings indicates the total impact of all shared environmental factors that make individuals growing up in the same family similar to one another. Unlike other domains of behavioral development for which adoptive sibling correlations are near zero, the median IQ correlation for adoptive siblings is typically reported to be about .30, suggesting that about a third of the total variance of IQ scores is due to shared environmental factors. However, adoptive siblings in previous studies were young—their average age was middle-childhood (Plomin, 1988). Four recent studies of older adoptive siblings yield IQ correlations of zero on average. Most impressive are the results of a 10-year longitudinal follow-up study of more than 200 pairs of adoptive siblings who, at the average age of 8, yielded an IQ correlation of .26 (Horn, Loehlin, & Willerman, 1979). Ten years later, this same sample tested on the Wechsler Adult Intelligence Scale yielded a correlation of .02 (Willerman, 1987). This suggests that although shared environmental factors are important for IQ in childhood, their influence wanes to negligible levels during adolescence. Results for specific cognitive abilities suggest similar results (Plomin, 1988).

The conclusion that environmental factors operate in a nonshared manner opens new opportunities for the study of environmental influences. It suggests that instead of thinking about environmental influences on a family-by-family basis, we need to think on an individual-by-individual basis. The critical question is: Why are children in the same family so different? The key to solving this puzzle is to study more than one child per family. The message is *not* that family experiences are unimportant. Rather, the point is that environmental influences in individual development are specific to each child rather than general to an entire family.

The first step in research on nonshared environment is to identify differences in siblings' experiences that relate to differences in their outcomes. Once such nonshared environmental associations are found, issues of cause and effect, including possible genetic mediation, can be worked out in a second step. The limiting factor in this research is the paucity of environmental measures specific to a child.

If research on cognitive abilities serves as a guide, we can hypothesize that learning disabilities will show shared environmental influence in childhood but that this influence will fade by adolescence. Long-lasting environmental influences on learning disabilities can be hypothesized to be of the nonshared variety.

SINGLE GENES AND POLYGENES

The conflict between biometricians and Mendelians 80 years ago was resolved by the realization that many genes can affect a trait and this will lead to the continuous distributions so characteristic of behavior. Although behavioral genetic methods can detect polygenic influences as well as single-gene effects, much current interest in genetic research has focused on the hope that single-gene or major-gene effects can be found. The major approach of this type involves attempts to find chromosomal linkage between genetic markers and disorders. However, reported linkages for manic–depression (Egeland, Gerhard, Pauls, Sussex, & Kidd, 1987), schizophrenia (Sherrington et al., 1988), and reading disability (Smith, Kimberling, Pennington, & Lubs, 1983) have not been replicated (Detera–Wadleigh et al., 1987; Gill, McKeon, & Humphries, 1988; Hodgkinson, Sherrington, Gurling, Marchbanks, & Reeders, 1987; Kennedy et al., 1988; Kimberling, Fain, Ing, Smith, & Pennington, 1985; McGuffin, 1987; St. Clair et al., 1989). Such lack of replication is consistent with the notion of genetic heterogeneity. However, it is possible that, by focusing on single pedigrees with a high incidence of rare disorders, linkage is found for a major mutation in a particular family that does not occur in the rest of the population. Other problems with linkage studies, including ascertainment biases, diagnoses, and significance levels, are beginning to surface (Buetow, 1988).

It is more likely that many genes (as well as environmental influences) affect the development of most aspects of complex disorders including learning disabilities (Plomin, 1990). Several lines of evidence are consistent with this hypothesis. First, selection studies for complex characteristics almost invariably result in slow, continuous progress after many generations of selection, suggesting that many genes are involved (Plomin, et al., 1990). Second, unlike medical disorders such as phenylketonuria (PKU) and Huntington's disease which have long been known to be single-gene characteristics, segregation analyses yield no clear evidence for single-gene or major-gene influences for behavioral phenotypes. For example, segregation analyses of reading disability for 133 pedigrees found no evidence of a single dominant or recessive gene (Lewitter, DeFries, Elston, 1980). Furthermore, although more than 100 rare single-gene disorders described mental retardation as part of the disorder (McKusick, 1989), their rarity implies that these single-gene disorders do not account for a detectable amount of IQ variance in the population. For example, one of the most frequent of these disorders is PKU with an incidence of about 1 in 20,000. PKU individuals are diagnosed early and treated with diets low in phenylalanine that ameliorate the otherwise devastating effects of this recessive gene when inherited in a double dose (homozygous). As many as 1 in 100 individuals are carriers for the PKU gene and these individuals show some IQ decrement (Bessman, Williamson, & Koch, 1978). Nonetheless, in the population as a whole, the slight effects on IQ of the PKU gene in the treated homozygous condition and in the untreated carrier condition are too small to be detected.

Third, recent research in plant genetics provides direct evidence that complex characteristics are influenced by many genes (e.g., Edwards, Stuber, & Wendel, 1987; Paterson, et al., 1988; Tanksley, Medina–Filho, & Rick, 1982). Fourth, the recent production of nearly complete linkage maps for human chromosomes has made it possible to detect single-gene linkage with a probability exceeding 95% (Donnis–Keller et al., 1987). However, replicated linkages have not as yet been detected for complex phenotypes.

For all these reasons, it seems unlikely that single genes will account for more than a small minority of rare learning disabilities. It seems much more likely that learning disabilities are intrinsically polygenic and multifactorial. That is, many genes as well as environmental influences affect learning disabilities and their subtypes. Defining narrower subtypes is important in clearing up heterogeneity but it is unlikely to lead to simple single-gene disorders. If this hypothesis is correct, genetic research on learning disabilities requires approaches that are probabilistic rather than deterministic and that recognize polygenic influences as well as nongenetic factors.

THE RELATIONSHIP BETWEEN
THE NORMAL AND ABNORMAL

Closer correspondence between studies of the normal and abnormal will benefit both types of research. For example, the abnormal provides societal significance for the study of the normal range of variability. That is, understanding genetic and environmental contributions to normal variability in reading ability may be important in its own right, but its societal value is enhanced by its possible applicability to reading disability.

Why should researchers interested in diagnosed disorders also pay attention to research in the normal range of variability? One answer could be that studying the normal range of variability elucidates processes that may be involved in the development of a disorder. There is now a more compelling answer to the question: Only by studying the abnormal in the context of the normal is it possible to assess the extent to which disorders represent the extremes of normal continua of variability. That is, the mechanisms responsible for abnormal behavior might be only quantitatively, not qualitatively, different from those that cause normal variability. There can be no presuppositions that normal and abnormal development do, or do not, involve the same mechanisms; rather there must be a concern empirically to test for similarities and dissimilarities (Rutter, 1988).

A key issue for the study of learning disabilities is the extent to which genetic factors that affect disorders—especially commonly occurring disorders such as learning disabilities—represent the quantitative extremes of genetic factors responsible for the normal continua of behavioral variability rather than qualitatively different genetic factors. That is, to what extent are learning disabilities the result of co-occurrence of many of the same genetic factors that are responsible for variability in the normal range? The purpose of this section is to describe a new behavioral genetic technique that addresses this question in terms of genetic and environmental etiology rather than symptomatology. This technique was first applied to reading disability (DeFries, Fulker, & LaBuda, 1987), and a chapter in this volume by Olson et al. describes an extension of this technique.

The new technique, developed by John DeFries and David Fulker (DeFries & Fulker, 1985, 1988), provides a powerful approach to the hoary problem of the relationship between the normal and abnormal. If quantitative (dimensional) data are obtained on probands, probands' relatives and the population, this technique makes it possible to assess the extent to which the genetic and environmental etiologies of abnormality (diagnosed disorders) differ from the etiologies of normality (dimensions).

Mental Retardation

The origins of this approach can be seen in an analysis by Roberts in 1952 involving mental retardation that used IQ as a continuous measure. Although Roberts's work has been criticized for methodological shortcomings (Kamin, 1974), recent work by Nichols (1984) using more adequate data has yielded results similar to those of Roberts. The essence of the method lies in the regression toward the population mean on a quantitative measure for relatives of diagnosed probands. The mean of the siblings of diagnosed probands will regress to the unselected population mean to the extent that familial factors are not important in the etiology of the disorder. In other words, if familial factors are important, the mean of the siblings of the probands will be greater than the population mean. The extent to which this mean difference between the siblings and the population approaches the mean difference between the probands and the population provides an estimate of the extent to which the mean difference between the probands and the population on the quantitative measure is due to familial factors. This estimate can be called "group" familiality to distinguish it from the usual "individual" familiality which is based on analyses of individual differences in the normal range. The point is that if group familiality differs from individual familiality, the disorder must be etiologically distinct from the dimension assessed by the quantitative measure.

Group familiality can differ from individual familiality. For example, individual differences in reading ability can differ from group familiality of the difference in reading performance between diagnosed reading-disabled individuals and the population if rare genetic or environmental factors affect reading disability. In Nichols's study, the IQ scores of siblings of severely retarded children (IQs less than 50) regressed all the way to the population IQ of 100 (mean IQ of 103), which indicates the absence of group familiality. In contrast, as shown in numerous studies, variability in IQ scores in the normal range shows substantial familial resemblance (e.g., Bouchard & McGue, 1981). Although numerical estimates of group and individual familiality for these data will be presented later, for now the point is that group familiality for severe retardation is substantially different from individual familiality for IQ. This implies that severe retardation is etiologically distinct from the rest of the IQ distribution. For example, severe retardation may arise from unusual genetic or environmental insults not experienced by nonretarded individuals.

In contrast, siblings of mildly retarded children (IQs from 50 to 69) show familial resemblance. Instead of regressing to the population IQ of 100, their

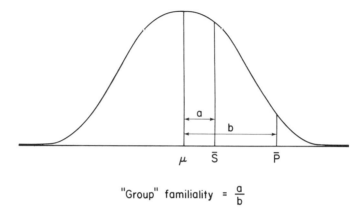

"Group" familiality $= \dfrac{a}{b}$

FIG. 4.1.   Hypothetical distribution of behavioral variation on a quantitative measure showing means of the probands ($\bar{P}$), of the siblings of the probands ($\bar{S}$), and of the population (μ) (adapted from twin analysis proposed by DeFries, Fulker, & LaBuda, 1987).

average IQ was 85. This average IQ occurred because the distribution was shifted downward, not because a few siblings were retarded. As will be shown, group familiality for mild retardation is similar to individual familiality for IQ scores. This suggests that mild retardation is etiologically connected with the rest of the IQ distribution. Similar results suggesting that mild retardation is familial but severe retardation is not have been found in parent–offspring analyses as well (Johnson, Ahern, & Johnson, 1976).

Estimating Group Familiality

The conceptual framework for estimating group familiality is illustrated in Figure 4.1. For a quantitative measure relevant to a particular disorder, diagnosed probands will fall toward the extreme of the distribution. The mean of the siblings ($\bar{S}$ in Figure 4.1) of diagnosed probands will regress to the unselected population mean (μ) to the extent that familial factors are unimportant in the etiology of the disorder. If familial factors are important, the mean of the siblings of the probands will be greater than the population mean. The extent to which this mean difference between the siblings and the population approaches the mean difference between the probands ($\bar{P}$) and the population provides a quantitative estimate of the extent to which the mean difference between the probands and the population is due to familial factors, which is group familiality. In other words, in Fig. 4.1, group familiality can be seen as *a/b*. In terms of genetics, this estimate of group familiality includes only half the genetic contribution to the mean difference between

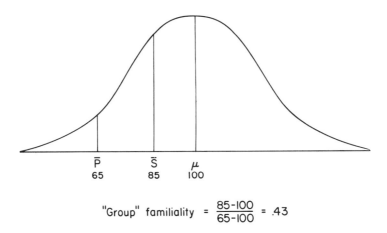

$$\text{"Group" familiality} = \frac{85\text{-}100}{65\text{-}100} = .43$$

FIG. 4.2. Familial retardation: IQ means for mildly retarded probands, their siblings, and the population (data from Nichols, 1984).

the probands and the population because siblings share only half of all segregating genes.

A rough estimate of group familiality can be obtained from Nichols's data for mild and severe retardation. For mild retardation, the probands had IQs between 50 and 69. Assuming an average IQ of 65, the mean IQ difference between the probands and the unselected population is –35 (i.e., 65 – 100) and the mean difference between the siblings of these probands and the unselected population is –15 (i.e., 85 – 100). This suggests a group familiality of .43 (i.e., the ratio of –15 to –35), as illustrated in Fig. 4.2.

In other words, about 40% of the difference between mildly retarded probands and the rest of the distribution is due to familial factors. This group familiality is quite similar to estimates of individual familiality. The average weighted sibling correlation for IQ is .45 in 69 studies involving 26,473 sibling pairs (Bouchard & McGue, 1981), which implies that individual familiality is 45% for IQ. Thus, this analysis of mild retardation suggests that group familiality is comparable with individual IQ familiality. We can conclude that mild mental retardation appears to represent the low end of the IQ distribution.

For severe retardation, in contrast, group familiality is negligible because the mean IQ of siblings of severely retarded probands regresses completely to the mean IQ of the population. This implies that the etiology of severe retardation differs from the rest of the distribution. The mean IQ difference between the siblings of severely retarded probands and the unselected population is 3 (i.e., 103 – 100). Selected probands had IQs less than 50. Assuming an average IQ of 40 for the probands, the difference between the probands and the unselected population is –60 (i.e., 40 – 100).   Group familiality is thus –.05 (i.e., the ratio of 3 to –40).

Estimating Group Heritability

Twins or adoptees are needed to establish that group and individual familialities in such sibling analyses are due to heredity rather than environment shared by siblings. Twin analyses of this sort have been formalized recently by DeFries and Fulker (1985, 1988), an approach that is applied to data on reading disability in a chapter in the present volume by Olson et al. This approach yields an estimate of group heritability (h^2_g) and its standard error. h^2_g refers to the proportion of the difference between the probands and the unselected population that is due to genetic differences. h^2_g is based on the differential regression to the mean for cotwins of identical and fraternal twin probands. That is, h^2_g is zero if identical and fraternal cotwins regress to the population mean to the same extent. h^2_g is 1.0 if identical cotwins do not regress to the population mean and if fraternal twins regress halfway back to the mean.

An easier way to think about h^2_g is to calculate an identical twin "group" correlation and a fraternal twin group correlation as in Figs. 4.1 and 4.2. As in the usual twin comparisons that yield "individual" heritability (h^2), h^2_g is indicated if the identical twin group correlation exceeds the fraternal twin group correlation. Both individual and group heritability can be estimated by doubling the difference between the identical and fraternal twin correlations. If h^2_g differs from h^2, we can conclude that the disorder differs genetically from the measured dimension.

Group Heritability for Reading Disability

In the first explicit analysis comparing h^2_g and h^2, DeFries and Fulker (1985) employed a continuous measure of reading ability for a nonclinical twin sample of disabled readers and their cotwins. The continuous measure was a discriminant function score whose weights were obtained from a battery of reading, perceptual speed, and memory tests in samples of 140 reading–disabled and 140 control nontwin children. The twin analysis of h^2_g included 64 pairs of identical twins and 55 pairs of fraternal twins in which at least one member of the pair met criteria for a diagnosis of reading disability.

Results of the analysis are depicted in Fig. 4.3. The data are expressed as standardized deviations from control means. The mean for probands is more than 2.5 standard deviations lower than the control mean for the discriminant function score, which is not surprising because the probands were diagnosed on the basis of low discriminant function scores. It can be seen that fraternal cotwins (DZ for "dizygotic" in Fig. 4.3) regress to the mean somewhat more than identical (MZ for "monozygotic") cotwins, which suggests genetic

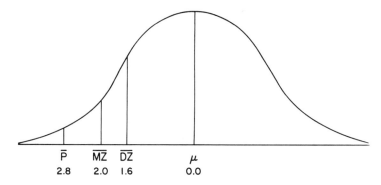

FIG. 4.3.   Group heritability for reading disability: Discriminant function score means for reading-disabled probands, MZ and DZ cotwins of
the probands, and the population.   Group correlation for MZ twins
(MZ r_g) = .71 and DZ r_g = .57. Group heritability (h^2_g) = 2 (MZ r_g – DZ r_g =
2 (.71 – .57) = .28.   Group shared environment (c^2_g) = is estimated as
MZ r_g – h^2_g = .71 – .28 = .43.

influence on the difference between the probands and the population mean.
It should also be noted that neither identical or fraternal cotwins regress very
far to the population mean. This suggests that shared environmental influences are also responsible for the difference between the probands and the
population mean. No unselected twin population is available to estimate
individual heritability for the reading discriminant function score. However,
h^2 of reading scores is generally substantial and c^2 is also substantial. Thus,
roughly speaking, these results for mild reading disability are similar to those
for the normal distribution of reading ability.

As indicated in Fig. 4.3, identical and fraternal twin group correlations can
be estimated from these data as .71 for identical twins and .57 for fraternal
twins. Doubling the difference between these group correlations estimates
h^2_g as 2(.71 – .57) = .28. In other words, over a quarter of the mean difference
between the probands and the population for the discriminant function score
is due to genetic factors. In twin analyses, shared environment (c^2) is estimated as the extent to which twin resemblance cannot be explained by
heredity. In the case of group parameter estimates, c^2_g is the difference between the identical twin group correlation and h^2_g: .71 – .28 = .43. In other
words, the mean difference between probands and the population is due 28%
to genetic factors and 43% to shared environment. The remainder of the
difference, 29%, is ascribed to nonshared environment (e^2_g). Although no
data are available for the reading discriminant function score for unselected
twins, this h^2_g estimate might be lower and the c^2_g might be higher than h^2 and
c^2 estimates of individual differences in reading ability. However, until
evidence for significant differences is found or other studies find similar

differences, parsimony suggests that the null hypothesis of no differences be accepted, a conclusion reached by DeFries and Fulker (1985, 1988) from their analyses of these data.

DeFries and Fulker (1985; 1988; DeFries, et al., 1987) offer a multiple regression approach to the estimation of h^2_g and its standard error. Their approach yields a significant estimate of $.29 \pm .10$ for these data (DeFries et al., 1987), which is similar to the estimate given. DeFries and Fulker also provide an approach to estimate h^2 from a selected sample and to test the significance of the difference between h^2_g and h^2. Although their estimate of h^2_g was not significantly different from their estimate of h^2, estimating h^2 from small selected samples of probands is hazardous in contrast to using estimates from large samples of unselected twins.

Two other aspects of the report by DeFries et al. are especially noteworthy. First, the analyses were rerun with IQ as a covariate and yielded essentially the same results, indicating that group heritability of reading disability is not attributable to IQ. Second, separate analyses were conducted for each of the six tests that comprise the discriminant function score. Reading recognition and spelling yielded results similar to those for the discriminant function score: h^2_g was about .30 and c^2_g was about .40. Reading comprehension, however, suggested lower h^2_g (.18) and higher c^2_g (.54). This finding suggests that, compared with reading recognition and spelling, reading comprehension contributes to reading disability more for reasons of shared environment than heredity.

The coding test produced odd results. The identical twin group correlation was .98 and the fraternal twin group correlation was .80, suggesting estimates of .36 for h^2_g and .62 for c^2_g. However, coding scores were less than a standard deviation different for probands and controls. This result illustrates an important point. In behavioral genetic analyses of covariance between traits (discussed earlier), when there is little phenotypic covariance between traits, estimates of genetic and environmental contributions to the covariance are not powerful. Analyses of h^2_g and c^2_g can be viewed as multivariate analyses of the covariance between a diagnosis and continuous measures of dimensions that are presumably related to the disorder. If there is little covariance between a diagnosis and a dimension (that is, if probands do not differ much from the population mean on the dimension), estimates of h^2_g and c^2_g are unreliable. This problem might also account for the results of the remaining two tests—another perceptual speed test and digit span—for which the differences between probands and controls were approximately one standard deviation. For the perceptual speed measures, h^2_g was high (.68) and c^2_g was low (.12). For digit span, the reverse finding emerged: h^2_g was low (.04) and c^2_g was high (.82).

Liability Correlations

A brief digression concerning liability correlations is in order. In psychiatric genetic research, concordances are usually converted to liability correlations, a tetrachoric correlation that assumes that a normal distribution of liability underlies a dichotomous diagnosis (Falconer, 1965; Smith, 1974). Liability correlations do not refer to the disorder as diagnosed but rather to a hypothetical construct of continuous liability. Group familiality is conceptually similar to the liability correlation with one critical difference: The liability correlation assumes an underlying continuous distribution although the data are dichotomous, whereas group familiality is based on an empirical assessment of continuous data for probands and their relatives (Plomin, in press). If the several assumptions that underlie the computation of the liability correlation from dichotomous data are correct and if the quantitative measure is strongly related to the disorder, the liability correlation will be similar to group familiality computed empirically from quantitative measures. Empirical comparisons between liability correlations and group correlations derived from continuous data show that they can differ dramatically (Plomin, in press).

For example, as noted, group correlations are .71 for identical twins and .57 for fraternal twins for reading disability in the Colorado Reading Project. Although twin concordances, needed to estimate liability correlations, were not reported for this sample, an earlier publication reported identical and fraternal twin concordances of 80% and 45%, respectively. The population base rate for this diagnosis of reading disability is not known, but assuming a base rate of 5%, liability correlations are estimated .97 and .76, respectively (Smith, 1974). (If the base rate is 10%, liability correlations are .96 and .68.) Thus, group correlations derived empirically from a continuous measure of reading performance differ dramatically from liability correlations derived from concordances for dichotomous diagnoses based on the same measure. Rather than assuming that continuous dimensions underlie diagnostic dichotomies, it makes more sense to assess the dimensions directly.

Group Heritability and Subtypes of Reading Disability

Behavioral genetic group analysis can be applied to subtypes of learning disabilities by showing that h^2_g or c^2_g differ for subtypes, as suggested by DeFries & Fulker, 1985). However, two subtypes could show the same h^2_g even though different genetic factors affect the same subtype. This is likely to be the case if, as discussed earlier, most learning disability subtypes show moderate heritability.

For this reason, multivariate analysis of the association between subtypes or components of learning disabilities will be especially useful for the analysis of heterogencity of learning disabilities. This approach is illustrated in the chapter by Olson et al. in the present volume. In the analyses that have been described (DeFries, et al., 1987), reading-disabled probands and their twins were compared on a reading disability discriminant score or tests that comprise the discriminant score. In contrast, although using the same Colorado Reading Project data set, Olson et al. compare probands' scores on PIAT Reading Recognition to their twins' scores on different dimensions: phonological coding and orthographic coding. Phonological coding is a measure of speed and accuracy in pronouncing one- and two-syllable nonwords, such as "ter" and "tegwop." Orthographic coding requires the subject to designate the word in pseudohomophone pairs, such as "room-rume." Both measures correlate highly with PIAT Reading Recognition (.68 and .57, respectively) but correlate only .25 with each other.

The analysis of Olson et al. yields a potentially important finding. Phonological coding shows a group heritability of nearly unity, whereas group heritability for orthographic coding is nearly zero. From their data, identical and fraternal twin group correlations can be computed as .81 and .34, respectively, for phonological coding. For orthographic coding, group correlations are .62 and .72 for identical and fraternal twins respectively, suggesting very substantial influence of shared environment.

PIAT Reading Recognition yields a group heritability of .40 based on identical and fraternal twin group correlations of .67 and .47. However, when phonological coding is partialed from PIAT Reading Recognition, group heritability for PIAT Reading Recognition is nearly zero: Group correlations are .54 for both identical and fraternal twins. This finding suggests that phonological coding may be a key genetic element in the heritability of PIAT Reading Recognition. Furthermore, when corrected for phonological coding, PIAT Reading Recognition scores appear to be substantially influenced by shared environmental factors as indicated by the high twin group correlations for both types of twins. When orthographic coding is partialed from PIAT Reading Recognition scores, the heritability of PIAT Reading Recognition scores increases: Group correlations are .68 for identical twins and .35 for fraternal twins.

In summary, these results can be interpreted to suggest that problems in phonological coding may represent a genetic subtype of reading disability whereas problems in orthographic coding represent a subtype caused by shared environmental factors. Because twin analyses of phonological and orthographic coding in unselected populations are not available, it is not possible to determine the extent to which these two RD subtypes represent the extremes of normal continua.

Another report in this vein concludes that reading disability with motor problems may be an inherited subtype of reading disability (Regehr &

Kaplan, 1988). For 10 reading-disabled probands with impaired balance and coordination, siblings and parents showed motor problems as well as reading problems. In contrast, siblings and parents of 10 reading-disabled probands with no motor problems showed reading problems but no motor problems. Mean scores of probands on the continuous measures of reading and motor performance were not reported so that it is not possible to compute sibling and parent–offspring group correlations. In addition to its small sample size, the study by Regehr and Kaplan is limited by its use of the family method. Although the authors conclude that reading disability with motor problems may be an inherited subtype, family studies cannot disentangle genetic and environmental sources of familial resemblance. The results of the analyses by the Colorado group suggest that shared environmental factors may be important in the etiology of reading disability.

Furthermore, there is a problem with the logic of this approach because it is possible that motor problems are transmitted in families independently of reading disability. As an analogy, reading-disabled individuals who are tall will have siblings who show reading problems and who are also taller than average, but this does not mean that there is an inherited subtype of tall reading-disabled individuals. It must be shown that reading-disabled children are more likely than controls to show motoric disturbances or that the processes involved in reading disability with motor disturbances differ from processes involved in reading disability without motor disturbances. Reading-disabled individuals are no taller than controls nor does height lead to different reading processes.

Summary

So far, the available data indicate only that some disorders such as mild mental retardation are part of the normal continuum of variability whereas severe mental retardation may be etiologically distinct. A quite speculative but reasonable hypothesis for learning disabilities is that severe, rare disorders, like severe retardation, are etiologically distinct from normal continua, whereas mild, common disorders, like mild retardation, represent the extremes of normal continua. It should be noted that severe disorders might be etiologically distinct from normal continua because their group heritability is lower or higher than individual heritability. Although for severe retardation group heritability is higher than individual heritability, for schizophrenia more severe schizophrenia shows greater genetic influence than mild schizophrenia. Identical twin concordances, for example, tend to be about 75% for severe schizophrenia but only about 25% for mild schizophrenia (Gottesman & Shields, 1982). Concordances for mild schizophrenia convert to heritabilities comparable with heritabilities for normal personality whereas the liability heritability for severe schizophrenia is much greater. This suggests that mild schizophrenia represents the extremes of normal continua whereas severe schizophrenia is etiologically distinct. However, unlike severe retardation, severe schizophrenia is distinct because it shows greater genetic influence than mild retardation as well as, presumably, the normal range of personality.

The implications of these concepts and methods are far reaching. If it is found that disorders are etiologically part of normal continua, as in the case of mild mental retardation, then causes and possibly cures can be sought in factors that affect the entire range of individual differences. Conversely, special factors unique to the disorder are not likely to explain it. On the other hand, if a psychosocial disorder is found to be etiologically distinct from individual differences in the normal range, as in the case of severe retardation, factors that affect variability in the normal range are not likely to explain the disorder. Although cures need not be related to causes, understanding the extent to which disorders are etiologically part of the normal continuum of variability is surely relevant to the goal of predicting and preventing disorders.

HYPOTHESES FOR LEARNING DISABILITIES AND THEIR SUBTYPES

By way of summary, the following 15 hypotheses for learning disabilities and their subtypes can be gleaned from the research described in this chapter. The hypotheses are accompanied by comments relevant to testing the hypotheses.

1. *All learning disabilities and their subtypes show genetic influence.* Adoption studies are needed to provide converging and convincing evidence testing this hypothesis.
2. *Genetic influence is substantial—heritabilities are as high as 50%.* Large samples are needed to test this hypothesis because of the large standard errors surrounding estimates of heritability.
3. *Some learning disabilities or subtypes of learning disabilities are more heritable than others.* Differential heritability is difficult to detect if all learning disabilities show some genetic influence. Extremely large samples or convergence of evidence from smaller studies are needed to test this hypothesis. Small studies will find that some disabilities or subtypes are significant and others are not, but this should not be taken as evidence for differential heritability.
4. *Assortative mating is important.* Because assortative mating leads to underestimates of heritability in twin studies and overestimates of heritability in adoption studies, it needs to be taken into account in estimating heritability of learning disabilities.

5. *Nonadditive genetic variance is significant, although most genetic variance is additive.* Studies of first-degree relatives will not detect nonadditive genetic variance, especially higher-order epistatic interactions. Studies of identical twins in comparison with first-degree relatives, such as fraternal twins, are needed to detect nonadditive genetic variance.

6. *Nongenetic influence is also substantial, typically accounting for more than half of the variance.* As evidence for significant genetic influence on learning disabilities mounts, overshooting the mark by assuming that learning disabilities are entirely genetic is likely to occur as it has in other areas such as psychopathology.

7. *The phenotypic covariance structure among learning disabilities and their subtypes largely reflects their underlying genetic structure.* To the extent that this hypothesis is proven correct, phenotypic associations among learning disabilities and their subtypes can be used to estimate genetic associations among them.

8. *Genetic effects of parental disorders on their children are diffuse rather than syndrome specific.* This hypothesis represents a developmental exception to the previous hypothesis.

9. *Heritability increases with age.* As in the case of differential heritability, very large samples are needed to detect age differences in heritability.

10. *Genetic effects on learning disabilities in childhood are highly correlated with genetic effects later in life even though heritability increases.* If heritabilities are modest, the contribution of genetic stability to phenotypic stability will be modest. The parent–offspring design can be used to provide an "instant" longitudinal analysis from childhood to adulthood and for screening childhood disorders for their ability to predict adult disorders.

11. *Shared environmental influence is important in childhood but fades by adolescence.* Studies of adoptive relatives are needed to provide direct tests of the importance of shared environmental influence for learning disabilities.

12. *Long-lasting environmental influence is of the nonshared variety.* Studies of differences in siblings' experiences, especially differences within pairs of identical twins, are needed to identify specific sources of nonshared environment.

13. *Genetic effects are polygenic.* Only a small minority of rare learning disabilities are likely to be affected only by one gene. Thus, quantitative genetic approaches are needed that are probabilistic rather than deterministic and that recognize polygenic influences as well as nongenetic factors. Nonetheless, efforts to search for major-gene

effects are needed because major-gene effects can be identified for disorders that are largely polygenic.

14. *Severe, rare disorders are etiologically distinct from normal continua.* As appears to be the case for schizophrenia, more severe symptoms can indicate greater genetic involvement. However, severe disorders can be etiologically distinct because they are less heritable than variation in the normal range, as in the case of severe mental retardation.

15. *Mild, common disorders represent the extremes of normal continua.* For this and the previous hypothesis, studies are needed that assess quantitative dimensions for diagnosed probands and their relatives. Quantitative measures of continuous variation sensitive to the extremes of dimensions as well as the normal range of variability need to be developed.

These hypotheses have been phrased somewhat dogmatically in order to encourage research to test them; they are all testable with available techniques and in some cases with available data. Although some of these hypotheses will undoubtedly be proven wrong, they will have served their purpose if they guide research in the relatively unexplored territory of the genetics of learning disabilities and their subtypes.

ACKNOWLEDGMENTS

Preparation of this chapter was supported in part by grants from the National Science Foundation (BNS–8806589), the National Institute of Child Health and Human Development (HD–10333 and HD–18426), and the National Institute of Mental Health (MH–43373 and MH–43899).

REFERENCES

Bessman, S. P., Williamson, M. L., & Koch, R. (1978). Diet, genetics, and mental retardation interaction between phenylketonuric heterozygous mother and fetus to produce nonspecific diminution of IQ: Evidence in support of the justification hypothesis. *Proceedings of the National Academy of Sciences, 78,* 1562–1566.

Bouchard, T. J., Jr., & McGue, M. (1981). Familial studies of intelligence: A review. *Science, 212,* 1055–1059.

Buetow, K. (1988). Large pedigrees for family and linkage studies. *Conference on genetic approaches to understanding health-damaging behaviors.* University of Pennsylvania, November.

Chipuer, H. M., Rovine, M., & Plomin, R. (1990). LISREL modelling: Genetic and environmental influences on IQ revised. *Intelligence, 14,* 11–29.

Decker, S. N., & Bender, B. G. (1988). Converging evidence for multiple genetic forms of reading disability. *Brain and Language, 33,* 197–215.

DeFries, J. C., & Fulker, D. W. (1985). Multiple regression analysis of twin data. *Behavior Genetics, 15,* 467–473.

DeFries, J. C., & Fulker, D. W. (1986). Multivariate behavioral genetics and development: An overview. *Behavior Genetics, 16,* 1–10.

DeFries, J. C., & Fulker, D. W. (1988). Multiple regression analysis of twin data: Etiology of deviant scores versus individual differences. *Acta Geneticae Medicae et Gemellologiae, 37,* 205–216.

DeFries, J. C., Fulker, D. W., & LaBuda, M. C. (1987). Evidence for a genetic aetiology in reading disability in twins. *Nature, 329,* 537–539.

DeFries, J. C., Johnson, R. C., Kuse, A. R., McClearn, G. E., Polovina, J., Vandenberg, S. G., & Wilson, J. R. (1979). Familial resemblance for specific cognitive abilities. *Behavior Genetics, 9,* 23–43.

DeFries, J. C., Plomin, R., & LaBuda, M. C. (1987). Genetic stability of cognitive development from childhood to adulthood. *Developmental Psychology, 57,* 348–356.

DeLisi, L. E., Mirsky, A. F., Buchsbaum, M. S., van Kammen, D. P., & Berman, K. F. (1984). The Genain quadruplets 25 years later: A diagnostic and biochemical followup. *Psychiatric Research, 13,* 59–76.

Detera–Wadleigh, S. D., Berrettini, W. H., Goldin, L. R., Boorman, D., Anderson, S., & Gershon, E. S. (1987). Close linkage of c-harvey-ras-1 and the insulin gene to affective disorder is ruled out in three North American pedigrees. *Nature, 325,* 806–808.

Donis–Keller, H., Green, P., Helms, C., Carinhour, S., Weiffenbach, B., Stephens, K., Keither, T. P., Bowden, D. W., & Smith, D. R. (1987). A human gene map. *Cell, 51,* 319–337.

Earls, F. (1987). On the familial transmission of child psychiatric disorder. *Journal of Child Psychology and Psychiatry, 28,* 791–802.

Edwards, M. D., Stuber, C. W., & Wendel, J. F. (1987). Molecular-marker-facilitated investigations of quantitative-trait loci in maize. I. Numbers, genomic distribution and types of gene action. *Genetics, 116,* 113–125.

Egeland, J. A., Gerhard, D. S., Pauls, D. L., Sussex, J. N., & Kidd, K. K. (1987). Bipolar affective disorders linked to DNA markers on chromosome 11. *Nature, 325,* 783–787.

Falconer, D. S. (1965). The inheritance of liability to diseases, estimated from the incidence among relatives. *Annals of Human Genetics, 29,* 51–76.

Farmer, A. E., McGuffin, P., & Gottesman, I. I. (1984). Searching for the split in schizophrenia: A twin study perspective. *Psychiatric Research, 13,* 109–118.

Fulker, D. W., DeFries, J. C., & Plomin, R. (1988). Genetic influence on general mental ability increases between infancy and middle childhood. *Nature, 336,* 767–769.

Gill, M., McKeon, P., & Humphries, P. (1988). Linkage analysis of manic depression in an Irish family using H-ras A and INS DNA markers. *Journal of Medical Genetics, 25,* 634–637.

Gottesman, I. I., & Shields, J. (1982). *Schizophrenia: The epigenetic puzzle.* Cambridge, England: Cambridge University Press.

Hodgkinson, S., Sherrington, R., Gurling, H., Marchbanks, R., & Reeders, S. (1987). Molecular genetic evidence for heterogeneity in manic depression. *Nature, 325,* 805–806.

Horn, J. M., Loehlin, J. C., & Willerman, L. (1979). Intellectual resemblance among adoptive and biological relatives: The Texas Adoption Project. *Behavior Genetics, 9,* 177–207.

Johnson, C. A., Ahern, F. M., & Johnson, R. C. (1976). Level of functioning of siblings and parents of probands of varying degrees of retardation. *Behavior Genetics, 6,* 473–477.

Kamin, L. J. (1974). *The science and politics of I.Q.* New York: Wiley.

Kennedy, J. L., Giuffra, L. A., Moises, H., W., Cavalli-Sforza, L. L., Pakstis, A. J., Kidd, J. R., Castiglione, C. M., Sjogren, B., Wetterberg, L., & Kidd, K. K. (1988). Evidence against linkage of schizophrenia to markers on chromosome 5 in a northern Swedish pedigree. *Nature, 336,* 167–170.

Kimberling, W. J., Fain, P. R., Ing, P. S., Smith, S. D., & Pennington, B. F. (1985). Linkage analysis of reading disability with chromosome 15. *Behavior Genetics, 15,* 597–598.

LaBuda, M., DeFries, J. C., & Fulker, D. W. (1987). Genetic and environmental covariance structures among WISC–R subtests: A twin study. *Intelligence, 11*, 233–244.
Lewitter, F. I., DeFries, J. C., & Elston, R. C. (1980). Genetic models of reading disability. *Behavior Genetics, 10*, 9–30.
McGuffin, P. (1987). The new genetics and childhood psychiatric disorder. *Journal of Child Psychology and Psychiatry, 28*, 215–222.
McKusick, V. A. (1989). *Mendelian inheritance in man* (9th ed.). Baltimore: Johns Hopkins University Press.
Nichols, P. L. (1984). Familial mental retardation. *Behavior Genetics, 14*, 161–170.
Nichols, R. C. (1978). Twin studies of ability, personality, and interests. *Homo, 29*, 158–173.
Orvaschel, H., Walsh–Allis, G., & Ye, W. (1988). Psychopathology in children of parents with recurrent depression. *Journal of Abnormal Child Psychology, 16*, 17–28.
Paterson, A. H., Lander, E. S., Hewitt, J. D., Peterson, S., Lincoln, S. E., & Tanksley, S. D. (1988). Resolution of quantitative traits into Mendelian factors by using a complete linkage map of restriction fragment length polymorphisms. *Nature, 335*, 721–726.
Plomin, R. (1986). *Development, genetics, and psychology.* Hillsdale, NJ: Lawrence Erlbaum Associates.
Plomin, R. (1988). The nature and nurture of cognitive abilities. In R. Sternberg (Ed.), *Advances in the psychology of human intelligence* (Vol. 4, pp. 1–33). Hillsdale, NJ: Lawrence Erlbaum Associates.
Plomin, R. (1989). Developmental behavioral genetics: Stability and change. In M. H. Bornstein & N. A. Krasnegor (Eds.), *Stability and continuity in mental development* (pp. 273–291). Hillsdale, NJ: Lawrence Erlbaum Associates.
Plomin, R. (in press). Genetic risk and psychosocial disorders: Links between the normal and abnormal. In M. Rutter (Ed.), *Biological risk factors for psychosocial disorders.*
Plomin, R., & Daniels, D. (1987). Why are children in the same family so different from each other? *Behavioral and Brain Sciences, 10*, 1–16.
Plomin, R., & DeFries, J. C. (1979). Multivariate behavioral genetic analysis of twin data on scholastic abilities. *Behavior Genetics, 9*, 505–517.
Plomin, R., & DeFries, J. C. (1980). Genetics and intelligence: Recent data. *Intelligence, 4*, 15–24.
Plomin, R., DeFries, J. C., & Fulker, D. W. (1988). *Nature and nurture during infancy and early childhood.* New York: Cambridge University Press.
Plomin, R., DeFries, J. C., & McClearn, G. E. (1990). *Behavioral genetics: A primer* (2nd ed.). New York: W. H. Freeman.
Plomin, R. & Loehlin, J. C. (1989). Direct and indirect IQ heritability estimates: A puzzle. *Behavior Genetics, 19*, 331–342.
Plomin, R., & Rende, R. (in press). Human behavioral genetics. *Annual Review of Psychology.*
Plomin, R., Rende, R. D., & Rutter, M. L. (in press). Quantitative genetics and developmental psychopathology. In D. Cicchetti (Ed.), *Rochester symposium on developmental psychopathology.* Hillsdale, NJ: Lawrence Erlbaum Associates.
Regehr, S. M., & Kaplan, B. J. (1988). Reading disability with motor problems may be an inherited subtype. *Pediatrics, 82*, 204–210.
Roberts, J. A. F. (1952). The genetics of mental deficiency. *Eugenics Review, 44*, 71–83.
Rüdin, E. (1916). *Zür verebung und neuentstehung der dementia praecos.* Berlin: Springer.
Rutter, M. (1988). Epidemiological approaches to developmental psychopathology. *Archives of General Psychiatry, 45*, 486–495.
Sherrington, R., Brynjolfsson, J., Petursson, H., Potter, M., Dudleston, K., Barraclough, B., Wasmuth, J., Dobbs, M., & Gurling, H. (1988). Localization of a susceptibility locus for schizophrenia on chromosome 5. *Nature, 336*, 164–167.
Smith, C. (1974). Concordance in twins: Methods and interpretation. *American Journal of Human Genetics, 26*, 454–456.

Smith, S. D. (1986). *Genetics and learning disabilities*. San Diego: College-Hill.

Smith, S. D., Kimberling, W. J., Pennington, B. F., & Lubs, H. A. (1983). Specific reading disability: Identification of an inherited form through linkage analysis. *Science, 219*, 1345–1347.

St. Clair, D., Blackwood, D., Muir, W., Baillie, D., Hubbard, A., Wright, A., & Evans, H. J. (1989). No linkage of chromosome 5qll-q13 markers to schizophrenia in Scottish families. *Nature, 339*, 305–308.

Tambs, K., Sundet, J. M., & Magnus, P. (1986). Genetic and environmental contributions to the covariation between the Wechsler Adult Intelligence Scale (WAIS) subtests: A study of twins. *Behavior Genetics, 16*, 475–491.

Tanksley, S. D., Medina–Filho, H., & Rick, C. M. (1982). Use of naturally-occurring enzyme variation to detect and map genes controlling quantitative traits in an interspecific backcross of tomato. *Heredity, 49*, 11–25.

Vandenberg, S. G., Singer, S. M., & Pauls, D. L. (1986). *The heredity of behavior disorders in adults and children*. New York: Plenum Press.

Vernon, P. E. (1979). *Intelligence: Heredity and environment*. San Francisco: W. H. Freeman.

Willerman, L. (1987). *Where are the shared environmental influences on intelligence and personality?* Paper presented at the Society of Research in Child Development, Baltimore, April.

II CURRENT RESEARCH ON SUBTYPING

5
Genetic Etiology of Individual Differences in Reading Disability

R. K. Olson
J. P. Rack
F. A. Conners
J. C. DeFries
D. W. Fulker
University of Colorado, and
Institute for Behavior Genetics

INTRODUCTION

Since 1979, the National Institute of Child Health and Human Development has supported a program Project at the University of Colorado entitled Differential Diagnosis in Reading Disability. As this title implies, a major goal of the project is to assess important individual differences in reading and cognitive profiles within a reading-disabled population. A related concern is with the genetic and environmental etiologies of reading disabilities and of individual differences among disabled readers.

Genetic and environmental influences are being assessed by comparing identical and fraternal twin pairs in which at least one member of each pair is reading disabled. Identical twin pairs are derived from the same fertilized egg (monozygotic), and therefore have the same genes. Fraternal twins are derived from two different eggs and sperm (dizygotic), and they share 50% of their genes on average. If environment shared by members of monozygotic and dizygotic twin pairs is similar, a greater resemblance for monozygotic pairs would provide evidence for genetic etiology (Plomin, DeFries, & McClearn, 1990).

Previous behavior-genetic analyses of twin data have shown that the deficit of disabled readers is significantly heritable (DeFries, Fulker, & LaBuda, 1987), although the level of heritability varies, depending on the component reading process examined (Olson, et al., in preparation; Olson, Wise, Conners, Rack, & Fulker, 1989). Our twin sample is now large enough to begin addressing questions about differential genetic etiology among disabled readers. The central question in this chapter is whether the heritability of deficits in reading varies significantly in relation to individual differences *within* the disabled group. If the genetic etiology of reading disability varies as a function of phenotypic within-group differences, this result would provide a powerful external validation for the differential diagnosis of reading disabilities.

In this chapter we will examine the genetic etiology of deficits in word recognition in relation to two major dimensions of individual differences: (1) the discrepancy between IQ and reading level; and (2) the profile of component processes in word recognition. In addition, we will examine the effects of severity of reading deficits, age, and gender on the heritability of reading disabilities.

The chapter is organized into three main sections. In the first section we discuss the historical background and measures for the selected dimensions of individual differences among disabled readers. The second section includes a brief discussion of the twin methodology for assessing the heritability of group differences between disabled and normal readers, and for assessing the differential heritability of deficits in reading as a function of disabled readers' performance on the dimensions of individual differences. In the third section we present and discuss the results of our analyses for differential genetic etiology.

DIMENSIONS OF INDIVIDUAL DIFFERENCES
AMONG DISABLED READERS

IQ

"Normal intelligence" has been a common inclusionary criterion for specific reading disability or dyslexia (Critchley, 1970). The usual rationale for requiring minimum IQ levels is that poor readers with "low IQ" are presumed to read poorly *because* of their low intelligence, while poor readers with "normal IQ" read poorly because of some other unique deficit presumed to be independent from general intelligence. Thus, it is often argued that the reading problems of "low" and "normal" IQ poor readers are fundamentally different in their origin and need for treatment. For example, remedial reading programs are often available for the "normal IQ" but not the "low IQ" poor readers, consistent with P.L. 94–142. Unfortunately, as we will see below, there is little empirical basis for this distinction.

Stanovich (1986) reviewed a number of problems associated with previous uses of IQ-reading discrepancy criteria. He noted that the minimal levels of IQ vary widely across studies, since IQ is normally distributed and there is no basis for selecting a specific cut-off point. Typically the IQ cutoff scores range from 80 to 100. A second problem is the use of different IQ measures. Some measures of "perceptual" or "performance" IQ, such as the Wechsler performance subscale, have low correlations with reading in the population. Correlations between measures of verbal intelligence such as the Wechsler verbal subscale are usually more highly correlated with reading. Thus, samples selected for reading discrepancies with different types of IQ could have different characteristics (Bishop & Butterworth, 1980; Bowers, Steffy, & Tate, 1988; Stanovich, in press-a). Also, Stanovich (in press-b) noted that measures used to define reading ability vary across studies and in their correlations with IQ. The correlation between verbal IQ and reading comprehension tends to be higher than the correlation between verbal IQ and word recognition (cf. Conners & Olson, in press). Therefore, the use of different reading-measure discrepancies with IQ could lead to different sample characteristics.

In addition to these concerns, the evidence is mixed for other differences between poor readers who are discrepant and nondiscrepant in reading and IQ. Studies by Bloom, Wagner, Reskin, and Bergman (1980), Fredman and Stevenson (1988), Taylor, Satz, and Friel (1979), and Siegel (1988) did not find significant discrepancy-group differences in a variety of component reading and cognitive skills, or in future progress in reading acquisition. A study often cited to support the distinction between discrepant and nondiscrepant groups is by Rutter and Yule (1975). In fact, this study found no significant differences between their "reading backwardness" group (mean IQ = 80) and their "specific reading retardation" group (mean IQ = 103) on proportions of family members with histories of reading difficulties, delays in language development, and right–left confusion. The primary difference between the groups was the greater progress in reading for the "reading backwardness" group in a follow-up assessment conducted 5 years later.

In view of the conflicting evidence on reading-IQ discrepancy, and the continuing widespread use of discrepancy criteria in research and practice, further study is warranted. In this chapter we will compare the genetic etiology for groups that are high and low in reading-IQ discrepancy, but as will be described, reading-IQ discrepancy will be evaluated with several different measures of IQ.

The IQ ascertainment criteria for the program Project included a minimum verbal or performance IQ of 90 on the Wechsler Intelligence Scale for Children–Revised (WISC–R; Wechsler, 1974), or the Wechsler Adult Intelligence Scale–Revised (WAIS–R; Wechsler, 1981). Subjects were excluded if school records indicated IQ scores substantially below our minimum criteria. However, IQ scores were not available in many of the poor readers' school records, and some were below 90 on both the verbal and performance subscales when tested in the laboratory (the criteria for reading deficits are described in the next section). These low-IQ subjects are included in the reading-IQ discrepancy analyses. In all the other analyses in the chapter, each twin met the minimum 90 IQ criterion on the verbal or performance subscales.

Although most twins in the sample met the minimum criterion, there was a substantial range in full-scale IQ within the disabled group. As described herein, there was also a wide range in severity of reading deficits. The correlation between full-scale IQ and reading was moderate within the disabled group (r = .35). Therefore, there was considerable variance in reading-IQ discrepancy that could be assessed for its effect on the genetic etiology of reading deficits.

In addition to assessing discrepancy effects with full-scale IQ, we will evaluate reading discrepancy with the Verbal Comprehension, Perceptual Organization, and Distractibility factors described by Kaufman (1975) for the Wechsler tests. Kaufman found that the Vocabulary, Similarities, Comprehension, and Information subtests of the WISC–R loaded strongly on a Verbal Comprehension factor, while Block Design, Picture Arrangement, Object Assembly, and Picture Completion loaded primarily on a Perceptual Organization factor. The Freedom from Distractibility factor included the Digit Span, Coding, and Arithmetic tests. We will see that the tests grouped under these three factors are differentially correlated with our measure of reading, and this could lead to different genetic contrasts based on their discrepancy with reading.

Word Recognition

Word recognition, rather than reading comprehension, is our basic measure of reading performance in the present analyses, for three reasons. First, word recognition was more deficient than reading comprehension for our reading disabled group (Conners & Olson, in press). This pattern is commonly found in studies of specific reading disabilities (Stanovich, 1986; in press-b). The second reason was pragmatic: The reliabilities for our word recognition measures were substantially higher (about .9) than for our reading comprehension measures (about .6). The third reason for focusing on word recognition was the importance of its component skills in previous discussions of subtype differences among disabled readers. Measures of these component skills will be presented following description of the word-recognition tests.

Our two tests of word recognition included the Peabody Individual Achievement Test (PIAT) (Dunn & Markwardt, 1970), and an experimental measure. The PIAT is a standardized test that contains 66 words ordered from easy to difficult. Subjects read words aloud from the test booklet until they made five errors on the last 7 words. The last word attempted was used to assign a grade level. Because the subjects' varied widely in age, their grade-level scores on the PIAT were divided by their grade-level expected by age.

TABLE 5.1
Word Recognition and IQ Levels for Disabled Twin Probands,
Cotwins, and the Normal Comparison Group

	N = 190 Pairs		N = 264
Variable	Probands	Cotwins	Comparison Group
Age	12.5 (2.9)	Same	12.4 (2.8)
PIAT Grade/Age grade	.78 (.20)	.98 (.28)	1.24 (.31)
Combined Word Rec. z	−2.41 (.97)	−1.35 (1.26)	0 (1)
WISC or WAIS IQ	101 (9.3)	103 (10.7)	113 (10.8)
Performance IQ	104 (10.4)	105 (11.5)	112 (11.7)
Verbal IQ	98 (9.7)	101 (11.2)	112 (11.2)

Note: Standard deviations are in parentheses.

The means for the PIAT-Grade/Age-Grade ratios are presented in Table 5.1 for the proband, cotwin, and comparison groups that will be described later.

Our experimental measure of word recognition included 183 words ranging from easy to difficult. The words were presented in order of difficulty, one at a time, on the computer screen. To be scored correct, the subjects had to initiate their correct response within 2 seconds of presentation (measured by a voice key). Subjects read through the list until they made 10 errors out of the last 20 words. This test had a more representative distribution of irregular words than the PIAT (which contains mostly regular words), and its 2-second limit for correct responses reflected speed requirements for fluent reading (there was no time constraint in the PIAT).

In previous analyses it was found that the two word recognition tests were highly correlated across the entire sample of disabled and normal readers ($r = .9$), and they yielded similar results in behavior-genetic analyses (Olson et al., 1989). For the present analyses, subjects' z scores on the two word-recognition measures were added to yield a single highly reliable measure of word recognition.

To be included in the disabled group for the genetic analyses, at least one member of each twin pair had to be at least one standard deviation below the word-recognition mean for a comparison group of twins who had not been identified as reading disabled by their school records. Some of the twins in the comparison group showed poor word recognition when tested in the laboratory, so they were also included in the disabled group. The mean levels and distribution of performance for the comparison group were fairly representative of the population in our testing area, although the comparison group did not include some of the poorest readers in the schools. The role of the comparison group in the genetic analyses will be discussed in the second section of the chapter.

A one standard deviation deficit in word recognition may seem a rather lax criterion for reading disability. However, the disabled group's average reading level was 2.4 SD below the reading level of the comparison group (see Table 5.1). The inclusion of disabled readers with relatively mild reading disability facilitates a test of differential genetic etiology for deficits in word recognition, depending on their severity.

2 Component Skills in Word Recognition

The third reason for focusing on word recognition is its relevance to a popular subtype hypothesis for reading disability. Many models of word recognition include two primary paths. A phonological decoding path involves the implicit sounding out and blending of orthographic segments to recognize words. A second "direct" path provides for the "visual" recognition of familiar whole words (see Carr & Pollatsek, 1985, for a review of dual-route models). A number of researchers have suggested that disabled readers may be deficient in either the "auditory" or "visual" processing modes (cf. Johnson & Myklebust, 1964). Boder (1973) has promoted a similar distinction between disabled readers labeled "dysphonetic" and "dyseidetic." Dysphonetics have unusual difficulty using phonological decoding rules in reading and spelling, while dyseidetics have unusual difficulty in remembering whole-word configurations in reading and spelling. This general subtype scheme is present in several recent and current research projects (Baron, 1979; Elbro, 1990; Malatesha & Dougan, 1982; Manis, Szeszulski, Holt, & Graves, in press; Mitterer, 1982; Newby, Recht, & Caldwell, 1989; Seymour, 1986).

We presented two tests of component skills in word recognition that were initially based on the dual-route model of word recognition described, and were intended to address the dyseidetic–dysphonetic subtype distinction (Olson, Kliegl, Davidson, & Foltz, 1985). Subjects' skill in the *phonological* coding path was measured in the present study by having them read 85 one- and two-syllable nonwords aloud (e.g., calch, tegwop). Their skill was represented by the combined z scores for percentage correct and latency for correct responses.

A second task measured subjects skill in the "direct" path. Eighty pairs of letter strings that would sound the same if pronounced were presented side by side on the computer screen (e.g., rain rane; room rume). One letter string in each of the pairs was a correctly spelled word. Subjects pushed a button on the right or left side as quickly as possible to designate the orthographically correct alternative. Their score in this task was derived by adding z scores for accuracy and latency on correct responses. The skill measured in this task was called *orthographic* coding because subjects had to remember the words' specific orthographic pattern to make a correct response (see Olson et al., 1989, and Olson, Wise, Conners, & Rack, in press, for further details on the phonological and orthographic coding tasks).

Several previous analyses indicated that phonological and orthographic coding reflected at least partly independent skills in disabled readers' word recognition (Olson et al., 1989; Olson et al., in press). First, both skills accounted for significant independent variance in word recognition. Second, when older disabled and younger normal readers were matched on word recognition, the older disabled readers were significantly worse in phonological coding, and significantly better in orthographic coding. Third, behavior-genetic analyses indicated that the genetic correlation between phonological coding and word recognition was significantly higher than that between orthographic coding and word recognition (see Plomin, this volume, for a more complete discussion of results from the genetic analyses of Olson et al., 1989).

Within the reading-disabled group, there was substantial variation in both phonological and orthographic coding skills relative to the subjects' level of word recognition. Although most of the disabled readers were much worse on the phonological task than expected from their level of word recognition, some were as good or even slightly better than the younger normal comparison group (Olson et al., 1989). The disabled readers' phonological coding was normally distributed with a mean about .8 standard deviation units below that expected from their word recognition, estimated from the younger normal comparison group. The disabled group's performance on orthographic coding was also normally distributed with a mean about .3 standard deviation units above that expected from their word recognition, based on the younger normal comparison group.

Phonological and orthographic coding were only marginally correlated ($r = .25$) for disabled readers in the reading-matched sample described in Olson et al. (1989). In the present sample the coding tasks' correlation was .23, and not significant ($r = -.06$) after partialing variance related to word recognition. Thus, it is appropriate to view orthographic and phonological coding as largely independent dimensions of individual differences within the disabled sample. The central question in the present analyses is whether disabled readers' scores on the orthographic and phonological coding dimensions are related to the genetic and environmental etiology of the deficits in word recognition. The statistical methods for answering this question are reviewed in the following section.

METHODS FOR ASSESSING HERITABILITY AND DIFFERENTIAL HERITABILITY

This section will be brief, because the basic methods for behavior-genetic analyses of twin data have been described by Plomin in this volume and in other articles cited herein.

In this chapter we are considering a particular type of heritability, the heritability of the disabled readers' *group deficit* relative to the normal population. This heritability, labeled h^2g, could be different from the heritability for individual differences in the normal population, which is commonly labeled h^2. As discussed by Plomin, differences between h^2g and h^2 for learning disabilities would be of considerable theoretical significance. DeFries and Fulker (1988) described a statistical test for the difference between h^2g and h^2, but because the standard errors for h^2 estimates tend to be large, the statistical power of this test is too low for our present sample size. However, statistical power is relatively high for heritability estimates of disabled readers' group deficit (h^2g) and for within-group differences in h^2g, which are the focus of this chapter.

The procedure for determining h^2g from identical (monozygotic or MZ) and fraternal (dizygotic or DZ) twin data is fundamentally simple. When twin pairs are selected so that at least one member of each pair is reading disabled (the lowest reader of each twin pair is called the proband), significant genetic etiology for the probands' reading deficits would lead to different expectations for MZ and DZ cotwins (the better readers in each pair). Because MZ probands and cotwins share all their genes while DZ probands and cotwins share half their genes on average, the presence of genetic influences on reading disability should result in DZ cotwin scores regressing more than MZ cotwin scores toward the mean of the unselected population. A hypothetical example of differential regression for MZ and DZ cotwin scores is diagramed in Figure 5.1.

The exact numerical value for h^2g, or the proportion of the probands' group deficit that is due to genetic factors, is based on the differential regression of MZ and DZ cotwin means toward the population mean. If the probands' group deficit has no genetic etiology, the MZ and DZ cotwins should regress the same amount toward the population mean. If the deficit is due entirely to genetic factors, and there is no test error, MZ cotwins should show no regression to the population mean. DZ cotwins, on the other hand, should regress one half the distance toward the population mean, because DZ probands and cotwins share half their genes on average. Intermediate levels of heritability would be indicated by differential MZ and DZ cotwin regression between these two extremes.

DeFries and Fulker (1985) proposed a convenient multiple regression model to assess the magnitude and statistical significance of h^2g, based on the differential regression of MZ and DZ cotwins described previously. In their basic model, the cotwin's score (C) is predicted from the proband's score (P), the coefficient of relationship (R), which is 1.0 for MZ twins and .5 for DZ twins, and the regression constant (A):

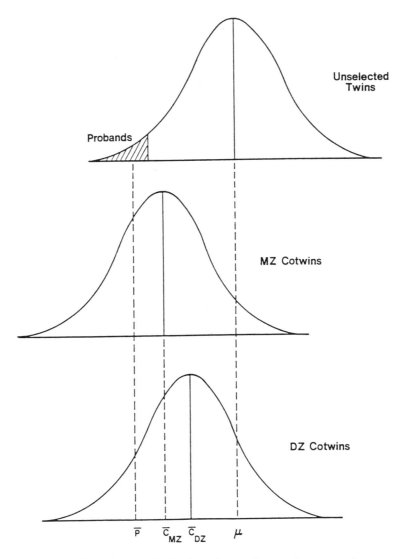

FIG. 5.1 Hypothetical distributions for reading performance of an unselected sample of twins, and of the identical (MZ) and fraternal (DZ) cotwins of probands with a reading disability. The differential regression of the MZ and DZ cotwin means toward the mean of the unselected population (fig. 1) provides a test of genetic etiology (from "Evidence for a Genetic Aetiology in Reading Disability of Twins," J. C. DeFries, D. W. Fulker, & M. C. LaBuda, 1987, *Nature, 329*, p. 537; Copyright © 1987, by Macmillan Magazines Ltd.; reprinted by permission).

$$C = B_1P + B_2R + A \qquad (1)$$

DeFries and Fulker showed that B_2, the partial regression of cotwins' scores on the coefficient of relationship, is equal to twice the difference between the means for MZ and DZ cotwins after covariance adjustment for differences between MZ and DZ probands. When the twin data are transformed by expressing each score as a deviation from the unselected population mean and dividing by the proband mean, B_2 provides a direct estimate of h^2g. The estimates of h^2g and their standard errors presented in the next section were based on this model.

DeFries and Fulker (1985) noted that an extension of the basic model in equation (1) could provide a test of differences in h^2g as a function of subtype variables. The extension simply requires including the probands' subtype designation (S) and the product of the coefficient of relationship and subtype designation (RS):

$$C = B_1P + B_2R + B_3S + B_4RS \qquad (2)$$

B_4 provides a test of the significance of differences in h^2g as a function of the subtype variable. Subtype variables in the model can range from dichotomous groups, such as gender, to continuously distributed variables such as word recognition and IQ that are examined in the following section.

HERITABILITY AND DIFFERENTIAL HERITABILITY
FOR DEFICITS IN WORD RECOGNITION

For reasons discussed in the first section of the chapter, word recognition was used as our measure of reading for the present analyses. To provide a reference frame for the subtype heritability analyses, we will begin by briefly presenting heritability estimates for word recognition, phonological coding, and orthographic coding for the whole sample. These analyses are presented in greater detail elsewhere (Olson et al., in preparation).

The heritability estimates for the probands' group deficit in word recognition, phonological coding, and orthographic coding are presented in Table 5.2, along with the respective means for the MZ and DZ probands and cotwins. The h^2g of .62 for the probands' deficit in word recognition on the combined test variable is somewhat higher than earlier estimates of about .4, which were based on less reliable separate word recognition measures and a smaller sample of twins (Olson et al., 1989). We can now say with greater assurance that about half of the probands' group deficit in word recognition is due to genetic influences. Of course, this estimate is relative to the range of environmental variance in our sample. Samples with less environmental homogeneity would be likely to yield lower heritability estimates. A second qualification is that the absolute level of h^2g estimates for word recognition and the coding tasks discussed here depend on our estimates of the popula-

TABLE 5.2
Heritabilities for Word Recognition, Phonological, and Orthographic
Coding

Variable	Identical (MZ) Proband	Cotwin	Fraternal (DZ) Proband	Cotwin	Heritability h^2g (SE)
Word recognition	−2.40	−1.68	−2.40	−.94	.62 (.09)
Phonological coding	−2.25	−1.27	−2.11	−.56	.57 (.12)
Orthographic coding	−2.13	−.97	−1.97	−.59	.29 (.12)

Note: Scores are mean standard deviation units from the comparison group.

tion means for these variables. If the present estimates of the population means are too high because some of the poorest readers were excluded from the comparison group, the present h^2g estimates would be slight under estimates.

The heritabilities presented in Table 5.2 for deficits in phonological coding (.57) and orthographic coding (.29) are also a bit higher than previous estimates by Olson et al. (1989), but the pattern of higher heritability for the phonological coding component, compared with orthographic coding, is again apparent. This contrast was most clear in the genetic correlation between the component skills and word recognition. As discussed by Plomin (this volume), the genetic correlation is an estimate of the degree to which genetic variation in one variable is correlated with genetic variation in another. The genetic correlation (more specifically, the phenotypically standardized genetic correlation) between word recognition and its component coding skills was estimated in the present sample by predicting the cotwin's score on one variable from the proband's score on another variable. We found that this "genetic correlation" between phonological coding and word recognition was significant (.62 ± .12), but that between orthographic coding and word recognition was not (.22 ± .17). Moreover, these two estimates are significantly different when tested in a LISREL model (Olson et al., in preparation). The results provide evidence for a strong genetic relationship between phonological coding and word recognition. In contrast, the relation between orthographic coding and word recognition is primarily due to environmental influences.

Next we turn to the heritability of probands' deficits in word recognition in relation to the subtype variables. We begin with differences in the severity of probands' deficits in word recognition.

Severity of Word Recognition Deficits

Evaluation of the heritability of word recognition deficits as a function of severity is a logical first step in the present series of analyses. Several of the other dimensions of individual differences examined subsequently are correlated with word recognition. If there are significant differences in the heritabilities of word recognition as a function of deficit severity, correlated dimensions of individual differences might also predict differential heritability in word recognition. Thus, it would be necessary to partial the variance associated with word recognition from the other dimensions to see if they independently predict differential heritability in word recognition. Of course, any differential heritability of word recognition deficits as a function of their severity is important in its own right.

Table 5.3 presents the heritabilities for deficits in word recognition for two groups of disabled readers who were divided at the mean deviation score for the whole disabled sample ($z = -2.41$). The larger number of subjects in the less severe group reflects the fact that the word recognition distribution is positively skewed. Note that h^2g for the more severe group is .51, while h^2g for the less severe group is .80. The results for the group split are presented to illustrate the magnitude of the difference in h^2g as a function of deficit severity. However, our statistical test for the interaction between h^2g for word recognition and deficit severity in equation (2) is based on the continuous variable rather than the groups indicated in Table 5.3. This approach is more statistically sensitive than dichotomous group contrasts to linear relations between h^2g for word recognition and continuous subtype variables such as deficit severity. Thus, the p value of .045 in Table 5.3 indicates a significant linear relation between h^2g and deficit severity: The more severe cases of reading disability tend to be significantly less heritable. However, the deficit for the more severe group still shows substantial genetic influence.

Plomin (this volume) reviewed evidence for differential heritabilities of severe and mild mental retardation and schizophrenia. The data suggest that severe retardation is less heritable and severe schizophrenia more heritable than their mild forms. This information has expanded our understanding of the genetic etiology for these disorders.

The present evidence for the differential heritability of reading deficits as a function of severity also provides important etiological information, but it does not specify the source of the additional environmental influences among the more severely disabled readers. We have examined parent questionnaire data for biological risk factors such as perinatal complications and congenital infections (Accardo, 1980; Schulman & Leviton, 1978), but their frequency of

TABLE 5.3
Differential Heritability of Word Recognition in Relation
to Deficit Severity

Group Division	n Twin Pairs	Mean Word Rec.	h²g (SE)	p
Worse than −2.4	85	−3.31	.51 (.11)	
				.045
Better than −2.4	105	−1.68	.80 (.17)	

Note: *p* value is two-tailed.

occurrence was low and unrelated to deficit severity. Unfortunately, we do not have data on the subjects' reading environment and exposure to print. This is certainly a major factor in determining reading progress among disabled readers (Stanovich & West, in press). We have begun to use some of Stanovich and West's techniques to assess print exposure, but it will be some time before sufficient data have been collected for further twin analyses.

Phonological and Orthographic Coding

We now turn to the differential heritability of word recognition deficits in relation to performance on the phonological and orthographic coding tasks. However, phonological and orthographic coding are both significantly correlated with word recognition in the present sample of reading-disabled probands ($r = .69$ and $.40$ respectively). We have already seen that h^2g levels for word recognition vary significantly with severity of deficit. To observe the coding tasks' relations to h^2g independently from deficit severity, the phonological and orthographic scores were adjusted for their linear relation with word recognition. In other words, we will now assess differences in h^2g for word recognition as a function of subjects' variance in phonological and orthographic coding that is independent from their word recognition.

The results are shown in Table 5.4. The mean deficits in word recognition were the same ($z = -2.4$) across the group splits, but the adjusted coding scores used to separate the groups, and the unadjusted coding scores were of course different. The h^2g estimates were higher for the groups that were lower in the coding tasks relative to their word recognition. However, the two-tailed p value approached an acceptable level of significance only for the h^2g interaction with phonological coding ($p = .057$).

The dissimilar p values for the coding tasks seem inconsistent with the similar group differences in h^2g. The reason became apparent when subjects were divided into three groups on the phonological and orthographic dimen-

TABLE 5.4
h^2g for Word Recognition in Relation to Phonological and Orthographic Coding

Group Division	n Twin Pairs	Unadjusted Mean Coding	Score h²g (SE)	p
Lower phonological	86	−2.81	.74 (.15)	
				.057
Higher phonological	104	−1.36	.54 (.11)	
Lower orthographic	77	−3.24	.74 (.13)	
				.404
Higher orthographic	113	−.67	.54 (.12)	

Note: p values are two-tailed.

sions. Heritabilities for word recognition at the three levels of phonological coding were .74 ± .16 for the low group, .58 ± .12 for the middle group, and .48 ± .19 for the high group. When three groups were divided on orthographic coding, the respective heritabilities were .74 ± .14, .54 ± .15, and .54 ± .19. The regression model (2) used to test the interaction between h^2g for word recognition and the continuous subtype variables was sensitive to the more linear changes with phonological coding.

Phonological Coding

The p value for the phonological coding interaction with h^2g for word recognition was significant enough to encourage speculation about its basis. It was noted earlier that most disabled readers were lower in phonological coding than expected from their word recognition, and there was a strong genetic correlation between deficits in phonological coding and word recognition (Olson et al., 1989; Olson et al., in preparation). We suggested that genetically based deficits in phonological coding and related segmental language skills hindered the development of word recognition in many disabled readers. However, there were also significant environmental influences on our disabled group's deficit in word recognition. Perhaps disabled readers who were not uniquely low in phonological coding may have tended to suffer from more environmentally based constraints on their progress in word recognition. Certainly, any environmental constraints on exposure to print and practice in reading would limit progress in word recognition (Olson et al., in press; Stanovich & West, in press). We are now collecting data on print exposure to test this hypothesis in future analyses.

We believe that the genetic pathway for the more severe deficits in phonological coding is through deficits in segmental language skills. Significant genetic correlations have been found between phonological coding deficits and deficits in rhyming and "pig-latin" games (Olson et al., 1989). The present group that was lower on the adjusted phonological coding variable was also significantly lower in their ability to play "pig-latin."

Orthographic Coding

It seems premature to speculate on the apparently higher heritability of word recognition deficits for the group that was low in orthographic coding. The interaction with h^2g did not reach an acceptable level of significance. Previous analyses showed that the genetic correlation between orthographic coding and word recognition was not significant, and was significantly lower than the genetic correlation between phonological coding and word recognition (Olson et al., 1989; Olson et al., in preparation). It was hypothesized that performance on the orthographic task and its correlation with word recognition was related primarily to environmental differences in subjects' print exposure (Stanovich & West, in press).

On the other hand, our sample is far too small to accept the null hypothesis for differences in h^2g. Assuming the present interaction of orthographic coding with h^2g remains and achieves significance in a larger sample, very poor performance on the orthographic task would indicate the existence of a possible subtype that is highly heritable. Based on the present data, this subtype would be orthogonal to h^2g differences along the phonological dimension because the two dimensions are not significantly correlated after controlling for word recognition ($r = -.06$).

It is not immediately clear what the cause of a heritable orthographic coding deficit might be. Boder (1973) suggested that her dyseidetic subjects' problems in whole-word recognition were related to deficits in visual-perceptual processes such as those measured by the WISC Performance subscale. Of course visual-perceptual skills are significantly heritable (see Plomin, this volume), and heritable deficits in these skills could mediate a heritable influence on reading deficits for some disabled readers. However, studies that have assessed the relationship between visual-perceptual deficits and orthographic coding problems have yielded negative results (Elbro, 1989; Olson et al., 1985; van den Bos, 1984). In the present sample of reading-disabled probands, the correlation between the Wechsler perceptual tests described here and the adjusted orthographic coding variable is not significant ($r = .05$). We must look elsewhere for an explanation if poor orthographic coding ultimately proves to be a marker for a more heritable subtype of reading disability.

IQ

The analyses for differential h^2g with IQ included 30 additional pairs of twins whose probands' verbal and performance IQ were both below the 90 minimum criterion used in the previous analyses. These additional twins increased the variance for IQ-reading discrepancies in the sample. The sample was further expanded by the inclusion of 27 additional twin pairs who had missing data on the phonological or orthographic coding tasks and were therefore excluded from the previous analyses. Thus, the present analyses included a total of 247 twin pairs wherein the probands were at least one standard deviation below the word recognition mean for the comparison group. Full-scale IQ ranged from 59 to 133 with a mean of 99 (SD = 11.1).

As discussed earlier, the WISC and WAIS IQ tests include 11 subtests that were divided into three groups based on Kaufman's (1975) factor analysis. In addition to assessing differential h^2g with subjects' full-scale score, we will observe differences in relation to the subtests grouped under Kaufman's

TABLE 5.5
Correlations Between IQ Scores and Word Recognition for Disabled
Probands

	Full-scale IQ	Verbal Comprehension	Perceptual Organization	Freedom Distract.
Verbal comprehension	.77			
Perceptual organization	.77	.40		
Freedom from distract.	.57	.26	.26	
Word recognition	.35	.24	.17	.37

Note: See text for subtests included in Kaufman's Verbal Comprehension, Perceptual Organization, and Freedom from Distractibility factor groups. All correlations are $p < .01$, $N = 247$.

Verbal Comprehension (Information, Similarities, Vocabulary, and Comprehension), Perceptual Organization (Picture Completion, Picture Arrangement, Block Design, and Object Assembly), and Freedom From Distractibility factors (Arithmetic, Digit Span, and Coding).

The probands' full-scale IQ and mean scaled scores for the three Kaufman test groups were significantly correlated with word recognition (see Table 5.5). Therefore, to observe IQ interactions with h^2g independently from deficit severity, the subjects' IQ scores were adjusted for their modest relations to word recognition. The correlations between word recognition and IQ scores in Table 5.5 are much lower than those commonly reported (see Torgesen, 1989, for a review). The correlations are constrained by restricted variance in both IQ and word recognition within the disabled sample. Also, the correlations are attenuated by the selection of most probands for poor reading and normal range IQ .

Levels of h^2g estimated from model (1) and the p values for the subtype interactions estimated from model (2) are presented in Table 5.6 for groups divided at the mean of the adjusted IQ scores. It is clear that regardless of the particular adjusted IQ score used, there were no statistically significant interactions with h^2g for word recognition.

Again, we caution against acceptance of the null hypothesis. Some potential subjects whose school records indicated low IQ were never invited for testing in the laboratory. Their inclusion would have further increased the variance for IQ–reading discrepancies in the sample, and might have led to stronger interactions with h^2g for word recognition than those presented here. Also, the interaction of h^2g with adjusted full-scale IQ was fairly large and approached significance even with the restricted IQ variance in our sample. It is interesting to note that in contrast to most of the other tests for interactions with h^2g, the significance level for full-scale IQ was higher when the subtype variable was based on the dichotomous group division ($p = .08$).

All of the trends in the group contrasts for heritability are the same across

TABLE 5.6
Differential Heritability for Word Recognition in Relation to IQ Scores

Group Division	n Twin Pairs	Unadjusted Mean Score	h^2g (SE)	p
Low full-scale IQ	123	90.7	.40 (.10)	
				.167
High full-scale IQ	124	107.2	.67 (.11)	
Low verbal comp.	127	8.3	.49 (.11)	
				.271
High verbal comp.	120	11.0	.59 (.12)	
Low percept. org.	124	9.2	.43 (.11)	
				.432
High percept. org.	123	12.1	.67 (.11)	
Low freedom dist.	119	7.4	.52 (.11)	
				.453
High freedom dist.	128	10.3	.57 (.11)	

the three Kaufman factors: heritabilities are higher for the groups with higher IQ. However, the sizes of the differences in h^2g for the group splits range from .27 for full-scale IQ to .05 for Freedom from Distractibility. These results suggest that different IQ measures may interact differently with h^2g for word recognition, but the p values show that a much larger sample would be needed to confirm this hypothesis.

A tentative two-part hypothesis is offered for the trends in h^2g differences for the group splits on adjusted IQ scores. First, subjects with more general intellectual deficits may tend to suffer more from environmental constraints on both reading and intellectual development. Stevenson and Fredman (in press) recently examined environmental correlates of reading ability in their twin study. They argued that several of these correlates affected reading through IQ.

The second part of our hypothesis is that disabled readers whose deficit is highly specific to reading may suffer more from heritable deficits in phonological coding and related segmental language skills. There is some support for differences in phonological coding for groups that are high and low in IQ. Rack and Olson (1989) found that the more specifically disabled individuals whose word recognition was below IQ-expected levels, tended to have a more specific phonological reading problem. The correlation between Verbal Comprehension and phonological coding, partialing out variance due to word recognition, was −.20 ($p < .01$). This correlation may not seem impressively large, but remember that the substantial variance shared between word recognition and phonological coding ($r = .69$) had been removed.

The presence of interesting trends in the foregoing group contrasts encourages further exploration of reading-IQ discrepancies with a larger twin sample. Certainly we have found nothing to support the exclusion of subjects with low IQ from the study of reading disabilities or from remedial services. The importance of IQ for the diagnosis, etiology, and remediation of reading disabilities can only be determined if we allow our reading-disabled samples to vary across a wide range of IQ scores (Fletcher & Morris, 1986; Lyon, 1989). At the present time, even the low cutoff scores of 80 suggested by Siegel (1989) or 85 suggested by Leong (1989) are not supported by research.

Age and Gender Differences in h^2g for Word Recognition

We will conclude our tests for differential h^2g with age and gender. Age differences in the heritability of word recognition were suggested by Stevenson, Graham, Fredman, and McLoughlin (1987) as a reason for their low estimate of $h^2 = .29$ for word recognition, and nonsignificant differences in MZ and DZ concordance rates for dyslexia in their sample of 13-year-old twins. Stevenson et al. noted that previous concordance studies indicating high heritabilities for reading disability included younger children. However, we found no support for this hypothesis in a previous study with a smaller twin sample (Olson et al., 1989). A more rigorous test of age differences in h^2g is provided here.

The possibility of a gender difference in the heritability of reading disabilities was raised by Harris (1986), who suggested that heritability analyses should be performed separately for male and female twin pairs. LaBuda and DeFries (in press) tested the interaction of gender with h^2g for several psychometric measures and a composite reading measure that included the word recognition, comprehension, and spelling tests from the PIAT. There were no significant differential effects of gender in the analyses, but the twin sample (62 female and 55 male pairs) was small. LaBuda, DeFries, and Pennington (in press) found no significant interaction between gender and the composite reading measure for a larger sample of 96 MZ and 72 DZ pairs.

TABLE 5.7
h^2g for Word Recognition in Relation to Sex and Age

Group Division	n Twin Pairs	Word Recognition	h^2g (SE)	p
Male	97	−2.54	.66 (.11)	
				.419
Female	93	−2.26	.58 (.14)	
Over 12 yr. (X = 14.8)	98	−2.41	.58 (.12)	
				.540
Under 12 yr. (X = 10.1)	92	−2.39	.66 (.14)	

Note: p values are two-tailed.

Their estimates of h^2g were .48 ± .17 for the males and .55 ± .17 for the females.

Results for Gender

In the present sample, there was no significant evidence that h^2g for deficits in word recognition differ for males and females (see Table 5.7). Of course for this comparison and all the other nonsignificant comparisons discussed earlier, larger samples may ultimately reveal significant differences. However, it does appear from the present sample that gender differences in h^2g for word recognition are not likely to be very large.

There were two other noteworthy results for the groups divided on gender. First, the ratio of 97 male probands to 93 female probands was not consistent with many previous studies of reading disability that reported male-female ratios of about three or four to one. LaBuda and DeFries (in press) discussed several possible reasons for the discrepancy in sex ratios across studies. These included a differential volunteer rate favoring female twins in a number of studies reviewed by Lykken, Tellegren, and DeRubeis, (1978), and a referral bias in previous nontwin studies (Finucci, 1978). LaBuda and DeFries reviewed several family studies, including one at Colorado (Vogler, DeFries, & Decker, 1985) that indicated the ratio of affected male and female relatives of reading disabled probands was less than 2 to 1 (family studies of probands' affected relatives are not contaminated by referral biases).

The second noteworthy result for gender in Table 5.7 is the significant difference in deficit severity for word recognition (gender was not adjusted for word recognition). The mean deficit for males was –2.54 SD, while the mean deficit for females was –2.26 SD. An examination of the distributions for word recognition in males and females revealed that males were disproportionately represented among the most severe cases. For example, there were 17 males and 4 females below –3.5 SD. For the more extreme deficits below –4.15 SD, there were 8 males and no females. These results are consistent with those reported by Finucci and Childs (1981). The disproportionate number of males in the extreme tail of the distribution may indicate a differential genetic etiology related to gender for these extreme cases. A much larger sample of such extreme cases would be needed to test for differences in h^2g

Results for Age

The lack of a significant difference as a function of age is clearly inconsistent with the hypothesis of Stevenson et al. (1987) that heritabilities for older subjects might be lower. In fact, the nonsignificantly higher h^2g heritability for word recognition in our older twins is consistent with the direction of age differences in h^2 heritability that have been found for a variety of cognitive skills (see Plomin, this volume). Olson et al. (1989) discussed several other possible reasons why the heritabilities reported for word recognition by Stevenson et al. were so low.

SUMMARY AND CONCLUSIONS

There were two dimensions of individual differences among disabled readers that were related to statistically significant differences in heritability for deficits in word recognition. First, the more severe deficits in word recognition were less heritable, although h^2g for the more severe half of the disabled sample was still substantial. Further research on environmental factors such as print exposure, education, and medical history is needed to clarify their greater influence on the more severe deficits in word recognition.

The second dimension that accounted for significant differences in h^2g was based on the subjects' phonological coding scores adjusted for word recognition. Disabled readers who were relatively poor in phonological coding tended to have more heritable deficits in word recognition. We argued that heritable deficits in phonological coding and related segmental language skills constrain the development of word recognition in most disabled readers. However, disabled readers' phonological coding deficits can be more or less severe, and some have phonological coding skills that are as good as those of normal readers at the same level of word recognition. Without the constraint of uniquely poor phonological coding, deficits in word recognition were more likely to be due to environmental factors.

There was a marginally significant trend toward higher h^2g for word recognition deficits in subjects with higher IQ scores. If this trend proves to be significant in a larger sample, it would indicate that environmental factors are relatively more influential in the co-occurrence of low IQ and low word recognition. Greater heritability for the co-occurrence of low word recognition and high IQ may be associated with relatively severe deficits in phonological coding (Rack & Olson, 1989).

Differences in h^2g related to age and gender did not approach statistical significance. A larger twin sample may ultimately reveal significant differences, although the present results suggest that these differences are likely to be small.

For all the contrasts in h^2g discussed in this chapter, the genetic factors causing individual differences in word recognition may differ in relation to the subtype dimensions, regardless of the presence or absence of significant differences in h^2g. For example, different sets of genes could be involved in reading disabilities for males and females, even though their respective levels of h^2g are similar. Significant differences in h^2g allow the important conclusion that there are changes in the relative influence of environmental and genetic factors along a subtype dimension; however, further research is needed to discover the specific mechanisms involved.

ACKNOWLEDGMENTS

The research was supported in part by NICHD Grant Nos. HD 11681 and HD 22223. We thank the staff members of the Colorado school districts and the families who participated in the study.

REFERENCES

Accardo, P. J. (1980). A *neurodevelopmental perspective on specific learning disabilities*. Baltimore: University Park Press.

Baron, J. (1979). Orthographic and word-specific mechanisms in children's reading of words. *Child Development, 50*, 60–72.

Bishop, D. V. M., & Butterworth, G. E. (1980). Verbal-performance discrepancies: Relationship to birth risk and specific reading retardation. *Cortex, 16*, 375–389.

Bloom, A., Wagner, M., Reskin, L. & Bergman, A. (1980). A comparison of intellectually delayed and primary reading disabled children on measures of intelligence and achievement. *Journal of Clinical Psychology, 36*, 788–790.

Boder, E. (1973). Developmental dyslexia: A diagnostic approach based on three atypical reading-spelling patterns. *Developmental Medicine and Child Neurology, 15*, 663–687.

Bowers, P., Steffy, R., & Tate, E. (1988). Comparison of the effects of IQ control methods on memory and naming speed predictors of reading disability. *Reading Research Quarterly, 23*, 304–319.

Carr, T. H., & Pollatsek, A. (1985). Recognizing printed words: A look at current models. In D. Besner, T. G. Waller, & G. E. MacKinnon (Eds.), *Reading research: Advances in theory and practice* (Vol. 5, pp. 1–82). Orlando, FL: Academic Press.

Conners, F., & Olson, R. K. (in press). Reading comprehension in dyslexic and normal readers: A component-skills analysis. In D. A. Balota, G. B. Flores d'Arcais, & K. Rayner (Eds.), *Comprehension processes in reading*. Hillsdale, NJ: Lawrence Erlbaum Associates.

Critchley, M. (1970). *The dyslexic child* (2nd ed.). London: Heinemann.

DeFries, J. C., & Fulker, D. W. (1985). Multiple regression analysis of twin data. *Behavior Genetics, 15*, 467–473.

DeFries, J. C., & Fulker, D. W. (1988). Multiple regression analysis of twin data: Etiology of deviant scores versus individual differences. *Acta Geneticae Medicae et Gemellologiae: Twin Research, 37*, 205–216.

DeFries, J. C., Fulker, D. W., & LaBuda, M. C. (1987). Evidence for a genetic aetiology in reading disability of twins. *Nature, 329*, 537–539.

Dunn, L. M., & Markwardt, F. C. (1970). *Examiner's manual: Peabody Individual Achievement Test*. Circle Pines, MN: American Guidance Service.

Elbro, C. (1990). *Differences in Dyslexia*. Copenhagen: Munksgaard International Publishers Ltd.

Finucci, J. M. (1978). Genetic considerations in dyslexia. In H. R. Myklebust (Ed.), *Progress in learning disabilities* (Vol. 4, pp. 41–63). New York: Grune & Stratton.

Finucci, J. M., & Childs, B. (1981). Are there really more dyslexic boys than girls? In A. Ansara,

N. Geschwind, A. Galaburda, M. Albert, & N. Gartrell (Eds.), *Sex differences in dyslexia* (pp. 11–19). Towson, MD: Orton Dyslexia Society.

Fletcher, J. M., & Morris, R. (1986). Classification of disabled learners: Beyond exclusionary definitions. In S. J. Ceci (Ed.), *Handbook of cognitive, social, and neuropsychological aspects of learning disabilities* (pp. 55–80). Hillsdale, NJ: Lawrence Erlbaum Associates.

Fredman, G., & Stevenson, J. (1988). Reading processes in specific reading retarded and reading backward 13-year-olds. *British Journal of Developmental Psychology, 6*, 97–108.

Harris, E. L. (1986). The contribution of twin research to the study of the etiology of reading disability. In S. D. Smith (Ed.), *Genetics and learning disabilities* (pp. 3–19). San Diego: College–Hill Press.

Johnson, D., & Myklebust, H. R. (1964). *Learning disabilities: Educational principles and practices.* New York: Grune & Stratton.

Kaufman, A. S. (1975). Factor analysis of the WISC–R at 11 age levels between 6 1/2 and 16 1/2 years. *Journal of Consulting and Clinical Psychology, 43*, 2, 135–147.

LaBuda, M. C., & DeFries, J. C. (in press). Genetic etiology of reading disability: Evidence from a twin study. In G. Pavlidis (Ed.), *Dyslexia.* New York: Wiley.

LaBuda, M. C., DeFries, J. C., & Pennington, B. F. (in press). Reading disability: A model for the genetic analysis of complex behavioral disorders. *Journal of Counseling and Development.*

Leong, C. K. (1989). The locus of so-called IQ test results in reading disabilities. *Journal of Learning Disabilities, 22*, 507–512.

Lykken, D. T., Tellegren, A., & DeRubeis, R. (1978). Volunteer bias in twin research: The rule of two-thirds. *Social Biology, 25*, 1–9.

Lyon, G. R. (1989). IQ is irrelevant to the definition of learning disabilities: A position in search of logic and data. *Journal of Learning Disabilities, 22*, 504–506.

Malatesha, R. N., & Dougan, D. R. (1982). Clinical subtypes of developmental dyslexia: Resolution of an irresolute problem. In R.N. Malatesha & P. G. Aaron (Eds.), *reading disorders: Varieties and treatments.* New York: Academic Press, pp. 69–92.

Manis, F. R., Szeszulski, P.A., Holt, L. K., & Graves, K. (1988). A developmental perspective on dyslexic subtypes. *Annals of Dyslexia, 38*, 139–153.

Manis, F. R., Szeszulski, P. A., Holt, L. K., & Graves, K. (in press). Variation in component word recognition and spelling skills among dyslexic children and normal readers. In T. H. Carr & B. A. Levy (Eds.), *reading and its development: Component skills approaches.* New York: Academic Press.

Mitterer, J. O. (1982). There are at least two kinds of poor readers: Whole- word poor readers and recoding poor readers. *Canadian Journal of Psychology, 36*, 445–461.

Newby, R. F., Recht, D., & Caldwell, J. (1989). *Phonological processing, verbal and nonverbal memory, and attention in dysphonetic and dyseidetic dyslexia.* Paper presented to the Society for Research in Child Development, Kansas City, April 27.

Olson, R. K., Conners, F., Rack, J., DeFries, J. C., Fulker, D. W., & LaBuda, M. C. (in preparation). *Genetic and environmental influences on word recognition and its component coding skills.*

Olson, R. K., Kliegl, R., Davidson, B. J., & Foltz, G. (1985). Individual and developmental differences in reading disability. In G. E. MacKinnon & T. G. Waller (Eds.), *Reading research: Advances in theory and practice* (Vol. 4, pp. 1–64). New York: Academic Press.

Olson, R. K., Wise, B., Conners, F., & Rack, J. (in press). Organization, heritability, and remediation of component word recognition and language skills in disabled readers. In T. H. Carr & B. A. Levy (Eds.), *reading and its development: Component skills approaches.* New York: Academic Press.

Olson, R. K., Wise, B., Conners, F., Rack, J., & Fulker, D. (1989). Specific deficits in component reading and language skills: Genetic and environmental influences. *Journal of Learning Disabilities, 22*, 6, 339–348.

Plomin, R., DeFries, J. C., & McClearn, G. E. (1990). *Behavioral genetics*. San Francisco: Freeman.

Rack, J., & Olson, R. K. (1989). *Sources of variance in the phonological deficit in developmental dyslexia*. Paper presented to the Rodin Remediation Society, Bangor, Wales, Sept. 14.

Rutter, M., & Yule, W. (1975). The concept of specific reading retardation. *Journal of Child Psychology and Psychiatry, 125*, 181–197.

Schulman, J., & Leviton, A. (1978). Reading disabilities: An epidemiologic approach. In H. R. Myklebust (Ed.), *Progress in learning disabilities* (Vol. 4, pp. 65–96). New York: Grune & Stratton.

Seymour, P. H. K. (1986). *Cognitive analysis of dyslexia*. London: Routledge & Kegan Paul.

Siegel, L. S. (1988). Evidence that IQ scores are irrelevant to the definition and analysis of reading disability. *Canadian Journal of Psychology, 42*, 201–215.

Siegel, L. S. (1989). IQ is irrelevant to the definition of learning disabilities. *Journal of Learning Disabilities, 22*, 469–479.

Stanovich, K. E. (1986). Cognitive processes and the reading problems of learning-disabled children: Evaluating the assumption of specificity. In J. K. Torgesen & B. Y. L. Wong (Eds.), *Psychological and educational perspectives on learning disabilities* (pp. 87–131). Orlando, FL: Academic Press.

Stanovich, K. E. (in press-a). *Discrepancy definitions of reading disability: Has intelligence led us astray?*

Stanovich, K. E., (in press-b). Explaining the differences between the dyslexic and garden-variety poor reader: The phonological-core variable-difference model. *Journal of Learning Disabilities*.

Stanovich, K. E., & West, R. F. (in press). Print exposure and orthographic processing. *reading Research Quarterly*.

Stevenson, J., & Fredman, G. (in press). The social environmental correlates of reading ability. *Journal of Child Psychology and Psychiatry*.

Stevenson, J., Graham, P., Fredman, G., & McLoughlin, V. (1987). A twin study of genetic influences on reading and spelling ability and disability. *Journal of Child Psychology and Psychiatry, 28*, 229–247.

Taylor, H. G., Satz, P., & Friel, J. (1979). Developmental dyslexia in relation to other childhood reading disorders: Significance and clinical utility. *reading Research Quarterly, 15*, 84–101.

Torgesen, J. K. (1989). Why IQ is relevant to the definition of learning disabilities. *Journal of Learning Disabilities, 22*, 484–486.

van den Bos, K.P. (1984). Letter processing in dyslexic subgroups. *Annals of Dyslexia, 34*, 179–193.

Vogler, G.P., DeFries, J. C., & Decker, S. N. (1985). Family history as an indicator of risk for reading disability. *Journal of Learning Disabilities, 18*, 419–421.

Wechsler, D. I. (1974). *Examiner's manual: Wechsler Intelligence Scale for Children—Revised*. New York: Psychological Corp.

Wechsler, D. I. (1981). *Examiner's manual: Wechsler Adult Intelligence Scale—Revised*. New York: Psychological Corp.

6 Can Learning-disabled Children Become Good Information Processors?: How Can We Find Out?

Michael Pressley
University of Maryland

My principal research interest for many years has been strategy instruction. In particular, I have studied memory and reading strategies (e.g., Pressley, Johnson, & Symons, 1987). There are a few basic assumptions that motivate this research. First, many people do not process information as efficiently and as effectively as they could. Second, there is the assumed potential for improving important human performances by teaching processing that is well matched to the demands of important educational tasks; that is, performance might improve my teaching strategies that are based on processes that accomplish the tasks in question. Third, many people can learn to use better strategies through direct instruction of those strategies. Fourth, instruction should vary, depending on the needs and characteristics of the learner (i.e., depending on the subtype of the student).

The first three assumptions can be supported by large data bases; the fourth is more debatable, enjoying only limited support at present (e.g., Hooper & Willis, 1989, Chap. 8). Relevant to the first assumption, not only do children often fail to use efficient strategies (e.g., Schneider & Pressley, 1989), but even "sophisticated" students enrolled in elite universities often fail to process information in efficient ways (e.g., Christopoulos, Rohwer, & Thomas, 1987). The second assumption is supported by research identifying many strategies accomplishing important educational goals, including effective procedures for reading (e.g., Bereiter & Bird, 1985), writing (e.g., Englert & Raphael, 1988), and computation (e.g., Reys, 1984). As for the third assumption, many of these strategies can be taught to children in school through direct instruction, with important insights in recent years about how to do such instruction so that students learn to apply strategies generally and continue to use them (e.g., Belmont, Butterfield, & Ferretti, 1982). The fourth assumption is supported by studies demonstrating more certain cognitive gains if teaching is directed at learners strengths rather than their weaknesses (e.g., Pressley, Cariglia-Bull, Deane, & Schreider, 1987). Nonetheless, it must be emphasized that study of occasions when instruction is matched to processing strengths is rare indeed (Hooper & Willis, 1989, Chap. 8).

All three purposes of this chapter are concerned with the issue of self-regulation, specifically self-regulated use of strategies appropriate to important academic tasks. In the first main section of the chapter, I will detail what is required for self-regulated use of strategies to occur. That is, there will be a description of what a really good information processor is like. It will become apparent from this analysis that learning deficiencies can follow from a number of information-processing deficits. The second main section of the chapter deals with how strategy instruction can be structured to promote the many subtleties of good information processing. It will become apparent that good strategy instruction is both intensive and extensive, cutting across the curriculum and over years of schooling. Moreover, a main theme will be that instruction at its best is tailored to the processing characteristics of the particular student—the subtyping classification should inform and guide instruction. The final section is motivated by the fact that a lot more could be known about strategic processing. I describe there the general questions that need to be addressed by researchers as part of comprehensive efforts to evaluate strategy instruction targeted at learning-disabled children who possess a variety of cognitive deficiencies.

Throughout the discussion, I will provide illustrations. Many of these (but not all) will be based on memory or reading tasks. Given my research interests, examples from these domains occur to me readily. They are appropriate here since learning disabilities, and particularly reading disabilities, are often problems of verbal processing. Even a cursory survey of learning disability journals makes it obvious that studies of memory and reading are at the forefront of research on exceptionality.

THE NATURE OF GOOD INFORMATION PROCESSING

Good information processing is not due to any one critical component, but rather a number of components operating in interaction. The good information processor model (see Pressley, Borkowski, & Schneider, in press) highlights the complexity of competent cognition; less-than-competent performance is also complex from the perspective of this model. Progress in understanding and remediating suboptimal performance is most likely to be achieved by confronting these complexities directly, a point of view consistent with other recent formulations of and treatments for learning disabilities (e.g., Farnham- Diggory, 1987).

Basic Competencies

The most basic competency required for good information processing is an intact brain functioning pretty much as most human brains function. Good information processing is almost never present when there are gross congenital brain abnormalities or when there has been severe brain injury (e.g., Kolb & Whishow, 1985).

"Symptoms" of healthy brain functioning include: (1) *Language skills* are intact. For instance, phoneme-grapheme correspondences are well known so that coding of both print to sound and sound to print is easily accomplished, usually automatically. The good information processor has an extensive receptive and productive vocabulary developed through lifelong language experiences. There is extensive tacit knowledge of the syntax of the language. (2) Good information processors have a lot of information stored in *long-term memory*, much of which can be accessed easily when needed. This information often enables strategy use. Thus, the list of friends attending a party can be remembered by imagining each guest in a unique spot in the house where the party will be held. This strategy can only be employed, however, if a detailed mental representation of the house is readily available in long-term storage. (3) Despite the importance of long-term knowledge for use of some strategies, the symbol manipulation that is part of strategy execution (e.g., rehearsal of information, construction of images, reorganization of input) largely occurs in *short-term memory*; hence, good information processing requires short-term capacity well within the normal range. Children who have little short-term capacity experience difficulty executing a variety of strategic processes that require conscious reflection and manipulation of content (e.g., Pressley, Cariglia-Bull et al., 1987). (4) Good information processors can attend to information appropriately (e.g., Anderson, Halcomb, & Doyle, 1973). One aspect of *attention* is simple vigilance, that is, the ability to remain on task for a period of time. In addition, it is also important to attend to the more relevant elements of the task—to attend selectively.

As critical as physiology is, however, it is not the entire explanation of good information processing. Good information processing also depends on well-developed "software" (i.e., strategies, metacognition, beliefs).

Strategies

Strategies are sequences of processes matched to the requirements of tasks. They are always potentially controllable, although sometimes they are carried out habitually and outside of conscious awareness. For instance, skilled readers often scan a chapter and its headings before reading it without doing so consciously; if they wished to do so, however, they could stop processing text in this fashion. There are strategies that are executed externally (e.g., placing a book that I want to take to the office by the door so that I do not forget it tomorrow) and ones that are executed entirely internally (e.g., using a "pegword" mnemonic to memorize a shopping list). Some strategies accomplish big tasks (e.g., writing a term paper), and others accomplish small

TABLE 6.1
Sample Strategies

Strategy	Operations	Demonstrated Effects
Story grammar (e.g., Short & Ryan, 1984)	Identify main characters of story, where and when it took place, what main characters did, how story ended, how main characters felt. OR Construct story map with setting, problem, goal, action, and outcome.	Improves free recall of stories and accuracy on short-answer questions. Effects probably more certain with poor readers.
Cognitive strategies in writing (e.g., Englert & Raphael, 1988)	1. Plan writing. Focus on audience and purpose. Access relevant information. 2. Organize. Identify comparisons and contrasts. Identify what is being explained and sequence the steps in the process. 3. Write first draft. 4. Edit. Self-edit, anticipate reader's questions. 5. Have peer editor read paper. 6. Revise. 7. Prepare final draft.	Improves the quality of student writing.
Spelling (Graham & Freeman, 1986)	1. Say word. 2. Write and say word. 3. Check the word. 4. Trace and say it. 5. Write word from memory, check. 6. Repeat first five steps.	Improves spelling in learning-disabled children.

tasks (e.g., remembering a French vocabulary word). Some additional examples of strategies are contained in Table 6.1.

Good information processors know a number of strategies. For memory, they might include rehearsal, organizational, and elaborative strategies (e.g., Schneider & Pressley, 1989); for comprehension, they know how to summarize text, create representational images, question themselves as they read, activate relevant prior knowledge, and reread selectively (e.g., Tierney, Readence, & Dishner, 1985). In addition, the good information processor knows some more generally useful strategies. One of the most important of these is checking and monitoring of performance (e.g., Markman, 1985). Another is trying to find similarities between a challenging task and a task one already knows how to do (e.g., Entwisle & Romsden, 1983). Good information processors search for environmental cues signaling what is important to remember or comprehend, although they do not get so involved in such cue seeking that nothing else gets done (Miller & Partlett, 1974).

Metacognitive Knowledge About Specific Strategies

Even if students know strategies, they will not use them appropriately if they do not understand their value (e.g., the procedure promotes memory and comprehension; Black & Rollins, 1982; Borkowski, Levers, & Gruenenfelder, 1976; Cavanaugh & Borkowski, 1979; Kennedy & Miller, 1976; Lawson & Fuelop, 1980; Paris, Newman, & McVey, 1982; Ringel & Springer, 1980) or do not know where or when to apply the strategies (e.g., Paris, Lipson, & Wixson, 1983; Pressley, Borkowski, & O'Sullivan, 1984, 1985). For instance, rehearsal strategies work well when lists of items are to be learned, but are not so effective if associations must be acquired. Awareness of this discriminative utility is required for flexible and appropriate deployment of rehearsal strategies. Each strategy possesses its own set of information specifying when the strategy can and should be deployed, and hence, my associates and I have dubbed this type of metacognition as metacognitive knowledge about specific strategies (for short, specific strategy knowledge).

Both naturalistic-correlational and experimental evidence is accumulating which indicates strategy use improves when students know where and when to use strategies (e.g., Duffy, Roehler, Sivan et al., 1987; Herrmann, 1986; O'Sullivan & Pressley, 1984). Such information is critical to the self-regulation of learning (Corno & Mandinach, 1983), since the heart of self-regulation is recognizing when procedural skills are appropriate to deploy.

Styles

Some students habitually respond to situations in a careful, reflective way; others respond more impulsively (e.g., Baron, 1985; Messer, 1976). Some people are habitually anxious; others much less so. Because strategy planning and use requires some time, reflective responding is more consistent with good information processing; because strategy use requires short-term capacity and unnecessary anxiety consumes short-term capacity, low anxiety is more consistent with good information processing than high anxiety. On the other hand, good information processors are not so reflective that they think themselves into inaction. Moreover, they are not so low anxious that they do not experience concern when there is a good reason (e.g., a test will occur tomorrow, and they have yet to study).

Motivational Beliefs

Although all children presumably begin life with an intrinsic motivation to learn and develop (e.g., White, 1959), that intrinsic motivation continues to operate in good information processors (e.g., Deci & Ryan, 1985). Good information processors have a history of success, and thus, generally feel good about themselves as students (e.g., McCombs 1986, 1987). They particularly understand that their success is largely due to their use of appropriate procedures on appropriate occasions (e.g., Clifford, 1984). Moreover, they, do not possess beliefs that could undermine their motivations to learn and use strategies. For instance, they do not attribute their successes to luck or their failures to lack of ability. They do not believe that the course of their intellectual success is determined by innate endowment alone; rather, they believe that their intellectual competence consists of a repertoire of skills expandable through their own efforts. In Dweck's (e.g., 1987) terms, good information processors are incremental theorists rather than people who believe that intelligence is a fixed entity. They recognize the skills and knowledge that they currently possess were acquired gradually, and that new situations may require the learning of more skills.

Good information processors know that exertion of effort is not a sign of low intelligence and recognize that challenging tasks should be confronted squarely rather than avoided for fear of failure. They recognize that effort expended in tackling challenging tasks and learning new strategies is investment in cognitive development, more than a risk to self-esteem (e.g., Brophy, 1986). They are aware that the road to knowing a strategy so that it can be applied consistently and effectively is often filled with errors and that failure does not imply low ability. In short, good information processors understand that normal cognitive development consists of mastering diverse strategies and skills.

Other Nonstrategic Knowledge

Besides knowledge of strategies and related metacognition and beliefs, good information processors also possess a lot of other knowledge. Sometimes this nonstrategic knowledge base diminishes the need to execute strategies. For instance, many avid baseball fans can watch an inning of a game and remember how every out was made without exerting any strategic effort. The fan's knowledge base permits automatic assimilation of new information about baseball (e.g., Spilich, Vesonder, Chiesi, & Voss, 1979). Possession of knowledge also enables use of some strategies. For instance, soccer-playing children process prose about soccer better when they intentionally activate prior knowledge about soccer before reading than when they do not engage in activation of prior knowledge about soccer. The same strategy does not benefit soccer novices (e.g., Hasselhorn & Körkel, 1986).

Summary of Good Information Processing

Although each component of good information processing was presented separately, these components interact constantly. When confronted with a task, the good information processor attends to it and almost automatically deploys effort, believing effort appropriately expended will lead to competent performance. For many familiar tasks, the situation automatically elicits appropriate strategic procedures. When good information processors face not-so-practiced tasks, they analyze situations in an attempt to identify similarities between the current problem and previous tasks that were strategically mediated. If similarities are identified, that triggers strategies associated with the previous situation. Performance is monitored while the strategy is being used to determine whether there is progress toward the goal. If there is no progress, and it becomes obvious that the current procedure is inadequate, the student might try hard to substitute other strategies until one is identified that works.

The explicit selection and conscious execution and monitoring of strategies consume short-term memory capacity (e.g., Baddeley, 1986; Case, 1985; Kahnemann, 1973). Strategy selection, execution, and monitoring all become more automatic with practice and hence require less capacity (e.g., Logan, 1985; Schneider, Dumais, & Shiffrin, 1984). Consider a child who is learning to use reading comprehension strategies. The child practices directing attention to relevant parts of text, self-testing, and summarizing from memory after completion of reading. At first, use of these strategies is clumsy, consuming most if not all of the child's short-term capacity, leaving little consciousness available for other cognitive demands of reading (e.g., integrating what is being read with prior knowledge). With practice, the strategies are carried out more quickly and efficiently, and much less short-term capacity is consumed in the process. The efficient execution of these comprehension strategies in turn results in a more complete memory trace being created and stored in long-term memory than would have occurred if the child had not employed the comprehension strategies.

How Do Learning-disabled Children Differ From Good Information Processors?

Learning-disabled children are a diverse population, with some of their problems comprehensible in terms of good information-processing components. That is, assessment of the various information-processing components can be used to define subtypes of disabled learners. Consider some of the possible deficiencies. Some learning-disabled children do not have normally functioning brains, even if the specific brain disorder is difficult to identify or pinpoint. The result can be language difficulties, limited short-term capacity, poor attention, and impulsivity (e.g., Gaddes, 1985). In addition, learning-disabled children use fewer strategies and seem to know less about the strategies they do use than do normal children (e.g., Forrest–Pressley & Waller, 1984; Schneider & Pressley, 1989, Chaps. 4 & 5). Some learning-disabled children are anxious about academic matters (Kasik, Sabatino, & Spoentgen, 1987; Perlmutter, 1987). Some make causal attributions undermining motivation to use strategies or exert effort at all, for example attributing academic failures to immutable ability factors (e.g., Pearl, 1982). A long history of learning difficulties and failures can result in a poorly developed knowledge base. Some learning-disabled children who possess knowledge have more difficulty accessing it and employing it during academic work than do normal child (e.g., Rabinowitz & Chi, 1987).

Implications of the Good information Processor Model for Planning Interventions With Learning-disabled Students

Although learning-disabled children as a group may be tremendously disadvantaged compared to normal peers, I am optimistic that their status can be improved. The first step is to evaluate the learner with respect to the components of good information processing before attempting a strategic intervention. The result should be a composite of information processing strengths and weaknesses, an analysis that can be especially helpful if interpreted in light of processing demands that might be required by a to-be-learned strategy. Of course this is consistent with subtyping approaches to assessment—learner characteristics theoretically linked to competent performance are assessed. The expectation is that learner differences in strengths and weaknesses can inform the design of instruction that takes advantage of the strengths and avoids the weaknesses.

What if I were considering teaching a learning-disabled child to use visual and first-letter mnemonics to aid learning of facts and associations, interventions often tried with learning-disabled children (Nagel, Schumaker, & Deshler, 1986)? I might assess the child's basic capacities. However, I would not worry too much about the intactness of the child's brain as far as mnemonic instruction is concerned, for I know that people suffering much more serious brain disorders than those commonly associated with learning disabilities can learn to use mnemonics (e.g., Wilson, 1987). Because some visual mnemonics require the child to make acoustic associations between to-be-learned materials and mnemonic elements (e.g., keyword method; Pressley, Levin, & Delaney, 1982), and because first-letter mnemonics often require students to construct new words composed of the first letters of to-be-learned pieces of information, language facility would be of greater concern. Similarly, since creation of visual images requires substantial short-term capacity (e.g., Pressley, Cariglia–Bull et al., 1987; Pressley & Levin, 1978), I would want to determine whether a candidate for mnemonics instruction has difficulties with tasks demanding short term capacity.

To be certain, there are great challenges here. The assessment should vary, depending on the goals of instruction (e.g., different strategy interventions depend on different processing capacities and thus the capacities assessed will vary depending on the strategy being considered). Thus, language difficulties might be given little weight when deciding how to teach a mathematics strategy, but enormous weight in evaluating whether a child might benefit from a particular type of reading comprehension strategy instruction. A good assessment provides other information as well. Some children may require more prompting or environmental support than others to benefit from strategy instruction, with a good assessment providing helpful hints as to what type of prompting or restructuring is necessary in order to provide learning, gains—that is, dynamic assessment is a good idea (e.g., Feurstein, 1979). To return to the mnemonics strategy example, children who are deficient in short-term capacity might experience difficulty with visual mnemonics. Because there is good reason to believe that verbal mnemonics make less demands on short-term memory than do visual mnemonics (Pressley, Levin, & McCormick, 1980), it would make sense to try teaching verbal mnemonics rather than visual to a child whose only deficiency was short-term memory. Alternatively, providing prompting in the form of some pictorial support for the construction of mnemonic images reduces short-term capacity demands during the construction of visual images. Thus, providing pictures that could be elaborated into mnemonic images might be profitable with children who are relatively low on short-term capacity (e.g., Pressley & Levin, 1978). At its best, assessment would provide such information.

I am willing to accept that some children may never get to the point that they can execute memory or reading comprehension strategies in a self-regulated fashion. Sensitive assessments before and during instruction aimed at illuminating children's processing proclivities and difficulties could be revealing about why some children fail to learn strategies to the point of self-regulation. These same assessments might also provide information about how to prompt the child or how to provide additional input so that the child nonetheless can be led to achieve memory and comprehension goals. More will be said later about less than fully self-regulated learning, but for now, I turn attention to how instruction can maximize the likelihood that self-regulated information processing will develop, for good information processing is sometimes possible, even with learning-disabled students.

STRATEGY INSTRUCTION

There has been a large investment in strategy instructional curriculum for learning-disabled students, with the best of this instruction aimed at developing the skills and knowledge that constitute good information processing. Such teaching includes directions about how to execute strategic procedures per se, metacognition about those strategies, and motivation to use strategies. There is also a recognition that it is important to build the nonstrategic knowledge base, given that a well-developed knowledge base can sometimes make strategy functioning unnecessary and that strategy functioning is often dependent on the knowledge base (Pressley, Borkowski, & Schneider, 1987, 1989).

As an example, consider the work of Donald Deshler and his associates at the Institute for Research on Learning Disabilities at the University of Kansas. They have developed a core group of strategies promoting the academic and social skills that are important for effective school functioning. For instance, the Kansas group has prepared instructional packages for a variety of memory and comprehension skills, including paraphrasing, self-questioning, visual imagery, first-letter mnemonics, test taking, and error monitoring (Hughes, Schumaker, Deshler, & Mercer, 1988; Lenz, Schumaker, Deshler, & Beals, 1984; Nagel, et al., 1986; Schumaker, Denton, & Deshler, 1984; Schumaker, Nolan, & Deshler, 1985; Schumaker & Sheldon, 1985; Sheldon & Schumaker, 1985). The particular skills that are the focus of instruction were selected on the basis of intense analyses of school requirements and demands (Deshler & Schumaker, 1986).

The instructional sequence was derived from analyses of the cognitive instruction and behavioral instructional literatures, but was also informed by years of teaching experience gained by Kansas personnel as they developed their methods in the field (e.g., Deshler & Schumaker, 1986). Strategy descriptions are presented first, including important metacognitive information, such as the rationale for the strategy and situations where the strategy can be applied. Then the teacher models the strategy, using think-aloud procedures. Students are provided teacher-guided practice and feedback. The steps of the procedure are rehearsed until they are memorized. Practice begins with fairly simple materials and progresses to grade-appropriate work. As practice continues, the teacher attempts to diagnose whether the child is using the strategy in question, and if so, whether the strategy is being employed as well as it could be. If not, the teacher provides additional feedback and additional instruction specifically tailored to the difficulties the student is experiencing. That is, students are supplied with responsive elaborations (Duffy & Roehler, 1987). Student practice with teacher-provided responsive elaborations continues until the child can execute the strategy with facility. The student is then ready to apply the procedure to more challenging materials, with the teacher continuing to supply responsive elaborations and prompting as needed. Throughout the process, the teacher provides information about benefits that follow from use of the strategy as well as information about where and when the procedure can be applied.

A main strength of this approach is its effect on generalized strategy use (Deshler, Schumaker, & Lenz, 1984; Ellis, Lenz, & Sabornie, 1987a, 1987b). Generalization is promoted through presentation of multiple exemplars at every phase of instruction and reminders about where strategies can be used. Students are given consistent guided practice at generalizing strategies to in-class assignments and are required to try to apply the skills to actual class assignments. Students are taught to prompt themselves to use strategies with self-talk (e.g., Meichenbaum, 1977), and they are instructed to be alert for cues that would suggest use of a strategy in a particular setting. Sometimes cue cards are provided containing summaries of the strategies, and students are instructed on how to use these cards in order to aid transfer.

Motivation is an important component, with students playing a role in deciding what strategies will be acquired and which educational goals will be targeted. Motivation is heightened by students charting, monitoring, and evaluating their own progress. Students are taught to self-reinforce good performance. They are also made aware of the important role of the strategic skills they are acquiring by the creation of a "strategic environment" in the classroom. This develops from teachers consistently modeling strategy use in class. Students get repeated in-class exposure to social role-taking, communication, and academic learning strategies.

In short, the Kansas approach is to provide explicit, intensive, and extensive teaching of strategies. Teaching involves a lot of feedback and a great deal of teacher explanation. Student progress is monitored throughout instruction with supplementary explanations and demonstrations provided as required. A great deal of effort is made to ensure that students understand the importance of the strategies they are learning, as well as where and when to apply these procedures. There are high expectations that strategy use will be transferred, with instruction fostering this goal. In general, the available evidence suggests that this approach improves the academic performance of children who otherwise do poorly in school (e.g., Ellis et al., 1987a, 1987b).

The Kansas approach has a lot in common with other strategy instructional models (e.g., Derry, Hawkes, & Tsai, 1987; Duffy & Roehler, 1986, 1987;

Duffy, Roehler, & Putnam, 1987), including the good information-processing perspective on instruction (Pressley et al., in press). All specify that strategies should be taught a few at a time and well (a "small is beautiful" approach; cf. Schumacher, 1973), rather than many simultaneously and superficially. All specify that students should be instructed to monitor performance consistently and to remediate cognitive problems once they are detected. All emphasize that students must be taught where and when to use strategies, since such knowledge is critical to effective generalization. All attend to motivation, including explicit highlighting of strategy utility and performance gains that follow from strategy use. Strategies are introduced and mastered in the context of ongoing reading, mathematics, and other content-area instruction, rather than as abstract skills separated from curriculum content. All of these models recognize the necessity of building the nonstrategic knowledge base, and all prescribe teaching that is explicit and extensive, with a great deal of supervised student practice and provision of feedback. Teachers are viewed as agents who can foster generalized strategy use by providing guidance and reminders about when and how strategies can be extended to new situations. In short, these strategy instructional models contrast strikingly to older approaches to strategy instruction in which a number of strategies were taught in a brief period of time (for examples, see Segal, Chipman, & Glaser, 1985) without metacognitive embellishment (for commentary, see Brown, Bransford, Ferrara, & Campione, 1983; Pressley, Heisel, McCormick, & Nakamura, 1982) or attention to monitoring, motivation, or the nonstrategic knowledge base (for commentary, see Brophy & Kher, 1986; Garner, 1987; Glaser, 1984).

This approach to instruction is an extremely social, interactive one. Teachers do not coerce students into being strategic, but rather convince them that these procedures are useful in achieving important academic goals. Such instruction provides students with the most effective cognitive tools that have been identified in research to date. Adoption of such procedures prepares students to cope with school demands and empowers them so that they can make the most of their abilities. The success experiences provided can do much to fuel additional academic activity. If children do well on important academic tasks because of strategy use and recognize that their competent performances are due to the use of cognitive tools, attitudes about school tasks should be improved.

For example, the Harford County, Maryland, public schools (1985; Hargest, Wood, Rose, & Coughlin, 1986) designed a 1-year learning strategies curriculum to teach functional mathematics skills to learning-disabled children in grades 7 and 8, with the affective data from their study summarized in Table 6.1. At the end of the year, the students in the strategy training classrooms

TABLE 6.2
Responses to Attitude Questionnaire Items About Mathematics at the
End of the Academic Year

Item	Percent Agreement Trained	Control
Working with numbers in math class is fun.	77%	55%
Math is good because it makes you think.	77%	64%
Math is fun.	69%	27%
Math is my favorite subject.	54%	9%
Solving math problems is exciting.	43%	32%
I like my math teacher.	91%	36%
I do well on math tests.	74%	41%
I try to avoid math whenever I can.	32%	68%
I can't use math skills in daily life.	17%	41%
Working on math is boring.	37%	59%
I would rather do anything else but math.	29%	64%
I don't like to do math at my school.	31%	55%
Time drags in math class.	34%	59%

From Hargest, Wood, Rose, and Coughlin, 1986.

clearly had more positive attitudes about mathematics than did the control students.

In short, there is ongoing instruction aimed at developing self-regulated cognition in learning-disabled students, instruction that targets the many dimensions of good information processing. The evaluations of this instruction that are available provide reason for optimism that extensive and intensive strategy instruction can often lead to sophisticated use of important academic skills. Those who identify strongly with the subtyping perspective featured in this volume, nonetheless, might object that the Kansas approach and related interventions are indifferent to student differences (e.g., Hooper & Willis, 1989, Chap. 8). That is probably too strong a claim, however. First, strategies are selected for instruction on the basis of individually diagnosed student needs. Although there is a fixed general sequence of instruction, teaching is constantly adjusted in light of student difficulties and the teacher's perceptions about the causes of difficulties, that is, there are continuous on-line assessments of performance by adults familiar with potential processing differences in learning-disabled students that might undermine instructional success. To be sure, however, there is an urgent need here to study formally how successful instruction varies with learner subtype. There is also a need for research on the dynamics of the informal assessment that goes on during instruction, for instance, what "tests" does the experienced teacher use to evaluate probable sources of student processing difficulties.

PROGRAMMATIC RESEARCH ON STRATEGY INSTRUCTION

In this section we explore how to determine whether a particular strategy should be taught to learning-disabled children, whether it can be taught to learning-disabled children, and what might be done if it proves either unteachable or difficult to teach. I first describe a sample family of strategies that will be used to develop the points made in this section. I selected summarization strategies to illustrate the points made here because summarization has high face validity as an important skill for students to acquire, and because it is a procedure that could be investigated profitably in the near future with learning-disabled students. A good deal of theoretical analysis of the strategy has already been done; many variations of the procedure have been worked out in studies of normal children, who seem to benefit from instruction to summarize as they read.

Summarization Strategies

A single reading of an expository text never permits recall of all of the information in the passage, although mature, capable readers can often remember the most important points—they remember the gist, with details forgotten. In Kintsch and van Dijk's (1978; van Dijk & Kintsch, 1983) terms, adults remember the macrostructure of the text. In contrast, children usually fail to abstract the macrostructure, and in fact, seem to require instruction in order to identify summary information at all (e.g., Brown & Day, 1983; Brown, Day, & Jones, 1983).

A family of summarization strategies have been developed that can be taught to children. Brown and Day (1983) devised instruction based on the rules that Kintsch and van Dijk (1978; van Dijk & Kintsch, 1983) argued were the basis for summaries constructed by competent readers. These rules were to delete trivial information, delete redundant information, substitute superordinate terms for lists of items, integrate a series of events with a superordinate action term, select a topic sentence, and invent a topic sentence if there is none. Bean and Steenwyk (1984) taught these rules to sixth-grade children, who applied them to expository paragraphs. Reading comprehension improved following this instruction in summarization. Barbara Taylor (1982) and her associates at Minnesota (e.g., Taylor & Beach, 1984) taught children to use headings, subheadings, and paragraphs to develop an outline of text, with a main idea statement then generated for every heading, subheading, and paragraph. This training improved free recall of expository passages, as did an intervention by Rinehart, Stahl, and Erickson (1986). Rinehart et al.'s treatment was an amalgamation of Brown and Day's (1983) rules derived from Kintsch and van Dijk and the outlining method devised by Taylor. Summaries can also have spatial components. Berkowitz (1986) taught sixth-grade students to construct maps of passages. They wrote the title of the passage in the middle of a sheet of paper. Then students searched the text for four to six main ideas, with these ideas placed in a circle around the title. The students were taught to use the graphic organizer to test themselves over the content of the text. Overall recall of passages was improved following this instruction, as it was in Armbruster, Anderson, and Ostertag (1987) who taught fifth-grade children to construct three-box diagrams when reading social studies passages. The boxes identified the problem specified by the article, the actions taken to deal with the problem, and the results of the actions. In short, normal children can be taught summarization strategies during the later grade-school years; in general, these procedures increase recall of expository content.

Do Learning-disabled Children Use Summarization Already? Another Strategy?

A question about naturalistic cognition needs to be answered before deciding whether to instruct summarization strategies. Do learning-disabled children already use such strategies? If they do not, perchance are they already doing something that would be equally or even more efficient in mediating learning of text? In either case, there would be little need to instruct summarization (Pressley, Heisel, et al., 1982). Of course, this type of diagnosis is at the heart of much research on cognitive development, with a great deal of information already generated about various strategies used naturalistically by both normal and disadvantaged students (see Schneider & Pressley, 1989, Chaps. 3 & 6, for examples).

There are many ways naturalistic strategy use can be tapped. Sometimes it is inferred from outcome patterns. When main ideas and few details are remembered following reading, use of a summarization strategy is suggested. Observation of actual memorization behaviors could support this inference. For instance, if the learner wrote down a sketchy, point-by-point summary when reading, this would be on-line evidence of summarization. In addition, self-reports of explicit attempts to abstract the gist and code main ideas might occur if the reader were using summarization. Confidence that summarization was being used would be especially high if the outcome, behavioral, and self-report measures converged, so that summarization was indicated by all measures.

What is known about naturalistic summarization skills? None of the investigators studying summarization has observed children naturally constructing verbal or spatial summaries. At least, they do not do it overtly. It seems unlikely that they do it covertly either (or at least they do not do it very well). When children are explicitly directed to create summaries, their synopses do not contain just the main points, with appropriate deletions and substitution of superordinate terms (Brown & Day, 1983; Brown, et al., 1983).

Although there have not been extensive analyses of summaries produced by learning-disabled children, Day (1986) documented that young adults with low and average verbal ability enrolled in junior college are not proficient at summarization even when they are told to do it. The little data that do exist on learning-disabled children's summaries suggest that there is much room for improvement (e.g., Jenkins, Heliotis, Stein, & Haynes, 1987; Kurtz & Borkowski, 1987).

Can Learning-disabled Students Be Taught to Use Summarization Strategies?

The fundamental question here is whether it is possible to get learning-disabled children to carry out the operations that define summarization in such a way that their comprehension and memory of text improve. Several sessions of intense instruction are required for normal children to learn how to carry out summarization strategies and thus, it is likely instruction for learning disabled children will need to be at least as extensive. Such instruction should follow the teaching principles reviewed earlier, with detailed modeling and explanation of the strategy followed by teacher-guided practice of the strategy and feedback.

Extensive analysis should be conducted to determine if learning of text really is better when learning-disabled children use summarization strategies, for even though summarization training improves memory in normal children, it may not do so with learning-disabled students. Far too many strategies are simply assumed to promote learning and other cognitive performances in normal and special populations, even though there are no substantiating data (see Pressley, Goodchild, Fleet, Zajdrowski, & Evans, 1989). The folly of such assumptions is evident when "well-regarded" strategies can be identified that simply do not deliver what they have been assumed to deliver. For example, despite countless recommendations in the literature that children's acquisition of vocabulary meanings can be facilitated by having them use new words in context, this strategy is no more efficient than simply providing the children with the vocabulary as paired associates and letting them learn the meanings in a rote fashion (Pressley, Levin, & McDaniel, 1987). It is important to determine whether strategies that seem like they should mediate important educational tasks actually *do* mediate those tasks.

Can Students Be Taught summarization So That They Continue to Use It and Use It Generally?

Brown, Bransford et al. (1983) proposed that maintenance of a strategy (i.e., use in situations similar to the training context) was likely if children were informed of the utility of the strategy. More general strategy use presumably follows from what they referred to as self-controlled strategy training. This training involves providing information about where and when to use the procedure and teaching the children to initiate use of the strategy on their own (e.g., through self-instructions). More recent models, including the good information processor perspective, emphasize other factors as well. For instance, motivation to use the strategy in question should be attended to as part of instruction. Moreover, students should be given diverse practice with generalization programmed, including teacher-guided opportunities to apply newly learned strategies to-be-learned materials.

How is it possible to know if the various instructional embellishments actually do promote transfer? Do experiments in which some subjects are taught how to execute the strategy, but receive little other input. In other conditions, subjects can be taught the strategic procedures, but with instructional embellishment, such as that recommended in the last paragraph. Four types of dependent variables are informative about the durability of strategy use. One, students should be given opportunity to apply the strategy (e.g., summarization) to previously trained tasks (e.g., elementary science texts) without prompting to do so. This provides information about strategy maintenance. Two, students should be directed explicitly to apply the strategy they have learned to trained tasks. This provides information about whether the strategy is still known by the subject at the time of the assessment. Three, students should be given the opportunity to apply the strategy to new tasks that can be mediated by the strategy (e.g., elementary history texts) but without prompting to do so. This provides information about strategy generalization. Four, students should be directed explicitly to apply the strategy they had learned to transfer tasks. This informs about whether any lack of transfer during phase three reflects failure to recognize that the strategy could be applied or inability to adapt the strategy to the new task.

Early in the game, it makes sense to throw every type of enrichment considered likely to promote transfer into the instructional pot, for a first question about generalization is whether it can be obtained at all. Suppose it proves possible to teach general use of the summarization strategy by providing lots of practice with different approaches to summarization applied to a variety of text types, when lots of information is provided during instruction about where and when to use summarization strategies, and when students are provided lots of motivational prompts (e.g., it is emphasized how much improved their text learning is following use of summarization strategies). Then, it might make sense to do studies in which the various instructional embellishments are titrated out of the complete mix. Such manipulations can be theoretically informative. For instance, if elimination of the motivational instruction greatly reduces transfer, that would be a telling sign that motivation is a critical determinant of transfer. These manipulations also can provide information that can be used to create a more economical treatment. Whether expensive components can be eliminated from instruction with little effect on generalization can be evaluated in true experiments constrasting the complete instruction to instruction that is identical except for the elimination of the costly component in question. See Pressley, Forrest–Pressley, and Elliott–Faust (1988) for more complete commentary on experimental analyses of instructional components.

What If It Proves Impossible to Teach Summarization Strategies So That Learning-disabled Students Can Use Them On Their Own?

Even if learning-disabled children cannot learn to use summarization in a self-regulated fashion, they may be able to analyze text for main ideas and supporting details if they are given consistent prompting to do so. Teachers can remind the students to summarize. Readings can be accompanied by work sheets including boxes for main and supporting ideas. In the case of a student who still could not generate summaries, it might make sense to provide summaries to accompany to-be-learned texts.

In making the recommendation to provide adjunct materials and consistent instructional prompting, I know there will be criticisms. Some will argue that self-regulated information processing is the goal, and that providing prompts as crutches will discourage development of self-regulated cognition. My first reply to this criticism is that provision of aids only should occur after it proves impossible or prohibitively expensive to teach self-regulated information processing. My second reply is that the content presented in textbooks needs to be acquired by learning-disabled students (e.g., Hirsch, 1987; Ravitch & Finn, 1987), and I believe it fair game to improve their acquisition of that content through any means possible. My third reply is that the long-term consequences of adjunct aids and prompting are not known. It may be that long-term exposure to effective summaries that are provided by a teacher or exposure to materials that aid summarization would improve understanding of the nature of summaries. To the extent that such prompting improves learning, and learning-disabled students recognize the benefits are due to the aids, they might be motivated to try summarization even when prompts are not provided. Although it is not known whether such cognitive gains would occur following exposure to learning aids, there is also no good reason to assume that provision of learning aids would necessarily lead to dependencies that impede the development of self-regulated cognition (Pressley, 1983). It is an empirical question that deserves attention as the potential benefits of adjunct learning aids (e.g., provided summaries) are evaluated in formal research studies.

Summary

When strategy instructional research follows a rational course, there are first studies of naturalistic strategy use, followed by determination of whether the population of interest can execute the strategic procedures at all. If the population can learn to carry out the strategy, research on generalization should follow. If they cannot carry out the procedures on their own, or cannot learn to generalize the procedures, then it is appropriate to begin research on materials modifications that might produce the gains that otherwise would be obtained with generalized strategy execution.

Throughout this evaluation process, researchers should be ever mindful of potential individual differences in students' responses to instruction; some types of learning disabled children will be able to execute particular strategies better than other strategies; some may be more likely to maintain and/or generalize strategies they have been taught; and some may be more in need of supplementary materials than others. Determining who benefits from what type of instruction is a focal concern for subtyping researchers. As individual differences in learning-disabled children are better understood, it should be possible to make increasingly sophisticated predictions about when strategy instruction will be successful, when it will generalize, and when it may need to be supported by prompts and aids.

CONCLUDING COMMENTS

Good information processing is complex and involves interacting cognitive, metacognitive, motivational, and knowledge-base factors. It does not develop quickly, but can be promoted by extensive and consistent instruction. Thus, strategy instruction at its best is a long-term intervention, extending across the curriculum. Such instruction is provided by patient and sensitive teachers who do all possible to model good strategy use, provide guided practice with strategies, and encourage general use of strategies by directly explaining when and where strategies should be used. My reading of the scientific community is that researchers are looking forward to contributing to these evaluations. Those interested in individual differences seem especially tantalized by the prospects that lie ahead, for instructional research is a real proving ground of subtyping theory; subtypes are only meaningful to the extent they predict differential success as a function of type of instruction. The perspective developed in this chapter is that the success of various types of instruction will be determined at least in part by how well the instruction makes demands of learners strengths rather than weaknesses. A lot of work remains to translate this theoretical proposal into a body of well-validated associations between learner subtypes and outcomes, given particular types of instruction.

ACKNOWLEDGMENT

This chapter was originally presented at the first annual conference on Research and Theory in Learning Disabilities, Pennsylvania State University, University Park , June 1, 1988

REFERENCES

Anderson, R. P. Halcomb, C. G., & Doyle, R. B. (1973). The measurement of attention deficits. *Exceptional Children, 39*, 534–539.

Armbruster, B. B. Anderson, T. H., & Ostertag, J. (1987). Does text structure/summarization instruction facilitate learning from expository text? *Reading Research Quarterly, 22*, 331–346.

Baddeley, A. (1986). *Working memory.* New York: Oxford University Press.

Baron, J. (1985). *Rationality and intelligence.* Cambridge, England: Cambridge University Press.

Bean, T. W., & Steenwyk, F. L. (1984). The effect of three forms of summarization instruction on sixth graders' summary writing and comprehension. *Journal of Reading Behavior, 16,* 297–306.

Belmont, J. M., Butterfield, E. C., & Ferretti, R. P. (1982). To secure transfer of training instruction self-management skills. In D. K. Detterman & R. J. Sternberg (Eds.), *How and how much can intelligence be increased?* (pp. 147–154). Norwood NJ: Ablex.

Bereiter, C., & Bird, M. (1985). Use of thinking aloud in identification and teaching of reading comprehension strategies. *Cognition and Instruction, 2,* 91–130.

Berkowitz, S. J. (1986). Effects of instruction in text organization on sixth-grade students' memory for expository reading. *Reading Research Quarterly, 21,* 161–178.

Black, M. M., & Rollins, H. A. (1982). The effects of instructional variables on young children's organization and free recall. *Journal of Experimental Child Psychology, 31,* 1–19.

Borkowski, J. G., Levers, S. R., & Gruenenfelder, T. M. (1976). Transfer of mediational skills in children: The role of activity and awareness during strategy acquisition. *Child Development, 47,* 779–786.

Brophy, J. (1986). *On motivating students.* Occasional Paper 101. East Lansing MI: Michigan State University, Institute for Research on Teaching.

Brophy, J., & Kher, N. (1986). Teacher socialization as a mechanism for developing student motivation to learn. In R. Feldman (Ed.), *Social psychology applied to education* (pp. 257–288). Cambridge, England: Cambridge University Press.

Brown, A. L., Bransford, J. D., Ferrara, R. A., & Campione, J. C. (1983). Learning, remembering, and understanding. In J. H. Flavell & E. M. Markman (Eds.), *Handbook of child psychology*, Vol 3: *Cognitive development* (pp. 177–266). New York: Wiley.

Brown, A. L., & Day, J. D. (1983). Macrorules for summarizing texts: The development of expertise. *Journal of Verbal Learning and Verbal Behavior, 22,* 1–14.

Brown, A. L., Day, J. D., & Jones, R. D. (1983). The development of plans for summarizing texts. *Child Development, 54,* 968–979.

Case, R. (1985). *Intellectual development.* Orlando, FL: Academic Press.

Cavanaugh, J. C., & Borkowski, J. G. (1979). The metamemory–memory "connection": Effects of strategy training and maintenance. *Journal of General Psychology, 101,* 161–174.

Christopoulos, J. P., Rohwer, W. D., Jr., & Thomas, J. W. (1987). Grade level differences in students' study activities as a function of course characteristics. *Contemporary Educational Psychology, 12,* 303–323.

Clifford, M. M. (1984). Thoughts on a theory of constructive failure. *Educational Psychologist, 19,* 108–120.

Corno, L., & Mandinach, E. B. (1983). The role of cognitive engagement in classroom learning and motivation. *Educational Psychologist, 18,* 88–118.

Day, J. D. (1986). Teaching summarization skills: Influences of student ability level and strategy difficulty. *Cognition and Instruction, 3,* 193–210.

Deci, E. L., & Ryan, R. M. (1985). *Intrinsic motivation and self-determination in human behavior.* New York: Plenum Press.

Derry, S. J., Hawkes, L. W., & Tsai, C. J. (1987). A theory for remediating problem-solving skills of older children and adults. *Educational Psychologist, 22,* 55–87.

Deshler, D. D., & Schumaker, J. B. (1986). Learning strategies: An instructional alternative for low-achieving adolescents. *Exceptional Children, 52,* 583–590.

Deshler, D. D., Schumaker, J. B., & Lenz, B. K. (1984). Academic and cognitive interventions for LD adolescents (Part I). *Journal of Learning Disabilities, 17,* 108–117.

Duffy, G. G., & Roehler, L. R. (1986). *Improving classroom reading instruction: A decision-making approach.* New York: Random House.

Duffy, G. G., & Roehler, L. R. (1987). Improving reading instruction through the use of responsive elaboration. *Reading Teacher, 40,* 514–520.

Duffy, G. G., Roehler, L. R., & Putnam, J. (1987). Putting the teacher in control: Basal textbooks and teacher decision making. *Elementary School Journal, 87,* 357–366.

Duffy, G. G., & Roehler, L. R., Sivan, E., Rackliffe, G., Book, C., Meloth, M., Vavrus, L. G., Wesselman, R., Putnam, J., & Bassiri, D. (1987). Effects of explaining the reasoning associated with using reading strategies. *Reading Research Quarterly, 22,* 347–368.

Dweck, C. (1987, April). *Children's theories of intelligence: Implications for motivation and learning.* Paper presented at the annual meeting of the American Education Research Association, Washington, DC.

Ellis, E. S., Lenz, B. K., & Sabornie, E. J. (1987a). Generalization and adaptation of learning strategies to natural environments: Part 1, Critical agents. *Remedial and Special Education, 8,* 6–20.

Ellis, E. S., Lenz, B. K., & Sabornie, E. J. (1987b). Generalization and adaptation of learning strategies to natural environments: Part 2, Research into practice. *Remedial and Special Education, 8,* 6–23.

Englert, C. S., & Raphael, T. E. (1988). Constructing well-formed prose: Process, structure, and metacognitive knowledge. *Exceptional Children, 54,* 513–520.

Entwisle, N. J., & Ramsden, P. (1983). *Understanding student learning.* New York: Nichols Publishing Co.

Farnham–Diggory, S. (1987). Time, now, for a little serious complexity. In S. J. Ceci (Ed.), *Handbook of cognitive, social, and neuropsychological aspects of learning disabilities* (Vol. 1, pp. 123–158). Hillsdale, NJ: Lawrence Erlbaum Associates.

Feurstein, R. (1979). *The dynamic assessment of retarded performers. The Learning Potential Assessment Device, theory, instruments, and techniques.* Baltimore: University Park Press.

Forrest-Pressley, D. L., & Waller, T. G. (1984). *Cognition, metacognition, and reading.* New York: Springer–Verlag.

Gaddes, W. H. (1985). *Learning disabilities and brain function* (2nd ed.). New York & Berlin: Springer–Verlag.

Garner, R. (1987). *Metacognition and reading comprehension.* Norwood, NJ: Ablex.

Glaser, R. (1984). Education and thinking: The role of knowledge. *American Psychologist, 29,* 93–104.

Graham, S., & Freeman, S. (1986). Strategy training and teacher- vs. student-controlled study conditions: Effects on learning disabled students, spelling performance. *Learning Disability Quarterly, 9,* 15–22.

Harford County Public Schools. (1985). *A learning strategies approach to functional mathematics for students with special needs.* Harford County Public Schools, Bel Air, MD.

Hargest, J. T., Wood, C., Rose, W. H., & Coughlin, L. P. (1986, June). *Preparing learning disabled adolescents for a state competency math test: A learning strategies approach.* Unpublished manuscript, Harford County Public Schools, Bel Air, MD.

Hasselhorn, M., & Körkel, J. (1986). Metacognitive versus traditional reading instructions: The mediating role of domain-specific knowledge on children's text processing. *Human Learning, 5,* 75–90.

Herrmann, B. A. (1986, April). *Effective instruction of math story problems.* Presented at the annual meeting of the American Educational Research Association, San Francisco.

Hirsch, E. D., Jr. (1987). *Cultural literacy: What every American needs to know.* Boston: Houghton Mifflin.

Hooper, S. R., & Willis, W. G. (Eds.). (1989). *Learning disability subtyping.* New York & Berlin: Springer–Verlag.

Hughes, C. A., Schumaker, J. B., Deshler, D. D., & Mercer, C. D. (1988). *The test-taking strategy.* Lawrence KS: EXCELLenterprises.

Jenkins, J. R., Heliotis, J., Stein, M. L., & Haynes, M. (1987). Improving reading comprehension by using paragraph restatements. *Exceptional Children, 54,* 54–59.

Kahnemann, D. (1973). *Attention and effort.* Englewood Cliffs, NJ: Prentice–Hall.

Kasik, M. M., Sabatino, D. A., & Spoentgen, P. (1987). In S. J. Ceci (Ed.), *Handbook of cognitive, social, and neuropsychological aspects of learning disabilities* (Vol. 2, pp. 251–272). Hillsdale NJ: Lawrence Erlbaum Associates.

Kennedy, B. A., & Miller, D. J. (1976). Persistent use of verbal rehearsal as a function of information about its value. *Child Development, 47,* 566–569.

Kintsch, W., & van Dijk, T. A. (1978). Toward a model of text comprehension and production. *Psychological Review, 85,* 363–394.

Kolb, B., & Whishaw, I. Q. (1985). *Fundamentals of human neuropsychology.* New York: Freeman.

Kurtz, B. E., & Borkowski, J. G. (1987). Development of strategic skills in impulsive and reflective children: A longitudinal study of metacognition. *Journal of Experimental Child Psychology, 43,* 129–148.

Lawson, M. J., & Fuelop, S. (1980). Understanding the purpose of strategy training. *British Journal of Educational Psychology, 50,* 175–180.

Lenz, B. K., Schumaker, J. B., Deshler, D. D., & Beals, V. L. (1984). *The word identification strategy.* Lawrence, KS: University of Kansas, Institute for Research on Learning Disabilities (Available by writing authors at P.O. Box 972, Lawrence, KS 66044).

Logan, G. D. (1985). Skill and automaticity: Relations, implications, and future directions. *Canadian Journal of Psychology, 39,* 367–386.

Markman, E. M. (1985). Comprehension monitoring: Developmental and educational issues. In S. F. Chipman, J. W. Segal, & R. Glaser (Eds.), *Thinking and learning skills, Vol. 2: Research and open questions* (pp. 275–292). Hillsdale, NJ: Lawrence Erlbaum Associates.

McCombs, B. L. (1986, April). *The role of the self-system in self-regulated learning.* Presented at the annual meeting of the American Educational Research Association, San Francisco.

McCombs, B. L. (1987, April). *The role of affective variables in autonomous learning.* Paper presented at the annual meeting of the American Educational Research Association, Washington, DC.

Meichenbaum, D. M. (1977). *Cognitive behavior modification*. New York: Plenum Press.
Messer, S. B. (1976). Reflection-impulsivity: A review. *Psychological Bulletin, 83*, 1026–1052.
Miller, C. M. L., & Partlett, M. R. (1974). *Up to the mark: A study of the examination game*. London: Society for Research in Higher Education.
Nagel, D. R., Schumaker, J. B., & Deshler, D. D. (1986). *The FIRST letter mnemonic strategy*. Lawrence, KS: Excel Enterprises, Inc. (Available from authors at P.O. Box 972, Lawrence, KS 66044).
O'Sullivan, J. T., & Pressley, M. (1984). Completeness of instruction and strategy transfer. *Journal of Experimental Child Psychology, 38*, 275–288.
Paris, S. G., Lipson, M. V., & Wixson, K. K. (1983). Becoming a strategic reader. *Contemporary Educational Psychology, 8*, 293–316.
Paris, S. G., Newman, R. S., & McVey, K. A. (1982). Learning the functional significance of mnemonic actions: A microgenetic study of strategy acquisition. *Journal of Experimental Child Psychology, 34*, 490–509.
Pearl, R. (1982). LD children's attributions for success and failure: A replication with a labeled LD sample. *Learning Disability Quarterly, 5*, 173–176.
Perlmutter, B. F. (1987). Personality variables and peer relations of children and adolescents with learning disabilities. In S. J. Ceci (Ed.), *Handbook of cognitive, social, and neuropsychological aspects of learning disabilities* (Vol. 1, pp. 339–359). Hillsdale NJ: Lawrence Erlbaum Associates.
Pressley, M. (1983). Making meaningful materials easier to learn: Lessons from cognitive strategy research. In M. Pressley & J. R. Levin (Eds.), *Cognitive strategy research: Educational applications* (pp. 239–266). New York: Springer–Verlag.
Pressley, M., Borkowski, J. G., & O'Sullivan, J. T. (1984). Memory strategy instruction is made of this: Metamemory and durable strategy use. *Educational Psychologist, 19*, 94–107.
Pressley, M., Borkowski, J. G., & O'Sullivan, J. T. (1985). Children's metamemory and the teaching of memory strategies. In D. L. Forrest–Pressley, G. E. MacKinnon, & T. G. Waller (Eds.), *Metacognition, cognition, and human performance* (pp. 111–153). New York: Academic Press.
Pressley, M., Borkowski, J. G., & Schneider, W. (1987). Cognitive strategies: Good strategy users coordinate metacognition and knowledge. In R. Vasta & G. Whitehurst (Eds.), *Annals of child development* (Vol. 4, pp. 89–129). Greenwich CT: JAI Press.
Pressley, M., Borkowski, J. G., & Schneider, W. (1989). Good information processing: What it is and how education can promote it? *International Journal of Educational Research, 13*, 857–867.
Pressley, M., Cariglia–Bull, T., Deane, S., & Schneider, W. (1987). Short–term memory, verbal competence, and age as predictors of imagery instructional effectiveness. *Journal of Experimental Child Psychology, 43*, 181–193.
Pressley, M., Forrest–Pressley, D. L., & Elliott–Faust, D., J. (1988). What is strategy instructional enrichment and how to study it: Illustrations from research on children's prose memory. In F. Weinert & M. Perlmutter (Eds.), *Memory development: Universal changes and individual development* (pp. 101–131). Hillsdale NJ: Lawrence Erlbaum Associates.
Pressley, M., Goodchild, F., Fleet, J. Zajchowski, R., & Evans, E. D. (1989). The challenges of classroom strategy instruction. *Elementary School Journal, 89*, 301–342.
Pressley, M., Heisel, B. E., McCormick, C. G., & Nakamura, G. V., (1982). Memory strategy instruction with children. In C. J. Brainerd & M. Pressley (Eds.), *Progress in cognitive development research: Verbal processes in children* (Vol. 2, pp. 125–159). New York: Springer–Verlag.
Pressley, M., Johnson, C. J., & Symons, S. (1987). Elaborating to learn and learning to elaborate. *Journal of Learning Disabilities, 20*, 76–91.

Pressley, M., & Levin, J. R. (1978). Developmental constraints associated with children's use of the keyword method of foreign language vocabulary learning. *Journal of Experimental Child Psychology, 26,* 359–372.

Pressley, M., Levin, J. R., & Delaney, H. D. (1982). The mnemonic keyword method. *Review of Educational Research, 52,* 61–92.

Pressley, M., Levin, J. R., & McCormick, C. B. (1980). Young children's learning of foreign language vocabulary: A sentence variation of the keyword method. *Contemporary Educational Psychology, 5,* 22–29.

Pressley, M., Levin, J. R., & McDaniel, M. A. (1987). Remembering versus inferring what a word means: Mnemonic and contextual approaches. In M. McGeown & M. E. Curtis (Eds.), *The nature of vocabulary acquisition* (pp. 107–127). Hillsdale, NJ: Lawrence Erlbaum Associates.

Rabinowitz, M., & Chi, M. T. H. (1987). An interactive model of strategic processing. In S. J. Ceci (Ed.), *Handbook of cognitive, social, and neuropsychological aspects of learning disabilities* (Vol. 2, pp. 83–102). Hillsdale NJ: Lawrence Erlbaum Associates.

Ravitch, D., & Finn, C. E. (1987). *What do our 17-year-olds know?* New York: Harper & Row.

Reys, R. E. (1984). Mental computation and estimation: Past, present, and future. *Elementary School Journal, 84,* 547–557.

Rinehart, S. D., Stahl, S. A., & Erickson, L. G. (1986). Some effects of summarization training on reading and studying. *Reading Research Quarterly, 21,* 422–438.

Ringel, B. A., & Springer, C. J. (1980). On knowing how well one is remembering: The persistence of strategy use during transfer. *Journal of Experimental Child Psychology, 29,* 322–333.

Schneider, W., Dumais, S. T., & Shiffrin, R. M. (1984). Automatic and control processing and attention. In R. Parasuraman & D. R. Davies (Eds.), *Varieties of attention* (pp. 1–27). Orlando, FL: Academic Press.

Schneider, W., & Pressley, M. (1989). *Memory development between 2 and 20.* New York & Berlin: Springer–Verlag.

Schumacher, E. F. (1973). *Small is beautiful: Economics as if people mattered.* London: Blood & Briggs.

Schumaker, J. B., Denton, P. H., & Deshler, D. D. (1984). *The paraphrasing strategy.* Lawrence, KS: University of Kansas. (Available by writing authors at P.O. Box 972, Lawrence, KS 66044).

Schumaker, J. B., Nolan, S. M., & Deshler, D. D. (1985). *The error monitoring strategy.* Lawrence, KS: University of Kansas. (Available by writing authors at P.O. Box 972, Lawrence, KS 66044).

Schumaker, J. B., & Sheldon, J. (1985). *The sentence writing strategy.* Lawrence, KS: University of Kansas. (Available by writing authors at P.O. Box 972, Lawrence, KS 66044).

Segal, J. W., Chipman, S. F., & Glaser, R. (Eds.). (1985). *Thinking and learning skills, Vol. 1.: Relating research to instruction.* Hillsdale, NJ: Lawrence Erlbaum Associates.

Sheldon, J., & Schumaker, J. B. (1985). *The sentence writing strategy: Student lessons volume.* Lawrence, KS: University of Kansas. (Available by writing authors at P.O. Box 972, Lawrence, KS 66044).

Short, E. J., & Ryan, E. B. (1984). Metacognitive differences between skilled and less-skilled readers: Remediating deficits through story grammar training. *Journal of Educational Psychology, 76,* 225–235.

Spilich, G. J., Vesonder, G. T., Chiesi, H. L., & Voss, J. F. (1979). Text processing of domain-related information for individuals with high and low domain knowledge. *Journal of Verbal Learning and Verbal Behavior, 18,* 275–290.

Taylor, B. M. (1982). Text structure and children's comprehension and memory for expository material. *Journal of Educational Psychology, 74,* 323–340.

Taylor, B. M., & Beach, R. W. (1984). The effects of text structure instruction on middle-grade students' comprehension and production of expository text. *Reading Research Quarterly, 19*, 134–146.

Tierney, R. J., Readence, J. E., & Dishner, E. K. (1985). *Reading strategies and practices: Guide for improving instruction* (2nd ed.). Boston: Allyn & Bacon.

van Dijk, T. A., & Kintsch, W. (1983). *Strategies of discourse comprehension.* New York: Academic Press.

White, R. W. (1959). Motivation reconsidered: The concept of competence. *Psychological Review, 66*, 297–333.

Wilson, B. A. (1987). *Rehabilitation of memory.* New York: Guilford Press.

7

Problem-solving Strategies and Academic Performance in Learning-disabled Students: Do Subtypes Exist?

Lynn Meltzer
Institute for Learning and Development, and
Tufts University, and
Harvard University Graduate School of Education

Learning-disabled students do not exhibit single areas of deficit, rather, they are characterized by multiple combinations of subtle weaknesses in different areas. Variability in learning-disability symptoms is affected by the complex interactions of individual characteristics (cognitive status, knowledge base, motivational level) with environmental influences (curriculum complexity, academic content, teaching style). This heterogeneous array of characteristics in the learning-disabled population can be better understood when examined in the context of problem solving and metacognitive strategies. Recent research indicates that learning-disabled students frequently use different processing routes and mental patterns, their metacognitive processes operate differently, and they often display inefficient and inflexible strategies for problem solving and learning (Meltzer, Solomon, Fenton, & Levine, 1989; Swanson, 1988,1989; Torgesen, 1978; Wong, 1986). Problem solving and metacognition can provide integrating themes which enhance our understanding of the heterogeneity of learning disabilities. Characterization of the multiple profiles of learning-disabled students and the eventual delineation of definitive subtypes may depend on the success with which researchers can integrate studies of problem solving and metacognition with studies of discrete processes (e.g., language, memory, perception, attention). Accurate descriptions of these interconnections will help clarify and explain the changes in students' symptomatology during different developmental stages as well as varying phases in the academic curriculum. Whether we label these various forms of learning disabilities as subtypes, subgroups, or profiles, seems less important than identification of the multiplicity of performance patterns in this population.

This chapter addresses the roles of problem solving and metacognitive strategies in shaping the learning profiles and academic performance of learning-disabled students. The term "metacognition" is used throughout the chapter to refer to the individual's awareness and knowledge of his or her own learning processes. The term "problem solving" denotes the behaviors or thought processes that are directed toward the performance of some specific, intellectually demanding task (Nickerson, Perkins, & Smith, 1985). The term "strategy" refers to the processes that facilitate performance and help students to learn (Pressley et al., 1988).

The chapter is divided into three major sections. The first section provides a context for the discussion by summarizing the current research on problem solving and metscognitive strategies in learning-disabled students. The second section addresses the interactions among problem solving and academic performance as they are reflected in different learning-disability profiles. The third section focuses on the implications of different problem solving and educational profiles for the assessment and teaching of learning-disabled students. Throughout, the chapter emphasizes the important roles of problem solving and metacognition in the delineation of meaningful subtypes. A number of questions will be addressed: (1) What is the relevance of problem solving for academic learning in learning-disabled students? (2) Are problem-solving and metacognitive deficits reflected in weaknesses in different academic domains, such as reading and math? (3) What are the implications of the problem-solving perspective for the assessment and teaching of learning-disabled students?

PROBLEM-SOLVING AND METACOGNITIVE STRATEGIES IN LEARNING-DISABLED STUDENTS

Students with learning disabilities represent a unique and fascinating population for investigation as they display major deficits in achievement despite average to above-average intelligence. A broad spectrum of symptoms characterizes this population. At one end, a link between learning disabilities and juvenile delinquency has been documented (Berman, 1974; Meltzer, Levine, Karniski, Palfrey, & Clarke, 1984; Poremba, 1975; Spreen, 1981). At the other end of the continuum, we are identifying more intellectually gifted students who nevertheless experience significant difficulty with reading and writing skills (Fox, Brody, & Tobin, 1983; Yewchuk, 1984,1986). Despite their scattered and spiked profiles, identification of learning-disabled students for research and instruction is often based on their most obvious deficits in the behavioral and learning realms. These deficits often eclipse the many strengths and talents that allow these students to succeed through reliance on compensatory strategies and bypass techniques.

One factor that has contributed to the deficit model of learning disabilities has been the emphasis on processes such as language, perception, and motor output, with less attention devoted to the role of metacognition and strategy use. In recent years, however, the field of learning disabilities has been increasingly influenced by research on normal achievers which has documented the importance of problem-solving, metacognition, and organizational strategies for spontaneous, independent learning (Brown, 1978; Brown, Bransford, Ferrara, & Campione, 1983; Brown & Campione, 1986; Pressley, Goodchild, Fleet, Zajchowski, & Evans, 1989; Torgesen, 1977; Wong, 1987). In 1986, Bernice Wong pointed out in a review article that metacognition had begun to exert a major impact on special education, primarily in the domains of research and theory. This influence is reflected in the currently popular view that learning-disabled students display inefficient strategies for approaching the complexities of academic tasks and therefore cannot perform at the level of which they are intellectually capable (Swanson, 1989).

How do these problem solving and metacognitive difficulties manifest in learning-disabled students? In his seminal work, Torgesen (1975, 1977, 1978) originally coined the term "maladaptive learners" to describe the ineffective and inefficient strategies that learning-disabled students apply in the school setting. More recently, Swanson (1989) has suggested that learning-disabled students should be viewed as "actively inefficient learners," rather than strategically inactive learners. In other words, learning-disabled students develop strategic thought patterns actively, albeit inefficiently because of the difficulties they experience with the flexible application of strategies. Swanson suggests that learning-disabled students do not process the organizational features of information in the same manner as normal achievers. Their metacognitive processes may operate differently and they use different mental patterns and processing routes (Swanson, 1989). Learning-disabled students are frequently unaware of the usefulness of specific strategies for solving particular tasks and they often display limited flexibility and inefficiency in accessing information at the appropriate times (Meltzer, 1984; Meltzer, et al., 1989). These students often have difficulty planning and regulating the effective use of their own cognitive resources in the same manner as "normal" children (Swanson, 1987, 1989).

The concept of the learning-disabled student as an inefficient learner suggests that the student often lacks specific strategies, has difficulty accessing the appropriate strategies, and does not apply adequate self-monitoring techniques. Research over the past few years indicates that learning-disabled children experience difficulty with self-regulatory mechanisms such as checking, planning, monitoring, and revising during learning or problem solving situations (Brown & Palincsar, 1982; Duffy, et al., 1986; Pressley & Levin, 1987; Short & Ryan, 1984; Swanson, 1989). Many of these students exhibit difficulties with the coordination and integration needed for the processing of complex, meaningful information (Hallahan & Bryan, 1981; Torgesen, 1982; review by Stone & Michals, 1986; Swanson, 1985, 1988, 1989). They also perform poorly on tasks that require the use of general strategies for solving problems (see review in Pressley & Levin, 1987). These students do not make efficient use of feedback concerning the relevance of their choices (Dykman, Ackerman, & Oglesby, 1979); for instance, they frequently do not correct spelling errors, even when they know they are wrong (Gerber & Hall, 1980, 1981). Finally, they often struggle to explain their solutions to specific tasks.

Recently, Borkowski, Estrada, Milstead, and Hale (1989) have proposed a metacognitive model that is relevant for the understanding of general problem-solving deficits in learning-disabled students. They note that their model is particularly applicable to children at the lower end of the average range of intelligence, who display general learning impairments across multiple domains such as comprehension, memorization, math, and general problem solving. Although this chapter concerns learning-disabled students with specific learning difficulties, many aspects of Borkowski's model are nevertheless relevant for conceptualizing the metacognitive deficits of these students. Their model emphasizes two components: executive processes and attributional beliefs. Borkowski et al. argue that learning-disabled students lack the higher-order executive processes needed to integrate information and to learn appropriately in novel situations. Learning-disabled students benefit from explicit training before they use executive processes to analyze task demands, monitor the effectiveness of strategy use, judge when a problem has been adequately solved, and develop a strong belief about the value of a specific strategy. Borkowski and his colleagues emphasize that maintenance and transfer of newly acquired strategies requires the presence of higher order executive processes (e.g., strategy selection and monitoring) as well as attributional beliefs about the critical importance of a specific strategy for learning. Strategy generalization will not occur until higher-order executive processes are addressed so that students can develop an awareness of the importance of using specific strategies and monitoring their own performance. In summary, their model emphasizes the critical interactions of metacognition and strategic processing as fundamental components of problem solving skills in learning-disabled students.

As regards other more specific studies of problem solving processes, findings have indicated a number of recurring themes (see review by Stone & Michals, 1986). Problem solving difficulties in learning-disabled students often manifest in different forms, depending on the presence of weaknesses in processing areas such as language, memory, visual-spatial ability, and conceptual reasoning (Stone, 1981; review by Stone & Michals, 1986). Investigators have identified qualitatively different approaches to concept learning tasks as well as discrepancies in the accuracy with which learning-disabled students learn. Studies of concept learning in learning-disabled students have used tasks ranging from object sorting and concept attainment to more complex hypothesis testing. Findings indicate that these students struggle to identify critical attributes in tasks and are inefficient in their use of feedback (Stone & Michals, 1986). Learning-disabled students also experience difficulty with problem solving in relation to academic content. Other studies have indicated that learning-disabled students fail to use the available information to solve problems (Gerber & Hall, 1981), they do not reason logically with the information provided (Kavale, 1980), and they frequently attend to extraneous information (Lee & Hudson, 1981). Studies of problem solving from a Piagetian perspective suggest that many of these students experience difficulties with Piagetian tasks and that difficulties vary as a function of the type of learning disability (Stone & Michals, 1986). Some learning-disabled children do not generate new information systematically in problem solving situations that require flexibility and they also do not make good use of the data they generate to develop or revise their explanations (Stone & Michals, 1986).

Other investigators have demonstrated that learning-disabled students often fail to plan systematically (Copeland & Weissbrod, 1983), they have difficulty identifying salient task features in different situations, and they frequently focus on isolated details rather than relying on the organization inherent in the context to create a plan of action (Copeland & Weissbrod, 1983; Levin, 1981). They also struggle to identify the critical attributes in a situation and may attend to irrelevant features (Harris, 1980). Deficiencies in the spontaneous application of problem solving and self-regulatory strategies have also been identified in these students, particularly when learning and social situations are unstructured (Borkowski & Kurtz, 1984; Hallanan & Kneedler, 1979; Torgesen, 1978; Torgesen & Licht, 1983).

To conclude this subsection, the caution suggested by Stone and Michals must be heeded: "It may be tempting, and in certain cases, appropriate, to reduce instances of poor problem solving to an underlying deficit such as auditory memory span or selective attention, but such efforts may distort the nature of some problems" (1986).

What other factors influence the efficiency with which learning-disabled students apply problem solving and metacognitive strategies in the learning situation? Three major influences are to be discussed: cognitive-motivational processes, automaticity, and problems coordinating multiple subskills and processes.

Processes such as language, perception, memory, and attention, are not detailed here as their impact on learning disabilities has been well documented in the literature (McKinney & Feagans, 1983; Swanson, 1987; Torgesen & Wong, 1986). An assumption underlying the current discussion is that weaknesses in problem solving and metacognitive strategies often interact with and contribute to the manifestation of deficits in language, memory, and attention.

Cognitive-Motivational Processes

One perspective that is currently gaining support emphasizes the role of motivation in strategy use (Pressley et al., 1988) and the cumulative influence of constant school failure (Licht, 1983; Torgesen & Licht, 1983). Failure experiences in school can lead students to believe that they do not have the ability to overcome their difficulties, which results in the development of learned helplessness. Evidence from research based on a number of cognitive-motivational perspectives, such as locus of control, learned helplessness, attribution theory, and self-efficacy theory, suggests that children's beliefs about their abilities can affect their achievement (Licht, 1983). Children who believe that their difficulties are caused by insufficient ability and factors beyond their control are likely to show reduced effort, to use less active problem solving strategies, and to avoid challenging tasks (Licht, 1983). In contrast, children who attribute their failure to controllable factors such as insufficient effort, usually maintain their effort and problem solving strategies in the face of failure and may even be challenged by the failure experience to use more sophisticated strategies (Diener & Dweck, 1978,1980; Dweck & Bush, 1976).

As we attempt to understand and more accurately describe the heterogeneity of learning disabilities, it becomes increasingly important to incorporate these cognitive-motivational processes into our investigations. This critical dimension of performance can enhance our understanding of students with diverse learning profiles.

Automaticity

Tasks such as reading, writing, and spelling are generally dependent on higher-order cognitive processes as well as automatic and rapid application of subskills. The difficulties experienced by learning-disabled students span a broad continuum ranging from conscious, effortful, strategic processing to automatic processing that occurs without effort or awareness (Swanson, 1989). One school of thought has attributed reading problems, in large part, to a lack of automaticity in naming and language skills (Denckla & Rudel, 1976; Doehring, 1976; Perfetti & Roth, 1981; Wolf, 1 986).The assumption underlying the automaticity literature is that when basic level reading and math concepts (such as letter and number identification) require too much time to process, insufficient processing time can be allocated to the more complex cognitive components of reading comprehension (La Berge &

Samuels, 1974; Wolf, 1984) or math problem solving (Garnett & Fleischner, 1983; Roditi, 1988). Recent research indicates an interaction between automaticity and strategy use so that children may often avoid using strategies that require a large expenditure of effort (Pressley, Borkowski, & Schneider, 1987). Pressley, Cariglia–Bull, and Snyder (1984) note that most research to date has been devoted to the controlled deployment of strategies even though many aspects of strategy use are automatized through frequent practice. They suggest that possible determinants of good strategy use include individual differences in attentional capacity and the facility for using available attentional resources to automatize relevant processes. Although this evidence reveals that deficits in processing speed and automaticity exert a disruptive influence on reading and math, we do not yet know how automaticity interacts with problem solving to affect academic achievement at different developmental levels.

Problems with Coordination
of Multiple Subskills and Processes

What about the interactions among these different processes? Recent research suggests that a major characteristic of learning disabilities relates to the struggle these students experience when they are required to coordinate the multiple subskills necessary for effective learning (Swanson, 1988, 1989). Learning-disabled children have difficulty accessing. organizing and coordinating incoming information that involves mental operations. They also experience difficulty with self-regulatory processes and tasks that require general control processes. Deficiencies in coordinating cognitive processes such as perception, memory, language and attention with other critical subskills involved in reading and writing reduce the effectiveness with which learning-disabled students can use active learning strategies. These weaknesses in coordination may also influence the efficiency and accuracy of their problem solving and learning. To quote Swanson

> It may also be argued that a learning disability may be related primarily to efficient regulation or coordination of mental processes rather than a specific type of processing deficiency per se. That is, specific processing deficiencies have shifted in their importance as accounting for learning disabilities, and higher order processes have become a focus of etiology, as well as intervention. (1989, p. 4)

In summary, it is clear that we need more research to determine how problem solving and metacognitive strategies interact with language, memory, perception, and attention to affect academic performance in learning-disabled students. It is particularly critical that we gain a better understanding of the influence of these cognitive processes on performance at various age levels and in different academic domains (e.g., reading, writing, and math). Once we obtain such baseline data, we can extend these multivariate studies to determine whether problem solving effectiveness varies as a function of subgroup membership.

IMPLICATIONS FOR ASSESSMENT

The findings of subtype and profile studies highlight the importance of developing a broader range of measures to identify the complex and multidimensional profiles of learning-disabled students. At this time, it is necessary to supplement and begin to replace the traditional, product-oriented measures of learning disabilities (e.g., IQ tests and standardized achievement tests) with process-oriented techniques which evaluate the processes and strategies which students apply to different tasks. Assessment techniques are needed which are geared not only toward identification of students' performance levels but also provide information about the processes used by students to reach specific solutions as well as the error patterns which characterize their performance (Campione, 1989; Feuerstein, Rand, Hoffman, & Miller, 1980; Feuerstein, Miller, & Jensen, 1981). These procedures need to incorporate a model with a multidimensional view of learning disabilities so that we can improve our methods of detecting the broad spectrum of learning deficits and strengths which characterize these children. Process-oriented assessment systems are critical for identifying students' learning profiles as well as the range of strategies they use to approach different learning situations. This information can provide valuable insights about students' learning disabilities as well as their strengths and compensatory strategies.

To begin to address these issues, a process-oriented identification procedure, the Surveys of Problem-Solving and Educational Skills (SPES), has been developed (Meltzer, 1984, 1987, Meltzer, et al., 1989). This procedure is derived from a specific problem solving paradigm (see Fig. 7.1), which is based on the metacognitive and problem-solving research discussed herein. The SPES also builds on recent theoretical work that suggests alternative models of intelligence (Gardner, 1983; Sternberg, 1981,1984) as well as clinical approaches that stress the importance of evaluating each child's learning potential (Feuerstein, et al., 1980; Feuerstein, et al., 1981). There is an emphasis on the close connections among problem solving strategies and educational performance.

The components of the SPES model focus on the major features of strategy selection that are essential for learning: efficiency, flexibility, methods, styles, and the ability to justify the solutions provided. These are detailed elsewhere (Meltzer, 1987; Meltzer, et al., 1989) and will be summarized briefly. There

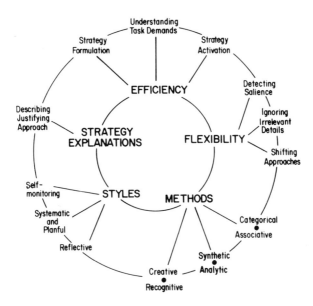

FIG. 7.1 Problem-solving strategies and learning difficulties: A paradigm. From Meltzer, L. J. (1987). Examiner's manual, *Surveys of
Problem-solving and Educational Skills (SPES)*. Cambridge, MA: Educators Publishing Service, Inc. Reprinted with permission.

is an emphasis on the efficiency with which students select strategies and
spontaneously structure tasks, processes which underlie effective planning,
self-monitoring, and organization. An important feature of the model relates
to the flexibility with which students problem solve, the manner in which they
shift among strategies, and the extent to which they can ignore irrelevant
details in order to categorize information. In summary, the SPES paradigm
incorporates critical strategy components and emphasizes the importance of
systematic observations of the learning strategies and processes used by
students in different situations.

   Based on this paradigm, the tasks incorporated in the SPES evaluate the
connections among problem-solving strategies, learning processes, and educational outcomes (Meltzer, 1987; Meltzer, Roditi, & Fenton, 1986). The
problem-solving and educational tasks derived from this model therefore
emphasize students' understanding of task instructions, their ease in formu-
lating strategies, their ability to identify salient details, and the flexibility with
which they shift problem-solving approaches. Students' methods and styles

of reasoning are assessed in conjunction with their ability to justify and explain their solutions. A systematic rating system guides the assessment procedure and is used to generate educational recommendations through analysis of individual performance profiles and error patterns. The functional profiles that are constructed can be matched with remedial and teaching techniques. These functional profiles represent different performance patterns and may, in fact, be associated with different learning disability subtypes.

PROBLEM SOLVING AND ACADEMIC PERFORMANCE

What are the impacts of problem-solving and metacognitive strategies on academic performance in different domains such as reading and mathematics? To date, a large proportion of the research has focused on the relationship between metacognition and reading comprehension (Brown, 1981; Palincsar & Brown, 1984; Wong, 1987), with less attention devoted to exploring the metacognitive components of math performance (Goldman, 1989). Findings are that learning-disabled students possess limited knowledge about effective reading strategies (Baker & Brown, 1984; Wong, 1987). In addition, they rarely use active strategies, such as identifying the main idea, ignoring irrelevant details, or asking questions as they read (Brown & Palincsar, 1982; Palincsar & Brown, 1984). Studies indicate that some poor readers believe that the main idea is the first idea in a paragraph, that summarizing a story means telling everything one can remember, and that skimming means reading little words as quickly as possible (Paris & Jacobs, 1984; Winograd, 1984). Further, as is emphasized by Paris and Oka (1989), there is little direct classroom instruction which specifically addresses reading strategies and explains the relevance and usefulness of these strategies. Although there have been fewer studies of math performance in learning-disabled students, the link with problem solving has been more specifically addressed (Polya, 1975; Garofalo & Lester, 1985). Garofalo and Lester describe four categories of activities involved in math-problem solving: orientation, organization, execution, and verification. Goldman (1989) conceptualizes math performance as a problem solving situation consisting of cognitive and metacognitive processes associated with representing the problem, planning a solution, carrying out the operations specified by the plan, and monitoring the course of the solution. Investigations of math performance in learning-disabled students have shown that these students experience significant difficulty with effective execution of math operations (Garnett & Fleischner, 1983; Russell & Ginsburg, 1984). Goldman notes that effective math instruction requires the teaching of problem representation and conceptual understanding of the task, task-specific planning and computational skills, and a framework for systematic monitoring of solutions.

Based on the findings summarized here, my colleagues and I have focused our research on determining whether discrete combinations of problem-solving strategies are associated with different academic outcomes, namely, reading and math (Meltzer & Fenton, 1989; Meltzer, Solomon, & Fenton, 1987; Meltzer et al., 1989). We were particularly interested in contrasting the profiles of students with and without learning disabilities on the basis of a process approach such as that incorporated in the SPES. In a number of studies over the past 5 years, we also studied the interactions of problem-solving strategies and automaticity and their effects on academic performance. The next section briefly summarizes the results of two selected studies and examines the implications for different learning disability subtypes. It should be noted that both studies used the same subjects and tasks.

Sample

The sample consisted of 626 students, 9 to 14 year olds of average intelligence from middle-class communities. The normally achieving group comprised 342 randomly selected competent learners. The learning-disabled group consisted of 284 students who were selected if they were enrolled in a special education program of a 502.2 prototype or above or if they met two or more of six criteria for learning disabilities. These broad selection criteria were used to sample the heterogeneous population of learning disabilities. All students were subdivided among three age-groups: 9–10-year-olds, 11–12-year-olds, and 13–14-year-olds.

Materials

Six process based problem-solving tasks were used from the SPES. These were designed in accordance with the problem solving paradigm (Meltzer, 1986) described above (see Fig. 7.1). These tasks are summarized in Table 7.1.

These six process-based problem-solving tasks were criterion-referenced and were developed to provide diagnostically useful information about the processes as well as the content of learning (Meltzer, 1984; Meltzer, Fenton, & Solomon, 1984; Meltzer, et al., 1986). Three of the six tasks emphasized primarily verbal, linguistic reasoning and three tasks stressed nonverbal, nonlinguistic reasoning. A number of tasks required explanations and questions were structured to elicit specific verbal categories. As is evident from Table 7.1, the six tasks included measures of categorization, concept formation, pattern analysis, flexibility in shifting strategies, and sequential reasoning. The tasks focused on two major areas: children's ability to provide

TABLE 7.1
Description of the Six Problem-solving Tasks

Task	Description	Focus
Nonlinguistic Tasks		
Series Completion (Pattern Analysis and Memory)	Series of geometrical patterns that change according to a specific rule. Students complete the series by selecting the correct solution from a multiple-choice array.	Measures the ability to identify salient features of the task and to ignore irrelevant details.
Categorization (Conceptual/Thematic Flexibility)	Five geometrical patterns, from which students must identify the three patterns that share the most common features. The two excluded items share some similar features but differ in other respects.	Assesses the ability to organize nonverbal information and to recognize that some patterns can belong to multiple categories.
Matrix Completion (Pattern Analysis and Memory)	Matrix format with complexity of items increasing by steps through the addition of visual details.	Measures spatial organization, attention to salient details, and pattern analysis.
Linguistic/Verbal Tasks		
Category Shift (Conceptual/Thematic Flexibility)	Four pictures or words that can be sorted in two different ways. A superordinate and an associative category are derived. Explanations are required.	Measures the ability to shift flexibly from one strategy to another. Identifies the student's awareness of the strategy used and his or her explanation of the answer.
Sequential Reasoning (Pattern Analysis and Memory)	Rote sequences that must be completed (e.g., numbers, letters, days of the week, months of the year). These rote sequences are often problematic for students with learning difficulties because of deficits in automaticity.	Measures automatic memory for sequences, working memory, and inferential reasoning.
Classification (Conceptual/Thematic Flexibility)	Word pairs that must be categorized.	Assesses categorization and verbal abstraction.

From Meltzer, L. J. (1987). Examiner's manual, *Surveys of Problem-solving and Educational Skills (SPES)*. Cambridge, MA: Educators Publishing Service, Inc. Reprinted with permission.

correct solutions to specific problems, and ability to reflect on the strategies they had used and to explain their judgments.

In the first study, we investigated the links among specific problem-solving profiles and various educational outcomes in children with and without learning disabilities (Meltzer, et al., 1987). We were particularly interested in determining whether different clusters of strategy and problem-solving weaknesses were associated with discrete educational outcomes in two academic domains: reading and mathematics. It could be hypothesized that discrepant problem-solving and academic profiles would provide information relevant to different learning-disability subgroups. The findings and conclusions are detailed elsewhere (Meltzer, et al., 1987) and are summarized herein.

Findings indicated differences in the constellations of problem-solving variables that predicted reading and math in the learning-disability (LD) group and the group of normal achievers (NA). These differences were directly related to the specific measure that was used to assess reading comprehension. When the LD group was compared with the NA group, a similar constellation of problem-solving tasks predicted oral formulation of reading material. In contrast, different profiles characterized the two groups when structured questions were used to measure reading comprehension. When reading comprehension was assessed on the basis of the student's oral retelling of the reading passage, cognitive flexibility, as measured on the Category Shift explanation task, exerted the most important influence. Findings indicated that oral formulation of reading material in LD and NA students was influenced by the same combination of processes, namely, flexible strategy use, verbal reasoning, pattern analysis, and working memory. In contrast, when reading comprehension was assessed on the basis of structured questions, LD and NA students displayed different profiles.

When the different measures of reading comprehension were compared within the two groups, interesting differences emerged. In the NAs, the same combination of problem-solving tasks predicted reading comprehension regardless of whether structured questions or oral retell were used. In contrast, in the LD group, the order of relative importance of the problem-solving tasks differed according to the specific measure of reading comprehension. These findings indicated that LD students relied on different problem-solving strategies to derive meaning from text and to memorize reading material, depending on the method used to assess their comprehension. Reading comprehension questions provided external structure whereas oral retell methods required students to impose their own structure on the material. In summary, LD students performed differently, depending on which measure of reading comprehension was used. In contrast, NA relied on similar processes to comprehend text regardless of the amount of external structure provided by the specific measure of reading comprehension. It can therefore be concluded that findings regarding the reading comprehension of LD students cannot be generalized without detailed task analysis of the demands of the specific reading comprehension measures.

In the math area, interesting differences characterized the LD and NA groups in terms of the constellation of problem-solving tasks which predicted performance. In the LD group, cognitive flexibility and spatial reasoning were critical predictors of academic performance. In contrast, in the NA group, cognitive flexibility assumed a less important role and sequential reasoning was the most critical predictor of math performance. Findings suggested that NAs relied more extensively on their store of knowledge, memorization, and verbal reasoning ability for successful math performance. In contrast, students with LD relied on cognitive flexibility and spatial organization, possibly to overcome weaknesses in memory for basic math facts.

In a second study, we added several measures of automaticity to the problem-solving tasks and examined their interactions and effects on reading and mathematics achievement in LD and NA students. We were particularly interested in investigating the similarities and differences in learning profiles which characterized students at different age levels and in different groups. Results from this study are detailed elsewhere (Meltzer, Fenton, Ogonowski, & Malkus, 1988) and are summarized herein.

Different combinations of variables were associated with reading comprehension in the LD and NA groups although there was some overlap. When reading was the outcome, the automaticity measure contributed the highest amount of variance to the regression equation for the LD students (Beta = .37) but was less important for the NA students (Beta = .15). Other group differences related to the types of problem-solving tasks which predicted reading, with measures of pattern analysis playing a predominant role for the LD students and measures of categorization and cognitive flexibility more critical for the NAs.

Math ability in LD and NA students was predicted by a similar combination of variables, with automaticity most significant. Findings suggested that addition of the automaticity measures to the equations significantly affected the relative importance for reading and math of different problem-solving measures. Once again, results highlighted the complexity of the relationships among problem-solving and academic performance.

An interesting developmental pattern emerged when students in three age-groups (9–10, 11–12, and 13–14) were compared. The profiles of each age-group differed with respect to the relative importance of the various measures of pattern analysis, cognitive flexibility, and categorization. The specific regression analysis results are not detailed here, rather, the findings are summarized briefly. In the LD group, comparison of the 9–10- and 11–12-year-old students indicated that automatic use of sight vocabulary was the most important predictor of reading comprehension. Cognitive flexibility and pattern analysis strategies were next in importance. By 13–14, reading comprehension in these LD students was more dependent on cognitive flexibility and abstract reasoning.

Such a clear developmental trend was not evident in the normal achievers where automaticity and problem solving interacted differently to predict reading comprehension for the three age-groups. Automatic sight vocabulary did not predict reading comprehension even for the 9–10-year-olds, as these students had already acquired automaticity in sight vocabulary. Instead, problem-solving processes constituted critical predictors of reading comprehension in all the NA age groups.

In the math domain, a very different developmental trend was evident. In the LD group, pattern analysis strategies were more critical predictors of math performance in the 9–10- and 11–12-year-olds. The 13–14-year-old LD students relied on the automatic recall of math facts to a much greater extent than the younger students, possibly because they had only recently acquired automaticity. In the NAs, math automaticity was of primary importance in all three age-groups.

These findings highlight the complexity of the interactions among the cognitive variables which underlie academic performance and suggest a number of major themes: First, automaticity, cognitive flexibility, and sequential reasoning influence performance differently in two academic domains, reading and math. Second, the manner in which automaticity interacts with problem-solving skills differs according to the area of academic achievement that is involved, the age-level of the child, and membership in a LD or NA group. Different profiles characterize LD and NA students at each of these age-levels for both reading and math, a result which emphasizes the importance of fine-tuning our subtype analyses even further.

IMPLICATIONS FOR TEACHING

As cognitive and metacognitive research have begun to filter into clinical and teaching areas, there has been a gradual shift away from attempts to diagnose students according to supposedly discrete diagnostic subgroups which may actually overlap. Practitioners are beginning to recognize the importance of identifying students' profiles of strengths and weaknesses and are conceptualizing cognitive processes as modifiable and susceptible to instruction. Remediation is now beginning to target students' individual learning profiles and strategy instruction is becoming more widespread. Teaching techniques for LD students increasingly emphasize modification of executive and self-regulatory processes and methods of training students to self-monitor. There is also greater recognition of the importance of linking strategy instruction with particular content domains, as has been advocated by Reid (1988), Schumaker and Deshler (1988), and Campione (1989).

As research results in a better understanding of LD subtypes, our teaching and treatment techniques will hopefully become more specific. We will also improve our methods for determining which teaching techniques are effective for which subgroups of learning disabled students. As we link identified subtypes with specific teaching methods, we must exercise caution so that we do not overinterpret findings or become rigid in our attempts to categorize students.

Specific methods of cognitive training which are directly relevant for the treatment and teaching of LD students, are summarized briefly herein. I have selected three different approaches, which are exemplified in the work of Vygotsky (1962, 1978), Feuerstein et al. (1980, 1981), and Deshler and Schumaker (1986). These encapsulate many issues of relevance for the teaching of problem-solving and metacognitive strategies. The relationship with learning disability subtype research will be discussed in the context of the profile approach elaborated previously.

The Influence of Adult–Child Interactions on Problem Solving and Learning

Recently, it has been suggested that some strategy deficiencies may occur as a consequence of impoverished adult–child interactions in the home and school settings (Stone, 1989; Stone & Wertsch, 1984). Stone and Wertsch also note that a better understanding of these adult–child interactions can yield important insights about the successes or failures of specific remedial and teaching situations (Stone, 1989). The critical role of parents and teachers in fostering psychological development and learning was originally proposed by the Soviet psychologist, Vygotsky (1962, 1978). Vygotsky's "zone of proximal development" conceptualizes newly developing skills as occurring in the context of social interactions so that parents and teachers stimulate the child to use more sophisticated approaches to tasks. Vygotsky also argued that higher cognitive activities are mediated by socially constructed symbol systems such as language.

What is the relevance of Vygotsky's approach for strategy training and remediation of problem solving in LD students? From his perspective, strategic behavior and higher psychological processes reside in the relationship between the child's development and the instruction provided by society. Students can achieve new levels of understanding of tasks or concepts through meaningful interactions with others, a process which he calls "proleptic instruction." Through the process of "scaffolding" (Palincsar, 1986; Stone, 1989; Wood, Bruner, & Ross, 1976), adults provide for children the temporary support they need to accomplish tasks that are beyond their current capabilities. Recently, Stone and Wertsch (1984) and Stone (1989) have analyzed remediation and strategy training efforts on the basis of Vygotsky's theory. They note that the frequent failure of remediation and strategy training efforts can be partly attributed to the fact that the dynamics of the remediation process have generally been ignored. These social interactions are critical as the precursors of independent strategic activity (self-regulation) occur in social interaction or other-regulation (Stone & Wertsch, 1984). The dialogue between the adult and child also embodies the strategies to be mastered by the child (Stone & Wertsch, 1984) and a better understanding of this interaction can yield important insights about the successes or failures of specific remedial and teaching situations (Stone, 1989).

Another concept that can enhance our understanding of learning disabilities is the process Vygotsky refers to as "compensation." He emphasizes that while handicaps involve certain limitations in functioning, they also stimulate the reorganization of functions into new, adaptive systems. The concept of compensation has particular relevance for students with specific LD profiles. They may use certain problem-solving strategies very effectively to overcome deficits in some domains, yet may be hampered by weaknesses in problem-solving strategies in other domains.

In summary, Vygotsky's notion of the critical interactions among adults and children has direct relevance for our understanding of the role of strategy use in the learning situation (Stone, 1989; Wertsch & Stone, 1985). Further research on these social interactions of LD students will hopefully clarify many of our fundamental questions relating to LD subtypes. As we design our subtype research studies, it is important that we begin to include procedures for assessing these adult–child interactions in conjunction with other process variables.

The Concept of Learning Potential

Teaching programs for enhancing cognitive and problem-solving strategies have been the subject of considerable controversy over the years and the validity of training cognitive processes has frequently been questioned (Mann, 1979). Many programs have been recently developed to teach thinking skills in the classroom context; however, these are diverse and often share very little in common (see Nickerson, et al., 1985, for a review). These programs differ in their theoretical orientation, scope, age level of subject population, type of instruction, and program length (Nickerson et al., 1985) so that it is often difficult to categorize them meaningfully.

One of the best-known training systems is the Instrumental Enrichment program of Feuerstein (Feuerstein, et al., 1981; Feuerstein, et al., 1980). He maintains that the "learning potential" of every child can be measured and enhanced. Instrumental Enrichment is based on the principle that intelligence is a set of changeable processes rather than fixed products. The underlying tenet of the program is that the purpose of assessment is to determine the extent to which a student's characteristics can be modified. Assessment of learning potential consists of actively instructing and teaching a child in the course of an evaluation to determine his or her responsiveness in the learning situation. Like Vygotsky, Feuerstein emphasizes the transmission of information through another individual, a process which he refers to as a "mediated learning experience." The Instrumental Enrichment program uses "content free" materials to help students develop reflective, insightful thinking in order to acquire the specific concepts, operations, and relationships necessary to perform certain cognitive tasks. The emphasis of the program is on "metalearning habits" and "learning how to learn" (Nickerson, et al., 1985).

Feuerstein's approach has direct relevance for the conceptualization of LD in terms of distinct subgroups of students who may profit from different forms of teaching. Linkages between subtype research and cognitive training approaches such as Feuerstein's could be extremely important for enhancing our understanding of LD from a theoretical and applied perspective.

Strategy Training Approaches

Over the past few years, strategy training programs have become more widespread as cognitive and metacognitive research findings have exerted their influence on educational practice. Over time, it has become increasingly clear that strategy training programs are not helpful for all LD students and that we need to identify the particular subgroups for whom such training is effective (DeBettencourt, 1987). The specificity of these programs has also revealed the importance of differentiating strategy training techniques that address particular processes such as metacognition, memory, and selective attention.

This section includes a brief discussion of Deshler's strategy training approach, which is currently one of the most widely used programs (Deshler & Schumaker, 1986; Deshler, Warner, Schumaker, & Alley, 1983). The Strategies Intervention Model developed by Deshler and his associates is designed to teach students how to learn more efficiently and how to apply these strategies to the secondary school curriculum by establishing goals, selecting techniques for meeting these goals, and monitoring their own progress (Lenz, 1989; Mayer, 1987). This strategy training approach incorporates planned opportunities for students to involve themselves in the instructional process and to discover ways in which the strategy can be helpful to their learning (Lenz, 1989). Each strategy intervention does not consist of a single strategy but instead incorporates several cognitive and metacognitive strategies arranged in a manner that facilitates task completion. The stepwise process involved in strategy instruction involves the following (Alley & Deshler, 1979; Schumaker, Deshler, Alley, Warner, & Denton, 1982; see Lenz, 1989): (a) test the student to determine his or her current learning habits, (b) describe the learning strategy, (c) model the strategy, (d) verbally rehearse the strategy, (e) practice on controlled materials, (f) provide feedback, (g) posttest.

An example of such a strategy system is the Paraphrasing strategy described by Ellis, Lenz, and Clark (1989). Here, the student is taught the mnemonic word "rap," where R = Read a paragraph, A = Ask yourself, "What were the main ideas and details in the paragraph?", P = Put the main idea and details in your own words. These steps cue the student to use the cognitive strategy of self-questioning, to organize the information and ask what is important and unimportant, and to transform and elaborate on the information that was read by describing the paragraph in his or her own words. These dimensions emphasize full participation by the student in the instructional process and require the student to use metacognitive strategies during the learning process (e.g., self-questioning, self-evaluation, goal setting, reviewing, and self-monitoring).

Advocates of strategy training emphasize the importance of characteristics and variables that are both internal and external to the individual. In fact, strategy intervention can only become effective when the entire teaching environment is modified to promote, model, and guide appropriate and efficient performance across all settings (Lenz, 1989; Nickerson, et al., 1985). Modification of the environment is therefore becoming a key factor in strategy training and teaching programs. Further research will help us determine whether specific strategy training programs are effective only for particular subgroups of students and will begin to explain possible selective effects. It is important that these studies incorporate variables which account for student characteristics in conjunction with critical features of the teaching environment. Although these variables add complexity to the design of our studies, they can ensure that findings are more holistic and provide an integrated perspective for addressing LD.

LINKING ASSESSMENT AND TEACHING

Effective instruction requires ongoing informal assessment of students' learning styles and evaluation of their responsiveness to different teaching techniques. The continuous spiral which connects process-oriented assessment with teaching is a fundamental principle of the Assessment for Teaching model (AFT; Meltzer & Roditi, 1989). Within the boundaries of this model, assessment always occurs in the context of teaching and has direct relevance for teaching. Teaching techniques are re-evaluated continually, resulting in refinements of the assessment process and modifications of teaching techniques. The AFT model emphasizes teacher involvement in the assessment process and the important roles teachers play as they develop profiles of students' strengths and weaknesses. Teachers refine their observations, become more proficient with error analysis, and link their observations of students' strategy use with performance on specific academic tasks such as reading, written language, and mathematics. These learning profiles are used prescriptively to tailor educational programming for the child. In doing so, teachers are conducting on-line assessment for the purposes of teaching, a basic principle of the AFT model.

The critical link between classroom-based assessment and instructional planning is also the kingpin of Zigmond and Miller's approach (1986). Their system provides information about each students' current level of academic performance, identifies objectives for remedial programming, and documents progress. Zigmond, Vallecorsa, and Silverman (1983) propose that assessment for the purpose of developing instructional objectives helps to target teaching which then becomes more efficient and successful. There is a focus on instructional objectives from two perspectives: analysis of students' learning styles and analysis of students' responsiveness to instruction (Zigmond et al., 1983). Zigmond proposes a 12-step informal assessment procedure which uses teacher-made and curriculum embedded tests. As a result of systematic observation, task analysis, and error analysis, the teacher identifies short- and long-term objectives which are modified over time. Assessment yields data of relevance for instructional decisions within subject matter or skill domains; these are used for the purposes of instructional planning.

In summary, it is important to ensure a consistent link between assessment and teaching via the development of learning profiles for each student. These learning profiles may suggest different clusters of performance patterns which will eventually improve our understanding of learning disabilities.

CONCLUSIONS

Over the course of development, students' learning profiles frequently change and their learning disabilities may manifest in different ways as a function of the complex interactions among their specific abilities and the demands of the curriculum. In fact, a child's latent learning disability may not immediately translate into academic difficulties but may only become evident during transition points in the curriculum. At these times, there is a perturbation in the previously established equilibrium and a mismatch is provoked between the child's skills and the demands and pressures of the learning environment. New and more complex tasks are introduced which require greater coordination of skills and strategies, for example, the introduction of timed multiple-choice tests, extensive writing requirements, and book reports. These challenges are increasingly evident during the more demanding transition points in the academic curriculum, namely, first grade, fourth grade, junior high school, high school, and college. These developmental and curriculum-based changes may exert a significant impact on subtype membership. Specific students may be classified in one LD subgroup if the study occurs when they are in the first few grades in school and in a different subgroup if the study occurs when they enter high school. Selection of different time-points for subtype analyses may yield discrepant findings, depending on the variables and measures used in the study. Consequently, it is important that subtyping studies include a cross-age or longitudinal component so that students are not classified at single time-periods (McKinney, 1989; McKinney & Speece, 1986). We also need to evaluate whether students in different LD clusters respond differentially to various curriculum and teaching methods (Speece & Cooper, 1989). For instance, certain children may only be at risk for failure in classes that do not support individual styles and rates of learning. Other students may be at increased risk in classes that emphasize predominantly oral instructions and provide no practical learning experiences. LD students who have not been placed in special education may also perform differently than those who have received special education services (Speece & Cooper, 1989). Developmental studies of these different subgroups in a variety of teaching settings can provide invaluable information regarding identification and appropriate treatment of learning disabilities.

In conclusion, subtype research has provided some systematization of our knowledge base and has enhanced our understanding of the heterogeneity and multiplicity of symptoms which characterize this population (Lyon & Watson, 1981; McKinney & Feagans, 1983; Speece, 1987; Speece & Cooper, 1989). However, we need to broaden the scope of subtype research toward a multidimensional approach which includes problem-solving and metacognitive strategies as they interweave among the other learning processes. We also need to understand how the forms and severity of learning disabilities are influenced by developmental changes as well as modifications in the academic content and curriculum. Investigations such as these can provide information about the variety of ways in which these processes interconnect to yield multiple LD profiles. Such research will eventually help to narrow the gap between system-identified and research-identified LD students and to improve the specificity of identification and intervention techniques.

ACKNOWLEDGMENTS

I express my appreciation to Bethany Roditi for her consistent support and excellent suggestions throughout the preparation of this manuscript. I would also like to thank Anita Brush for her valuable comments about earlier drafts of this chapter. Finally, thanks to Matt Goodman, Lisa Guarneri, and Thelma Segal, for their help with manuscript preparation.

REFERENCES

Alley, G., & Deshler, D. (1979). *Teaching the learning-disabled adolescent: Strategies and methods.* Denver: Love.

Baker, L., & Brown, A.L. (1984). Metacognitive skills and reading. In P. D. Pearson, M. Kamil,

R. Barr, & P. Mosenthal (Eds.), *Handbook of reading research* (pp. 353–394). New York: Longman.

Berman, S. (1974). Delinquents are disabled. In B. Kratovile (Ed.), *Youth in trouble* (pp. 39–63). San Raphael, CT: Academic Therapy Publications.

Borkowski, J. G., Estrada, M. T., Milstead, M., & Hale, C. A. (1989). General problem-solving skills: Relations between metacognitive and strategic processing. *Learning Disability Quarterly, 12*(1), 57–70.

Borkowski, J. G., & Kurtz, B. E. (1984). Metacognition and special children. In B. Gholson & T. L. Rosenthal (Eds.), *Applications of cognitive-developmental theory* (pp. 193–213). Orlando, FL: Academic Press.

Brown, A. L. (1978). Knowing when, where, and how to remember: A problem of metacognition. In R. Glaser (Ed.), *Advances in instructional psychology* (Vol. 1, pp. 131–165). Hillsdale, NJ: Lawrence Erlbaum Associates.

Brown, A.L. (1981). Metacognitive development and reading. In R. J. Shapiro, B. Bruce, & W. F. Brewer (Eds.), *Theoretical issues in reading and comprehension*. Hillsdale, NJ: Lawrence Erlbaum Associates.

Brown, A.L., Bransford, J. D., Ferrara, R. A., & Campione, J. (1983). Learning, remembering and understanding. In P. H. Mussen (Ed.), *Handbook of child psychology* (Vol. 3, pp. 77–166). New York: Wiley.

Brown, A. L., & Campione, J. C. (1986). Psychological theory and the study of learning disabilities. *American Psychologist, 41*,1059–1068.

Brown, A. L., & Palincsar, A. S. (1982). Inducing strategic learning from texts by means of informed self-control training. *Topics in Learning and Learning Difficulties, 2*,1–18.

Campione, J. C. (1989). Assisted assessment: A taxonomy of approaches and an outline of strengths and weaknesses. *Journal of Learning Disabilities, 22*,151–165.

Cronbach, L. J., & Snow, R. B. (1976). *Aptitude and instructional methods*. New York: Irvington.

Copeland, A. P., & Weissbrod, C. S. (1983). Cognitive strategies used by learning disabled children: Does hyperactivity always make things worse? *Journal of Learning Disabilities, 16*, 473–477.

DeBettencourt, L. U. (1987). Strategy training: A need for clarification. *Exceptional Children, 54*(1), 24–30.

Denckla, M.B., & Rudel, R. (1976). Rapid "automatized" naming (R. A. N.). Dyslexia differentiated from other learning disabilities. *Neuropsychologia, 14*, 471–479.

Deshler, D. D., & Schumaker, J. B. (1986). Learning strategies: An instructional alternative for low achieving adolescents. *Exceptional Children, 52*(6), 583–590.

Deshler, D. D., Warner, M. M., Schumaker, J. B., & Alley, G. R. (1983). Learning strategies intervention model: Key components and current status. In J. D. McKinney & L. Feagans (Eds.), *Current topics in learning disabilities* (pp. 245–283). Norwood, NJ: Ablex.

Diener, C. l., & Dweck, C. S. (1978). An analysis of learned helplessness: Continuous changes in performance, strategy, and achievement cognitions following failure. *Journal of Personality and Social Psychology, 36*, 451–462.

Diener, C.I., & Dweck, C. S. (1980). An analysis of learned helplessness: II. The processing of success. *Journal of Personality and Social Psychology, 39*, 940–952.

Doehring, D. G. (1976). Acquisition of rapid reading responses. *Monographs of the Society for Research in Child Development, 41* (2, Serial No. 165).

Duffy, G. D., Roehler, L. R., Meloth, M. S., Vavrus, L. G., Book, C., Putnam, J., & Wesselman, R. (1986). The relationship between explicit verbal explanations during reading skill instruction and student awareness and achievement: A study of reading teacher effects. *Reading Research Quarterly, 21*, 237–252.

Dweck, C. S., & Bush, E. S. (1976). Sex differences in learned helplessness: 1. Differential debilitation with peer and adult evaluators. *Developmental Psychology, 12*, 147–156.

Dykman, R. A., Ackerman, P.T., & Oglesby, D. M. (1979). Selective and sustained attention in hyperactive, learning disabled, and normal boys. *Journal of Nervous and Mental Disease, 167*, 288–297.

Ellis, E. S., Lenz, B.K., & Clark, F. L. (1989). *TACTIC: Procedures for developing strategy interventions.* Lawrence, KS: Edge Enterprises.

Feuerstein, R., Miller, R., & Jensen, M. R. (1981). Can evolving techniques better measure cognitive change? *Journal of Special Education, 15*(2), 201–270.

Feuerstein, R., Rand, V., Hoffman, M., & Miller, R. (1980). *Instrumental enrichment: An intervention program for cognitive modifiability.* Baltimore: University Park Press.

Fox, L. H., Brody, L., & Tobin, D. (1983). *Learning-disabled gifted children: Identification and programming.* Baltimore: University Park Press.

Gardner, H. (1983). *Frames of mind: The theory of multiple intelligences.* New York: Basic Books.

Garnett, K., & Fleichner, J. E. (1983). Automatization and basic fact performance of normal and learning disabled children. *Learning Disability Quarterly, 6*, 223–230.

Garofalo, J., & Lester, F. K., Jr. (1985). Metacognition, cognitive monitoring, and mathematical performance. *Journal for Research in Mathematics Education, 16*, 163–176.

Gerber, M. M., & Hall, R. J. (1980). *Spelling errors and cognitive strategies in attentionally disordered learning disabled children* (Tech. Rep. No. 27). Charlottesville: University of Virginia, Learning Disabilities Research Institute.

Gerber, M. M., & Hall, R. J. (1981). *Development of orthographic problem solving strategies in learning disabled children* (Tech. Rep. No. 37). Charlottesville: University of Virginia, Learning Disabilities Research Institute.

Goldman, S. R. (1989). Strategy instruction in mathematics. *Learning Disability Quarterly, 12*(1), 43–55.

Hallahan, D.P., & Bryan, T. H. (1981). Learning disabilities. In J. M. Kaufman & D.P. Hallahan (Eds.), *Handbook of special education* (pp. 141–164). Englewood Cliffs, NJ: Prentice-Hall.

Hallahan, D.P., & Kneedler, R. D. (1979). *Strategy deficits in the information processing of learning-disabled children* (Tech. Rep. No. 6). Charlottesville: University of Virginia, Learning Difficulties Research Institute.

Harris, G. (1980). *Classification skills in normally achieving and learning disabled seven and nine year old boys: A study in conceptualization.* Unpublished doctoral dissertation, Northwestern University, Evanston, IL.

Kavale, K. A. (1980). The reasoning abilities of normal and learning disabled readers on measures of reading comprehension. *Learning Disability Quarterly, 3*, 34–45.

Kollegian, J., & Sternberg, R. J. (1987). Intelligence, information processing and specific learning disabilities: A triarchic synthesis. *Journal of Learning Disabilities, 20*, 8–17.

La Berge, D., & Samuels, S. J. (1974). Toward a theory of automatic information processing in reading. *Cognitive Psychology, 6*, 293–323.

Lee, W. M., Hudson, F. G. (1981). *A comparison of verbal problem-solving in arithmetic of learning disabled and non-learning disabled seventh grade males* (Tech. Rep. No. 43). Lawrence: University of Kansas, Institute for Research in Learning Disabilities.

Lenz, B.K. (1989). *In the spirit of strategies instruction: Cognitive and metacognitive aspects of the strategies intervention model.* Paper presented at the second annual conference of the National Institute of Dyslexia, Washington, DC.

Levin, B. E. (1981). *Organization deficits among dyslexic children.* Unpublished doctoral dissertation, Temple University, Philadelphia.

Licht, B. G. (1983). Cognitive-motivational factors that contribute to the achievement of learning-disabled children. *Journal of Learning Disabilities, 16*, 483–489.

Licht, B. G., & Dweck, C. S. (1984). Determinants of academic achievement: The interaction of children's achievement orientations and skill area. *Developmental Psychology, 20*, 628–636.

Lyon, R., & Watson, B. (1981). Empirically derived subgroups of learning disabled readers: Diagnostic characteristics. *Journal of Learning Disabilities, 14*, 356–361.

Mann, L. (1979). *On the trail of process: A historical perspective on cognitive processes and their training.* New York: Grune and Stratton.

Mayer, R. E. (1987). *Educational psychology: A cognitive approach.* Boston: Little, Brown.

McKinney, J. D. (1989). Longitudinal research on the behavioral characteristics of children with learning disabilities. *Journal of Learning Disabilities, 22*(3),141–150.

McKinney, J. D., & Feagans, L. (1983). *Current topics in learning disabilities.* Norwood, NJ: Ablex.

McKinney, J. D., & Speece, D. L. (1986). Academic consequences and longitudinal stability of behavioral subtypes of learning disabled children. *Journal of Educational Psychology, 78*(5), 365–372.

Meltzer, L. J. (1984). Cognitive assessment and the diagnosis of learning problems. In M.D. Levine & P. Satz (Eds.), *Middle childhood: Development and dysfunction* (pp. 131–152). Baltimore: University Park Press.

Meltzer, L J. (1987). *The surveys of problem-solving and educational skills.* Cambridge, MA: Educator's Publishing Service.

Meltzer, L. J., & Fenton, T. (1989). *The influence of automaticity and cognitive flexibility on academic achievement in learning disabled students.* Paper presented at the Joint Conference on Learning Disabilities, Ann Arbor, MI.

Meltzer, L. J., Fenton, T., Ogonowski, M., Malkus, K. (1988). *Automaticity. cognitive strategies and academic achievement in students with and without learning disabilities.* Paper presented at the annual meeting of the American Educational Research Association, New Orleans.

Meltzer, L. J., Fenton, T., & Solomon, B. (1984, August). *Automatization and abstract problem-solving as predictors of academic achievement.* Paper presented at the meeting of the American Psychological Association, Toronto.

Meltzer, L. J., Levine, M., Karniski, W., Palfrey, J., & Clarke, S. (1984). An analysis of the learning styles of adolescent delinquents. *Journal of Learning Disabilities, 17*(10), 600–608.

Meltzer, L. J., & Roditi, B. (1989). *Assessment for Teaching: An alternative approach to the diagnosis of learning disabilities.* Manuscript in preparation.

Meltzer, L. J., Roditi, B., & Fenton, T. (1986). Cognitive and learning profiles of delinquents and learning disabled adolescents. *Adolescence, 21*, 581–591.

Meltzer, L. J., Solomon, B., & Fenton, T. (1987). *Problem-solving strategies in children with and without learning disabilities.* Paper presented at the 95th annual convention of the American Psychological Association, New York.

Meltzer, L. J., Solomon, B., Fenton, R., & Levine, M.D. (1989). A developmental study of problem-solving strategies in children with and without learning difficulties. *Journal of Applied Developmental Psychology, 10*, 171–193.

Nickerson, R. S., Perkins, D. N., & Smith, E. E. (1985). *The teaching of thinking.* Hillsdale, NJ: Lawrence Erlbaum Associates.

Palincsar, A. S. (1986). The role of dialogue in providing scaffolded instruction. *Educational Psychologist, 21*, 73–98.

Palincsar, A. S., & Brown, A.L. (1984). Reciprocal teaching of comprehension—fostering and monitoring activities. *Cognition and Instruction, 1*, 117–175.

Paris, S. G., & Jacobs, J. E. (1984). The benefits of informed instruction for children's reading awareness and comprehension skills. *Child Development, 55*, 2083–2093.

Paris, S. G., & Oka, E.R. (1989). Strategies for comprehending text and coping with reading difficulties. *Learning Disability Quarterly, 12*(1), 32–42.

Perfetti, C. A., & Roth, S. (1981). Some of the interactive processes in reading and their role in reading skill. In A.M. Lesgold & C. A. Perfetti (Eds.), *Interactive process in reading.* Hillsdale, NJ: Lawrence Erlbaum Associates.

Polya, G. (1975). *How to solve it.* New York: Doubleday Anchor Books.

Poremba, C. D. (1975). Learning disabilities, youth and delinquency: Programs for intervention. In H. R. Myklebust (Ed.), *Progress in learning disabilities* (Vol. 3, pp. 123–149). New York: Grune and Stratton.

Pressley, M., Borkowski, I. G., & Schneider, W. (1987). Cognitive strategies: Good strategy users coordinate metacognition and knowledge. In R. Vasta and G. Whitehurst (Eds.), *Annals of Child Development, 5,* 89–129.

Pressley, M., Cariglia-Bull, T., & Snyder, B. L. (1984). Are there programs that can really teach thinking and learning skills? Review of *Thinking and learning skills: Vol. 1. Relating instruction to research. Contemporary Education Research, 3,* 435–444.

Pressley, M., Goodchild, F., Fleet, J., Zajchowski, R., & Evans, E. (1988). The challenges of classroom strategy instruction. *Elementary School Journal, 89,* 301–342.

Pressley, M., & Levin, J. R. (1987). Elaborative learning strategies for the inefficient learner. In S. J. Ceci (Ed.), *Handbook of cognitive social and neuropsychological aspects of learning disabilities* (Vol. 2, pp. 175–212). Hillsdale. NJ: Lawrence Erlbaum Associates.

Reid, D. K. (1988). *Teaching the learning disabled: A cognitive developmental approach.* Needham: Allyn and Bacon.

Roditi, B. (1988). Automaticity, cognitive flexibility, mathematics and problem solving: A longitudinal study of children with and without learning disabilities. (Doctoral dissertation, Tufts University), *Dissertation Abstracts International, 49,* 2396B.

Russell, R. L., & Ginsburg, H.P. (1984). Cognitive analysis of children's mathematics difficulties. *Cognition and Instruction, I,* 217–244.

Schumaker, J. B., & Deshler, D. D. (1988). Implementing the regular education initiative in secondary schools: A different ball game. *Journal of Learning Disabilities. 21*(1), 36–41.

Schumaker, J. B., Deshler, D. D., Alley, G. R., Warner. M. M., & Denton, P. H.(1982). Multipass: A learning strategy for improving reading comprehension. *Learning Disability Quarterly, 5*(3), 295–304.

Short, E. J., & Ryan, E. B. (1984). Metacognitive differences between skilled and less skilled readers: Remediating deficits through story grammar and attribution training. *Journal of Educational Psychology, 76,* 225–235.

Speece, D. (1987). Information processing subtypes of learning-disabled readers. *Learning Disabilities Research, 2,* 91–102.

Speece, D. L., & Cooper, D. H. (1989). *Subtype membership and the risk for referral in the primary grades.* Paper presented at the first annual conference on Research and Theory in Learning Development. Pennsylvania State University.

Spreen, O. (1981). The relationship between learning disability, neurological impairment and delinquency: Results of a follow up study. *Journal of Nervous and Mental Diseases, 169,* 791–802.

Sternberg, R. J. (1981). The evolution of theories of intelligence. *Intelligence, 5,* 209–230.

Sternberg, R. J. (1984). What should intelligence tests test? Implications of a triarchic theory of intelligence for intelligence testing. *Educational Researcher, 13,* 5–15.

Stone, C. A. (1981). Reasoning disorders in learning-disabled adolescents. *Exceptional Child, 28,* 43–53.

Stone, C. A. (1989). Improving the effectiveness of strategy training for learning-disabled students: The role of communicational dynamics. *Remedial and Special Education, 10,* 35–42.

Stone, C. A., & Michals, D. (1986). Problem solving skills in learning disabled children. In S. J. Ceci (Ed.), *Handbook of cognitive, social and neuropsychological aspects of learning disabilities* (Vol. 1, pp. 291–315). Hillsdale, NJ: Lawrence Erlbaum Associates.

Stone, C. A., & Wertsch, J. V. (1984). A social interactional analysis of learning disabilities remediation. *Journal of Learning Disabilities, 17*(4), 194–199.

Swanson, H. L. (1985). Assessing learning disabled children's intellectual performance: An information processing perspective. In K. Gadow (Ed.), *Advances in learning and behavior disabilities* (pp. 225–272). Greenwich, CT: JAI Press.

Swanson, H. L. (1987). The influence of verbal ability and metamemory on future recall. *British Journal of Educational Psychology, 53,*179–190.

Swanson, H. L. (1988). Information processing theory and learning disabilities: A commentary and future perspective. *Journal of Learning Disabilities. 20*(3), 155–166.

Swanson, H. L. (1989). Strategy instruction: Overview of principles and procedures for effective use. *learning Disability Quarterly, 12*(1), 3–14.

Torgesen, J. K. (1975). Problems and prospects in the study of learning disabilities. *Review of Child Development Research, 5,* 385–440.

Torgesen, J. K. (1977). The role of non-specific factors in task performance of learning disabled children: A theoretical assessment. *Journal of learning Disabilities, 10,* 27–34.

Torgesen, J. K. (1982). The learning-disabled child as an inactive learner: Educational implications. *Topics in Learning and Learning Disabilities, 2,* 45–51.

Torgesen, J. K., & Licht, B. (1983). The learning-disabled child as an inactive learner: Retrospects and prospects. In J. McKinney & L. Feagans (Eds.), *Current topics in learning difficulties* (Vol. 1, pp. 3–31). Norwood, NJ: Ablex.

Torgesen, J. K., & Wong, B. (1986). *Psychological and educational perspectives on learning disabilities.* Orlando, FL: Academic Press.

Vygotsky, L. S. (1962). *Thought and language.* Cambridge, MA: MIT Press.

Vygotsky, L. S. (1978). *Mind in society.* Cambridge, MA: Harvard University Press.

Wertsch, J. V., & Stone, CA. (1985). The concept of internalization in Vygotsky's account of the genesis of higher mental functions. In J. V. Wertsch (Ed.), *Culture, communication, and cognition: Vygotskian perspectives* (pp. 162–179). New York: Cambridge University Press.

Winograd, P. (1984). Strategic difficulties in summarizing texts. *Reading Research Quarterly, 19,* 404–425,

Wolf, M. (1984). Naming, reading and the dyslexias: A longitudinal overview. *Annals of Dyslexia, 34,* 87–115.

Wolf, M. (1986). Rapid alternating stimulus naming in the developmental dyslexias. *Brain and language, 29,* 360–379.

Wong, B. Y. (1986). Metacognition and special education: A review of a view. *Journal of Special Education, 20,* 9–29.

Wong, B. Y. L. (1987). How do the results of metacognitive research impact on the learning disabled individual? *Learning Disability Quarterly, 10,*189–195.

Wood, A., Bruner, J., & Ross, G. (1976). The role of tutoring in problem solving. *Journal of Child Psychology and Psychiatry, 17,* 89–100.

Yewchuk, C. (1984). Learning disabilities among gifted children. *Special Education in Canada, 58,* 95–96.

Yewchuk, C. (1986). Identification of gifted learning disabled children. *School Psychology International, 7,* 61–68.

Zigmond, N., & Miller, S. (1986). Assessment for instructional planning. *Exceptional Children, 52,* 501–509.

Zigmond, N., Vallecorsa, A., & Silverman, R. (1983). *Assessment for instructional planning in special education.* Englewood Cliffs, NJ: Prentice–Hall.

8

Arithmetic Disability: Theoretical Considerations and Empirical Evidence for this Subtype

Sylvia R. Morrison
Linda S. Siegel
Department of Special Education,
Ontario Institute for Studies in Education

INTRODUCTION

In this chapter we will discuss the evidence for the existence of a subtype of learning disabilities called an arithmetic disability. According to Siegel (1988a), it is characterized by difficulties in one or more of the following: computational arithmetic, rote learning (for example memorizing the times tables or number facts), written work, and/or fine motor coordination in spite of good oral language and reading skills. This disability has been also known by a variety of names, "developmental output failure," "dysgraphia," "writing backwardness," and arithmetic/written work disability (Siegel, 1988a), and described in publications such as Kinsbourne and Warrington (1963), Siegel and Feldman (1983), Siegel and Heaven (1986), and Spellacy and Peter (1978).

Rourke (1983) has argued that until recently many educators have ignored the child with poor arithmetic skills but with normal reading scores. Weinstein (1980) estimates that as many as 6% of the school-aged population may form just such a specific arithmetic-disabled group. A survey of 114 intermediate and secondary learning resource room teachers (McLeod & Armstrong, 1982), found 66.5% of LD students seen for remediation of learning disabilities had difficulties in mathematics; in 26.2%, it was the primary difficulty and in 40.3% of the students it was a supplementary factor. In children with reading disabilities, Siegel and Ryan (1984, 1988, 1989) could find few without accompanying severe arithmetic deficits except at the youngest age groups, 7 to 8 years old. They suggest that the absence of arithmetic deficits in these younger children may be due to the oral content of the Wide Range Achievement Test–WRAT (Jastak & Jastak, 1978) in the early school years. Clearly the importance of arithmetic/mathematics in the field of learning disabilities must not be underestimated.

In this chapter we shall attempt to clarify some of the issues relating arithmetic to learning disabilities by (1) by describing the definitional controversy as it applies to the subtyping literature in general and arithmetic in particular, (2) critically examining some of the evidence for a specific arithmetic subtype and delineating some of its possible characteristics, (3) reviewing some of the research on learning disabilities and arithmetic, and (4) suggesting some areas for future research.

DEFINITIONAL ISSUES

Historically, the term learning disabilities has been used to refer to the problems manifested by a group of children whose difficulties in one or more of the basic school subjects cannot be explained as a function of their intelligence (ability), physical handicap, or some other extrinsic factor in their environment. However, the definition and classification of the actual population to be serviced or investigated has remained controversial (Algozzine & Ysseldyke, 1988; Fletcher & Morris, 1986; Keogh, 1987; Wong, 1986). Some studies (Siegel, 1988b, Wong, 1986) have suggested that at least one of the difficulties with current definitions is that they are hard to operationalize, which has led to a variety of interpretations. These interpretational difficulties have allowed different school boards, administrators, and investigators to apply a variety of classification criteria to the same definitional names and the same classification criteria to different names (Epps, Ysseldyke, & Algozzine, 1985; Keogh, 1986; Wong, 1986). Hooper and Wallis (1989) conclude "a major obstacle that impedes progress in learning disability research is the lack of a universally accepted, operational definition" (p. 93).

Siegel (1988b) maintains that these inconsistencies in definition have led to problems in specificity. That is, should learning disabilities be characterized as a phenomenon in which all children share the same strengths and weaknesses in basic information-processing systems or is it a generic label which refers to a group of children who have heterogeneous cognitive and psychoneurological profiles and who can be subdivided into more homogeneous subgroups? McKinney and Speece (1986) claim that the "problem of sample heterogeneity has not only frustrated efforts to build a generalizable body of knowledge about learning disabilities but has also contributed greatly to the present controversy over misclassification and appropriate education for learning disabled students" (p. 369).

SUBTYPING ISSUES

Given the heterogeneity of LD groups, Siegel (1988b) contends that if all LD children are grouped together then inaccurate conclusions may be reached. Evidence in support of this position have been found by many investigators (e.g., Fletcher, 1985a, 1985b; McKinney, Short, & Feagans, 1985; Rourke & Finlayson, 1978; Siegel & Linder, 1984; Siegel & Ryan, 1984, 1988, 1989) For example, Siegel and Ryan (1984, 1988, 1989) and Fletcher (1985b) found differences between specific arithmetic-disabled children without reading problems and reading-disabled children in both short-term and working memory. McKinney et al., using a cognitive battery designed to assess a wide range of linguistic and perceptual abilities, were able to classify 55 first- and second-grade, school-identified learning-disabled children into six subtypes. They then demonstrated that the three subtypes with atypical cognitive profiles had poorer academic outcomes than the three groups with normal or near-normal profiles. These differences might not have been evident had these children been grouped together and not divided into subtypes.

Because of this heterogeneity of LD groups, considerable effort has been made to identify specific subgroups of learning-disabled children who share common attributes that distinguish them from other subtypes. Not only do subtypes exist, but they seem to take several forms in terms of achievement patterns and/or associated cognitive information-processing abilities. Further these subtypes may vary as a function of etiology and age (e.g., McKinney, et al., 1985; Rourke & Finlayson, 1978; Satz & Morris, 1981; Short, Feagans, McKinney, & Appelbaum, 1986; Siegel & Heaven, 1986). For example, McKinney and Speece (1986) found that in a sample of learning-disabled children divided into behavioral subtypes, subtype membership was not stable over a 3-year period although most (55%) were likely to remain maladjusted after the 3 years.

Subtyping Models

Early subtype approaches are based on clinical inferences which have attempted to reduce complex data sets of subjects into presumably homogeneous classes largely based upon a priori considerations and visual inspection techniques. These methods have been criticized for their inability to manage simultaneously large quantities of information in an objective fashion as well as the subjectivity that results from the bias of clinical decisions made at various stages during the subtype development and subject classification (see Satz & Morris, 1981, and Hooper & Willis, 1989, for a complete review).

More recently, with the availability of advanced computer technology, empirical classification models using applied descriptive multivariate statistics have been developed. This approach has involved a search for hidden structure in complex multidimensional data sets generally involving cognitive linguistic skills or direct measures of achievement or behavior (e.g., Doehring & Hoshko, 1977; Feagans & Appelbaum, 1986).

These methods also have difficulties. Hooper and Willis (1989) contend that standards of reliability and validity have frequently been overlooked or marginally addressed by investigators using these classification techniques. In addition they suggest that "the adequacy and strength of models derived by empirical classification methods are influenced by many a priori clinical decisions including those regarding theoretical orientation, sample selection, and variable selection" (p. 104). Thus, the appropriate subtyping model remains an open question and may depend on the type of research undertaken.

Academic Performance Models

In spite of the difficulties inherent in subtyping models, a number of investigators (e.g., Fletcher, 1985a; Rourke & Finlayson, 1978; Rourke & Strang, 1978; Siegel & Feldman, 1983; Siegel & Linder, 1984; Siegel & Ryan 1984, 1988, 1989) have suggested that learning-disabled students in general and children with computational arithmetic problems in particular, can be divided on the basis of their academic achievement as measured by Wide Range Achievement Test (WRAT) scores in reading, spelling, and arithmetic. Although each investigator has created his or her classification scheme, two broad categories of subtype groups have emerged. The first contains children with at least reading deficits and the second contains children with at least arithmetic deficits and normal-to-above-normal reading scores. Some authors (e.g., Fletcher, 1985b; Rourke & Finlayson, 1978; Rourke & Strang, 1978) have subdivided these groups further, based on the presence of other deficits. For example, Siegel and Linder (1984) and Siegel and Ryan (1984, 1988, 1989) have used only two academic subtypes, an arithmetic-disabled group, defined by scores equal to or below the 25th percentile on the WRAT Arithmetic Subtest and scores equal to or above the 30th percentile on the WRAT Reading Subtest and a reading-disabled group, defined by scores equal to or below the 25th percentile on the WRAT Reading Subtest and no cutoffs for the other two WRAT subtests. Fletcher (1985b) has developed the following four subtypes: (1) a reading-spelling-disabled group, (2) a reading-spelling-arithmetic-disabled group, (3) an arithmetic-disabled group, and (4) a spelling-arithmetic-disabled group. According to this categorization, the reading-spelling-disabled group is defined as consisting of children with (1) WRAT Reading and Spelling Subtest scores below the 31st percentile, (2) WRAT Arithmetic Subtest scores above the 30th percentile, and (3) the arithmetic score must be at least one-half standard deviation above their reading score on the appropriate WRAT subtest. The reading-spelling-arithmetic-disabled group is characterized by children with scores on all three WRAT subtests below the 31st percentile. The arithmetic-spelling-disabled group contains children who have (1) WRAT Spelling and Arithmetic Subtest scores below the 31st percentile, (2) WRAT Reading Subtest scores above the 39th percentile, and (3) at least one standard deviation between their reading and arithmetic scores. The arithmetic-disabled group consists of children who have (1) WRAT Reading and Spelling Subtest scores above the 39th percentile, (2) WRAT Arithmetic Subtest scores below the 31st percentile, and (3) at least a one standard deviation difference between their reading and arithmetic scores. In contrast a series of studies by Rourke and his associates (Rourke & Finlayson, 1978; Rourke & Strang, 1978; Strang & Rourke, 1983) have identified the following three subtypes: (1) a general disabled group (reading-spelling-arithmetic-disabled), (2) a reading-disabled group, and (3) an arithmetic-disabled group. These investigators defined their reading-spelling-arithmetic groups as consisting of children with WRAT Subtest scores below the 19th percentile on all three subtests. The reading-spelling-disabled group consisted of children with (1) WRAT Arithmetic Subtest scores at least 1.8 years higher than their WRAT Reading and Spelling Subtest scores and (2) WRAT Reading and Spelling Subtest below the 15th percentile. The arithmetic-disabled group contained children whose WRAT Reading and Spelling Subtest scores were at least 2 years above the WRAT Arithmetic Subtest scores. It is important to recognize that the Rourke reading-spelling-arithmetic-disabled group and the reading-spelling-disabled group are equated on reading and spelling scores while the reading-spelling-disabled group and the arithmetic-disabled group are equated on (deficient) arithmetic scores.

Regardless of the exact criteria used, this method of subtyping has identified groups of learning-disabled children whose arithmetic difficulties are not confounded by deficits in reading (word recognition). The emergence of a specific arithmetic-disabled subgroup has permitted investigators to clarify some of the characteristics which distinguish this group from other learning-disabled children with reading deficits.

Arithmetic-disabled Subtype

Investigators (e.g., Fletcher, 1985b; Rourke & Finlayson, 1978; Rourke & Strang, 1978; Siegel & Feldman, 1983; Siegel & Ryan, 1984,1988, 1989) have found evidence that children with specific arithmetic deficits and average or above-average word recognition scores on the WRAT appear to have a variety of cognitive and neuropsychological deficits which differentiate them from children with at least reading deficits as defined by depressed scores on the Reading Subtest on the WRAT. The cognitive and neuropsychological profiles of children identified as specific arithmetic-disabled are also different from normally achieving children.

Evidence (Fletcher, 1985b; Siegel & Linder, 1984; Siegel & Ryan, 1984, 1988, 1989) suggests that those children meeting the criteria of the specific arithmetic-disabled subtype have deficits in short-term and working memory that are dependent on the type of stimulus and the aspect of memory assessed. Specifically, Siegel and Linder (1984), in a study of the role of phonemic coding in short-term memory, compared three groups of children, one with reading disabilities (as defined by scores on the WRAT Reading Subtest of equal to or below the 25th percentile and no cutoff on the other two WRAT Subtests), a second with arithmetic disabilities (as defined by scores on the WRAT Arithmetic Subtest of equal to or below the 25th percentile and scores on the WRAT Reading Subtest of equal to or above the 30th percentile), and a normally achieving group (as defined by scores of greater than or equal to the 30th percentile on all three WRAT Subtests). The children, aged 7 to 13, were administered a series of tasks that involved the visual or auditory presentation of rhyming and nonrhyming letters and either an oral or written response. Patterns and levels of performance were compared statistically across three age groups (7–8, 9–11, 12–13) and between each subtype and normally achieving children. Due to statistical problems, noncomparable age distributions, and small sample sizes, it was not possible to compare across subtypes. Results indicated that both older disabled groups, like their normal counterparts, had significantly poorer recall of rhyming as opposed to nonrhyming letters (except for the oldest—12 to 13 years—arithmetic-disabled group, where the authors suggest that the children may be functioning at the upper limit of their visual, short-term memory). For stimuli presented visually the overall performance levels of both learning-disabled groups were significantly lower than the normally achieving group. For the auditory stimuli, only the reading-disabled group differed significantly from the normally achieving peers.

Fletcher (1985b) found differences in memory tasks between learning-disabled groups as defined by WRAT scores. He compared four groups of learning-disabled children (a reading-spelling-disabled group, a reading-spelling-arithmetic-disabled group, a spelling-arithmetic-disabled group, and an arithmetic-disabled group) and a normally achieving group of children on storage and retrieval aspects of memory for verbal and nonverbal stimuli. He found that relative to the normally achieving controls, both the arithmetic and the arithmetic-spelling-disabled subgroups had significantly lower storage and retrieval scores on the nonverbal task but did not differ from each other; the reading-spelling subgroup differed only on retrieval scores on the verbal task; while the reading-spelling-arithmetic subgroup differed on the retrieval scores on the verbal task and storage and retrieval scores on the nonverbal task. As with Siegel and Linder (1984), the differences between subgroups depended on the type of stimulus (verbal vs. nonverbal) and the aspect of memory (storage or retrieval) being assessed.

Siegel and Ryan (1988) also compared reading-disabled (as defined by WRAT subtest scores), specific arithmetic-disabled (as defined by WRAT subtest scores), and normally achieving children on a variety of skills involving grammatical sensitivity, phonology, and short-term memory. In general, it was found that older specific arithmetic-disabled children performed in a manner similar to the normally achieving group and were significantly different from the reading-disabled group in grammatical sensitivity and phonological tasks. Some exceptions were found in that the arithmetic-disabled children in the 7–10 age-group who performed more poorly on a sentence repetition task, with this difficulty attributed to the short-term memory component of the task. As well, this age group performed more poorly than normally achieving children on the nonword spelling section (a writing task) of the phonics tasks. However, in tasks that measure short-term memory (phonological coding) the specific arithmetic-disabled group performed in a manner similar to the reading-disabled group and significantly more poorly than the normally achieving group. The authors conclude that while both the two disabled groups, compared with normally achieving children, have deficits in short-term memory, only the reading-disabled group had deficits in tasks said to represent a language disorder.

Siegel and Ryan (1989) examined the same groups, using two working memory tasks, one involving sentences and the other involving counting. Again the disabled groups differed from each other on the types of memory deficits observed. The reading-disabled group differed from the normally achieving children on both tasks while the arithmetic-disabled children differed from their normally achieving peer only on the counting task. It would appear from the research (Fletcher, 1985b, Siegel & Linder, 1984; Siegel & Ryan, 1988, 1989) that while both subtypes of learning-disabled children have deficits in short-term and working memory, those in children with reading deficits are more generalized involving both verbal and nonverbal aspects of memory while those in children with arithmetic deficits and normal or above-normal reading are more limited to visually, nonverbal, and numerical material.

Evidence from a number of sources (Fletcher, 1985b; Rourke & Finlayson, 1978; Share, Moffitt, & Silva, 1988; Siegel & Feldman, 1983; Spellacy & Peter, 1978; Webster, 1979) indicates that specific arithmetic-disabled children (as defined by deficient scores on the WRAT Arithmetic Subtest and age-appropriate scores on the WRAT Reading and Spelling Subtests–Group 3) have age-appropriate auditory-perceptual and verbal abilities but are deficient on measures of visual-perception and visual-spatial abilities. However, reading-disabled children (as defined by being relatively proficient at arithmetic as compared with their WRAT Reading and Spelling Subtest scores–Group 2) have age-appropriate visual-perception and visual-spatial abilities but are deficient on measures of auditory-perceptual and verbal abilities (Rourke & Finlayson, 1978). Also, Group 3 (arithmetic-disabled) children exhibit difficulty in tasks such as the Halstead Category Test, which require "higher-order" visual-spatial analysis and visual-perceptual organization (Strang & Rourke, 1983). They also appear to exhibit deficits in measures of psychomotor abilities and on tests such as the Tactile Performance Test (Reitan & Davison, 1974), the Grooved Pegboard Test (Klove, 1963), and the Maze Test (Klove, 1963); designed to identify tactile-perceptual impairment (Rourke & Strang, 1978; Siegel & Feldman, 1983; Spellacy & Peter, 1978). On the other hand Rourke and Strang (1978) and Strang and Rourke (1983) found that Group 2 children (relatively proficient in arithmetic, compared with their reading and spelling) are proficient at these tasks.

In addition Rourke and Strang (1978) claim that the arithmetic subgroup (Group 3) exhibited normal right-hand performance but impaired left-hand performance, the exact opposite of the Group 2 children, who had impaired right-hand performance but normal left-hand performance. Strang and Rourke (1983) suggest that the arithmetic-disabled subgroup has deficiencies in nonverbal concept-formation, compared with other disabled subgroups. Specifically, when the types of errors made of the Arithmetic Subtest of the WRAT were analyzed, it was found that the specific arithmetic subtype tended to make a larger number of errors, make a greater variety of errors, and attempted to answer questions without an apparent understanding of the strategies needed to solve the problems (Strang & Rourke, 1985). This error pattern was not found in children with reading disabilities–Group 2.

As with the research with memory deficits cited earlier, Rourke and Finlayson (1978), Rourke and Strang (1978), and Strang and Rourke (1983) suggest that the characteristics described are different from other learning-disabled students (who showed deficits on all the WRAT subtests–Group 1, or just on the reading and spelling subtests, compared with the arithmetic subtest–Group 2). This has led Rourke et al. (Rourke, 1982; Rourke, 1983; Rourke, 1985; Rourke, 1987; Rourke & Finlayson, 1978; Rourke & Fisk, 1988) to hypothesize that those children with arithmetic deficits belong to the larger nonverbal learning-disabled group with right-hemisphere processing problems, while those children with deficits in reading as well as arithmetic belong the larger linguistic learning-disabled group with left-hemisphere processing problems. Clearly, however, children who only have severe deficits in arithmetic can be differentiated from children with reading difficulties and from normally achieving children on cognitive and neuropsychological profiles.

ARITHMETIC AND LEARNING DISABILITIES

In spite of the research in the area of subtyping, much of the information about the relationship of arithmetic to learning disabilities comes from studies which have tended to treat learning-disabled children as a homogeneous group. Historically, the research in this area has developed from two quite different approaches, a neuropsychological model and an educational deficits model. Recently much of the work in this area has focused on cognitive processing models.

Neuropsychological Approach

Historically, the neuropsychological approach as it relates to mathematics and arithmetic disabilities has centered on neurological dysfunction. In this approach, the focus is on internal processes. Here, investigators have concentrated their efforts in determining the deficits in neurological functioning that have reduced the learner's mental abilities for mathematics. Within the neurological approach, two general types of conditions have been described. If the person is an adult, he or she can be described as acalculia, or having a complete or partial disturbance in some aspect of mathematical ability because of a specific lesion in some area of the brain. However, if the person is a child with no history of neurological dysfunction, then he or she can be described as dyscalculia. (Gaddes, 1985; Kosc, 1981-1982).

Typically, research in this area has developed as an outgrowth of studies of mathematical behavior in adults with acquired brain injuries. Investigators (see Gaddes, 1985; Luria, 1966; McEntire, 1981–1982) concerned with mapping the brain for centers of mathematical ability—occipital, frontal, parietal, and temporal lobes all have been suggested—have tried to establish a cause-and-effect relationship that injury to particular sections of the brain results in particular deficits in mathematical ability. Specifically, Luria (1966) has found that lesions of the posterior (occipitoparietal) systems are associated with deficits in the patient's idea of number and arithmetic operations. Although they could perceive names denoting quantity, their categorical structure of number was disturbed so that they made mistakes when writing or reading numbers. Further, these patients had great difficulty in situations requiring the internal recognition of numerical relationships and frequently could do no more than recite a series of numbers. Luria (1966) also cited evidence of loss of mathematical ability in patients with frontal system lesions. In these instances, the damage appeared to have affected the patient's ability to recode information in a problem-solving situation. Specifically, they showed no appreciable difficulty in understanding the systems of concepts and the logic-grammatical or numerical relationships. However, they had marked difficulties when it was necessary to analyze (reword) the problem before forming a preliminary plan of solution.

Ojemann (1974) has shown that electrostimulation of the left and right thalamus has been found to impair arithmetic ability differently. Specifically, the left thalamic stimulation has tended to accelerate the rate of counting backwards while right thalamic stimulation tended to decrease the rate of counting backwards. However, in both cases, calculation errors increased. These findings have led neuropsychologists (e.g., Gaddes, 1985; Obrzut, 1981), to draw analogies that children with similar mathematical behavior patterns were assumed to have similar neurological disorders even in the absence of identifiable pathology (Kosc, 1981 to 1982; Luria, 1966,1980; McEntire, 1981–1982; Rourke, 1982). Therefore, specific cognitive deficits and behavior syndromes themselves became indicators for the diagnosis that children had neurological dysfunctions and resulting mental abilities deficits (Gaddes, 1985; Kosc, 1981–1982; McEntire, 1981–1982). Hence the central theme of this neuropsychological approach was that certain neurological damage (as measured in brain-injured adults) resulted in specific cognitive deficits which could be measured on specific psychometric tests. This led to the hypothesis that children with learning disabilities, as diagnosed by specific psychometric tests, had some types of central processing deficits that made them significantly different from children with normal learning abilities.

These earlier approaches have been criticized on several levels. Luria (1980) in his reexamination of the concepts of functions and localization suggests that earlier evidence for localization theories have been overstated. Others (McEntire, 1981–1982; Rourke, 1975, 1982) fault these models for a view of mental processes that is "innate, static, and unaffected by the environment" (McEntire, 1981–1982, p. 6) and for failing "to account for the development of the brain as well as the development of the individual's approach to material-to-be-learned" (Rourke, 1982, p. 3).

Educational Tasks Approach

The second historical reference point for research in mathematics and learning disabilities has focused on an education tasks approach. This area of research represents a shift away from deficiencies in internal processes to deficiencies in external performance. Here, the basic theoretical assumption is that deficits in mathematics should be addressed without hypothesizing about deficits in mental processes or brain function. The only factors to be concerned about are the educational tasks. These approaches were based on the psychological theory (Thorndike, 1922, cited in McEntire, 1981–1982) that it is an association between external stimuli and external response that constitutes learning. Further, these associations are strengthened by similarity, contrast, and continuity. Learning occurs when the organism makes an association between a stimulus and a response. As the organism is exposed to similar, contrasting, and continuous stimulus–response situations, these associations become stronger.

This theory had a strong influence on educational thought and teaching in that learning was considered to result as a consequence of connections between situations and responses enforced by satisfying results and habituation of thought and action. Also, increased knowledge concerning the relationship between amount, rate, and conditions of practice and habituation influenced the types of programs that were developed (i.e., the Diagnostic–Prescriptive teaching model, DISTAR Arithmetic program). The development of standardized tests and scales allowed measurement of precise changes in amount of knowledge which then were equated to precise measurement of learning change. Finally these changes led to the development of an hierarchical scheme in the content of mathematical learning (McEntire, 1981–1982).

In this educational atmosphere, students' mathematical difficulties are attributed to such factors as failure to master prerequisite skills, lack of instruction, inadequate stimulus presentation, insufficient reinforcement, use of inefficient procedures, and limited opportunities for practice. Since the etiology of the mathematical deficiency in the education task approach could be traced to incorrectly learned responses and poor selection of instructional stimuli, it was suggested that remediation lay in the use of programs that used the appropriate instructional strategies and material. This led to the development of programs using (1) scope and sequence skill approaches to expand the mathematical content as in the Diagnostic–Prescriptive teaching model (e.g., Brown, 1975; Glennon & Wilson, 1972), (2) changing the instructional strategy as in the DISTAR Arithmetic Program (Engelmann & Carnine, 1975), and (3) manipulating the external contingencies to condition the learners response as in the Applied Behavior Analysis model (Lovitt, 1975). In any case, proponents believe that analysis of the student's errors will lead to discovery of the missing subskill and appropriate teaching will lead to mastery (Ashlock, 1976; Blankenship, 1985; Roberts, 1968).

Critics of the educational tasks deficits approach argue that it represents an objective view of children that sees them as reactive rather than an active human being and ignores the internal subjective developmental processing of information by the learner (McEntire, 1981–1982; Reid & Hresko, 1981). Further it is argued that "external manipulation to condition predetermined responses appears detrimental to the development of meaningful useful information and active, risk-taking, self-confident, problem-solving persons." (McEntire, 1981–1982, p. 9).

Cognitive Models Approach

Recently interest in learning disabilities in general, and specific arithmetic-learning disabilities in particular has focused on cognitive-processing and cognitive models. These models provide an alternative explanation of how children with specific arithmetic disabilities process arithmetic information. Much of our understanding in this area has come from research involving normally achieving children. Here, the emphasis has been on analyses of errors made by these children as they solve computational arithmetic problems. As in other areas of education and psychology, errors are thought to be especially informative in revealing factors relevant to the psychological and learning processes underlying performance.

Fixed-rule Approach

Although these studies (e.g., Ashlock, 1976; Brown & Burton, 1978; Brown & VanLehn, 1980, 1982; Young & O'Shea, 1981) vary in methodology and theory, one common conclusion is that a substantial part of children's errors are not random or capricious but are systematic and consistent. From this evidence it has been inferred that children's knowledge of arithmetic can be adequately represented by a set of procedural rules or internal algorithms that are thought to remain reasonably stable between instructional episodes. Further these rules are problem-type-specific, that is they specify certain problem-solving actions for certain problem types.

Reid and Hresko (1981) suggest that this internalization of procedural rules occurs in the classroom during instruction when the teacher explicitly verbalizes the appropriate procedural rule and the child practices them in drills. According to this model of arithmetic learning, once the rules are internalized, they can be accessed by presenting the student with the relevant problem. In general, systematic computations result from learning procedural rules and specifically systematic errors result from learning incorrect rules. Arithmetic-disabled children for reasons unspecified and/or unknown appear to use inappropriate rather than appropriate procedural rules.

Contextual Approach

Linder (1985) has argued that the foregoing models are flawed in that they are based on the following two assumptions: (a) that systematic error interpretation relies on an understanding of fixed internalized rules and (b) that arithmetic problem solving is context-independent or "decontextualized" (that is direct access to knowledge can be made by presenting the relevant arithmetic problem without consideration of contextual conditions which underlie the original learning and diagnostic assessment). He presents evidence that children's systematic errors and problem-solving activities are not fixed but fluctuate depending on the contextual conditions present in tests. Specifically Linder (1985) found that under one set of contextual conditions (e.g., drills using 1 × 1 subtraction facts) children answer a problem type (e.g., involving 2 × 1 digit subtraction facts) correctly but during the same testing session under different contextual condition(s) (e.g., 2 × 2 digit subtraction problems involving 2-digit answers) the same children answered the same problems *consistently* incorrectly.

As opposed to seeing children as operating in much the same way as a computer, that is, responding to moment-to-moment stimulus input with actions specified by the procedural rules, Linder (1985) argues that children's problem solving is much more variable in nature. The procedure selection process is not exclusively based on the information contained in the current problem to be solved, but depends on the types of problems, the problem-solving activity, and the context in which they are presented.

Because Linder (1985) has demonstrated that children's arithmetic errors can be influenced by the contextual conditions present at and before tests are administered, he has suggested that a "lexical analogies" mechanism similar to the one identified by Brooks (1978) for reading. According to this model, the child identifies a similar, already known problem-solving technique and then gives the new unknown stimulus the category label associated with the known problem-solving technique. The analogy mechanism is context-dependent, that is to some extent the analogy selected depends on the technique used in the immediately preceding problem. The advantage of the analogy model is that it accounts for cognitive behavior which is apparently regular and systematic on the surface but does not rely on the use of explicit rules. Therefore, this model suggests that the child solves new arithmetic problems by drawing analogies to the way he or she has solved other previous problems. Whether the child is correct depends on the appropriateness of the analogy. If this model is correct, the arithmetic-disabled child is unable to apply appropriate analogies. Several reasons could be offered for this failure, including lack of previous success, inability to retrieve the appropriate algorithm, or failure to recognize the appropriate algorithm.

Mental Arithmetic Models

Ashcraft (1982) has argued that neither error analysis nor contextual clues are enough to provide the necessary information about mathematical cognition, the development of reasoning, and thought based on numerical and mathematical knowledge. He suggests that the use of reaction time paradigms are important as they provide "a window through which the normally unseen mental operations and processes of computational arithmetic can be viewed" (p. 213). In this approach the operation to be examined is modeled, usually by an additive model (Stemberg, 1969). Frequently more than one model is suggested and reaction time data are used to determine the "best" model. For example, in mental addition, research suggests that young children use a counting algorithm. Specifically, according to this algorithm's model, children need to encode the stimulus, set their internal counter, increment the counter, and produce a response. The lapsed time between presentation of a stimulus and the subject's response is then a composite, reflecting the additive contribution of several separate stages or operations which have occurred between presentation and response. Usually it can be assumed that all but one stage have constant reaction times. Therefore, differences in the lapsed times reflect differences in the times needed for that particular stage (Sternberg, 1969). Again, using the mental arithmetic model, the time needed for children to encode the stimulus, set their internal counters, and produce a response is assumed to be constant for all trials. The differences in reaction time must then result from incrementing the counter. Then using "least squares" criteria the "best fit" line can be drawn and the most appropriate model can be determined (Ashcraft, 1982). A number of investigators (e.g., Ashcraft & Fierman, 1982; Groen & Parkman, 1972; Woods, Resnick, & Groen, 1975) have attempted to explain children's arithmetic development using this method.

Groen and Parkman (1972), using reconstructive memory to explain young children's simple single-digit addition, postulated five models. Based on the Sternberg (1969) model, they suggest that simple addition of single-digit numbers presented horizontally can be modeled as follows: (1) The counter is set to zero, then both addends are added in by increments of one. (2) The counter is set to the first addend—the leftmost number, then the second is added by increments of one. (3) The counter is set to the first addend—the rightmost number, and the second addend is added by increments of one. (4) The counter is set to the first addend—the minimum number, and the second addend is added by increments of one. (5) The counter is set to the first addend—the maximum number, and the second addend is added by increments of one. Using reaction time data, Groen and Parkman (1972) determined that model 5 provided the best explanation. They also found that except for ties and doubles, assuming that the internal counter is set for the maximum addend, the greater the second addend the longer the reaction time. They concluded that this model provided the best explanation for mental addition in young children.

In further experiments, Groen and Parkman (1972) attempted to apply this model to adults' mental arithmetic processing. They found that the adults' reaction times were significantly faster. This lead them to suggest an alternative model. Here, number facts are stored in a fast access memory and adults use a memory look-up process with homogeneous retrieval times and occasionally revert back to the counting process used by young children.

Woods, et al., (1975) modified the procedure used by Groen and Parkman (1972) and were able to model the subtraction process. The data in this study suggest that in younger children (up to grade three) subtraction is also explained by an increment or counting strategy. That is children either count down from the larger number or up from the smaller.

Ashcraft (1982) argues that by grade three, children switch from a counting or increment strategy to a fact retrieval strategy, similar to the one suggested by Groen and Parkman (1972). That is, with extensive practice, these arithmetic facts switch from procedural to declarative knowledge and are best explained by a fact retrieval model.

Geary, Widaman, Little, and Cormier (1987), using true/false, reaction time verification paradigm for cognitive arithmetic, have confirmed this strategy shift from implicit counting to memory retrieval for normal children. However, children with specific learning disabilities in mathematics (scores below the 34th percentile on the mathematics sections of the Stanford Achievement Test) took longer and appeared deficient in the ability to make this strategy shift. Specifically, the shift from implicit counting to memory retrieval was evident in grades four and six for normally achieving children but absent in learning-disabled children. By grade eight the learning-disabled students appeared to make the shift but they were still slower. They conclude that specific arithmetic-disabled students differ academically in the developmental maturity of the component processes used in problem solving, the temporal duration required to execute this strategy, and the ability to self-monitor the problem-solving process. Although the authors (Geary et al., 1987) report that these children were not receiving extra help in any other academic area, unfortunately no reading scores were reported, so it is impossible to determine if these results could have been confounded by reading problems.

Kirby and Becker (1988) have used a reaction time paradigm to examine differences between normally achieving and two disabled groups: reading-disabled and arithmetic-disabled. The sample of 48 children (three groups of 16) was selected from a larger population of 200 fifth-grade children in regular classrooms. All 200 were given the Standard Progressive Matrices (Raven, 1938, cited in Kirby & Becker, 1988), the Reading Comprehension Subtest of the Progressive Achievement Test and an arithmetic computation test designed for the experiment. The groups were determined through a discrepancy definition. The arithmetic-disabled group consisted of children whose (1) intelligence and reading levels were within plus or minus one standard deviation of the mean for the 200 students; (2) arithmetic scores had to fall at least 0.7 standard deviations below the group mean; (3) there was at least a one standard deviation discrepancy between an individual's arithmetic and reading scores, and (4) there was at least a one standard deviation discrepancy between an individual's arithmetic and intelligence scores. The reading-disabled group was chosen the same way, using reading scores as the discrepant criteria. The control group of normally achieving students had (1) all three (reading, arithmetic, and intelligence) test scores within 1.2 standard deviations of the population mean and (2) had less than one standard deviation difference among all three test scores. Unfortunately no test scores were reported, making it impossible to determine if these children were truly disabled or simply below the norm for that school population.

In spite of these sampling problems, Kirby and Becker's (1988) results appear to indicate that the arithmetic-disabled children were no different from the controls in the areas of encoding and strategy application but significantly poorer in "operational efficiency" (speed as measured by reaction time). This is in contrast to the findings of Geary et al. (1987), who suggest that specific arithmetic-disabled children not only have poorer "operational efficiency" (speed) but use different strategies as well. Given the sampling problems of Kirby and Becker (1988) cited previously, it is possible that the samples used in the two experiments do not represent comparable populations. As well it is not clear that children with reading problems were excluded from the arithmetic-disabled subgroups. It is evident that much research remains to be undertaken in this field.

CONCLUSIONS

Clearly the field of learning disabilities as it applies to computational arithmetic has many difficulties ahead. First, definitional issues tend to confuse and misclassify children deemed learning-disabled. Secondly, many studies fail to distinguish between reading disabilities and specific arithmetic disabilities. However, research making this discrimination has demonstrated that there are clear differences between these groups in cognitive processes such as short-term and working memory and in neuropsychological processes such as visual-spatial analysis, nonverbal concept formation, and visual-perceptual organization. Further, there appears little application of this subtype research to the investigation of the evolution of children's underlying cognitive structures and processes in mathematics. This provides results which only can tend to confuse any attempt to illuminate the possible role of cognitive variables. Finally as Rourke (1983) notes, "Arithmetic disabilities as separated from reading difficulties are only just beginning to capture the interest of serious investigators" (p. 570). In order for these discriminations to be meaningful, it is necessary to look at children's cognitive processing using a subtype approach. Regardless of the approach, there is much work to be done before the multitude of questions related to arithmetic disabilities can be answered.

ACKNOWLEDGMENT

The preparation of this chapter was supported by a grant from the Natural Sciences and Engineering Research Council of Canada to L. Siegel.

REFERENCES

Algozzine, B., & Ysseldyke, J. E. (1988). Questioning discrepancies: Retaking the first step 20 years later. *Learning Disability Quarterly, 11,* 307–318.

Ashcraft, M. H. (1982). The development of mental arithmetic: A chronometric approach. *Developmental Review, 2,* 213–236.

Ashcraft, M. H., & Fierman, B. A. (1982). Mental addition of third, fourth, and sixth graders. *Journal of Experimental Child Psychology, 33,* 216–234.

Ashlock, R. B. (1976). *Error patterns in computations.* Columbus, OH: Charles E. Merrill.

Blankenship C. S. (1985). A behavioral view of mathematical learning problems. In J. F. Cawley (Ed.), *Cognitive strategies and mathematics for the learning disabled.* Rockville, MD: Aspen Systems Corp.

Brooks, L. R. (1978). Nonanalytic concept formation and memory for instances. In E. Rosch & B. B. Lloyd (Eds.), *Cognition and categorization.* Hillsdale, NJ: Lawrence Erlbaum Associates.

Brown, J. S., & Burton, R. B., (1978). Diagnostic models for procedural bugs in basic mathematical skills. *Cognitive Sciences, 2,*155–192.

Brown, J. S., & VanLehn, K. (1980). Repair theory: A generative theory of bugs in procedural skills. *Cognitive Science, 4,* 379–426.

Brown, J. S., & VanLehn, K. (1982). Towards a generative theory of "bugs." In T. D. Carpenter, J. M. Moser, & T.A. Romberg (Eds.), *Addition and subtraction: A cognitive perspective.* New York: Academic Press.

Brown, V. (1975) Learning about mathematics instruction. *Journal of Learning Disabilities, 8,* 476–485.

Doehring, D. G., & Hoshko, I. M. (1977). Classification of reading problems by the Q-technique of factor analysis. *Cortex, 13,* 281–294.

Engelmann, S., & Carnine, D. (1975). *Distar R Arithmetic I.* Chicago: Science Research Associates.

Epps, S., Ysseldyke, J., & Algozzine, B. (1985). An analysis of the conceptual framework underlying definitions of learning disabilities. *Journal of School Psychology, 23,* 133–144.

Feagans, L., & Appelbaum, M. I. (1986). Language subtypes and their validation in learning disabled children. *Journal of Educational Psychology, 78,* 385–364.

Fletcher, J. M. (1985a). External validity of learning disability subtypes. In B.P. Rourke (Ed.), *Neuropsychology of learning disabilities: essentials of subtype analysis* (pp. 187–211). New York: Guilford Press.

Fletcher, J. M. (1985b). Memory for verbal and nonverbal stimuli in learning disability subgroups: Analysis of selective reminding. *Journal of Experimental Child Psychology, 40,* 244–259.

Fletcher, J. M., & Morris, R. (1986). Classification of disabled learners: Beyond exclusionary definitions. In S. J. Ceci (Ed.), *Handbook of cognitive, social, and neuropsychological aspects of learning disabilities* (Vol. 1, pp. 55–80). Hillsdale, NJ: Lawrence Erlbaum Associates.

Gaddes, W. H. (1985). *Learning disabilities and brain function: A neuropsychological approach.* New York: Springer–Verlag.

Geary, D. C., Widaman, K. F., Little, T. D., & Cormier, P. (1987). Cognitive addition: Comparison of learning disabled and academically normal elementary school children. *Cognitive Development, 2,* 249–269.

Glennon, V. J., & Wilson, J. W. (1972). Diagnostic-prescriptive teaching. In W. C. Lowrey (Ed.), *The slow learner in mathematics.* Thirty-fifth Yearbook of the National Council of Teachers of Mathematics. Washington, DC: NCTM.

Groen, G. J., & Parkman, J. M. (1972). A chronometric analysis of simple addition. *Psychological Review, 79,* 329–343.

Hooper, S. R., & Willis, W. G. (1989). *Learning disability subtyping: Neuropsychological foundations, conceptual models, and issues in clinical differentiation.* New York: Springer–Verlag.

Jastak, J. F., & Jastak, S. R. (1978). *Wide Range Achievement Test* (2nd ed.). Wilmington, DE: Guidance Associates.

Keogh, B. (1986). Marker system for describing LD samples. In S. J. Ceci (Ed.), *Handbook of cognitive, social, and neuropsychological aspects of learning disabilities* (pp. 81–94). Hillsdale, NJ: Lawrence Erlbaum Associates.

Keogh, B. (1987). Future of the LD field: Research and practice. *Journal of Learning Disabilities, 21,* 196–209.

Kinsbourne, M., & Warrington, E. K. (1963). Developmental factors in reading and writing backwardness. *British Journal of Psychology, 54,* 145–156.

Kirby, J., & Becker, L. (1988). Cognitive components of learning problems in arithmetic. *Remedial and Special Education, 9,* 7–16.

Klove, H. (1963) Clinical neuropsychology. In F. M. Forster (Ed.), *The medical clinics of North America.* New York: Saunders.

Kosc, L. (1981–1982). Neuropsychological implications of diagnosis and treatment of mathematical learning disabilities. *Topics in Learning and Learning Disabilities, 1,* 19–30.

Linder, B. (1985). *The effect of content on children's arithmetic problem solving.* Unpublished doctoral dissertation, McMaster University, Hamilton, Canada.

Lovitt, T. C. (1975). Applied behavior analysis and learning disabilities, Part II: Specific research recommendations and suggestions for practitioners. *Journal of Learning Disabilities, 8,* 36–50.

Luria, A. R. (1966). *Human brain and psychological processes.* New York: Harper & Row.

Luria, A. R. (1980). *Higher cortical functions in man* (2nd ed.). New York: Basic Books.

McEntire, E. (1981–1982). The relationship between learning disabilities and mathematics: A research review. *Topics in Learning and Learning Disabilities, 1,* 1–18.

McKinney, J. D., Short, E. J., & Feagans, L. (1985). Academic consequences of perceptual-linguistic subtypes of learning disabled children. *Learning Disabilities Research, 1,* 6–17.

McKinney, J. D., & Speece, D. L. (1986). Academic consequences and longitudinal stability of behavioral subtypes of learning disabled children. *Journal of Educational Psychology, 78,* 365–72.

McLeod, T., & Armstrong, S. (1982). Learning disabilities in mathematics-skill deficits and remedial approaches at the intermediate and secondary lever. *Learning Disability Quarterly, 5,* 305–311.

Obrzut, J. E. (1981). Neuropsychological procedures with school-age children. In G. W. Hynd & J. E. Obrzut (Eds.), *Neuropsychological assessment and the school-age child: Issues and procedures* (pp. 237–277) New York: Grune & Stratton.

Ojemann, G. A. (1974). Mental arithmetic during human thalamic stimulation. *Neuropsychologia, 12,* 1–10.

Reid, D. K., & Hresko, W. (1981). *A cognitive approach to learning disabilities,* New York: McGraw-Hill.

Reitan, R. M., & Davison, L. A. (Eds.). (1974). *Clinical neuropsychology: Current status and applications.* Washington, DC: Winston & Sons.

Roberts, G. H. (1968). The failure strategies of third grade arithmetic pupils. *Arithmetic Teacher, 15,* 442–446.

Rourke, B. R. (1975). Brain–behavior relationships in children with learning disabilities: A research program. *American Psychologist, 30,* 911–920.

Rourke, B. P. (1982). Central processing deficiencies in children: Toward a developmental neuropsychological model. *Journal of Clinical Neuropsychology, 4,*1–18.

Rourke, B. P. (1983). Outstanding issues in learning disabilities research. In M. Rutter (Ed.), *Developmental neuropsychology* (pp. 1–25). New York: Guilford Press.

Rourke, B. P. (1985). An overview to learning disability subtypes. In B. P. Rourke *Neuropsychology of Learning Disabilities: Essentials of Subtype Analysis,* (pp. 3–17) New York: Guilford Press.

Rourke, B. P. (1987). Syndrome of nonverbal learning disabilities: The final common pathway of white-matter disease/dysfunction? *Clinical Neuropsychologist, 1,* 209–234.

Rourke, B. P., & Finlayson, M. A. J. (1978). Neuropsychological significance of variations in pattern of academic performance: Verbal and visual-spatial abilities. *Journal of Abnormal Child Psychology, 6,*121–133.

Rourke, B. P., & Fisk, J. L. (1988). Subtypes of learning-disabled children: Implications for a neurodevelopmental model of differential hemispheric processing. In D. L. Molfese & S. J. Segalowitz (Eds.), *Brain lateralization in children: Developmental implications.* (pp. 547–567) New York: Guilford Press.

Satz, P., & Morris, R. (1981). Learning disability subtypes: A review. In F. J. Pirozzole & M. C. Wittrock (Eds.), *Neuropsychological and cognitive processes in reading.* (pp. 109–145) New York: Academic Press.

Share, D. L., Moffitt, T. E., & Silva, P. A. (1988). Factors associated with arithmetic-and-reading disability and specific arithmetic disability. *Journal of Learning Disabilities, 21,* 313–321.

Short, E. J., Feagans, L., McKinney, J. D., & Appelbaum, M. I. (1986). Longitudinal stability of LD subtypes based on age-and IQ-achievement discrepancies. *Learning Disability Quarterly, 9,* 214–224.

Siegel, L. S. (1988a). De rerum novarum, Agatha Christie's learning disability. *Canadian Psychology, 29,* 213–216.

Siegel, L. S. (1988b). Definitional and theoretical issues and research on learning disabilities. *Journal of Learning Disabilities, 21,* 264–266.

Siegel, L. S., & Feldman, W. (1983). Non-dyslexic children with combined writing and arithmetic learning disabilities. *Clinical Pediatrics, 22,* 241–244.

Siegel, L. S., & Heaven, R. (1986). Categorization of learning disabilities. In S. J. Ceci (Ed.), *Handbook of cognitive, social and neuropsychological aspects of learning disabilities* (pp. 95–123) Hillsdale, NJ: Lawrence Erlbaum Associates.

Siegel, L. S., & Linder, B. (1984). Short-term memory processes in children with reading and arithmetic learning disabilities. *Developmental Psychology, 20,* 200–207.

Siegel, L. S., & Ryan, E. B. (1984). Reading disability as a language disorder. *Remedial and Special Education, 5,* 25–33.

Siegel, L. S., & Ryan, E. B. (1988). Development of grammatical sensitivity, phonological, and short-term memory skills in normally achieving and learning disabled children. *Developmental psychology, 24,* 28–37

Siegel, L. S., & Ryan, E. B. (1989). The development of working memory in normally achieving and subtypes of learning disabled children. *Child Development, 60,* 973–980.

Spellacy, F., & Peter, B. (1978). Dyscalculia and elements of the developmental Gerstmann Syndrome in school children. *Cortex, 14,*197–206.

Sternberg, S. (1969). The discovery of processing stages: Extensions of Donder's method. *Acta Psychologia, 30,* 276–315.

Strang, J. D., & Rourke, B. P. (1983). Concept-formation/non-verbal reasoning abilities of children who exhibit specific academic problems with arithmetic. *Journal of Clinical Child Psychology, 12*, 33–39.

Strang, J. D., & Rourke, B. P. (1985). Arithmetic disability subtypes: The neuropsychological significance of specific arithmetical impairment in childhood. In B. P. Rourke (Ed.), *Neuropsychology of learning disabilities: Essentials of subtype analysis.* (pp. 167–187) New York: Guilford Press.

Thorndike, E. L. (1922). *The psychology of arithmetic.* New York: Macmillan.

Webster, R.E. (1979). Visual and aural short-term memory capacity deficits in mathematics disabled students. *Journal of Educational Research, 72* 272–283.

Weinstein, M. L. (1980). A neuropsychological approach to math disability. *New York University Education Quarterly, 11*, 22–28.

Wong, B. (1986). Problems and issues in the definition of learning disabilities. In J. K. Torgesen & B. Wong (Eds.), *Psychological and educational perspectives on learning disabilities* (pp. 3–26) New York: Academic Press.

Woods, S. S., Resnick, L. B., & Groen, G.J. (1975). An experimental test of five process models for subtraction. *Journal of Educational Psychology, 67*, 17–21.

Young, R. M., & O'Shea, T. (1981). Errors in children's subtraction. *Cognitive Science, 5*, 153–177.

9
A Subgroup Analysis of Learning-disabled and Skilled Readers' Working Memory: In Search of a Model for Reading Comprehension

H. Lee Swanson
University of California at Riverside

INTRODUCTION

A number of studies have produced some conflicting results related to learning disabled readers' memory problems. For example, some investigators (e.g., Bauer, 1987; Bauer & Emhert, 1984; Dallego & Moely; 1980; Swanson, 1989; Tarver, Hallahan, Kauffman, & Ball, 1976; Wong, Wong, & Foth, 1977) have attributed learning-disabled readers' poor memory to a failure to use effective encoding strategies. On the other hand, other investigators implicate deficits in selective attention, organization, and/or retrieval (e.g., Tarver et al., 1976; Torgesen, 1978), whereas still others (e.g., Baker, Ceci, & Herrman, 1987; Brainerd, Kingma, & Howe, 1986; Liberman, Mann, Shankweiler, & Werfelman, 1982; Olson, Wise, Conners, Rack, & Fulker, 1989; Swanson, 1986; Wagner & Torgesen, 1987) have argued that learning-disabled readers' memory problems reflect difficulties in storage and coding of verbal information. Two possibilities may account for these discrepant findings, one related to task selection and the other related to sample heterogeneity.

First, measures commonly used in assessing differences between learning-disabled (LD) and nondisabled children's memory performance (e.g., digit or word span tasks) are weakly correlated with academic measures (e.g., reading ability, Dempster, 1985; Perfetti & Lesgold, 1977). Indeed, the majority of these memory tasks do not capture the essence of reading, namely the combination of memory processing and storage (Daneman, 1987).

A second reason for discrepant research findings is that LD children are a heterogeneous group (Fletcher, 1985; McKinney, Short, & Feagans, 1985;

Short, Feagans, McKinney & Appelbaum, 1984; Siegel & Linder, 1984). One strategy to deal with such variability is to identify distinct LD subgroups (e.g., Fletcher, 1984; Short et al., 1984; Speece, 1987; Speece, McKinney, & Appelbaum, 1985; Tarnowski & Nay, 1989). The purpose of the present chapter is to present some preliminary information suggesting that LD children known to have reading comprehension problems yield a distinct subtype of working memory performance. Before exploring the possibility that distinct memory subtypes are related to reading performance, however, a process model of working memory related to LD readers' comprehension must be provided.

Rationale

There are three important reasons why the development of a process-model specifically related to LD readers comprehension is important. First, a focus on working memory processes may be contrasted to the current view of learning-disabilities that focuses on short-term memory processes. Although some researchers view the processes related to short-term memory as interchangeable with working memory (Jorm, 1983), or as a subset of working memory (Baddeley, 1986), some studies suggest that processes related to short-term memory and working memory do not overlap but instead operate independently of each other (Brainerd & Kingma, 1985; Klapp, Marshburn, & Lester, 1983). To address this issue, the present chapter will briefly sketch the results of two studies that compare one model with another.

Second, the majority of studies on working memory have included only a narrow range of reading ability groups and, thus, one cannot adequately determine if these effects can be generalized to younger skilled or LD readers (Dempster, 1985). Finally, models of working memory performance have explained traditionally the variance between and within ability groups as error variance (i.e., Geiselman, Woodward, & Beatty, 1982, for a discussion). It is my assumption that variations in reading can be accounted for in terms of specific working memory processes, and that the variance in memory performance observed between and within skilled and LD reading groups can be reduced in some theoretically interpretable manner.

Models of Memory

In order to provide a theoretical framework, some competing models must be considered. The prevailing opinion is that short-term memory tasks are a subset of working memory processes. As stated by Ellis and Hunt (1983), "Working memory shares some of the characteristics of short-term memory . . . it (working memory) describes the active processes involved in retention, rehearsal, chunking. . ." (p. 78). Short-term memory is partly understood as a component of a limited capacity system for accumulating and holding segments of speech or orthographic units as they arrive during a listening or reading task. Material in short-term memory is maintained if it is restructured in some way, such as by rehearsal or by item association (Baddeley, 1986; Case, Kurland, & Goldberg, 1982; Shankweiler & Crain, 1986). Thus, the short-term memory system is limited in capacity, but the limits are modified by the use of working memory strategies such as rehearsal and/or by association.

In contrast to this opinion, Brainerd and Kingma (1985) suggest that "short-term memory and working memory do not overlap and develop independently of each other" (p. 210). There are two lines of evidence suggesting that short-term and working memory may be independent systems. First, activities related to short-term memory do not interfere with working memory tasks. For example, Klapp et al. (1983) presented subjects with a series of digits, followed by two digit mathematical or reasoning problems; the subjects were then tested on their recall of the digits. The data were analyzed to determine whether or not the interpolated activity (performance of the problem-solving tasks) had any effects on memory for digits. It was reasoned that if short-term memory and the interpolated task rely on the same memory resources, then the interpolated task should interfere with digit span performance. They found, however, that digit span did not react to the presence or absence of the interpolated task (also see Brainerd & Kingma, 1985).

Second, the correlations between working memory tasks and reading are higher than those found between short-term memory tasks and reading. Evidence suggests that measures of short-term memory (such as digit or word span tasks) are weakly correlated with reading comprehension (Daneman & Carpenter, 1980; Perfetti & Lesgold, 1977), whereas working memory tasks, such as Daneman and Carpenter's sentence span task, yield correlations from .72 to .90 between memory and reading comprehension. It is assumed that the high correlations between reading and working memory are due to the fact that working memory tasks simultaneously assess processing and storage functions of memory, both of which are thought to play an active role in reading comprehension.

Although there is some controversy concerning the nature of short-term and working memory tasks, there is also some agreement that a *transformation* or *inference* is required on working memory tasks (e.g., Daneman, 1987; Daneman & Carpenter, 1980). Likewise, it is assumed that working memory tasks require the monitoring of multiple resources (Baddeley & Hitch, 1974); short-term memory tasks, on the other hand, access a passive storage system that draws upon a common pool of resources (Brainerd & Kingma, 1985). For the sake of parsimony, the present chapter views working memory tasks as those that require some inference, transformation and executive processing, whereas short-term memory tasks require the storage of information with minimal processing requirements.

Components of Working Memory

A key roadblock to understanding the relationship between reading ability and working memory performance is the lack of specificity as to which particular components of working memory are involved (Baddeley, Logie, Nimmo–Smith, & Brereton, 1985; Daneman, 1987; Hitch, Woodin, & Baker, 1989). Therefore, it is necessary that subsequent subtyping research identify which components of working memory contribute to the variability in LD readers performance. The multiple-component model proposed by Baddeley and colleagues may shed some light on this issue.

According to Baddeley and colleagues (Baddeley, 1986; Baddeley & Hitch, 1974; Hitch et al., 1989), working memory is comprised of at least three components: a central executive, which is the control system that selects and operates various processes; the articulatory loop, which specializes in verbal storage; and the visuospatial scratch pad, which specializes in imagery and spatial store. An important assumption of Baddeley's model is that the peripheral systems (i.e., the articulatory loop and visuospatial scratch pad) and the central executive system occupy separate though interrelated capacity pools. Provided that storage demands can be met by the peripheral systems, the central executive system uses its capacity for processing activities, such as information organization and long-term memory retrieval. However, when the storage demands exceed storage capacity in the peripheral systems, some central executive capacity must be devoted to storage, with the result that fewer resources will be available for processing activities. Traditionally, inferences related to peripheral system involvement in memory performance are derived from tasks that vary verbal and visuospatial processing demands, such as those with high-low imagery words (Paivio, 1971). In contrast, inferences related to the central executive are derived from multiple or concurrent memory load tasks (e.g., Baddeley, 1986).

The two studies I have recently completed attempt to assess whether a working memory model adequately accounts for subtype differences in learning-disabled children who have difficulty in reading comprehension.

STUDY 1

The purpose of Study 1 is to compare two process models of LD children's memory performance that focus on four hypothetical constructs: central executive, verbal store, visuospatial store, and short-term memory. Multiple indicators were taken from the literature on working memory, and the different relationships among the four constructs were tested, using a confirmatory statistical analysis of the correlational data (Joreskog, 1977). Composite scores related to the factor analysis of memory scores were computed for a later analysis of subtypes. Table 9.1 provides a brief overview of some of the memory components assessed utilizing these tasks (for an extensive discussion of these tasks, see Swanson, Cochran, & Ewars, 1989). Three tasks, which included a total of 16 scores, were utilized in Study 1 to derive these factor scores.

A brief description and rationale for task selection shown in Table 9.1 follows. In the sentence span task, subjects were presented a series of sentences that they were required to process (comprehend), while concurrently trying to retain the last word of each sentence. Working memory performance was measured as the maximum number of sentences processed, while correctly recalling the last word. The contribution of memory components related to long-term store were evaluated by manipulating the type of words to be recalled. Recall of high- and low-imagery words can be seen to be influenced by the verbal and visual store processes (Paivio, 1971).

TABLE 9.1
Components That Are Assumed to be Assessed with Memory
Measures

Task: Concurrent Task: specific conditions	Demands made by the peripheral systems on the central executive
Control	Minimal demands on central executive
Nonverbal shape sorting	Demands on central executive by visual-spatial system
Verbal categorical sortingDemands on the central executive by the verbal store system	Demands on the central executive by the verbal store system
Component Measures	
	Component Measures
Task: Sentence span task specific conditions	General processing and storage
low-imagery words	Verbal abstract information accessed from a verbal store
high-imagery words	Concrete verbal and visual information accessed from a verbal and/or visual store
Task: Preload task: specific conditions	Demands made on a unitary short-term memory capacity
1. 3- vs. 6- digit preload	Alternating preload demands on short-term memory capacity
2. Word span task	Interpolated task, which includes components of short-term memory, i.e., recency effect
A. Low imagery words on interpolated task	Demands made on verbal store
B. High imagery words on interpolated task	Demands made on Verbal and Visual store

In the preload condition, subjects were given a sequence of three or six digits followed by a word list. The subject recalls the words in their correct order and then recalls the digits in order of the original presentation. Short-term and long-term store contributions to recall can be evaluated by analyzing word recall serial position performance under high and low preload conditions, since it is commonly assumed that recency performance reflects short-term memory processes (e.g., Glanzer, 1982). Thus, in order to determine if learning-disabled children's poor recall performance is a function of a short-term memory deficiency versus a generalized working memory deficiency, demands on storage load and the type of words to be recalled (high- vs. low-imagery words) were varied.

In the concurrent memory task, digit strings were verbally presented while the subject attempted to sort cards into categories. Manipulation of memory load is accomplished by varying digit string length (three vs. six digits); and the demands of the peripheral systems on the central executive are manipulated through the type of sorting required. Sorting that utilizes the verbal store would be the sorting of pictures into semantic categories, whereas sorting that makes demands on the visuospatial scratch pad would require discrimination between nonverbal shapes. The sorting of blank cards served as a control condition. Baddeley and Hitch (1974) found that in such activities, the main task difficulty (sorting) interacts with concurrent memory load, but only with a memory load of six digits. These results suggest that demands are being made on the central executive, thereby interfering with the main task.

Two major predictions were relevant to my first study. First, it was anticipated that the factor analysis procedure would yield a model of memory performance roughly characteristic of the multiple-component theory discussed in the review of literature. Second, individual differences in memory and reading performance were predicted to represent distinct subgroups. That is, it was my hope that subgroups would vary in the degree to which components of memory functioning relate to their reading performance. It was expected that components related to working memory would most likely be related to reading comprehension performance, whereas the relationship between short-term memory and reading would be weak for all subgroups.

Thirty-one learning-disabled readers and 70 skilled readers from grades four to six, participated in the study. The performance means and standard deviations on memory measures for all subjects are shown in Table 9.2. The dependent measures for the span task are the number of words correctly recalled in order for each sentence set, and the remaining dependent measures are the proportion of correct recall. A MANOVA comparing ability groups across the measures was significant, as were all univariates.

In order to simplify the results related to model testing, only the factor model that included the total sample was subjected to further model testing. The results of our Liseral testing model indicated that the concurrent memory

TABLE 9.2
Performance Means on the 16 Memory Scores of Experiment 1

	Average of all 101 Children	SD	Skilled Reader (n=70) Average SD	Learning-disabled Reader (n=31) Average SD
Concurrent task				
Recall order-shape	.54	.23	.62(.19)	.36(.20)
Recall order-blanks	.62	.23	.69(.21)	.44(.19)
Recall order-categories	.53	.26	.62(.22)	.31(.20)
Item recall-shape	.82	.12	.86(.09)	.72(.13)
Item recall-blanks	.86	.11	.89(.11)	.80(.09)
Item recall-categories	.82	.12	.87(.09)	.70(.12)
Span task				
High imagery	2.37	2.15	3.42(3.04)	1.32(1.27)
Low imagery	3.37	2.80	4.60(3.56)	2.06(2.0)
Preload task (6-digit)				
Interpolated activity				
Low imagery-words (item recall)	.32	.13	.35(.13)	.25(.09)
High imagery-word (item recall)	.39	.16	.41(.17)	.34(.11)
Low imagery-recency (order)	.13	.12	.16(.13)	.09(.11)
High imagery-recency (order)	.20	.18	.23(.18)	.13(.13)
Digit recall				
Low imagery-digits (order)	.18	.11	.19(.12)	.14(.09)
High imagery-digits (order)	.18	.11	.20(.11)	.12(.08)
Low imagery-digits (item)	.23	.09	.20(.12)	.29(.07)
High imagery-digits (item)	.31	.10	.32(.09)	.28(.094)

load task loaded heavily on Factor 1. This factor was interpreted as reflecting measures of the central executive. Factor 2 reflects measures of immediate word recall on the preload task, and is interpreted as measuring short-term memory. Factor 3 clearly reflects the memory span task. Factors 4 and 5 relate to the recall of the digit string following the presentation of low and high imagery words. Factor 4 has a high loading for low imagery word span recall. This loading reflects the possibility that Factor 4 is related to a peripheral verbal store system. The final factor, Factor 5, reflects high-imagery recall and suggests that resources associated with a peripheral visual-spatial store may be involved. Utilizing a procedure outlined by Schmid and Leiman (1957), overlapping variance between the factors was removed (see Carroll, 1983, for further discussion of this procedure). The model structure is expressed as high-order factors (in this case as independent factors) with a second-order factor designated as g. The important finding related to this analysis is that Factor 2 (short-term memory) loads poorly on g, suggesting independence between this factor and the other factors. In contrast, the factors related to the sentence span and concurrent tasks load highly on g.

Individual Differences

It was necessary that these factors represent independent (uncorrelated) components of memory for the subsequent analysis. Then, based on the hierarchical factor model, memory composite scores were used to analyze individual differences.

The first step was to divide the sample into groups such that a MANOVA of the differences between residual values was maximized. This hierarchical cluster analysis was performed on the five composite scores, plus the classification variable of reading ability and the general memory (g) factor. The reading measure was included because this measure was the primary classification variable. Further, it was important to determine whereby subgroups would emerge on specialized components of working memory when the general memory factor was entered into the equation. For the 101 children, five clusters were judged as being optimal in producing subgroup patterns in memory performance.

Cluster solutions are consistently subject to criticisms related to internal validity. Thus, further validation was necessary to support the five-cluster solution. The validation procedures utilized are outlined in Short et al. (1984), Speece et al. (1985) and McKinney et al. (1985), and include using an alternative algorithm, split-sample replication and discriminant analysis. To assess alternative solutions, the sample was reclustered using the average linkage method. The assumption is that little overlap should exist between the subgroups if the clusters are stable. A discriminant analysis indicated 100% correct classification for all subgroups. Milligan and Cooper's (1985) psychometric criteria were also used to determine the stability of the five clusters. These criteria include analyzing pseudo F and t statistics and a cubic clustering criterion (ccc).

As expected, a MANOVA on cluster variables indicated that all subgroups were significantly differentiated. Because these subgroup differences were expected (the cluster procedure minimized within-cluster variance across the measures), a further analysis of the memory profiles was considered profitable. Thus, cluster profiles were plotted for all children relative to the total group scores. Z-scores near 0 were considered average memory performance, and scores above or below 1.0 were considered exceptional strengths or weaknesses, respectively. The standard scores, as well as the gender, demographic, and psychometric scores relevant to each subgroup, are presented in Table 9.3.

As shown in Table 9.3, Subgroup 1 represents learning-disabled readers with low memory scores in all areas of functioning, except for scores related to short-term memory and visual-spatial store. Correlations of the composite scores within this subgroup indicate that *none* of the memory composite scores correlated significantly with reading. This finding suggests that although some of the memory scores in this particular subgroup are low, compared with the higher reading subgroups, low memory ability may be a necessary but not sufficient condition for low reading ability. Subgroup 2 showed a profile in memory and reading ability within the average range. Correlations between the reading subtest and memory measures were significant for general memory and verbal processing (Factor 3). Subgroup 3 was considered an outlier, and the *n* was too small to compute correlations. Subgroup 4 was also in the average range of reading ability, with exceptional performance in general memory, central executive processing, and general verbal processing. There were substantial correlations among reading and general memory, general verbal processing, and the peripheral verbal system. Subgroup 5 was a high reading group, which had no particular strengths in memory processing. The only noteworthy correlation existed between reading and general verbal processing.

Psychometric Scores

It was of interest to determine whether (a) patterns of working memory performance are maintained on measures separate from those used to define the original clusters, and (b) whether the classification and working memory measures were relevant to performance measures that are assumed to be concurrently related.

Because of sample size, subgroup 3 was removed from the subsequent analysis. Significant ANOVAs comparing subgroups on the CTBS mathematics and spelling subtests occurred. This was expected because of the high intercorrelations among reading, mathematics and spelling measures. A Duncan multiple range test indicated that significant differences in achievement were isolated to the low reading ability groups for mathematics ($1 < 3 = 4 = 5$) and spelling ($1 < 2 = 4 = 5$). An ANOVA comparing subtypes was also significant for verbal and performance intelligence measures. Post hoc analysis indicated that significant differences between the subgroups were localized to the LD readers and high readers for verbal IQ ($5 > 4 = 2 = 1; 4 > 1$) and performance IQ ($5 > 4 = 2 = 1$). No significant differences were found between subgroups in terms of gender, ethnicity, or chronological age.

TABLE 9.3

Mean standard Scores for Memory Classification and Demographic and Psychometric Data as a Function of Subgroup (N = 101)

Subgroups	Reading General	Central Executive Processing	Short-term Memory	General Verbal Processing	Peripheral Verbal Store	Peripheral Visual Spatial Store	Math (%)	Spell (%)	VIQ	PIQ	CA	% Male Readers	% LD
Subgroup 1 (n = 19)	-.69(19)	-1.12	-1.01	-.03	-1.01	-1.37	-.83	22.9	22.26	92.33	99.83	12.71	47.37%	(100%)
Subgroup 2 (n = 36)	-.50(51.77)	-.44	-.49	-.51	-.43	-.16	-.17	47.41	46.25	94.10	102.90	12.07	69%	(30%)
Subgroup 3 (n = 2)	.54(69.00)	-2.27	-.72	-3.55	-2.10	-1.27	-1.87	61.00	14.00	103.35	108.00	12.00	50%	(0%)
Subgroup 4 (n = 14)	.55(78.00)	1.22	1.53	.18	1.33	.40	.26	61.64	62.71	103.00	104.00	12.13	35%	(0%)
Subgroup 5 (n = 30)	.85(79.00)	.82	.56	.78	.68	.56	.74	66.34	73.63	115.50	118.93	12.08	60%	(0%)

Brackets ( ) indicate percentile.

Summary of Findings

The results provide unique profiles related to memory and reading performance. Subgroup 1 clearly consists of the learning-disabled readers who were deficient in all measures of memory, except short-term memory and a factor possibly related to the visual-spatial store system. These findings are consistent with the literature (Swanson, 1984b; Vellutino, 1979), which suggests that visual coding is not deficient in poor readers. The results are in conflict, however, with studies attributing short-term memory deficits to disabled readers. Therefore, the value of citing short-term memory as an explanation for reading disabilities may be overestimated. Subgroup 2 represents a mix of poor and average readers with no apparent strengths or weaknesses in memory functioning. In fact, this profile is similar to the profile for Subgroup 5, except that this latter subgroup has significantly higher reading scores. Subgroup 4 is also a skilled reading group and is proficient in general working memory and in the specified working memory components related to executive central processing and verbal storage. Subgroup 3 includes children who, despite adequate reading skills, perform poorly on short-term memory tasks, as well as on the majority of working measures. No attempt will be made to explain this subgroup pattern except to suggest that other mechanisms beside the measures utilized in the present study must be taken into account when establishing a process model of memory and reading function.

STUDY 2

The previous study suggests that working memory and short-term memory are independent systems. The results also confirm findings from previous studies which suggest that short-term memory functioning is a rather poor predictor of reading comprehension. Of course, it is possible that the short-term memory measures in Study 1 were rather general and did not assess processing activities commonly attributed to short-term store, such as phonological coding. To examine this possibility, the next study was conducted to examine the effect of presenting word span tasks that disrupt the parsing of words into phonological units. One task sensitive to this storage is a span task of phonologically similar items (e.g., Shankweiler et al., 1979). Similar items are assumed to disrupt subvocal rehearsal and the functions of the articulatory loop (e.g., Shankweiler & Crain, 1986).

Study 2 also introduced new tasks for measuring working memory. Two tasks were administered in Study 2 that required the transformation and monitoring of information. The first task, a semantic orienting task, required subjects to *reorganize* information prior to recall. The other task required subjects to make difficult decisions about which word fit into a sentence, while *simultaneously* requiring subjects to attend to secondary information. This latter task was adapted from the literature on cognitive effort (Ellis, Thomas,

& Rodriquez, 1984; Swanson, 1984a). These encoding tasks generally include manipulations of high- and low-processing effort that require the use of executive processes to direct attention to primary and secondary information.

Three predictions were relevant to this next study. First, we anticipated that the results would replicate those of Study 1 by showing both that short-term memory and working memory tasks do not share a common factor and that only the factors related to working memory correlate significantly with reading. Second, the factor analysis was expected to divide along tasks that are assumed to assess short-term memory versus those designed to tap working memory. For example, tasks that require a transformation prior to output will load on a separate factor from tasks that require the voluntary monitoring of attention resources; however, these factors are both assumed to assess components of working memory. Finally, we predicted the emergence of unique reading subgroups as a function of the various memory components.

Twenty-five skilled and 49 disabled readers were randomly selected from a larger sample of identified children in the school districts. The same criteria as Experiment 1 were used to determine LD readers. Mean and standard deviation scores for reading, verbal IQ, and chronological age (CA) were as follows: 14.78, (SD = 9.26); 94.54, (SD = 18.41); 12.12, (SD = 1.10). The 25 nondisabled readers were selected randomly (matched, however, as closely as possible for CA, gender, and SES) from students in a regular classroom who had normal reading achievement scores.

Task Materials, Procedures, and Measures

Semantic Orienting Task. Children were told they would be asked to remember words from two visually presented word lists. Children were instructed to say each word individually from the list aloud. After saying each word, they were asked to place a letter beside each word that went with a particular category (e.g., put an "r" beside things you ride on). The purpose of the semantic orienting task was to direct children to engage in concurrent processing (i.e., subjects determine whether a word to be remembered matches a particular category) and storage activity (recall of all words in the lists). The task was viewed as a working memory measure because some transformation (reorganization of words into semantic categories) of information was required prior to output (e.g., Greeno, 1973).

Phonemic Disruption (Rhyming) Task. Children were presented two word lists from which they were to recall two categories (e.g., words that rhyme with cat or pit) of five rhyming words (e.g., cat, rat, fat, sat) within each word list.

Each word list contained 10 words. Words of similar sound were next to each other. After the two lists had been represented, children were asked to recall the words that rhymed together. It was assumed that the rhyming quality of words would interfere with phonological coding (Conrad, 1964; Shankweiler et al., 1979). No doubt this task has a processing component, but we reasoned that the transformation of information prior to output would be disrupted because of acoustic interference. This is because it is more difficult to recall an item if there are other similar items in memory; recall of items in short-term memory is assumed to be sensitive to acoustic interference (rhyming words) because the learner usually (but not necessarily) relies on acoustic codes (e.g., Conrad, 1964).

Besides the proportion correct recall, dependent measures for both the semantic and phonemic recall tasks also included an index score of memory organization independent of the number of words recalled (for ARC formula, see Murphy & Puff, 1982). This measurement of clustering is particularly important for the semantic orienting task because children were asked to reorganize (transform) the words prior to recall.

Sentence Elaboration Task. As with the other two tasks, the purpose of the sentence elaboration task was to assess children's ability to recall words. The elaboration task facilitates the matching of external information to information in long-term memory, but requires little *transformation* of the stored information prior to output. Thus, it is my assumption that the elaboration task measures short-term memory.

Effortful Encoding Task. The purpose of this task was to assess more directly the demands made on central executive processing. Such demands on central executive processing were evaluated by varying encoding difficulty (e.g., Ellis et al., 1984; Swanson, 1984a). Twenty base sentences were constructed. Each sentence consisted of a one-word omission followed by a pair of nouns from which the child selected the word that correctly completed the sentence. Sentences were further divided in terms of the degree of difficulty (low or high effort) in choosing the missing word (Ellis et al., 1984). For low-effort choices, incorrect distractions were used to minimize choice errors (i.e., words that did not fit meaningfully into the sentence). For high-effort choices, the choice of words was less obvious or less self-evident when compared with the low-effort items. Children were told that they would be asked to recall the words they had circled *first* and then the words they did not circle.

Digit Span Task. The forward digit span task from the WISC–R test was also used to compare ability groups. This task is generally assumed to be a popular measure of short-term memory (Dempster, 1985).

Summary of Findings

The performance means across 74 subjects are shown in Table 9.4. A MANOVA comparing skilled and disabled readers for the 10 memory measures was significant, and Univariates were significant for low effort encoding, high effort encoding, recall of semantically organized lists, and semantic organization.

The model testing procedure suggested that a three-factor model best captured the data set. The general memory factor, g was best characterized by the central recall task. A moderate loading was also found with semantic organization, suggesting that long-term memory processing is an important component of general working memory, a finding consistent with Greeno (1973). Poor loadings on the g factor were found for the phonemic (rhyming) task, which suggests that this short-term memory measure reflects a separate system. In general, the results replicate those described in Study 1 in showing that working memory and short-term memory represent functionally independent systems. The results were generally disappointing, however, when correlations were computed within subgroups relating reading performance to Factor scores. Only Factor 2 (semantic manipulation) was significantly correlated with reading, whereas Factor 3, which was assumed to assess an isolated component of working memory, correlated poorly with reading. Despite the poor correlations, the results are consistent with Study 1 in suggesting that the short-term memory factor and the working memory factor vary in their loadings on the common factor. In addition, tasks that make up the short-term memory factor are poorly correlated to reading whereas some

TABLE 9.4
Performance Means on the 10 Memory Scores of Experiment 2

	Average of 74 Children	SD	Skilled Readers Avg. SD	LD Readers Avg. SD
1. Nonelaborative task recall	37.02	24.63	41.25(22.09)	31.52(27.18)
2. Elaborative task recall	36.62	31.94	40.25(22.35)	32.42(19.68)
3. Low-effort encoding task central recall	34.72	17.29	42.50(16.32)	25.15(13.94)
4. Low-effort encoding task secondary recall	28.51	15.68	30.25(16.51)	26.06(14.34)
5. High-effort encoding task central recall	36.63	19.23	43.15(18.88)	28.51(17.19)
6. High-effort encoding task secondary recall	29.78	18.50	31.85(19.87)	26.84(16.70)
7. Semantic recall	50.40	23.37	62.50(19.1)	34.54(17.51)
8. Semantic organization	35.00	36.6	48.3(39.6)	18.16(25.12)
9. Phonetic recall	44.59	21.40	45.0(17.34)	43.63(25.47)
10. Phonetic organization	32.6	36.33	35.00(39.00)	30.30(33.66)

TABLE 9.5

Mean Standard Scores for Memory Classification, Psychometric, and
Demographic Information as a Function of Subgroup

	Classification Variables									Variable		LD
Subgroup	Reading	General Memory	Short-term Memory	Semantic Manipulation	Secondary Recall	Math	Digit Span	Verbal IQ	Performance IQ	Male (%)	Anglo (%)	Readers (%)
Subgroup 1 (n = 16)	.786(74.3)	.505	.263	.180	1.32	72.93	10.31	113.25	117.50	43.75%	81.25%	0%
Subgroup 2 (n = 33)	.349(57.84)	-.583	-.387	-.529	-.387	49.75	8.72	103.03	109.69	63.64%	69.70%	27.27%
Subgroup 3 (n = 1)	1.25(6.0)	3.54	3.54	3.76	-1.21	8.00*	4.00*	80.00*	78.00*	100%	100%	100%
Subgroup 4 (n = 23)	-.939(14.43)	-.201	.044	.340	-.315	18.60	9.39	96.43	93.47	60.87%	56.52%	100%

Brackets ( ) indicate % score.

*Raw Score.

Mathematics score are in percentiles; digit span scores are in scale scores (range = 1 to 19), and Verbal IQ and Performance IQ are in standard scores.

tasks, but not all, that load on a working memory factor (in this case Factor 2) significantly correlated with reading here as in Study 1.

Similar procedures to those in Study 1 were used to subgroup the readers. Dependent measures for the subgroup analysis were reading ability, the composite scores related to general memory ability (g factor composite score) and the three orthogonalized factors. The main composite scores for each subgroup are shown in Table 9.5. Cluster profiles were plotted in terms of total group z-scores. The results again yielded a distinctly poor reading group (Subgroup 4). A post hoc analysis indicated significant differences between subgroups on reading (1 = 2 > 4), general memory (1 = 4 > 2), short-term memory (1 = 4; 1 > 2), semantic manipulation (4 = 1 > 2), and secondary recall (1 > 4 = 2). Because of the small n, Subgroup 3 was removed from the analysis.

In order to determine if the differences between subgroups might be extended to measures other than memory and reading ability, an analysis was conducted, comparing subgroups on mathematical achievement, verbal and performance IQ, and digit span performance. The latter measure was included to establish divergent validity; in other words, if short-term memory is poorly related to reading ability and working memory (Dempster, 1985; Perfetti & Lesgold, 1977), one would predict little relationship between digit span performance and subgroup classification.

An ANOVA comparing subgroups on mathematical performance was significant, and a post hoc analysis indicated significant differences ($p < .05$) between the high- and low-memory subgroups: 1 > 2 > 4. An ANOVA between subgroups on the digit test was not significant, $F < 1$, supporting earlier research suggesting that the digit span task is not directly related to working memory and reading comprehension. In addition, no significant differences were found between subgroups in terms of gender, ethnicity, or chronological age.

SUMMARY AND CONCLUSIONS

It is typically assumed that individuals who experience the same task differ in performance when they experience the same processing instructions (Geiselman et al., 1982). The primary aim of reviewing two preliminary studies was to suggest that a significant proportion of that variance could explain memory differences between skilled and learning-disabled readers. Collectively, the analyses point to a model of memory in which short-term memory and working memory operate independently and confirm that certain processes in working memory, such as the central executive, account for a large part of the individual differences in reading comprehension. The results also seem to suggest that although individual differences in performance are related to general working memory functioning (g), they are also related to specialized components of working memory. Of the working memory components identified in Studies 1 and 2, activities related to the central executive are possibly the most important in predicting reading comprehension ability.

Taken together, the two studies confirmed that a multiple-process conception of memory functioning in learning-disabled and skilled readers is plausible, and a uniprocess model that combines the functions of short-term memory and working memory is rejected. One advantage of this multiple-process memory model in accounting for skilled and learning-disabled readers' performance is that it may account for the inadequacy of short-term memory in explaining reading comprehension. The present studies suggest that the central executive does not appear to have direct access to short-term memory as a means for processing verbal material. This interpretation is consistent with Baddeley (1981), who has pointed out that central executive processing does not itself have access to phonological codes, although it has access to semantic codes in long-term memory. Thus, working memory and short-term may be indirectly related.

In terms of subtyping, the two studies clearly demonstrate that children of various reading ability can be subdivided in terms of the various memory components, strengths, and weaknesses. Further, the results indicate that learning-disabled readers can be differentiated from average readers on a number of measures of working memory. For example, the LD subgroup has distinct deficiencies in general working memory, central executive processing, and verbal storage. The results support the hypothesis that some pervasive, as well as isolated working memory processes, underlie poor reading comprehension ability.

REFERENCES

Baddeley, A. D. (1981). The concept of working memory: A view of its current state and probable future development. *Cognition, 10*, 17–23.

Baddeley, A. D. (1986). *Working memory*. Oxford, England: Clarendon Press.

Baddeley, A. D., & Hitch, G. (1974). Working memory. In G. H. Bower (Ed.), *The Psychology of learning and motivation* (Vol. 8, pp. 199–239) New York: Academic Press.

Baddeley, A. D., Lewis, V., Eldridge, M., & Thomson, N. (1984). Attention and retrieval from long-term memory. *Journal of Experimental Psychology: General, 113*, 518–540.

Baddeley, A. D., Logie, R., Nimmo–Smith, T., & Brereton, N. (1985). Components of fluent reading. *Journal of Memory and Language, 24*, 119–131.

Baker, J. G., Ceci, S. J., & Herrmann, N. D. (1987). Semantic structure and processing: Implications for the learning disabled child. In H. L. Swanson (Ed.), *Memory and learning disabilities* (pp. 85–110). Greenwich, CT: JAI Press.

Bauer, R. H. (1987). Control processes as a way of understanding, diagnosing and remediation. In H. L. Swanson (Ed.), *Memory and learning disabilities*. Greenwich, CT: Jai Press.

Bauer, R. H., & Emhert, J. (1984). Information processing in reading-disabled and nondisabled children. *Journal of Experimental Child Psychology, 37*, 271–281.

Bentler, P. M., & Bonnett, D. (1980). Significance test and goodness of fit in the analysis of covariance structures. Psychological Bulletin, 88, 588–606.

Brainerd, C. J. & Kingma, J. (1985). On the independence of short-term memory and working memory in cognitive development. *Cognitive Psychology, 17*, 210–247.

Brainerd, C. J., Kingma, J., & Howe, M. L. (1986). Long-term memory development and learning disability: Storage and retrieval loci of disabled/nondisabled differences. In S. Ceci (Ed.), *Handbook on cognitive, social, and neurological aspects of learning disabilities.* Hillsdale, NJ: Lawrence Erlbaum Associates.

Carroll, J. B. (1983). Studying individual differences in cognitive abilities: Through and beyond factor analysis. In R. Dillon & R. Schmeck (Eds.), *Individual differences in cognition* (pp. 1–28). New York: Academic Press.

Case, R., Kurland, D. M., & Goldberg, J. (1982). Operational efficiency and the growth of short-term memory span. *Journal of Experimental Child Psychology, 33*, 386–404.

Conrad, R. (1964). Acoustic confusion in immediate memory. *British Journal of Psychology, 3*, 75–84.

Dallego, M., & Moely, B. (1980). Free recall in boys of normal and poor reading levels as a function of task manipulation. *Journal of Experimental Child Psychology, 30*, 62–78.

Daneman, M. (1987). Reading and working memory. In J. R. Beech & A.M. Colley (Eds.), *Cognitive approaches to reading* (pp. 57–86). New York: Wiley.

Daneman, M., & Carpenter, P. A. (1980). Individual differences in working memory and reading. *Journal of Verbal Learning and Verbal Behavior, 19*, 450–466.

Dempster, F. N. (1985). Short-term memory development in childhood and adolescence. In C. J. Brainerd & M. Pressley (Eds.), *Basic processes in memory development: Progress in cognitive development research.* New York: Springer–Verlag.

Ellis, H., & Hunt, R. (1983). *Fundamentals of human learning and cognition.* Dubuque, IA: Brown.

Ellis, H. D., Thomas, R. L., & Rodriquez, I. A. (1984). Emotional mood states and memory: Elaborative encoding, semantic processing, and cognitive effort. *Journal of Experimental Psychology: Learning, Memory and Cognition, 10*, 470–432.

Fletcher, J. M. (1985). Memory for verbal and nonverbal stimuli in learning disability subgroups: Analyses by selective reminding. *Journal of Experimental Child Psychology, 40*, 244–259.

Geiselman, R. E., Woodward, J. A., & Beatty, J. (1982). Individual differences in verbal performance: A test of alternative information processing models. *Journal of Experimental Psychology: General, 111*, 109–134.

Glanzer, M. (1982). Short-term memory. In C.R. Puff (Ed.), *Handbook of research methods in human memory and cognition* (pp. 63–93), New York: Academic Press.

Greeno, J. G. (1973). The structure of memory and the process of solving problems. In R. C. Soslo (Ed.), *Contemporary issues in cognitive psychology.* Washington, DC: Winston.

Halford, G. S., Bain, J. D., & Mayberry, M. T. (1986). Working memory and representational processes: Implications for cognitive development. In H. Bouman & D. G. Bowhuis (Eds.), *Attention and performance X: Control of language processes* (pp. 459–470). Hillsdale: Lawrence Erlbaum Associates.

Hitch, G. J., Woodin, M. E., & Baker, S. (1989). Visual and phonological components of working memory in children. *Memory and Cognition, 17*, 175–185.

Joreskog, K. G. (1977). Structural equation models in the social sciences: Specification, estimation, and testing. In P.R. Krishnaiah (Ed.), *Proceedings of the symposium on applications of statistics.* Amsterdam: North-Holland.

Jorm, A. F. (1983). Specific reading retardation and work memory: A review. *British Journal of Psychology, 74*, 311–342.

Klapp, S., Marshburn, E., & Lester, P. (1983). Short-term memory does not involve the "working memory" of information processing: The demise of a common assumption. *Journal of Experimental Psychology: General, 112*, 240–263.

McKinney, J. D., Short, E. J., & Feagans, L. (1985). Academic consequences of perceptual-linguistic subtypes of learning disabled children. *Learning Disabilities Research, 1*, 6–17.

Milligan, G. W., & Cooper, M. C. (1985). An examination of procedures for determining the number of clusters in a data set. *Psychometrica, 50*, 159–179.

Murphy, M., & Puff, C. (1982). Free recall: Basic methodology and analysis. In C. Puff (Ed.), *Handbook of research methods in human memory and cognition* (pp. 99–128). New York: Academic Press.

Olson, R., Wise, B., Conners, F., Rack, J., & Fulker, D. (1989). Specific deficits in component reading and language skills: Genetic and Environmental Influence. *Journal of Learning Disabilities, 22*, 339–348.

Paivio, A. (1971). *Imagery and verbal processes*. New York: Holt, Rinehart, & Winston.

Perfetti, C. A., & Lesgold, A. N. (1977). Discourse comprehension and sources of individual differences, In M. Just & P. Carpenter (Eds.), *Cognitive processes in comprehension*. Hillsdale, NJ: Lawrence Erlbaum Associates.

Schmid, J., & Leiman, J. M. (1957). The development of hierarchical factor solutions. *Psychometrica, 22*, 53–61.

Shankweiler, D., & Crain, S. (1986). Language mechanisms and reading disorder: A modular approach. *Cognition, 24*, 139–168.

Shepard, L. A., Smith, M. L., & Vojir, C.P. (1983). Characteristics of pupils identified as learning disabled. *American Educational Research Journal, 20*, 309–331.

Short, E. J., Feagans, L., McKinney, J. D., & Appelbaum. (1984). Longitudinal stability of LD subtypes based on age and IQ-achievement discrepancies. *Learning Disability Quarterly, 9*, 214–225.

Siegel, L. S., & Linder, B. A. (1984). Short-term memory processes in children with reading and arithmetic disabilities. *Developmental Psychology, 20*, 200–207.

Speece, D. L. (1987). Information processing subtypes of learning disabled readers. *Learning Disability Research, 2*, 91–102.

Speece, D. L., McKinney, J. D., & Appelbaum, M. I. (1985). Classification and validation of behavioral subtypes of learning disabled children. *Journal of Educational Psychology, 77*, 67–77.

Swanson, H. L. (1984a). Effects of cognitive effort and work distinctiveness and learning disabled and nondisabled readers' recall. *Journal of Educational Psychology, 76*, 894–908.

Swanson, H. L. (1984b). Semantic and visual memory codes in learning disabled readers. *Journal of Experimental Child Psychology, 37*, 124–140.

Swanson, H. L. (1986). Do semantic memory deficiencies underlie disabled readers encoding process? *Journal of Experimental Child Psychology, 41*, 461–488.

Swanson, H. L. (1989). The effects of central processing strategies on learning disabled, mildly retarded, average and gifted children's elaborative encoding abilities. *Journal of Experimental Child Psychology, 41*, 370–397.

Swanson, H. L., Cochran, K., Ewars, C. (1989). Working memory and reading ability. *Journal of Abnormal Child Psychology, 17*, 145–156.

Tarnowski, K. J., & Nay, S. M. (1989). Locus of control in children with learning disabilities and hyperactivity: A subgroup analysis. *Journal of Learning Disabilities, 122*, 381–383.

Tarver, S., Hallahan, D., Kauffman, J., & Gall, D. (1976). Verbal rehearsal and selective attention in children with learning disabilities: A development lag. *Journal of Experimental Child Psychology, 22*, 375–385.

Thorndike, E., & Lorge, T. (1944). *The teacher's word book of 30,000 words*. New York: Teachers College, Columbia University.

Torgesen, J. K. (1978). Memorization processes in reading disabled children. *Journal of Educational Psychology, 69*, 471–478.

Torgesen, J. K., & Houck, D. G. (1980). Processing deficiencies of learning-disabled children who perform poorly on the Digit Span Test. *Journal of Educational Psychology, 72,* 141–160.

Wagner, K., & Torgesen, J. K. (1987). The nature of phonological processing and its causal role in the acquisition of reading skills. *Psychological Bulletin, 101,* 192–212.

Vellutino, F. R. (1979). *Dyslexia: Theory and research.* Cambridge, MA: MIT Press.

10 Subtypes as Prototypes: Extended Studies of Rationally Defined Extreme Groups

Joseph K. Torgesen
Florida State University

In this chapter, I will discuss the utility of studying carefully defined extreme groups of learning-disabled children as a method for coping with the heterogeneity of the learning-disabled population in our schools and clinics. Whatever the source of this heterogeneity—be it the result of misdiagnosis or real variation in the cognitive factors that underly learning difficulties—it has created enormous problems for the establishment of scientific understanding of learning disabilities (Senf, 1986). One solution to the problem is to search for useful ways to form subgroups within the larger population of LD children. Presumably, the identification of such subgroups will allow us to make preventive, treatment, and prognostic statements with greater accuracy and specificity than is possible if the LD population is treated as a single entity.

At the outset, I want to express my pessimism about the idea that there are naturally occurring, discrete clusters, or syndromes, within the learning-disabled population. I agree with Andrew Ellis (1985), Keith Stanovich (1988), and others, that the best analogy for all types of learning disabilities at present is a condition like obesity, rather than a condition like pregnancy. That is, it seems extremely likely that the factors that produce specific learning disabilities of various types are continuously distributed in the entire population. Just as it is possible to be a little, or a lot, obese (but not a little or a lot pregnant), it is also possible to possess different cognitive weaknesses associated with learning disabilities to varying degrees. This idea that the factors responsible for learning disabilities "are continuously arrayed in a multidimensional space and not distributed in clusters" (Stanovich, 1988, p.

229

599), suggests that the proper way to think about the variability within the LD population involves heterogeneity, without homogeneity of subtypes (Olson, Kliegl, Davidson, & Foltz, 1985). Although there may be different types of learning disabilities, we should not expect the boundaries between the different subtypes to be naturally defined, nor should we expect there to be little important variability among children in a given subtype.

Just because we cannot expect to find naturally occurring discrete clusters, or subtypes, within samples of LD children does not mean that research focusing on subgroups will not produce valuable information. It does mean, however, that whatever methods we use to divide children into subgroups need to be recognized as rationally imposed and arbitrary to some degree. For example, if one is interested in a subgroup of learning-disabled children with several salient characteristics, the decision about whom to include in this subgroup involves the setting of arbitrary criteria along a continuum from normal to maximally impaired on each characteristic. The fact that arbitrary selection criteria must be established does not lessen the value of studying the subgroups that are formed. As long as the criteria are explicit, as they are in many studies of individuals of varying degrees of obesity, useful and replicable knowledge can be obtained.

Given that the characteristics of subgroups are likely to vary along a continuum, potentially important distinctions among different groups will become "fuzzy" as the selection criteria become less extreme. Children falling at the boundary between one subtype and another will not look strikingly different from each other, nor will they be likely to have significantly different treatment or prognostic outcomes. Thus, I would argue that, at this preliminary stage of investigation, our best strategy is to identify subjects that are the most extreme exemplars of the subgroup or subgroups we are studying. If our goal is to create knowledge about learning disabilities by discovering specific preventative, treatment, and prognostic information that is imbedded within a coherent theory of etiology, a good place to start is with "prototypical" subgroups that possess characteristics differing substantially from those of other LD children.

To illustrate the utility of forming subgroups that represent reasonable extremes in terms of their identifying characteristics, it is useful to consider the kinds of questions we might want to answer about a specific subtype, or subgroup of LD children. As we ask each question, it will become clear that sensible answers can only be obtained by restricting as much as possible the relevant heterogeneity of the groups we are studying. These questions were selected from both a scientific and educational perspective. That is, answers to questions like these are essential to both the establishment of a science of learning disabilities, and to effective educational practices.

RESEARCH QUESTIONS ABOUT SUBGROUPS

One of the first questions we want to answer about a specific subgroup concerns the stability of its identifying features. That is, subgroups will likely be identified by their performance on neuropsychological (Lyon, 1985), cognitive (Torgesen, 1988), or behavioral measures (McKinney, 1989). Assessment of both the short-term (reliability) and long-term (stability) consistency of performance on these measures by individuals in the subgroups would seem to be a prerequisite for further study of the entire group. Although there may be good reasons to expect that the composition of subgroups might change over long periods of time (measured in years), subgroups for which the defining characteristics are not stable over shorter periods are certainly of questionable value.

After establishing the stability of the characteristics that define a subgroup, it is important to develop an adequate conceptualization of the fundamental cognitive and/or neuropsychological difficulties of the group. Most empirical subtyping studies rely on psychometric instruments to provide initial assessment of identifying characteristics. However, the actual information-processing requirements of these tasks are often poorly understood (Estes, 1974), so that further experimentation is almost always essential to eliminate competing hypotheses about reasons for the group's deviant performance on the measures. Our confidence in the group's essential cohesiveness will be increased to the extent that we can show that their performance problems on the defining measures have a common explanation.

For example, a subgroup of elementary-school-aged LD children might be defined by the fact that they show specially impaired performance on measures of individual word reading while manifesting adequate listening comprehension and math skills. Further studies of this group might demonstrate differences among the children in the factors most responsible for their word-reading difficulties. Since these different etiologies might each have different preventive, prognostic, or treatment implications, they suggest the possibility that the previously identified subgroup was defined at too general a level.

Work to answer questions about the fundamental cognitive or neuropsychological difficulties of a given subgroup provides an opportunity to test the foundational assumptions of our field, which are currently under vigorous attack from a variety of sources (Coles, 1987; Stanovich, 1986a). These foundational assumptions are: (1) that learning disabilities are caused by deficiencies in basic psychological processes that do not produce broad cognitive impairment, but which do affect performance on specific academic tasks; and, (2) that these cognitive limitations are caused by naturally occurring variation in the neurological substrate that supports all intellectual activity, or by damage to this substrate caused by accident or disease. These assumptions about the basic causes of learning disabilities do not exclude the possibility that much important variation in academic performance is the result of general intellectual characteristics, home and family background, teaching effectiveness, motivation and attitudes, or peer influences. Neither do they deny that learning outcomes are always the result of an interaction between specific student and environmental characteristics. They do assert, however, that a complete account of student variability in achievement must acknowledge an important role for inherent (within the child) variability in specific intellectual abilities. Using extreme and relatively homogeneous groups of LD children to study this intellectual variability should allow more convincing demonstrations of the uniqueness, and specificity, of LD children's problems than has been possible in the past.

Fortunately, our attempts to build a coherent theory of the individual differences that produce learning disabilities is aided by the recent emergence of both information processing and neuropsychology as rapidly maturing scientific paradigms that can supply methods and concepts to help answer questions in this area (Torgesen, 1986). My own preference is first to establish clearly a description of a subgroup's deficits in terms of specific information-processing limitations, and then to focus on developing a neurologically based explanation for these difficulties.

A third important question about subgroups is how processing limitations affect the acquisition of academic skills. This is actually a very difficult scientific problem. It is not sufficient, for example, to assume a causal relationship because a given processing disability and certain academic deficits co-occur within a subgroup. Establishing causal relationships between processing disabilities and academic problems requires a complex set of converging experiments involving at least longitudinal studies, instructional studies, and systematic constrasts with appropriate control groups (Bradley & Bryant, 1985). Fortunately, future efforts in this area will be aided by our increasing understanding of the specific mental requirements for learning various academic skills (Butterfield & Ferretti, 1987; Campione, 1989).

Related to this previous question, but extending beyond it to practical concerns, are questions about specific types of remediation that might apply to the subgroup being studied. A primary reason for identifying reasonably coherent subgroups of LD children is to find a more efficient way of programming instruction than simple trial and error. Hopefully, children with very similar patterns of processing disabilities will respond similarly to specific instructional methods. This also is one of the foundational assumptions of our field that has been very difficult to verify.

I am not discouraged by previous failures to find aptitude by treatment interactions with LD children (Arter & Jenkins, 1979). It is relatively easy to understand these failures as the result of inadequate conceptualization of both the processing disabilities of the groups being treated, and of the treatments themselves. (Torgesen, 1979). It may turn out that the instructional techniques that different subgroups require in common (need for increased number of learning trials, need for close supervision and careful feedback), are more numerous than those that require differential application. However, some of the preliminary work by Lyon (1985) suggests that the performance of at least some subgroups can be markedly, and differentially, affected by variation in important instructional techniques.

A final question that should be the focus of any systematic study of subgroups involves long-term prognosis. Of course, prognosis, and especially educational prognosis, is dependent on the instructional environment to which the individual is exposed. Therefore, prognostic statements are never complete, but they can be useful in determining the long-term adequacy of current educational programs for specific subgroups. Long-term prognostic studies are also required in order to establish the developmental course of the characteristics that are used to define subgroups. For example, 20% of LD children may constitute a specific subgroup in the third grade, but half of these children may no longer possess the essential characteristics of the subgroup in high school, or these characteristics may be expressed in a different way during adolescence. Having this type of information is helpful, not only in understanding more about the homogeneity of our original subgroup, but also in understanding how these characteristics impact on various academic tasks.

TWO CAVEATS

Having illustrated the kinds of questions that are easier to answer if we focus on relatively homogeneous, extreme, or prototypical subgroups of LD children, at least two caveats are in order. The first involves a reminder that any selection criteria we use to define our groups are likely to be arbitrarily chosen along a continuum of severity. Thus, to ask how prevalent a given subgroup is within the total population of LD children ". . . will be as meaningful, and as meaningless, as asking how prevalent obesity is. The answer will depend entirely upon where the line is drawn" (Ellis, 1985, p. 172).

The second caveat involves both a virtue and a vice of studying extreme subgroups. On the one hand, a virtue of studying extreme groups is that the relationships between specific processing disabilities and academic achievement are likely to be relatively clear. Academic achievement is complexly determined, so that the effect of mild handicaps may be substantially altered by variations in other intellectual skills, teaching effectiveness, motivational patterns, and even the skill levels of classmates (Share, Jorm,

Maclean, & Matthews, 1984). Unless one has a very large sample in which these other determinants of achievement can be systematically covaried, one is more likely to identify clear relationships between processing skills and academic achievement by studying extreme subgroups.

On the other hand, a drawback of this method is that the techniques that are required for extreme examples of a particular subgroup may not be required for children who possess the same characteristics, but to a lesser degree. Thus, in making both treatment and prognostic statements, a careful specification of the degree of impairment is likely to be very important. Of course, children's responses to their learning disabilities are complexly determined, which makes "degree of impairment" individually meaningful only within a broad personal and social context. However, in reporting aggregate data on specific subtypes, objective measures describing the extent to which the subtypes differ from an appropriate normal comparison group on the defining measures should always be reported.

A RESEARCH EXAMPLE

The best way for research on extreme subgroups to proceed is to start with a large-scale empirical classification study followed by systematic study of samples that are prototypical of the major subgroups identified (Torgesen, 1987). The initial classification study would help establish the context for the systematic research on specific subtypes, and might also suggest appropriate control groups against which the performance of the target subgroup should be compared.

The studies I am going to discuss will not be presented in the order in which they occurred, but rather in a manner that is consistent with this "ideal" pattern. I will first present two classification studies, both of which identified a particular subgroup of LD children within heterogeneous samples. Thereafter, I will present studies that provide follow-up information about that specific subgroup. Although this method of presentation is not accurate historically, it does not distort the essential meaning of the research, and it helps to illustrate the role of follow-up studies in the development of knowledge about subtypes.

In 1981, Lyon and Watson reported the results from an empirical classi-fication study of 10- to 12-year-old LD children, using a battery of common neuropsychological instruments as the basis of classification. Altogether, six different subgroups were identified. Approximately 13% of their sample showed relatively isolated difficulties on tasks that measured the ability to retain verbatim sequences of verbal information briefly. This subgroup performed four standard deviations (S.D.) below the mean on one measure

(Token Test), and differed by 2.4 S.D.'s from a normal control group on another (Auditory memory). An additional 23% of children in this sample showed slightly less severe impairments on these measures in conjunction with more pervasive cognitive limitations.

In a more recent study (Speece, 1987), 15% of a sample of carefully selected 9- and 10-year-old children with reading disabilities showed isolated difficulties on a digit span task. This task has similar performance requirements to the two used by Lyon and Watson, except that children must retain verbatim sequences of digits, instead of words. The subgroup with isolated deficits on this task performed 1.8 S.D.'s below normal. Another group (20% of the sample) performed 1.2 S.D.'s below normal on the span task, and they also showed extreme difficulties on rapid naming tasks. The converging result from both of these studies is that a substantial part (15%–35%) of 9–12-year-old children with learning disabilities show extreme deficits on tests of verbal short-term memory in the presence of otherwise normal intellectual development.

The identification of this group within the context of these classification studies is only the first step in research on subtypes. All of the questions listed earlier in this chapter must now be addressed with regard to this specific subtype of LD children. For example, there are a number of reasons why children might perform poorly on tasks requiring the verbatim retention of verbal information. They might be inattentive, use inefficient mnemonic strategies, be highly anxious or poorly motivated, have difficulties perceiving or coding temporal order between stimuli, or have a limitation in the capacity of general short-term memory. In addition, considerable work must be done in order to establish a theoretical and empirical link between failure in recalling sequences of digits or words and difficulties learning important academic tasks. We have performed 18 experiments on groups of LD children selected because of their extremely poor performance on tests of short-term memory, and we have also been able to obtain 8–9-year follow-up data on some of the children in our original studies. I will now discuss some of the information we have obtained about children in this subgroup, starting with a description of our definitional criteria.

Defining the Subgroup

We used five exclusionary criteria to define our subgroup of LD children with serious problems in the short-term retention of information (LD-S). First, we required all subjects to have Full-scale IQs of 85 or above. Second, the children were between the ages of 9 and 11 y at the time they were selected. Our third criterion was that all children show delays of at least 1.5 grade levels (relative to their present grade placement) in either math or reading achievement. The fourth criterion, absence of gross behavioral problems, was assessed on the basis of the psychological evaluations made on each child by school psychologists.

Our final criterion involved measurement of the central defining feature of the subgroup—their deficiencies in the short-term retention of information. We used a two-level screening procedure to select LD children with the most serious problems in this area. From information in psychological reports, we formed an initial group of children identified by school psychologists as deficient in memory span. At this level, tasks we relied on to indicate memory span deficiencies were those requiring children to repeat sequences of verbal information such as strings of digits or words verbatim. Most of these tasks involved presentation of items at a rate of one per second and required immediate recall of sequences of varying length. We then individually administered a digit span task (requiring memory for sequences of randomly arranged digits). Subjects whose variable performance on the task appeared to reflect problems in concentration or cooperation were eliminated from the sample. Any child who could reliably recall digit strings longer than four items was also not included in our subgroup. We did not explicitly control for socioeconomic background, race, or sex of subject in our experiments, because we wanted to determine if the short-term memory problems of children who varied on these dimensions would have different causal explanations.

In all our experiments except one (in which an additional control group was used), we contrasted the performance of eight LD-S children (who performed extremely poorly on the digit span task) to that of eight children in each of two other groups. LD-N children were LD children from the same classrooms as the LD-S children, who met all the same criteria, but performed normally on digit span tasks. N children were equivalent to the LD-N group, except that they were achieving normally in school. Table 10.1 summarizes

TABLE 10.1
Characteristics of Subjects in Early Studies

	LD-S N = 24	LD-N N = 24	N N = 24
Age (years)	10.3	124.1	122.5
Reading (grade)	2.6	3.3	5.5
Math (grade)	3.4	3.6	5.2
Intelligence	98.6	98.7	——
Sex of subject			
Males	21	22	17
Females	3	2	7

Note. LD-S = learning disabled children who perform poorly on digit span tests; LD-N = learning-disabled children who perform in average range on digit span tests; N = children with normal academic achievement and average scores on digit span tests.

the characteristics of children in all three groups who participated in our experiments over a span of 4 years.

Description of Defining Disability

The performance deficits of the LD-S group on digit span tasks were extreme, as their mean performance was 3.8 S.D.'s below that of the LD-N group, and none of the children in the LD-S group had scores within three S.D.'s of the groups that performed normally on the task. The average number of digits that could be recalled in the correct order by children in the LD-S group was 4.0, while that for the LD-N and N groups was 5.8 and 5.9 respectively. Although this difference, in itself, may not seem large, the LD-S children recalled digits about as well as normal 5- to 6-year-olds, while children in the other groups performed like 9- to 12-year-olds.

Our early work (Torgesen & Houck, 1980) also established that the performance deficits of children in the LD-S group on the digit span task were very stable over both the short (within a half-hour session) and long (within a year) term. In another study (Torgesen, Rashotte, Greenstein, & Portes, in press) we examined the generality of the memory deficit experienced by children in the LD-S group. We administered nine different memory tasks to groups of LD-S, LD-N, and N children. The most important finding from this study was that the LD-S children did not perform poorly on all the tasks. For example, they performed normally on a task that required them to retain briefly sequences of abstract visual forms. Furthermore, their ability to retain meaningfully organized material over longer periods (3 to 4 minutes) was also unimpaired. They also did not show deficits, compared with other LD children on recognition memory tasks. In other words, they could distinguish just as well as the LD-N group between items that they had seen or heard earlier in a sequence and those they had not. The LD-S children had difficulties only on four different tasks that required verbatim repetition of sequences of verbal information. It did not matter whether this verbal information was presented visually, or whether it was embedded within meaningful sentences. Although they could recall the gist of verbal expressions as well as other children (Torgesen, Rashotte, & Greenstein, 1988), they did not remember the actual words in a sentence or passage as well as children in the same-age control groups.

Developing Theoretical Understanding of the Problem

Having established that the memory difficulties of children in the LD-S group are both stable and specific, the next step was to develop an adequate theoretical account of the problem. We have conducted several different studies designed to examine various hypotheses that might account for the extreme performance problems of children in this subgroup. As this research has been recently reviewed elsewhere (Torgesen, 1988), I will present only the conclusions here. At present, the most viable explanation for the verbatim retention problems of children in this group involves:

> Difficulties utilizing phonologically based codes to store information in working memory. Since phonological codes are particularly well adapted for storage of information about the order of items as well as their identity (Drewnowski & Murdock, 1980; Salame & Baddeley, 1982), performance on a wide variety of verbatim recall tasks is affected. In fact, this processing disability should limit performance on any task that depends critically on the use of phonological codes to represent information while it is being processed." (Torgesen, 1988, p. 609)

Although there is strong evidence that children in the LD-S subgroup experience special difficulties processing phonological representations in working memory, there are still at least two different ways to conceptualize this problem. For example, it may be the case that the memory codes utilized by these children are degraded in some manner. If LD-S children have subtle difficulties in the perception of speech sounds (Brady, Shankweiler, & Mann 1983; Godfrey, Syrdal-Lasky, Millay, & Knox, 1981; Tallal, 1980), phonological representations of words in their lexicon may include fewer, or more variable, distinctive phonological features. These degraded codes would not be as reliably distinct from one another as those available to children able to perceive speech sounds more accurately. In contrast to this explanation, it might also be the case that LD-S children simply have special difficulties accessing phonological codes that are in other respects quite normal. If this were true, these children might experience a kind of temporal, or attentional interference on verbatim recall tasks caused by their difficulties in accessing appropriate codes. (Baddeley, 1986)

There is evidence in support of both of these interpretations (Torgesen, Kistner, & Morgan, 1987), and it is not possible to choose one over the other. At present, we prefer a more general hypothesis which involves the concept of operational efficiency in the use of phonological information in working memory. This is a more general hypothesis because operational inefficiency might result from degraded codes, slow access to codes, or some combination of both. The concept of operational efficiency was used by Case, Kurland, and Goldberg (1982) to explain age-related changes on memory span tasks. Essentially, the hypothesis states that differences in short-term memory performance are not caused by actual limitations in memory capacity, but rather are the result of differences in the efficiency with which processes necessary for memory are executed. Within this framework, the critical difficulty for LD-S children lies in a lack of operational efficiency in dealing with phonologically based information. Although their actual memory capacity may be the same as other children, their *functional capacity* for verbatim storage of verbal material is limited by difficulties they have in accurately and rapidly processing phonological information.

Effects of Processing Disability on Academic Tasks

In our attempts to understand how LD-S children's processing difficulties affect their performance on important academic tasks, we have conducted a general examination of their math skills, and a more specific examination of their reading, spelling, and language comprehension skills. Although they are behind in the development of math skills (see Table 10.1), they are not more impaired in this area than other LD children.

They do appear to have special difficulties, however, in the acquisition of reading skills. Furthermore, their difficulties in reading are most pronounced in comparisons involving the rapid and accurate pronunciation of individual words (Torgesen, Rashotte, Greenstein, Houck, & Portes, 1987). In one experiment, for example, we asked the subjects to name series of digits, familiar single-syllable words, and single-syllable nonwords as rapidly and accurately as possible. They performed these tasks in three different sessions, and between sessions, they received intensive computer-based practice in naming the nonwords. The naming rates for these stimuli across the three sessions are presented in Fig. 10.1. The differences in naming rate between

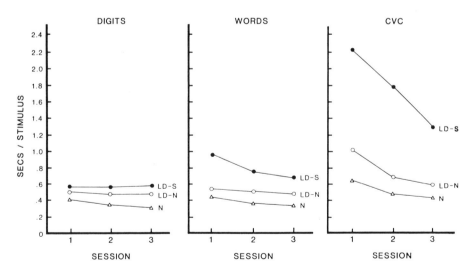

FIG. 10.1 Naming rates across three sessions for digits, words, and nonsense syllables (LD-S = learning-disabled with short-term memory deficits; LD-N = learning-disabled who performed in average range on short-term memory tests; N = children with normal academic achievement) '(from "Academic difficulties of learning disabled children who perform poorly on memory span tasks," J. K. Torgesen, C. A. Rashotte, J. Greenstein, G. Houck, & P. Portes. In H. L. Swanson (Ed.), *Memory and learning disabilities: Advances in learning and behavior disabilities*, 1987, Greenwich, CT: JAI Press. Copyright 1987 by JAI).

the LD-S and control groups were significant for all three types of material, but they were especially large for words and nonwords. These findings are understandable in terms of the operational efficiency hypothesis.

For example, naming either a word or a nonsense syllable almost certainly requires many more processing operations utilizing phonemic codes than does digit naming. To identify a nonsense syllable correctly, the child must extract a phonetic code for each letter while simultaneously storing these representations in working memory long enough to integrate them into a single response. If LD-S children are operationally deficient in the manipulation of phonemic codes, tasks that require them to identify multiple codes and perform integrative operations on them should be specially difficult. In the pattern or results we obtained, tasks requiring simultaneous operations on multiple phonemic codes produced the most striking differences among the groups. Furthermore, the pattern of differences was similar to that obtained for the digit span task. Thus, "LD-S children might have extreme difficulties on span tasks and word identification tasks for the same reason: both kinds of tasks require them to efficiently extract and operate on multiple phonemic codes over brief periods of time" (Torgesen, *et al.*, 1987, p. 329).

This explanation implies that children in the LD-S group should have particular difficulties mastering reading skills that involve utilization of the "alphabetic principle" in decoding new words. That is, they will be at a striking disadvantage in the early stages of learning to read, when many words must be processed as a series of separately encoded phonological elements.

At this point, a brief digression is required in order to place our research on the LD-S subgroup within the context of general theoretical developments in the study of specific developmental dyslexia, or severe reading disability. There is now considerable evidence that the primary reading difficulties of dyslexic children lie at the word, rather than the text, level of processing (Stanovich, 1986b). The difficulties these children experience in mastering basic word recognition processes are thought to be fundamental to their general inability to develop efficient skills in reading for meaning. In fact, Siegel (in press) has recently suggested that the best single measure of dyslexia is ability to read pronounceable nonwords fluently. Difficulty on this measure presumably reflects dyslexic children's difficulties in mastering basic phonological decoding strategies.

At present, the most likely cause of dyslexic children's word recognition difficulties involves inherent deficits in their ability to process the phonological elements of language (Liberman, 1987; Wagner & Torgesen, 1987). Stanovich (1988) has recently demonstrated how the large majority of the most extreme cases of specific developmental dyslexia are likely to be those children with the most severe phonological processing difficulties. Although phonological coding processes are only one aspect of overall phonological processing efficiency (Wagner & Torgesen, 1987), they are clearly an important one

(Wagner, *et al.*, 1987). Thus, there may be a high degree of overlap between a subgroup of LD children identified by their poor performance on span tests (phonological coding), and one identified by extremely poor performance on measures of analytical, or phonological decoding skills in reading. That is, it is possible that we may have identified the same subgroup within a hetero-geneous sample of LD children if we had used measures of nonword reading instead of measures of memory span as our defining criteria.

The empirical classification studies mentioned earlier shed some light on this issue. Lyon and Watson (1981) identified various subgroups of LD children using a battery of neuropsychological tests and then examined the academic performance patterns of each subtype. Their data suggest that, of the LD subgroups who showed a pattern of specific impairment, Subgroup 5 (similar to the LD-S group), was most impaired in word identification processes. In fact, "the major academic characteristic that distinguished subtype 5 youngsters from the other children was their consistently poor application of word attack (phonetic) skills to the reading and spelling process"(p. 27). Speece's (1987) data are more complicated, but tell essen-tially the same story. That is, the children in her cluster 1, who had the most severe deficits on memory span performance, also showed the poorest performance on a standardized measure of phonological decoding skills (the Word Analysis subtest from the Woodcock Reading Mastery Test). The data are complicated by the fact that children in cluster 2, who were relatively less impaired on the memory span task (although still more than one S.D. below normal), showed the most severe deficits on naming speed for digits and familiar words. These deficits on the "recoding" tasks led Speece to speculate that children in cluster 2 may have been the most severely reading impaired of all the subtypes. However, at least as far as basic word recognition skills are concerned, this speculation was not confirmed in the results from the standardized reading measure. Speece's data, in fact, suggest that, for children in the middle elementary grades, verbal memory span, not naming rate, is the measure of phonological processing skills that is most closely tied to level of analytical decoding skills. The point of this digression, then, is to show that it may be appropriate to label our LD-S children as the "most dyslexic" of children in a public school sample of LD children. In order to confirm this possibility, of course, we would have to examine the actual overlap between a group of children selected because of extreme analytical decoding difficulties and one selected because of extremely poor performance on span tasks.

Our other investigations of the academic skills of children in the LD-S group suggest that, as might be anticipated, they are specially impaired in the ability to learn new spelling words (Foster & Torgesen, 1983). In contrast to their difficulties on basic reading and spelling tasks, however, these children do not appear to be impaired in their ability to comprehend normal prose that is presented orally (Torgesen, Rashotte, & Greenstein, 1988). Our findings in this area are in contrast to those reported by Mann and her colleagues (Mann, Cowen, & Schoenheimer, 1989), who have attempted to show that children with severe reading disabilities (and, presumably, phonological coding difficulties) do have problems in sentence comprehension because they cannot remember individual words effectively. The differences in our findings are most likely due to variation in the memory demands of the material used in our respective experiments. That is, we had children listen to sentences and paragraphs taken from material that they would normally be exposed to in school. In contrast, Mann, Shankweiler, and Smith (1984) used sentences that were specially constructed so that verbatim retention of specific words in order was required for comprehension to occur. These latter sentences were almost like memory span tasks themselves in that almost every individual word (and their order) had to be remembered in order to represent sentence meaning adequately.

Developmental and Prognostic Issues

Another of the questions about subgroups outlined earlier in this chapter requires long-term investigation of intellectual development and academic outcomes. We are currently engaged in a longitudinal study of the phonological processing skills of 300 children beginning at age 5 in kindergarten. This study is designed to provide information about the manner in which specific aspects of phonological processing efficiency are related to the acquisition of specific types of reading skill. It should help us understand more about the early emergence of problems similar to those shown by children in the LD-S group.

Further, we have recently had the opportunity to obtain follow-up data on a small sample of the LD-S and LD-N children we studied between 1979 and 1982. The average age of the youths is now 19 y. Although our sample is still very small (eight LD-S children and nine LD-N children), the data are intriguing. For example, Table 10.2 presents information about performance on IQ and academic achievement measures. The large divergence in vocabulary test score is interesting in light of the original similarities between groups in full scale IQ and their continued equivalence on the block design subtest. It is also consistent with research suggesting that the Vocabulary scores of children with extreme reading disabilities will deteriorate significantly over time because of lack of exposure to new words through reading (Stanovich, 1986). The groups are clearly divergent on individual word reading skills, while their math skills are essentially equivalent (and relatively less impaired in both groups).

Both groups improved substantially in their performance on memory span tests. In our research, we have always used as our primary dependent

TABLE 10.2
Performance on Measures of Intelligence and Academic Achievement
at 19 years

	LD-S	LD-N
Intelligence		
Block Design WAIS[1] (raw score)	31.9	34
Vocabulary WAIS (raw score)	31	53
FS IQ WISC[2] (age 10) for children in follow-up sample	101.3	104.7
Reading		
Word identification[3] (grade level)	4.8	9.6
Word attack[3] (grade level)	3.7	5.8
Mathematics		
Calculation[4] (grade level)	9.6	8.4
Spelling		
Accuracy[5] (grade level)	3.6	6.7

[1]Wechsler Adult Intelligence Scale
[2]Wechsler Intelligence Scale for Children
[3]Woodcock Reading Mastery Test
[4]Woodcock-Johnson Psycho-Educational Battery
[5]Wide Range Achievement Test

measure the total score for a digit span series, which measures performance on increasingly longer spans until the child makes a specified number of errors. In our follow-up testing, the average series score for the LD-S group was 39.1, and that for the LD-N group was 56.8. The corresponding scores for the same children at age 10 had been 20.3, and 38.9, respectively. The overall correlation between span measured at age 10 and 19 was .78. Although the pattern of differences between the groups has remained stable over the past 9 years, there is now more overlap between the groups than when they were 10 years old. At age 10, none of the LD-S children performed within 3 S.D.'s of the average score for the LD-N children. At age 19, however, three of the eight were close to, or within one S.D. of the LD-N average. In other words, three of the LD-S children were now much less impaired relative to the LD-N children than they were when originally tested.

If the reading scores for the LD-S subjects who improved in their relative standing on span measures are compared with those who did not, some interesting differences emerge. For example, the LD-S subjects who improved on the memory span measure read about as well as the LD-N children (Word identification = 8.7, Word attack = 5.9). However, the children who continued to show severe span difficulties have made almost no improvement in reading skills over the last 9 years (Word identification = 3.9, Word attack = 2.8) despite being exposed to the same remedial opportunities as the other LD children.

Although the three subjects who showed relative improvement in span performance over the past 9 years are interesting for a variety of reasons (Torgesen, in press), more important for this chapter is the fact that 60% of the LD-S children showed striking continuities in their span performance over a very long period of time. Furthermore, their continued difficulties on span tasks were associated with virtually no improvement in basic reading skills over the same period of time. If this same pattern holds up as we are able to locate more students for follow-up testing, it will provide strong support for phonological coding deficiencies as a possible explanation for the intransigent nature of many reading difficulties.

CONCLUDING COMMENTS

In conclusion, I would like to return to the basic point that large-scale classification studies are only a starting point in our attempts to understand important sources of variability within the LD population. Although comprehensive classification efforts are important in describing the overall variability within the population, they contain inherent ambiguities that can only be resolved by careful, systematic study of prototypical extreme groups. Such follow-up studies are the only method currently available to develop the rich knowledge base that is required to make accurate preventive, treatment, and prognostic statements.

ACKNOWLEDGMENT

Preparation of this manuscript was partly supported by Grant No. HD23340 from the National Institute of Child Health and Human Development.

REFERENCES

Arter, J. A., & Jenkins, J. R. (1979). Differential diagnosis-prescriptive teaching: a critical appraisal. Review of Educational Research, 49, 517–555.

Baddeley, A. D. (1986). Working memory. New York: Oxford University Press.

Brady, S., Shankweiler, D., & Mann, V. (1983). Speech perception and memory coding in relation to reading ability. Journal of Experimental Child Psychology, 35, 345–367.

Bradley, L., & Bryant, P. (1985). Rhyme and reason in reading and spelling. Ann Arbor: University of Michigan Press.

Butterfield, E. D., & Ferretti, R. P. (1987) Toward a theoretical integration of cognitive hypotheses about intellectual differences among children. In L. Borkowski & L. D. Day (Eds.), Cognition in Special Children: Comparative approaches to retardation, learning disabilities, and giftedness (pp. 195–234) New York: Ablex.

Campione, J. C. (1989). Assisted assessment: A taxonomy of approaches and an outline of strengths and weaknesses. Journal of Learning Disabilities, 22, 151–165.

Case, R., Kurland, D. M., & Goldberg, L. (1982). Operational efficiency and the growth of short-term memory span. Journal of Experimental Child Psychology, 33, 386–404.

Coles, G. S. (1987). The learning mystique: A critical look at "learning disabilities." New York: Pantheon.

Drewnowski, A., & Murdock, B. (1980). The role of auditory features in memory span for words. Journal of Experimental Psychology: Human Learning and Memory, 6, 315–332.

Ellis, A. W. (1985). The cognitive neuropsychology of developmental (and acquired) dyslexia: A critical survey. Cognitive Neuropsychology, 2, 169–205.

Estes, W. K. (1974). Learning theory and intelligence. American Psychologist, 29, 740–749.

Foster, K., & Torgesen, J. K. (1983). The effects of directed study on the spelling performance of two subgroups of learning-disabled children. Learning Disabilities Quarterly, 6, 252–257.

Godfrey, J. J., Syrdal–Lasky, A.K., Millay, K. K., & Knox, C.M. (1981). Performance of dyslexic children on speech perception tests. Journal of Experimental Child Psychology, 32, 401–424.

Liberman, I. Y. (1987). Language and literacy: The obligation of schools of education. In R. F. Bowler (Ed.), Intimacy with language. Baltimore: Orton Dyslexia Society.

Lyon, G. R. (1985). Identification and remediation of learning disability subtypes: Preliminary findings. learning Disabilities Focus, 1, 21–35.

Lyon, R. & Watson, B. (1981). Empirically derived subgroups of learning-disabled readers: Diagnostic characteristics. Journal of learning Disabilities, 14, 256–261.

Mann, V. A., Cowin, E., & Schoenheimer, J. (1989) Phonological processing, language comprehension, and reading ability. Journal of learning Disabilities, 22, 76–89.

Mann, V. A., Shankweiler, D., & Smith, S. T. (1984). The association between comprehension of spoken sentences and early reading ability: The role of phonetic representation. Journal of Child Language, 11, 627–643.

McKinney, J. D. (1989). Longitudinal research on the behavioral characteristics of children with learning disabilities. Journal of learning Disabilities, 22, 141–150.

Olson, R., Kliegl, R., Davidson, B., & Foltz, G. (1985). Individual and developmental differences in reading disability. In T. Waller (Ed.), Reading research: Advances in theory and practice (Vol. 4, pp. 1–64). London: Academic Press.

Salame, P., & Baddeley, A. (1982). Disruption of short-term memory by unattended speech: Implications for the structure of working memory. Journal of Verbal Learning and Verbal Behavior, 21, 150–164.

Senf, G. M. (1986). LD research in sociological and scientific perspective. In J. K. Torgesen & B. Y. L. Wong (Eds.), Psychological and educational perspectives on learning disabilities. New York: Academic Press.

Share, D. L., Jorm, A. F., Maclean, R., & Matthews, R. (1984). Sources of individual differences in reading acquisition. Journal of Educational Psychology, 76, 1309–1324.

Siegel, L. S. (in press). IQ is irrelevant to the definition of learning disabilities. Journal of learning Disabilities.

Speece, D. L. (1987). Information processing subtypes of learning-disabled readers. learning Disabilities Research 2, 91–102.

Stanovich, K. E. (1986a). Cognitive processes and the reading problems of learning-disabled children: Evaluating the assumption of specificity. In J. K. Torgesen & B. Y. L. Wong (Eds.), Psychological and educational perspectives on learning disabilities. New York: Academic Press.

Stanovich, K. E. (1986b). Explaining the variance in reading ability in terms of psychological processes: what have we learned? Annals of Dyslexia, 35, 67–96.

Stanovich, K. E. (1986c). Matthew effects in reading: Some consequences of individual differences in the acquisition of literacy. Reading Research Quarterly, 21, 360–406.

Stanovich, K. E. (1988). Explaining the differences between the dyslexic and the garden-variety poor reader: The phonological-core variable-difference model. Journal of learning Disabilities, 21, 590–604.

Tallal, P. (1980). Auditory temporal perception, phonics, and reading disabilities in children. *Brain and Language, 9*, 182–198.

Torgesen, J. K. (1979). What shall we do with psychological processes? *Journal of learning Disabilities, 12*, 514–521.

Torgesen, J. K. (1986). Learning disabilities theory: Its current state and future prospects. *Journal of Learning Disabilities, 19*, 399–407.

Torgesen, J. K. (1987). Thinking about the future by distinguishing between issues that have answers and those that do not. In S. T. Vaughn & C. S. Bos (Eds.), *Issues and future directions for research in learning disabilities* (pp. 55–67) San Diego: College Hill Press.

Torgesen, J. K. (1988). Studies of children with learning disabilities who perform poorly on memory span tasks. *Journal of learning Disabilities, 21*, 605–612.

Torgesen, J. K. (in press). Cross-age consistency in phonological processing. In S. Bradey & D. Shankweiler (Eds.), *Phonological processes in literacy*. Hillsdale, NJ: Lawrence Erlbaum Associates.

Torgesen, J. K., & Houck, G. (1980). Processing deficiencies in learning disabled children who perform poorly on the digit span task. *Journal of Educational Psychology, 72*, 141–160.

Torgesen, J. K., & Kistner, J. A., & Morgan, S. (1987). Component processes in working memory. In J. Borkowski & J. D. Day (Eds.), *Memory and cognition in special children: Perspectives on retardation, learning disabilities, and giftedness* (pp. 49–86). Norwood, NJ: Ablex.

Torgesen, J. K., Rashotte, C. A., & Greenstein, J. (1988). Language comprehension in learning disabled children who perform poorly on memory span tests. *Journal of Educational Psychology, 80*, 480–487.

Torgesen, J. K., Rashotte, C. A., Greenstein, J., Houck, G., & Portes, P. (1987). Academic difficulties of learning disabled children who perform poorly on memory span tasks. In H. L. Swanson (Ed.), *Memory and learning disabilities: Advances in learning and behavioral disabilities* (pp. 305–333). Greenwich, CN: JAI Press.

Torgesen, J. K., Rashotte, C. A., Greenstein, J., & Portes, P. (in press). *Further studies of learning disabled children who perform poorly on memory span tests. Learning Disabilities Research.*

Wagner, R. K., Balthazar, M., Hurley, S., Morgan, S., Rashotte, C., Shaner, R., Simmons, K., Stage, S. (1987). The nature of prereaders' phonological processing abilities. *Cognitive Development, 2*, 355–373.

Wagner, R. K., & Torgesen, J. K. (1987). The nature of phonological processing and its causal role in the acquisition of reading skills. *Psychological Bulletin, 101*, 192–212.

Author Index

Note: Italicized page numbers refer to bibliography pages.

A

Accardo, P. J., 124, *133*
Ackerman, P. T., 166, *184*
Adams, K. M., 33, *49*
Adams, N. A., 36, *50*
Adelman, H. S., 61, *78*
Ahern, F. M., 96, *107*
Alberg, J., 7, 8, *26*
Aldenderfer, M.S., 14, *26*, 38, 46, *49*
Alexander, D., 45, *49*
Algozzine, B., 6, 8, *31*, 57, 62, *82*, 190, *205*
Alley, G. R., 180, *183*, *184*, *187*
Altus, G. T., 5, *26*
Anderberg, M. R., 14, *27*, 46, *49*
Anderson, B., 54, *79*
Anderson, R.P., 139, *156*
Anderson, S., 92, *107*
Anderson, T. H., 151, *156*
Appelbaum, M. I., 19, 20, 21, 24, 25, 26, *27*, *30*, 38, 39, 40, 41, *50*, *52*, 59, 60, *79*, 191, 192, *205, 207*, 210, 216, *227*
Applebee, A. N., 34, *49*
Argyris, C., 55, *78*
Armbruster, B.B., 151, *156*
Armstrong, S., 189, *206*
Arter, J. A., 232, *244*
Ashcraft, M. H., 201, 202, 203, *205*

Asher, S. R., 33, *52*
Ashlock, R. B., 199, 200, *205*

B

Baddeley, A. D., 143, *156*, 210, 211, 212, 214, 225, 225, 238, *244*, *245*
Baillie, D., 92, *109*
Bain, J. D., *226*
Baker, J. G., 209, *225*
Baker, L., 172, *183*
Baker, S., 212, *226*
Balthazar, M., 241, *246*
Banntyne, A., 5, *27*
Barclay, C. R., 64, 65, *78*, *79*
Baron, J., 118, *133*, *156*
Barraclough, B., 92, *108*
Bassiri, D., 141, *157*
Bateson, G., 54, *78*
Bauer, R. H., 209, *225*, *226*
Bayliss, J., 9, *27*
Beach, R. W., 150, *160–161*
Beals, V. L., 146, *158*
Bean, T. W., 150, *156*
Beatty, J., 210, 224, *226*
Becker, L., 203, 204, *206*
Belmont, J. M., 66, *79*, 138, *156*

247

Belmont, L., 6, 27
Bender, B. G., 89, 106
Bentler, P. M., 226
Benton, A. L., 25, 27
Bereiter, C., 137, 156
Bergen, P. L., 57, 79
Bergman, A., 115, 133
Berkowitz, S. J., 150–51, 156
Berman, K. F., 89, 107
Berman, S., 164, 184
Berrettini, W. H., 92, 107
Bessman, S. P., 93, 106
Birch, H. G., 6, 27
Bird, M., 137, 156
Bishop, D. V. M., 115, 133
Black, F. W., 6, 27
Black, M. M., 141, 156
Blackburn, I., 8, 28
Blackwood, D., 92, 109
Blankenship, C. S., 199, 205
Blashfield, R. K., 14, 16, 26, 26, 30, 38, 41, 26, 49, 51
Bloom, A., 115, 133
Boder, E., 8, 9, 27, 118, 127, 133
Boliek, C. A., 39, 51
Bonnett, D., 226
Book, C., 141, 157, 165, 184
Boorman, D., 92, 107
Boorse, C., 56, 79
Borkowski, I. G., 169, 187
Borkowski, J. G., 70, 81, 138, 141, 146, 152, 156, 157, 158, 159, 166, 167, 184
Boron, 141
Bouchard, T. J., Jr., 95, 97, 106
Bowden, D. W., 93, 107
Bowers, P., 115, 133
Bradley, L., 3, 5, 11, 12, 27, 232, 244
Brady, S., 238, 244
Brainerd, C. J., 209, 210, 211, 226
Bransford, J. D., 148, 151, 152, 156, 165, 184
Brereton, N., 212, 225
Brody, L., 164, 185
Broman, S., 58, 79
Brooks, L. R., 201, 205
Brophy, J., 142, 148, 156
Brown, A. L., 61, 65, 80, 148, 150, 151, 152, 156, 165, 172, 183, 184, 186
Brown, D. A., 80
Brown, J. S., 200, 205
Brown, V., 199, 205
Bruce, P., 6, 27
Bruner, J., 178, 188

Bryan, T. H., 166, 185
Bryans, B. N., 15, 27
Bryant, P., 3, 5, 11, 12, 22, 23, 27, 232, 244
Brynjolfsson, J., 92, 108
Buchsbaum, M. S., 88, 107
Buetow, K., 93, 106
Burks, H. F., 6, 27
Burton, R. B., 200, 205
Bush, E. S., 168, 184
Butler, J. A., 44, 52
Butler, S. R., 43, 49
Butterfield, E. C., 66, 79, 138, 156
Butterfield, E. D., 232, 244
Butterworth, G. E., 115, 133

C

Caldwell, J., 118, 134
Camp, B. W., 8, 9, 27
Campbell, D., 55, 79
Campbell, D. T., 36, 50
Campione, J. C., 148, 151, 152, 156, 165, 170, 177, 184, 232, 244
Cariglia-Bull, T., 138, 139, 145, 159, 169, 187
Carinhour, S., 93, 107
Carnine, D., 199, 205
Carpenter, P. A., 211, 226
Carr, T. H., 118, 133
Carroll, J. B., 216, 226
Case, R., 143, 157, 211, 226, 238, 245
Castiglione, C. M., 92, 107
Cavalli-Szforze, L. L., 92, 107
Cavanaugh, J. C., 141, 157
Ceci, S. J., 209, 225
Chandler, C. L., 61, 74, 79
Chi, M. T. H., 144, 160
Chiesi, H. L., 143, 160
Childs, B., 131, 133–134
Chipman, S. F., 148, 160
Chipuer, H. M., 85, 106
Christopoulos, J. P., 137, 157
Chronbach, L. J., 184
Clark, F. L., 180, 185
Clarke, S., 164, 186
Clifford, M., 19, 29
Clifford, M.M., 142, 157
Cochran, K., 213, 227
Cole, M., 54, 55, 79
Coleman, M., 5, 31
Coles, G. S., 58, 59, 61, 79, 231, 245
Cone, T. E., 7, 27

Conners, F., 113, 115, 116, 117, 118, 119, 122, 123, 126, 130, 132, 133, 134, 209, 227
Conrad, P., 57, 79
Conrad, R., 221, 226
Cook, T. D., 36, 50
Cooper, D. H., 39, 45, 46, 48, 52, 183, 187
Cooper, M. C., 33, 38, 51, 216, 227
Copeland, A. P., 167, 184
Cormack, 59
Cormier, P., 203, 204, 206
Corno, L., 141, 157
Coughlin, L. P., 148, 149, 158
Cowen, E., 242
Cowin, E., 245
Crain, S., 211, 219, 227
Crim, D., 54, 57, 61, 62, 81
Critchley, M., 114, 133
Cronbach, L. J., 37, 50
Cross, D. R., 33, 44, 50
Cruickshank, W. M., 25, 28, 61, 80

D

Dallego, M., 209, 226
Daneman, M., 209, 211, 212, 226
Daniels, D., 91, 108
Darby, R. O., 16, 27
Davidson, B. J., 118, 127, 134, 230, 245
Davison, L. A., 196, 207
Day, J. D., 150, 151, 152, 156, 157
Deane, S., 138, 139, 145, 159
DeBettencourt, L. U., 180, 184
Deci, E. L., 61, 74, 79, 142, 157
Decker, S. N., 89, 106, 131, 135
DeFries, J. C., 84, 86, 87, 88, 89, 90, 91, 93, 94, 96, 98, 100, 101, 102, 107, 108, 113, 120, 121, 122, 123, 126, 130, 131, 133, 134, 135
Delaney, H. D., 145, 160
Del Dotto, J. E., 59, 60, 79
DeLisi, L. E., 88, 107
Demo, S., 57, 62, 82
Dempster, F. N., 209, 210, 221, 224, 226
Denckla, M. B., 10, 27, 168, 184
Denton, P. H., 146, 160, 180, 187
Derry, S. J., 147, 157
DeRubeis, R., 131, 134
Deshler, D. D., 65, 81, 144, 146, 147, 157, 158, 159, 160, 177, 178, 180, 183, 184, 187
Detera-Wadleigh, S. D., 92, 107

Diener, C. I., 168, 184
Dishner, E. K., 141, 161
Dobbs, M., 92, 108
Doehring, D. G., 10, 14, 15, 27, 168, 184, 192, 205
Delcourt, J. L., 8, 9, 27
Donis-Keller, M., 93, 107
Dougan, D. R., 118, 134
Doyle, R. B., 139, 156
Drewnowski, A., 238, 245
Dudleston, K., 92, 108
Duffy, G. D., 165, 184
Duffy, G. G., 141, 147, 148, 157
Dumais, S. T., 143, 160
Dunn, L. M., 66, 79, 116, 133
Dweck, C. S., 142, 157, 168, 184, 185
Dykman, R. A., 166, 184

E

Earls, F., 89, 107
Edwards, M. D., 93, 107
Egeland, J. A, 92, 107
Ehri, L. C., 46, 50
Elbro, E., 118, 127, 133
Eldridge, M., 225
Elliott-Faust, D. J., 154, 159
Ellis, A. W., 229, 233, 245
Ellis, E. S., 65, 81, 147, 157, 180, 185
Ellis, H., 210, 226
Ellis, H. D., 219, 221, 226
Elston, R. C., 93, 108
Emhert, J., 209, 226
Englemann, S., 199, 205
Englert, C. S., 137, 157
Entwisle, N. J., 141, 157
Epps, S., 6, 8, 31, 190, 205
Erickson, L. G., 150, 160
Estes, W. K., 231, 245
Estrada, M. T., 166, 184
Evans, E. D., 152, 159, 164, 165, 168, 187
Evans, H. J., 92, 109
Everitt, B. S., 14, 27, 59, 79
Ewars, C., 213, 227

F

Fabrega, H., 54, 57, 79
Fain, P. R., 92, 107

Falconer, D. S., 101, *107*
Farmer, A. E., 88, *107*
Farnham-Diggory, S., 139, *157*
Farran, D., 20, 21, *28*
Feagans, L., 6, 12, 18, 19, 20, 21, 24, 25, 26, 27, *28*, *29*, 38, 41, 48, *50*, *51*, 59, 60, 63, *79*, *80*, 167, 183, *186*, 191, 192, *205*, *206*, *207*, 209, 210, 216, *227*
Feinstein, A., 56, 57, *79*
Feldman, W., 189, 192, 193, 195, 196, *207*
Fenton, R., 165, 170, 173, *186*
Fenton, T., 163, 171, 173, 174, 175, 176, *186*
Ferrara, R. A., 148, 151, 152, *156*, 165, *184*
Ferretti, R. P., 138, *156*, 232, *244*
Feuerstein, R., 170, 178, 179, *185*
Feuerstein, R., 145, *157*
Fiedorowicz, C. A. M., 10, 15, *27*
Fierman, B. A., 202, *205*
Finlayson, M. A. J., 13, *30*, 191, 192, 193, 195, 196, *207*
Finn, C. E., 154, *160*
Finucci, J. M., 131, *133–134*
Fish, E., 42–43, *52*
Fisk, J. L., 14, 16, *28*,196, *207*
Fleet, J., 152, *159*, 164, 165, 168, *187*
Fleichner, J. E., 169, *185*
Fleischner, J. E., 172
Fletcher, J. M., 13, 16, 26, *28*, *30*, 33, 42, 43, 46, 48, *50*, *51–52*, 130, *134*, 190, 191, 192, 193, 194, 195, *205*, 209, 210, *226*
Foltz, G., 118, 127, *134*, 230, *245*
Forness, S. R., 7, 24, 25, *28*, *29*, 35, 36, 37, 45, 46, 48, *50*, 59, 60, *80*
Forrest-Pressley, D. L., 144, 154, *157*, *159*
Foster, G., 54, *79*
Foster, K., 12, *28*, 241, *245*
Foth, 209
Foucault, M., 54, 55, *79*
Fox, B., 12, *28*
Fox, L. H., 164, *185*
Fredman, G., 115, 129, 130, 131, 132, *134*, *135*
Freedman, D., 17, *29*, 38, *51*
Freeman, S., *158*
French, D. C., 33, *50*
French, J. H., 9, 10, 25, *29*
Friel, J., 36, 43, *52*, 115, *135*
Frostig, M., 3, *28*
Fuelop, S., 141, *158*
Fulker, D. W., 87, 88, 89, 90, 91, 94, 96, 98, 100, 101, *107*, *108*, 113, 117, 118, 119, 120, 121, 122, 123, 126, 130, 132, *133*, *134*, 209, *227*

G

Gaddes, W. H., 144, *157*, 197, 198, *206*
Gall, D., 209, *227*
Gallagher, J. J., 4, 5, *28*
Gardner, H., 170, *185*
Garner, R., 148, *157*
Garnett, K., 169, 172, *185*
Garofalo, J., 172, *185*
Gayor, P., 5, *31*
Geary, D. C., 203, 204, *206*
Geiselman, R. E., 210, 224, *226*
Gerber, M. M., 166, 167, *185*
Gerhard, D. S., 92, *107*
Gershon, E. S., 92, *107*
Giere, R. N., 55, *79*
Gil, E., 14, *29*
Gill, M., 92, *107*
Ginsburg, H. P., 172, *187*
Giuffra, L. A., 92, *107*
Glanzer, M., 214, *226*
Glaser, R., 148, *158*, *160*
Glennon, V. J., 199, *206*
Godfrey, J. J., 238, *245*
Goldberg, J., 211, *226*
Goldberg, L., 238, *245*
Golden, R. R., 45, *50*
Goldgar, D. E., 18, *31*
Goldin, L. R., 92, *107*
Goldman, S. R., 172, *185*
Goldstein, K., 3
Goodchild, G., 152, *159*, 164, 165, 168, *187*
Gottesman, I. I., 88, 103, *107*
Grabow, J. M., 5, *29*
Graden, J., 57, 62, *82*
Graham, P., 130, 131, 132, *135*
Graham, S., *158*
Graves, K., 118, *134*
Green, P., 93, *107*
Greeno, J. G., 220, 222, *226*
Greenstein, F., 12, *31*
Greenstein, J., 237, 239, 240, 242, *246*
Groen, G. J., 202, 203, *206*, *208*
Gruenenfelder, T. M., 141, *156*
Guarino, E. A., 5, *29*
Gunderson, C. W., 61, *79*
Gurling, H., 92, *107*, *108*
Guthrie, D., 7, *28*

H

Haaf, R. G., 23, *30*, 48, *52*
Habermas, J., 55, *79*

Hagen, J. H., 65, *79*
Hagen, J. W., 61, 64, 65, 66, *78, 79, 80*
Halcomb, C. G., 139, *156*
Hale, C. A., 166, 184
Halford, G. S., 226
Hall, R. J., 166, 167, 185
Hallahan, D., 209, 227
Hallahan, D. P., 19, 25, 28, 61, 80, 166, 167, 185, 209
Hamill, D. D., 6, 28
Happmanen, R. M., 39, 51
Hardesty, R. A., 36, 50
Hargest, J. T., 148, 149, *158*
Harris, E. L., 130, 134
Harris, G., 167, 185
Harter, S., 66, 80
Harwood, A., 54, *80*
Hasselhorn, M., 143, *158*
Havinghurst, R. L., 64, *80*
Hawkes, L. W., 147, *157*
Haynes, M., 152, *158*
Heaven, R., 189, 191, *207*
Hegion, A., 42–43, *52*
Heisel, B. E., 148, 151, *159*
Heliotis, J., 152, *158*
Helms, C., 93, *107*
Henriques, J., 57, *80*
Herrmann, B. A., 141, *158*
Herrmann, N. D., 209, *225*
Hewitt, J. D., 93, *108*
Hirsch, E. D., Jr., 154, *158*
Hitch, G., 211, 214, *225*
Hitch, G. J., 212, *226*
Hobbs, N., 63, *80*
Hodgkinson, S., 92, *107*
Hoffman, M., 170, 178, 179, *185*
Holcomb, W. R., 36, *50*
Hollway, W., 57, *80*
Holroyd, J., 6, *28*
Holt, L. K., 118, *134*
Hooper, S. R., 33, 48, *50, 52*, 137, 138, 149, *158*, 190, 191, 192, *206*
Horn, J. M., 91, *107*
Horne, D., 3, *28*
Hoshko, I. M., 14, 15, 27, 192, *205*
Houck, D. G., 12, *31, 228*
Houck, G., *31*, 237, 239, 240, *246*
Howe, M. L., 209, *226*
Hresko, W., 199, 200, *206*
Hubbard, A., 92, *109*
Hudson, F. G., 167, *185*
Hufford, D. J., 57, *80*

Hughes, C. A., 146, *158*
Humphries, P., 92, *107*
Hunt, R., 210, *226*
Hurley, S., 241, *246*

I

Ing, P. S., 92, *107*
Ingram, T. T. S., 8, *28*
Ireton, H., 42, *50*

J

Jacobs, J. E., 172, *186*
Jastak, J. F., 190, *206*
Jastak, S. R., 190, *206*
Jenkins, J. R., 152, *158*, 232, *244*
Jensen, M. R., 170, 178, 179, *185*
Jessop, D. J., 63, *81*
Johnson, C. A., 96, *107*
Johnson, C. J., 137, *159*
Johnson, D., 118, *134*
Johnson, D. J., 8, *29*
Johnson, R. C., 86, 96, *107*
Jones, R. D., 150, *156*
Jones, R. L., 37, *51*
Joreskog, K. G., 213, *226*
Jorm, A. F., 210, *226*, 233, *245*

K

Kahnemann, D., 143, *158*
Kallos, G. L. 5, *29*
Kamberelis, G., 61, 64, *79*
Kamin, L. J., 95, *107*
Kaplan, A., 36, *50*
Kaplan, B. J., 103, *108*
Karniski, W., 164, *186*
Kasik, M. M., 144, *158*
Kauffman, J., 209, 227
Kauffman, J. M., 19, 28
Kaufman, A. S., 6, 7, *29*, 116, 127, *134*
Kavale, K. A., 7, 23, 24, *29*, 35, 36, 37, 45, 47, *50*, 58, 59, 60, *80*, 167, *185*
Keither, T. P., 93, *107*
Kennedy, B. A., 141, *158*
Kennedy, J. L., 92, *107*
Keogh, B. K., 33, 34, 37, 41, *50, 51*, 190, *206*
Kerlinger, F. N., 47, *50*

Kher, N., 148, *156*
Kidd, J. R., 92, *107*
Kidd, K. K., 92, *107*
Kimberling, W. J., 92, *107, 109*
Kingma, J., 209, 210, 211, *226*
Kinsbourne, M., 59, *82*, 189, *206*
Kintsch, W., 150, *158, 161*
Kirby, J., 203, 204, *206*
Kirk, S., 58, *80*
Kirk, S. T., 3, *29*
Kirk, W., 3, *29*
Kistner, J.A., 238, *29*
Klapp, S., 210, 211, *226–227*
Kliegl, R., 118, 127, *134*, 230, *245*
Kiove, H., 196, *206*
Kneedler, R. D., 167, *185*
Knox, C. M., 238, *245*
Koch, R., 93, *106*
Kolb, B., 139, *158*
Kollegian, J., *185*
Körkel, J., 143, *158*
Kosc, L., 197, 198, *206*
Kuhn, T. S., 55, *80*
Kurland, D. M., 211, *226*, 238, *245*
Kurtz, B. E., 152, *158*, 167, *184*
Kuse, A. R., 86, *107*

L

LaBerge, D., 168, *185*
LaBuda, M.C., 88, 90, 94, 96, *107, 108*, 113,
    121, 122, 123, 126, 130, 131, *133, 134*
Lander, E. S., 93, *108*
Larsen, S. C., 6, *28*
Laughlin, C. D., 54, 55, *81*
Lawson, M. J., 141, *158*
Laywell, E. D., 64, *80*
Lee, W. M., 167, *185*
Leiman, J. M., 216, *227*
Lenz, B. K., 146, 147, *157, 158*, 180, 181, *185*
Leong, C. K., 130, *134*
Lesgold, A. N., 209, 211, 224, *227*
Lessig, E. E., 14, *29*
Lester, F. K., Jr., 172, *185*
Lester, P., 210, 211, *226–227*
Levers, S. R., 141, *156*
Levin, B. E., 167, *185*,
Levin, J. R., 145, 152, *160*, 165, 166, *187*
Levine, M., 164, *186*
Levine, M. D., 163 165, 170, 173, *186*
Leviton, A., 124, *135*

Lewis, V., *225*
Lewitter, F. I., 93, *108*
Liberman, I. Y., 209, 240, *245*
Licht, B. G., 61, *80*, 167, 168, *185, 188*
Lichtenstein, R., 42, *50*
Lincoln, S. E., 93, *108*
Linder, A., 13, *30*
Linder, B., 191, 192, 194, 195, 200, 201, *206, 207*
Linder, B. A., 210, *227*
Lipson, M. V., 141, *159*
Little, T. D., 203, 204, *206*
Liversey, P. J., 9, *27*
Lloyd, J. W., 19, *28*
Loehlin, J. C., 84, 91, *107, 108*
Logan, G. D., 143, *158*
Logie, R., 212, *225*
Lorge, T., *227*
Lorr, M., 14, *29*, 46, *50*
Lovitt, T. C., 199, *206*
Lubs, H. A., 92, *109*
Luckmann, T., 57, *79*
Luria, A. R., 197, 198, *206*
Lykken, D. T., 131, *134*
Lyon, G. R., 33, 38, 39, 40, 46, 47, *50, 51*, 130,
    134, 233, *245*
Lyon, R., 17, 22, *29*, 183, *185*, 231, 234, 241,
    245

M

Maclean, R., 234, *245*
MacMillan, D. L., 37, *51*
Maesch, C., 61, *79*
Magnus, P., 88, *109*
Major-Kingsley, S., 34, *50*
Malatesha, R. N., 118, *134*
Malkus, K., 176, *186*
Mandinach, E. B., 141, *157*
Manis, F. R., 118, *134*
Mann, 209
Mann, A.W., 8, *28*
Mann, L., 179, *185*
Mann, V., 238, *244*
Mann, V. A., 242, *245*
Marchbanks, R., 92, *107*
Markman, E. M., 141, *158*
Markwardt, F. C., 116, *133*
Markwardt, F. C., Jr., 66, *79*
Marsh, H. W., 43, *49*
Marshburn, E., 210, 211, *226–227*
Mason, J., 19, *29*

Matthews, R., 234, *245*
Mattis, S., 9, 10, 25, *29*
Mayberry, M. T., *226*
Mayer, R. E., 180, *186*
McCarthy, J., 3, *29*
McClearn, G. E., 84, 86, *107*, *108*, 113, *135*
McCombs, B. L., 142, *158*
McCormick, C. B., 145, *160*
McCormick, C. G., 148, 151, *159*
McDaniel, M. A., 152, *160*
McEntire, E., 197, 198, 199, *206*
McGue, M., 95, 97, *106*
McGuffin, P., 88, 92, *107*, *108*
McKeon, P., 92, *107*
McKinney, J. D., 6, 8, 18, 19, 20, 21, 24, 25, 26, *28*, *29*, *30*, 33, 39, 40, 41, 44, 48, *51*, *52*, 59, 63, *80*, 167, 183, *186*, 190, 191, *206*, *207*, 209, 210, 216, *227*, 231, *245*
McKnight, R. T., 61, *80*
McKusick, V. A., 93, *108*
McLeod, T., 189, *206*
McLoughlin, V., 130, 131, 132, *135*
McManus, J., 54, 55, *81*
McVey, K. A., 141, *159*
Medina-Filho, H., 93, *109*
Meehl, P., 36, 45, *50*, *51*
Meichenbaum, D. M., 147, *159*
Meloth, M. S., 141, *157*, 165, *184*
Meltzer, L. J., 163, 164, 165, 170, 171, 173, 174, 175, 176, 181, *186*
Mercer, C. D., 146, *158*
Merriwether, A., 12, *28*
Messer, S. B., 141, *159*
Michals, D., 166, 167, *187*
Millay, K. K., 238, *245*
Miller, C. M. L., 141, *159*
Miller, D. J., *158*
Miller, R., 170, 178, 179, *185*
Miller, S., 182, *188*
Milligan, G. W., 33, 38, 47, *51*, 216, *227*
Milstead, M., 166, *184*
Mirsky, A. F., 88, *107*
Mitterer, J. D., 118, *134*
Moats, L. C., 39, *50*
Moely, B., 209, *226*
Moffitt, T. E., 195, *207*
Moises, H. W., 92, *107*
Moos, R. H., 66, *80*
Morey, L. C., 38, *51*
Morgan, S., 238, 241, *246*
Morris, R., 10, 11, 14, 16, 17, 22, 26, *30*, 33,

41, 42, 46, 48, *50*, *51–52*, 59, 60, *81*, 130, *134*, 190, 191, *205*, *207*
Moscovitch, M., 59, *82*
Muir, W., 92, *109*
Murdock, B., 238, *245*
Murphy, M., 221, *227*
Myklebust, H. R., 8, *29*, *30*, 118, *134*

N

Nagel, D. R., 144, 146, *159*
Nakamura, G. V., 148, 151, *159*
Nay, S. M., 210, *227*
Newby, R. F., 118, *134*
Newell, A., 55, *80*
Newman, R. S., 141, *159*
Nichols, P. L., 95, 97, *108*
Nichols, R. C., 86, *108*
Nickerson, R. S., 164, 179, 180, 181, *186*
Nimmo-Smith, T., 212, *225*
Nolan, S. M., 146, *160*
Nye, C., 58, *80*

O

Obrzut, J. E., 9, *30*, 39, *51*, 198, *206*
Oglesby, D. M., 166, *184*
Ogonowski, M., 176, *186*
Ojemann, G. A., 198, *206*
Oka, E. R., 172, *186*
Olson, R. K., 113, 115, 116, 117, 118, 119, 122, 123, 126, 127, 129, 130, 132, *133*, *134*, *135*, 209, *227*, 230, *245*
Omori-Gordon, H., 34, *50*
Orvaschel, H., 89, *108*
Orza, M., 44, *52*
Osborne, L. T., 54, 57, 61, 62, *81*
Osborne, S. S., 44, *51*
O'Shea, T., 200, *208*
Ostertag, J., 151, *156*
O'Sullivan, J. T., 141, *159*

P

Pacey, A., 55, *80*
Paivio, A., 212, 213, *227*
Pakstis, A. J., 92, *107*
Palfrey, J. S., 44, *52*, 164, *186*
Palincsar, A. S., 61, 65, *80*, 165, 172, 178, *184*, *186*

Paris, S. G., 33, 44, *50*, 141, *159*, 172, *186*
Parker, T., 42–43, *52*
Parkman, J. M., 202, 203, *206*
Partlett, M. R., 141, *159*
Pascarella, E. T., 61, *80–81*
Patel, T. P. G., 10, 15, *27*
Paterson, A. H., 93, *108*
Pauls, D. L., 88, 92, *107*, *109*
Pearl, R., 144, *159*
Pedhazur, E. J., 47, *50*
Penfold, P. S., 57, *80*
Pennington, B. F., 92, *107*, *109*, 130, *134*
Perfetti, C. A., 168, *186*, 209, 211, 224, *227*
Perkerson, K., 19, *29*
Perkins, D. N., 164, 179, 180, 181, *186*
Perlmutter, B. F., 144, *159*
Perrin, J., 63, *80*
Peter, B., 189, 195, 196, *207*
Peterson, S., 93, *108*
Petrauskas, R., 15, *30*
Petursson, H., 92, *108*
Pflaum, S. W., 61, *80–81*
Phillips, D. C., 55, *80*
Pinkerton, P., 63, *80*
Pless, I. B., 63, *80*
Plomin, R., 84, 85, 87, 88, 89, 90, 91, 92, 93, 101, *106*, *107*, *108*, 113, *135*
Pollatsek, A., 118, *133*
Polovina, J., 86, *107*
Polya, G., 172, *186*
Ponder, H. M., 36, *50*
Poplin, M. S., 35, 36, 37–38, *51*, 61, *80*
Porch, B., 17, *29*
Poremba, C. D., 164, *186–187*
Portes, P., 12, *31*, 237, 239, 240, *246*
Potter, M., 92, *108*
Pressley, M., 70, *81*, 137, 138, 139, 141, 144, 145, 146, 148, 151, 152, 154, *159*, *160*, 164, 165, 166, 168, 169, *187*
Puff, C., 221, *227*
Putnam, J., 141, 148, *157*, 165, *184*

Q

Quine, 55

R

Rabinowitz, M., 144, *160*
Rack, J., 113, 117, 118, 119, 122, 123, 126, 129, 130, 132, *134*, *135*, 209, *227*

Rackliffe, G., 141, *157*
Ramsden, P., *157*
Rand, V., 170, 178, 179, *185*
Raphael, T. E., 137, *157*
Rapin, I., 9, 10, 25, *29*
Rashotte, C. A., 12, *31*, 237, 239, 240, 241, 242, *246*
Ravitch, D., 154, *160*
Readence, J. E., 141, *161*
Reason, P., 61, *81*
Recht, D., 118, *134*
Reeders, S., 92, *107*
Rees, J. W., 61, *79*
Regehr, S. M., 102, *108*
Reid, D. K., 177, *187*, 199, 200, *206*
Reid, H. P., 34, *50*
Reitan, R. M., 196, *207*
Reitter, S., 17, *29*
Rende, R., 84, 89, *108*
Reskin, L., 115, *133*
Resnick, L. B., 202, *208*
Rettinger, V., 35, 36, 37–38, *51*
Reyes, R. E., 137, *160*
Rhodes, J., 17, *29*
Rhu, A. H., 54, 57, 61, 62, *81*
Rick, C. M., 93, *109*
Rinehart, S. D., 150, *160*
Ringel, B. A., 141, *160*
Risucci, D., 33, 40, 47, *51*
Roberts, G. H., 199, *207*
Roberts, J. A. F., 95, *108*
Roditi, B., 169, 171, 173, 181, *186*, *187*
Rodriquez, I. A., 220, 221, *226*
Roehler, L. R., 141, 147, 148, *157*, 165, *184*
Rohwer, W. D., Jr., 137, *157*
Rollins, H. A., 141, *156*
Romsden, P., 141
Rose, W. H., 148, 149, *158*
Ross, G., 178, *188*
Roth, S., 168, *186*
Rourke, B. P., 11, 13, 14, 15, 16, *28*, *30*, 33, *51*, 55, 58, 59, 60, *79*, *81*, 189, 191, 192, 193, 195, 196, 198, 204, *207*, *208*
Rourke, R. B., *207*
Routh, D. K., 12, *28*
Rovine, M., 85, *106*
Rowan, J., 61, *81*
Rubinstein, R. A., 54, 55, *81*
Rudel, R., 168, *184*
Rudin, E., 88, *108*
Russell, R. L., 172, *187*
Rutter, M., 89, 94, *108*, 115, *135*

Ryan, E. B., 3, *30*, 61, *81*, *160*, 165, *187*, 189, 191, 192, 193, 194, 195, *207*
Ryan, R. M., 142, *157*
Ryschon, K. L., 18, *31*

S

Saarnio, D., 64, *80*
Sabatino, D. A., 144, *158*
Sabornie, E. J., 147, *157*
Salame, P., 238, *245*
Salmon, W. C., 54, *81*
Salvia, J., 46, *51*
Samuels, S. J., 169, *185*
Sandoval, J., 39, *51*
Satz, P., 10, 11, 13, 14, 16, 17, 22, 26, *28*, *30*, 33, 36, 41, 43, 44, 48, *51–52*, 59, 60, *81*, 115, *135*, 191, *207*
Schmid, J., 216, *227*
Schneider, J., 57, *79*
Schneider, W., 70, *81*, 137, 138, 139, 141, 143, 144, 145, 146, 151, *159*, *160*, 169, *187*
Schoenheimer, J., 242, *245*
Schön, D., 55, *81*
Schulman, J., 124, *135*
Schulte, A. C., 44, *51*
Schumacher, E. F., 148, *160*
Schumaker, J. B., 65, *81*, 144, 146, 147, *157*, *158*, *159*, *160*, 177, 178, 180, *184*, *187*
Schwethelm, B., 64, 65, *79*
Scribner, S., 54, 55, *79*
Segal, J. W., 148, *160*
Selzer, S. C., 48, *52*
Senf, G. M., 229, *245*
Seymour, P. H. K., 118, 135
Shaner, R., 241, *246*
Shankweiler, D., 209, 211, 219, 221, *227*, 238, 242, *244*, *245*
Share, D. L., 195, *207*, 233, *245*
Sheldon, J., 146, *160*
Shepard, L., 7, *30*
Shepard, L. A., 34, *52*, 227
Sheppard, J. L., 43, *49*
Sheppard, M. J., 43, *49*
Sherrington, R., 92, *107*, *108*
Shields, J., 103, *107*
Shiffrin, R. M., 143, *160*
Short, E. J., 3, 20, 21, 25, 26, *28*, *29*, *30*, 59, 61, *80*, *81*, *160*, 165, *187*, 191, *206*, *207*, 209, 210, 216, *227*
Siegel, L. S., 13, *30*, 115, 130, *135*, 189, 190,

191, 192, 193, 194, 195, 196, *207*, 210, *227*, 240, *245*
Silva, P. A., 195, *207*
Silverman, R., 182, *188*
Simons, K., 241, *246*
Simon, H. A., 55, *81*
Sinclair, E., 7, *28*
Singer, J. D., 44, *52*
Singer, S. M., 88, *109*
Sivan, R., 141, *157*
Sjogren, B., 92, *107*
Skinner, H. A., 38, 46, 47, *51*, *52*
Sleeter, C. E., 61, *81*
Smith, C., 101, *108*
Smith, D. R., 93, *107*
Smith, E. E., 164, 179, 180, *181*, *186*
Smith, M. L., 34, *52*, 81, 227
Smith, R. W., 54, 57, 61, 62, *81*
Smith, S. D., 83, 92, *107*, *109*
Smith, S. T., 242, *245*
Snow, R. B., *184*
Snow, R. E., 37, *50*
Snyder, B. L., 169, *187*
Solomon, B., 163, 165, 170, 173, 174, 175, *186*
Speece, D. L., 19, 20, 21, 22, 24, 25, 26, *29*, *30*, 33, 34, 38, 39, 40, 41, 44, 45, 46, 48, *51*, *52*, 58, *81*, 183, *186*, *187*, 190, 191, *206*, 210, 216, *227*, 235, *245*
Spellacy, F., 189, 195, 196, *207*
Spilich, G. J., 143, *160*
Spoentgen, P., 144, *158*
Spreen, O., 23, *30*, 48, *52*, 164, *187*
Springer, C. J., 141, *160*
St. Clair, D., 92, *109*
Stage, S., 241, *246*
Stahl, S. A., 150, *160*
Stanovich, K. E., 3, 5, 12, *30*, 65, *79*, 114, 115, 116, 125, 126, 127, *135*, 229–230, 231, 240, 242, *245*
Steenwyk, F. L., 150, *156*
Steffy, R., 115, *133*
Stein, M. L., 152, *158*
Stein, R. E. K., 63, *81*
Stemberg, 201, 202
Stephens, K., 93, *107*
Sternberg, R. J., 170, *185*, *187*
Sternberg, S., *207*
Stevenson, H. W., 42–43, *52*
Stevenson, J., 115, 129, 130, 131, 132, *134*, *135*
Stewart, N., 17, *29*, 38, *51*
Stone, C. A., 166, 167, 178, 179, *187*, *188*

Strang, J. D., 13, *30*, 192, 193, 196, *208*
Strauss, A. A., 3, *30*
Strawser, S., 39, 40, *52*
Stuber, C. W., 93, *107*
Sundet, J. M., 88, *109*
Sussex, J. N., 92, *107*
Swanson, H. L., 23, *30*, 163, 165, 166, 167, 168, 169, *188*, 209, 213, 219, 220, 221, 227
Symons, S., 137, *159*
Syrdal-Lasky, A. K., 238, *245*
Szeszulski, P. A., 118, *134*

T

Tallal, P., 238, *246*
Tambs, K., 88, *109*
Tanksley, S. D., 93, *108, 109*
Tarnowski, K. J., 210, *227*
Tarver, S., 209, *227*
Tate, E., 115, *133*
Taylor, A. R., 33, *52*
Taylor, B. M., 150, *160–161*
Taylor, H. G., 36, 43, *52*, 115, *135*
Taylor, L., 61, *78*
Tellegren, A., 131, *134*
Thomas, J. W., 137, *157*
Thomas, R. L., 219, 221, *226*
Thomson, N., *225*
Thorndike, E. L., 198, *208, 227*
Thurlow, M., 57, 62, *82*
Tierney, R. J., 141, *161*
Tobin, D., 164, *185*
Torgesen, J. K., 3, 5, 11, 12, 13, 25, *28, 30–31*, 33, 34, 35, 39, *52*, 58, 59, 61, 70, *81*, 128, *135*, 163, 165, 166, 167, 168, *188*, 209, *227, 228*, 231, 232, 233, 234, 237, 238, 239, 240, 241, 242, 244, *245*, 246
Tramontana, M. G., 48, *52*
Triter, R. L., 10, 15, *27*
Tsai, C. J., 147, *157*

U

Urwin, C., 57, *80*

V

Vallecorsa, A., 182, *188*
Vance, H., 5, *31*

Vandenberg, S. G., 86, 88, *107, 109*
van den Bos, K. P., 127, *135*
van Dijk, T. A., 150, *158, 161*
van Kammen, D. P., 88, *107*
VanLehn, K., 200, *205*
Vavrus, L. G., 141, *157*, 165, *184*
Vellutino, F. R., 219, *228*
Venn, C., 57, *80*
Vernon, P. E., 85, *109*
Vesonder, G. T., 143, *160*
Vogler, G. P., 131, *135*
Vojir, C. P., 34, *52*, 227
Voss, J. R., 143, *160*
Vygotsky, L. S., 178, *188*

W

Wagner, K., 209, *228*
Wagner, M., 115, *133*
Wagner, R. K., 3, 5, 12, 31, 240, 241, *246*
Walker, D. K., 44, *52*
Walker, G., 57, *80*
Walkerdine, R., 57, *80*
Waller, T. G., 144, *157*
Wallis, W. G., 190
Walsh-Allis, G., 89, *108*
Warner, M. M., 180, *184, 187*
Warrington, E. K., 189, *206*
Wasmuth, J., 92, *108*
Waters, W., 35, 36, 37–38, *51*
Watson, B., 17, 22, *29*, 183, *185*, 234, 241, *245*
Watson, B. V., 18, *31*
Webster, R. E., 195, *208*
Wechsler, D. I., 66, *81*, 115, *135*
Weed, K. A., 3, *30*, 61, *81*
Weiffenbach, B., 93, *107*
Weinstein, M. L., 189, *208*
Weissbrod, C. S., 167, *184*
Weller, C., 39, 40, *52*
Wendel, J. F., 93, *107*
Wenger, M., 44, *52*
Werfelman, 209
Werner, H., 3, *30*
Wertsch, J. V., 178, 179, *187, 188*
Wesselman, R., 141, *157*, 165, *184*
Wesson, C., 57, 62, *82*
West, R. F., 125, 126, 127, *135*
Wetterberg, L., 92, *107*
Whishaw, I. Q., *158*
Whishow, I. Q., 139
White, R. W., 142, *161*

Whitehead, A. N., 54, *81*
Widaman, K. F., 203, 204, *206*
Wilkinson, A., 42–43, *52*
Willerman, L., 91, *107*, *109*
Williams, G. A., 33, *52*
Williams, V., 14, *29*
Williamson, M. L., 93, *106*
Willis, W. G., 33, *50*, 137, 138, 149, *158*, 191,
    192, *206*
Wilson, B. A., 145, *161*
Wilson, J. R., 86, *107*
Wilson, J. W., 199, *206*
Wilson, L. R., 7, *27*
Wimsatt, W., 54, *81*
Winograd, P., 172, *188*
Wise, B., 113, 117, 118, 119, 122, 123, 126,
    130, 132, *134*, 209, *227*
Wixson, K. K., 141, *159*
Wolf, M., 168, 169, *188*
Wolfus, B., 59, *82*
Wong, 209
Wong, B., 167, *188*, 190, *208*
Wong, B. Y., 3, *31*, 163, *188*

Wong, B. Y. L., 165, 172, *188*
Wood, A., 178, *188*
Wood, C., 148, 149, *158*
Woodin, M. E., 212, *226*
Woods, S. S., 202, *208*
Woodward, J. A., 210, 224, *226*
Wright, A., 92, *109*
Wright, F., 6, *28*

Y

Ye, W., 89, *108*
Yewchuk, C., 164, *188*
Young, R. M., 200, *208*
Ysseldyke, J. E., 6, 8, *31*, 46, *51*, 57, 62, *82*,
    190, *205*
Yule, W., 115, *135*

Z

Zajchowski, R., 152, *159*, 164, 165, 168, *187*
Zigmond, N., 182, *188*

Subject Index

A

Academic performance
  arithmetic disabilities and, 192–193
  dimensional approach to, *see* Dimensional
    approach
  problem-solving strategies and, 172–177
  in rationally defined subgroups, 232, 234,
    239–242
Academic subtypes, 8–9
Acalculia, 197
Achievement/IQ discrepancy, 7–8, 58
Achievement tests, 58, 76, 170, *see also*
    specific tests
Actively inefficient learners, 165
Additive genetic variance, 105
Adoption studies, 84, 104, 105
  developmental analysis in, 90
  environmental variables in, 91–92
  group heritability and, 98
  IQ data in, 84, 85
  multivariate analysis in, 89
  on specific cognitive abilities, 85–86
AFT, *see* Assessment for Teaching
Age
  arithmetic disabilities and, 194, 195
  clinical/inferential classification and, 11

in dimensional approach, 66
problem-solving strategies and, 176–177
reading disabilities and, 114, 130–132
significance of in rationally defined
  subgroups, 243
Alcoholism, 89
Alexics, 8, 9
Alphabetic principle, 240
ANOVAs
  in dimensional approach, 66, 71, 73
  in working memory analysis, 217, 224
Applied Behavior analysis model, 199
Aptitude-by-treatment interactions (ATI),
  36, 37
Arithmetic disabilities, 3, 4, 189–204
  cognitive models approach to, 197, 200–
    204
  definitional issues in, 109
  educational tasks approach to, 198–199
  neuropsychological approach to, 197–198
  problem-solving strategies and, 164, 169,
    170, 172–173, 175, 176, 177
  in rationally defined subgroups, 11, 13,
    235–236, 239, 242
  subtyping issues in, 191–196
Articulatory loop, 212, 219
Assessment for Teaching (AFT) model, 181

Assortative mating, 85, 104
ATI, *see* Aptitude-by-treatment interactions
Attention span, 4
    dimensional approach and, 61
    empirical classification of deficits in, 19, 44
    information processing and, 139, 144
    problem-solving strategies and, 180
    working memory and, 209
Attribution theory, 166, 168
Auditory dyslexia, 8
Auditory memory, 235
Automaticity, 167, 168–169, 176, 177

B

Behavioral genetic approach, 83–106
    developmental analysis in, 89–91
    environmental variance in, 83, 91–92
    longitudinal analysis in, 83, 90–91, 105
    multivariate analysis in, 83, 87–89, 90, 100, 101–102
    relationship between normal and abnormal in, 83, 94–103
    single vs. polygenes in, 83, 92–94, 105–106
    univariate analysis in, 83, 84, 88
Boys Town Study, 16, 18
Brain damage, 3, 9–10, 197

C

Carolina Longitudinal Project, 16, 18–23, 26
Category Shift explanation task, 175
Central executive processes, *see* Executive processes
Central/Incidental Serial Recall Task, 66, 70
Central nervous system (CNS), 58,59
Chronic illnesses, *see* specific types
Clinical/inferential subtypes, 4, 5–11
Cluster analysis, 5
    in dimensional approach, 59, 60
    in empirical classification, 14, 16–23, 26, 33, 34, 38–29, 40, 41, 44, 46–47
    of working memory performance, 216
Coding abilities, 3, 6, 209, specific types
Cognition, dimensional approach to, *see* Dimensional approach
Cognitive flexibility, 175, 176, 177
Cognitive limitations, 231–232

Cognitive-motivational processes, 167, 168
Cognitive processing models, 197, 200–204
Colorado Reading Project, 101, 102
Computational arithmetic, 189
Conceptual reasoning, 166, 167
Constructivist view, 56–58
Contextual approach, 200–201
Correlation coefficients, 34
Critical theory, 54
Cybernetics, 54

D

Decoding abilities, *see* Coding abilities
Depression, hereditary factors in, 85, 88
Developmental analysis
    in behavioral genetic approach, 89–91
    in empirical classification, 40, 42–44, 45, 49
Developmental output failure, 189
Diabetes mellitus, 64, 65, 66, 76, 77
    test results and, 67, 68, 69, 70, 71
Diagnostic categorization
    history of, 56, 58–63
    logic of, 56–58
Diagnostic-Perscriptive teaching model, 199
Differential Diagnosis in Reading Disability program, 113
Differential heritability, *see* Heritability
Digit span task, 221, 236, 240
Dimensional approach, 53–78
    diagnostic categorization in, 55, 56–63
    empirical support for, 65–67
    interview data in, 72–73
    model of, 63–65
    principal components analysis in, 66, 73–76
    tests used in, 66, 67–72
Direct path tasks, 118
DISTAR Arithmetic program, 199
Dizygotic twins, *see* Fraternal twins
Dyscalculia, 197
Dyseidetics, 8, 9, 118, 127
Dysgraphia, 189
Dyslexia, *see also* specific types
    brain damage in, 9–10
    genetic factors in, 114
    in rationally defined subgroups, 240–241
    subtypes of, 8–9
Dysphonetics, 8, 9, 118

E

Educational tasks approach, 198–199
Effortful encoding task, 221
Empirical classification, 5, 33–49
  advancing in, 33, 34, 47–49
  cluster analysis in, 14, 16–23, 26, 33, 34,
    38–39, 40, 41, 44, 46–47
  Q-factor analysis in, 14–16
  regrouping in, 33, 34, 38–47
  retreat from, 33–34, 35–38
Environmental variables
  in behavioral genetic approach, 83, 91–92
  in dimensional approach, 55, 59, 61, 63
  in empirical classification, 48
Etiological perspective, 44, 45
Executive processes, 3
  in problem-solving strategies, 166
  in working memory, 212, 219, 220, 221,
    224, 225
External validity, 36, 37, 114
Extreme subgroups, *see* Rationally defined
  subgroups

F

Factor analysis, 14, 214, *see also* Q-factor
  analysis
Family studies, 83, 84, 86, 89, 103
Fine motor coordination, 189
Five-cluster solution, 216
Fixed-rule approach, 200
Florida Longitudinal Project on Under-
  achievement, 16–17, 26
Focus symptoms, 61
Fraternal twins
  IQ studies on, 84
  multivariate analysis of, 88
  nonadditive genetic variance in, 105
  reading disabilities in, 113
    group heritability and, 98, 99, 100, 102
    liability correlations and, 101
    methods for assessing, 120–122
    word recognition and, 122, 130
  schizophrenia in, 103

G

Genain quadruplets, 88
Gender
  clinical/inferential classification and, 11

in dimensional approach, 62, 66
reading disabilities and, 114, 130–131
Genetic factors, *see* Behavioral genetic
  approach; Reading disabilities,
  genetic factors in
Gifted children, 61
Grammatical sensitivity, 195
Gray Oral Reading Test, 22
Grooved Pegboard Test, 196
Group deficits, *see also* Group familiarity;
  Group heritability
  IQ scores and, 127, 128–120
  methods for assessing, 120–122
  orthographic coding and, 125–126, 127
  phonological coding and, 125–126
  word recognition and, 122–123, 124, 130–
    132
Group familiality, 95, 96–98, 101, *see also*
  Group deficits; Group heritability
Group heritability, 98–100, 101–103, *see also*
  Group deficits; Group familiality

H

Halstead Category Test, 196
Harford County school system, 148–149
Hawaii Family Study of Cognition, 86
Heritability, *see also* Group heritability
  methods for assessing, 119–122
  in word recognition, 122–132
Heterogeneity
  arithmetic disabilities and, 190, 191
  dimensional approach and, 58
  empirical classification and, 34, 37, 41, 44
  problem-solving strategies and, 183
  in rationally defined subgroups, 229, 230,
    234, 241
  working memory and, 209–210
Hit-rate model, 42–44
Homogeneity
  empirical classification and, 45
  in rationally defined subgroups, 230, 232,
    233
Hyperactivity, 3

I

Identical twins
  IQ studies of, 84, 85
  multivariate analysis of, 88, 89
  nonadditive genetic variance in, 105

Identical twins (continued)
  reading disabilities in, 89, 113
    group heritability and, 98, 99, 100, 102
    liability correlations and, 101
    methods for assessing, 120–122
    word recognition and, 122, 130
  schizophrenia in, 103
Illinois Test Psycholinguistic Abilities
    (ITPA), 4, 6
Individual familiality, 95, 96, 97
Information processing, 137–156
  basic competencies required for, 139
  dimensional approach to, 58, 59, 76, 77
  interventions for, 144–146
  metacognition in, 139, 141, 146, 148
  motivation in, 142, 146, 147, 148
  nonstrategic knowledge in, 142–143
  problems specific to learning disabilities
    in, 144
  in rationally defined subgroups, 232, 234
  strategies in, 139–141, 143, 144, 146–149,
    150–155
  styles in, 141–142
Institute for Research on Learning
    Disabilities, 146–147, 149
Instrumental Enrichment program, 179–180
Intelligence quotient (IQ), 26, see also
    Intelligence tests
  achievement discrepancy and, 7–8, 58
  dimensional approach to, 61, 73
  empirical classification and, 16, 21, 22
  genetic factors influencing, 84–85
    environmental variables and, 48, 91–92
    group heritability and, 100
    longitudinal analysis of, 90–91
    in mental retardation, 95–96, 97–98
    reading disabilities and, 1144–116, 127–
      130
  in rationally defined subgroups, 12, 242
Intelligence test, 58, 76, 170, see also
    Intelligence quotient; specific tests
  subtest scatter on, 5–7
Internal consistency, see Reliability
Internal validity, 37
IQ, see Intelligence quotient
ITPA, see Illinois Test of Psycholinguistic
    Abilities

J

Journal of Learning Disabilities, 37
Juvenile delinquency, 164

K

Kaufman's Freedom From Distractibility
    factors, 128, 129
Kaufman's Perceptual Organization, 128
Kaufman's Verbal Comprehension, 127–128
Keyword method, 145

L

Language deficits
  empirical classification of, 20–21
  information processing and, 139, 144, 145
  problem-solving strategies and, 166
  in rationally defined subgroups, 239
Learned helplessness, 168
Learning potential, 179–180
Left-hand performance impairment, 196
Left-hemisphere processing problems, 196
Liability correlations, 101
Liseral testing model, 214
LISREL testing model, 123
Locus of control, 168
Longitudinal analysis
  in behavioral genetic research, 83, 90–91,
    105
  empirical classification and, 48, 49
  of subtype stability, 44
Long-term memory
  in information processing, 139, 143
  in rationally defined subgroups, 237
  working memory compared with, 212,
    213, 214, 222
Lumpers, 85

M

Maladaptive learners, 165
Manic-depression, 88
MANOVAs, 214, 216, 222
Math disabilities, see Arithmetic disabilities
McGill studies, 14–15
Memory, 4
  arithmetic disabilities and, 194–195, 202
  auditory, 235
  dimensional approach to, 61, 65, 66
  empirical classification and, 23
  in information processing, 137, 138, 139,
    141, 143, 144

long-term, *see* Long-term memory
working, *see* Working memory
Mental arithmetic models, 201–204
Mental retardation, 4, 58
  genetic factors in, 93, 95–98, 103, 104, 106, 124
Metacognition, 3, 163
  academic performance and, 172
  implications for teaching in, 177, 180, 181
  in information processing, 139, 141, 146, 148
  specific strategies in, 164–170
Metalearning habits, 180
Mnemonics
  in information processing, 144–145
  in problem-solving strategies, 180
  in rationally defined subgroups, 12, 235
Monozygotic twins, *see* Identical twins
Moos Family Environment scale, 66, 72
Motivation, *see also* Cognitive-motivational processes
  dimensional approach to, 61
  in information processing, 142, 146, 147, 148
Motor problems
  arithmetic disabilities and, 189
  reading disabilities and, 102–103
Multiple regression model, 120
Multiple subskills, 167, 169–170
Multivariate analysis, *see also* Empirical classification
  of arithmetic disabilities, 191–192
  in behavioral genetic approach, 83, 87–89, 90, 100, 101–102

N

National Institute of Child Health and Human Development, 113
Neurological factors
  in arithmetic disabilities, 197–198
  classification of, 9–10
  in dimensional approach, 53–54, 55, 58, 59, 60, 63
  in rationally defined subgroups, 231, 232
Nonadditive genetic variance, 85 105
North Carolina Study, *see* Carolina Longitudinal Project
Northwestern Study, 16, 17–18

O

Operational efficiency, 238, 240

Organizational strategies
  information processing and, 141
  working memory and, 209
Orthographic coding, 102, 118, 119, 122, 123, 125–127

P

Pairwise comparisons, 71
Pause-Time Free Recall Task, 66, 70
Peabody Individual Achievement Test (PIAT)
  in dimensional approach, 66, 68–69, 70, 71, 773
  in empirical classification, 17, 20
  in genetic studies, 102, 116–117, 130
Perceived Competence Scale, 66, 71, 73, 74
Phenotypic covariance, 87, 105
Phenylketonuria (PKU), 93
Philosophy of science, 54
Phonemic coding, 194, 240
Phonemic disruption task, 220–221, 222
Phonological coding
  arithmetic disabilities and, 195
  genetic factors and, 102, 118, 119, 122, 123, 125–126, 129, 132
  in rationally defined subgroups, 12, 238, 240–241, 242
  working memory and, 219, 225
Piagetian perspective on problem-solving, 167
PIAT, *see* Peabody Individual Achievement Test
Pig-latin, 126
PKU, *see* Phenylketonuria
Pleiotropy, 87
Polygenes, 83, 92–94, 105–106
Porch Index of Communicative Ability, 17
Principal components analysis, 66, 73–76
Problem-solving strategies, 163–183
  academic performance and, 172–177
  automaticity and, 167, 168–169, 176, 177
  cognitive-motivational processes in, 167, 168
  implications for assessment and, 170–172
  influence of adult–child interactions on, 178–179
  learning potential concept in, 179–180
  linking assessment and teaching in, 181–182
  multiple subskill coordination in, 167, 169–170
  specific to the learning disabled, 164–170
  training approaches in, 180–181

Progressive Achievement Test, 203
Proleptic instruction, 178
Prototypes, *see* Rationally defined subgroups
Public Law 94–142, 114

Q

Q-factor analysis, 5, 14–16, 59

R

Race, 10, 11, 62
Rationally defined subgroups, 11–13, 229–244
    academic performance of, 239–242
    caveats concerning, 233–234
    defining of, 235–237
    description of defining disability in, 237
    developmental and prognostic issues in,
        242–244
    empirical classification compared with, 34,
        35
    research on, 231–233
    theoretical understanding of, 237–239
Reading comprehension, Reading
    disabilities
    information processing and, 137, 138, 143,
        150
    role of working memory in, *see* under
        Working memory
Reading disabilities, 3, 4, *see also* Reading
    comprehension; specific types
    arithmetic disabilities and, 192–193, 194,
        195–196, 203–204
    empirical classification of, 14–16, 22
    genetic factors in, 83, 89, 94, 113–133
    group familiality and, 95
    group heritability and, 98–100, 101–103
    IQ and, 114–116
    liability correlations of, 101
    methods for assessing, 199–122
    orthographic coding and, *see* Ortho-
        graphic coding
    phonological coding and, *see* Phono-
        logical coding, genetic factors and
    word recognition and, *see* Word
        recognition
    problem-oriented strategies and, 164, 168,
        169, 170, 172, 175, 176–177
    in rationally defined subgroups, 11, 12, 13,
        235–236, 239, 240–242, 243
    subtest scatter and, 5–6
    types of, 8–9

Realist view, 56, 57
Recombinant DNA, 84
Reconstructive memory, 202
Reductive fallacy, 35
Regression analysis, 7, 8, 47, 66
Regression to the mean, 95, 97, 98, 99, 120, 122
Rehearsal, 141, 219
Reliability, 38, 45, 46
Replicability, 46, 47
Rhyming
    genetic deficits in, 126
    working memory and, 220–221, 222
Right-hand performance impairment, 196
Right-hemisphere processing problems, 196
Rote learning, 189
R-technique, *see* Factor analysis

S

SCAN observational system, 19
Schizophrenia, 88–89, 103–104, 106, 124
Secondary analysis, 41
Seizure disorders, 54, 64, 65, 66, 75–76, 77
    interview data and, 72–73
    test results and, 67, 68–69, 70, 71
Semantic orienting task, 220
Sensitivity index, 42–43
Sentence elaboration task, 221
Sequential reasoning, 176, 177
SES, *see* Socioeconomic status
Short-term memory (STM)
    arithmetic disabilities and, 194, 195
    in dimensional approach, 65
    empirical classification and, 23
    in information processing, 139, 143, 144
    in rationally defined subgroups, 11, 12,
        235–237, 238
    working memory compared with, 210–
        212, 214, 215, 216, 217, 219, 220, 221,
        222, 224, 225
Single genes, 83, 92–94, 105
Socioeconomic status (SES)
    in dimensional approach, 60, 62, 66
    empirical classification and, 17, 21
Soft neurological signs, 9, 16, 17, 26
Specificity index, 42, 43
Spelling
    problem-solving strategies and, 168
    in rationally defined subgroups, 11, 13, 241
SPES, *see* Survey of Problem-Solving and
    Educational Skills
Splitters, 85

Standard Progressive Matrices, 203
Standard score difference method, 8
Stanford Achievement Test, 203
STM, *see* Short-term memory
Strategies Intervention Model, 180–181
Subtest scatter, 4, 5–7
Subvocal rehearsal, 219
Summarization strategies, 150–154
Survey of Problem-Solving and Educational
    Skills (SPES), 170–172, 173

T

Tactile Performance Test, 196
Twin studies, 83, 84, 103, 105, *see also*
    Fraternal twins; Identical twins
    developmental analysis in, 90
    IQ data in, 84, 85
    multivariate analysis in, 88, 89
    of reading disabilities, 89, 98–100, 101,
        102, 113–133, *see also* Reading
        disabilities, genetic factors in
    of specific cognitive abilities, 86–87
Two-group schemes, 44

U

Underachievers, 64, 65, 66, 76, 77
    interview data for, 73
    test results of, 67, 68, 69, 70, 71, 72
Univariate analysis, 37, 83, 84, 88
University of Colorado, 113
University of Kansas learning disability
    program, *see* Institute for Research
    on Learning disabilities

V

Validity, 114
    in dimensional approach, 53, 54, 58
    in empirical classification, 36, 37, 38, 42,
        45, 48
Verbal storage, 212, 215, 219
Visual-spatial ability
    problem-solving strategies and, 166
    working memory and, 212, 214, 215–216,
        217, 219

Visuospatial dyslexia, 8

W

WAIS, *see* Wechsler Adult Intelligence
    Scale
Wechsler Adult Intelligence Scales (WAIS),
    91, 115, 127
    in dimensional approach, 66, 67–68, 69,
        70, 73
    in empirical classification, 21, 22, 23
    for reading disabled individuals, 115, 116,
        127
    subtest scatter on, 5, 6, 7
    working memory analysis and, 221
Wechsler Intelligence Scales for Children
    (WISC), 10, *see also* Wechsler
    Intelligence Scale for Children-
    Revised
Wide Range Achievement Test (WRAT)
    arithmetic disability testing with, 190,
        192–196
    in empirical classification, 16, 23, 46
    for rationally defined subgroups, 13
    Windsor studies, 14–16
WISC, *see* Wechsler Intelligence Scales for
    Children
Woodcock-Johnson Achievement Battery,
    22
Woodcock Reading Mastery Test, 18, 241
Word recognition, 114, 116–118, 122–132
    age and gender in, 130–132
    component skills in, 118–119
    severity of, 123–125
Working memory
    arithmetic disabilities and, 194, 195
    in rationally defined subgroups, 238, 240
    reading comprehension and, 209–225
        components in, 212
        models in, 210–212
        studies on, 212–224
Writing backwardness, 189
Writing skills, 168, 169, 170, *see also* specific
    disabilities in

Z

Zone of proximal development, 178